A critical introduction to twentieth-century American drama

To the memory of Alan Schneider

A critical introduction to twentieth-century American drama

2

Tennessee Williams
Arthur Miller
Edward Albee

C. W. E. BIGSBY

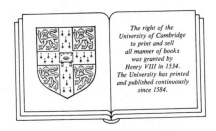

The right of the
University of Cambridge
to print and sell
all manner of books
was granted by
Henry VIII in 1534.
The University has printed
and published continuously
since 1584.

CAMBRIDGE UNIVERSITY PRESS

Cambridge
London   New York   New Rochelle
Melbourne   Sydney

Published by the Press Syndicate of the University of Cambridge
The Pitt Building, Trumpington Street, Cambridge CB2 1RP
32 East 57th Street, New York, NY 10022, USA
10 Stamford Road, Oakleigh, Melbourne 3166, Australia

First published 1984
Reprinted 1986

Printed in Great Britain by
the University Press, Cambridge

Library of Congress catalogue card number: 81 – 18000

British Library Cataloguing in Publication Data
Bigsby, C. W. E.
A critical introduction to twentieth-century American drama.
2: Tennessee Williams, Arthur Miller, Edward Albee
1. American drama – 20th century – History and criticism
I. Title
812'.52'09   PS351
ISBN 0 521 25811 1 hard covers
ISBN 0 521 27717 5 paperback

Publisher's acknowledgements
    From 'Burnt Norton' and 'East Coker' in *Four Quartets*, copyright 1943 by T. S. Eliot; renewed 1951 by Esme Valerie Eliot. Reprinted by permission of Harcourt Brace Jovanovich, Inc.
    From 'The Hollow Men' and 'Ash-Wednesday' in *Collected Poems 1909–1962* by T. S. Eliot, copyright 1936 by Harcourt Brace Jovanovich, Inc.; copyright © 1963, 1964 by T. S. Eliot. Reprinted by permission of the publisher.
    From *The Cocktail Party*, copyright 1950 by T. S. Eliot; renewed 1978 by Esme Valerie Eliot. Reprinted by permission of Harcourt Brace Jovanovich, Inc.
    From *The Confidential Clerk*, copyright 1954 by T. S. Eliot; renewed 1982 by Esme Valerie Eliot. Reprinted by permission of Harcourt Brace Jovanovich, Inc.
    From *The Family Reunion*, copyright 1939 by T. S. Eliot; renewed 1967 by Esme Valerie Eliot. Reprinted by permission of Harcourt Brace Jovanovich, Inc.

UP

CONTENTS

ILLUSTRATIONS

PREFACE

If the American theatre prior to 1940 was dominated by the work of one man — Eugene O'Neill — in the post-war world it was Tennessee Williams and Arthur Miller who brought American drama to prominence. And when their careers seemed to falter at the end of the 1950s not only did another major figure obligingly appear, in the person of Edward Albee, but the diminishing significance of Broadway ushered in a period of radical experimentation of a kind unmatched in American theatrical history. Aesthetic innovation coexisted with political revolt.

I have chosen to tell the story of these developments in two separate volumes. Despite Albee's early roots in Off-Broadway theatre and Tennessee Williams's late enthusiasm for its freedoms and its protective environment, the division seems a natural one, and the only way to do justice both to the achievement of America's major dramatic talents and to those whose aesthetic experiments and political enthusiasms made the American theatre of the 1960s and 1970s such an exciting and fascinating phenomenon. Accordingly, this volume concerns itself with the work of Tennessee Williams, Arthur Miller and Edward Albee, while the next examines the variety of dramatic and theatrical forms to be found beyond Broadway. In a sense it is plainly an arbitrary division. They all inhabited the same cultural and political world, shared certain critical, social and moral anxieties and sought new ways in which to express those anxieties. And yet there were differences: they turned to different models, assumed different audiences, and proposed different ways in which the theatre could operate as fact and image; they placed a different weight on language and, on the whole, made rather different assumptions about the nature of character and the role of that ritualised action which is the basis of theatrical performance. In the end, therefore, the division is a logical as well as a pragmatic one; just how logical, however, is for the reader to decide.

ACKNOWLEDGEMENTS

I wish to acknowledge the generosity of Arthur Miller, Edward Albee and the late Tennessee Williams in allowing me access to unpublished material. I also wish to thank for their assistance the librarians and staff at the Humanities Research Center, the University of Texas at Austin, and at the New York Public Library at Lincoln Center.

Permission to reproduce illustrations is gratefully acknowledged: for numbers 1, 4, 5, 6, 7, 8, 11, 12, 13 and 18 from the Hoblitzelle Theatre Arts Library, Humanities Research Center, the University of Texas at Austin; for numbers 2, 3, 9, 16 and 17 the Billy Rose Theatre Collection, New York Public Library at Lincoln Center; and for numbers 10, 14 and 15 from Inge Morath.

The discussion of Arthur Miller's *The Price* first appeared in a slightly different form in *Twentieth-Century Literature*. Extracts from the Works of T. S. Eliot appear by kind permission of Faber and Faber Limited and Harcourt Brace Jovanovich, Inc.

Introduction

The theatre is the most public of arts. It offers the opportunity of acting out anxieties and fears which are born in the conflict between private needs and public values. In America in the 1930s it staged the battle between capital and labour, reflected a desperate pacifism, and dramatised the diminishing space allowed the individual by the encroaching city and an increasing mechanisation. Frequently utopian or visionary in spirit, it tended to pitch love against the sheer density of social experience and the coercions of an economic system which seemed to find no place for the self. The mere placing of the individual on the stage was an assertion of priorities while the co-operative nature of theatre implied a possible social strategy. The post-war theatre, by contrast, seemed more intensely psychological, less convinced that experience could be subordinated to idea, altogether less assured. It seemed to reflect a sense of bafflement, the war having apparently drawn a line across a particular kind of historical development. And yet, of course, those who emerged as playwrights after 1945 had, in a sense, been shaped by the as-sumptions of the previous decade. It was there that they found their images no less than a language of liberal possibility often curiously at odds with the social reality which they chose to render as simple threat.

Tennessee Williams and Arthur Miller, who dominated the American theatre for nearly a decade and a half, both began their careers as political playwrights. Formed by the 1930s, they responded to the economic and social realities of the age. Though their first works appeared on Broadway in the 1940s, they had both been writing for more than a decade, and in the case of Tennessee Williams those early works were actually staged by a radical theatre company in St Louis. There seemed to be a simple coherence to the world which they dramatised then. It resolved itself into contending forces in which the necessities of justice seemed clear, and evil was an unexamined force expressing itself through a wayward capitalism or an inherent corruption. And in that they scarcely differed from those whose work dominated the public stage, people like Sidney Kingsley, Clifford Odets, Maxwell Anderson and William Saroyan. Though these all differed from one another in many ways, they seemed to share a radically simplified vision of human relations and social process.

The war changed this. For Arthur Miller, a Jew, the enormity of the events in Europe challenged equally his model of human nature and his sense of history as an account of progress. For Williams it intensified his feeling of

1

society as threat; it deepened a sense of insecurity rooted in private experience but intensified by the new realities of a post-nuclear age. The pieties of pre-war America no longer seemed capable of sustaining the individual or the culture – though both writers were capable of invoking them, ironised by their own deepening sense of unease. The new materialism bred its own discontents and the word 'alienation' infiltrated the language of sociologist and literary critic alike. Affluence, proudly proclaimed as a value, seemed to locate the individual primarily as consumer. Babbitt was welcomed back into the clan after two decades of naive rebellion. After all, was this not the America which possessed most of the world's consumer goods? It was a period of conspicuous consumption. It is, thus, not for nothing that Willy Loman makes his car and refrigerator criteria of value, and is dismissed from his job by a man distracted by his pride in possession of a new wire recorder (precursor of the tape recorder). For much the same reason Tennessee Williams, in *Cat on a Hot Tin Roof*, uses as a central prop and metaphor:

> a monumental monstrosity peculiar to our times, *a huge* console combination of radio-phonograph (Hi-Fi with three speakers) TV set *and* liquor cabinet, bearing and containing many glasses and bottles, all in one piece, which is a composition of muted silver tones, and the opalescent tones of reflecting glass, a chromatic link, this thing, between the sepia (tawny gold) tones of the interior and the cool (white and blue) tones of the gallery and sky. This piece of furniture (?!), this monument, is a very complete and compact little shrine to virtually all the comforts and illusions behind which we hide from such things as the characters in the play are faced with.[1]

In both cases the stance is more than a little informed with nostalgia for an older, gentler America, more lyrical, more in touch with the reality of human need. And if that time also had its betrayals then at least the individual had seemed more in tune with his environment. Now that environment was changing. The countryside was giving way to suburbia and suburbia to the city (though that is a world for the most part ignored by Tennessee Williams). Nor was the individual invited to assume a personal relationship to his society, to play an active role in the moral and political issues of the age. New Deal liberalism was deferring to a conservatism which, following the explosion of the Soviet bomb in 1949, sought to expose and punish those whose Americanness seemed suspect or whose loyalty might be in question. Indeed in many ways the principal victims were those who had been most closely associated with Roosevelt's policies, and those in the arts and education unwilling to disavow values not immediately compatible with the orthodoxies of the moment. It is perhaps not altogether strange that total disaffection, a determined bohemianism, should have emerged as a principal literary stance in the decade. It was a tactic which seemed culturally subversive but which was safely apolitical.

There is, of course, something entirely familiar in this role of alienated intellectual (Irving Howe discusses precisely this in his essay, 'The Age of Conformity'), while the romantic stance of the poet in a prosaic age is a comfortable one, springing from a natural sense of superiority. But in the 1940s and 1950s these positions were not without a certain subversive *frisson*. The moral and spiritual charge to be derived from a stance of alienation (in Miller's case still with vague Marxist overtones, in Williams's with equally vague Freudian ones) was not without its attraction. Unsurprisingly, neither Miller nor Williams had much time for the new model citizen: an organisation man (in the words of William Whyte); a member of the lonely crowd (according to David Reisman), who made a virtue of submerging his identity in the team: a consumer, a realist, a conformist, prepared to trade independence of mind and spirit for immunity from social pressure. It was, indeed, a period which distrusted the idealist (had he not turned traitor?), the artist (on the one hand a hopeless dreamer; on the other perversely critical of the society which protected him), and the non-conformist (by definition un-American). Writing in the 1950s, James Thurber became convinced that McCarthyism had turned the word 'security' into a term to be 'employed exclusively in a connotation of fear, uncertainty and suspicion'. He felt that the world was faced with 'the smokescreen phrases of the political terminologists' which left it threatened with a 'menacing Alice in Wonderland meaninglessness'.[2] And not the least of Miller's concerns was the necessity of rescuing language from its debasement: to make his characters responsible for the words they uttered no less than the deeds they committed. Not the least of Williams's obsessions was the need to restore a sense of poetry to lives rendered void by the banality of the world in which they were nurtured.

For a time it seemed that the only legitimate stance for an intellectual to take was one of resolute rejection of public values. But, denied a retreat to the radical ideology of the 1930s, they had relatively little purchase on those values. Miller did adopt a forthright stance, denouncing informers, refusing to be infected by hysteria, and forcibly expressing a distrust of materialism, but he was rather less sure of what could replace it, beyond a kind of instinctively felt existentialism allied to a sense of natural decency. At the heart of his work was an insistence that the individual had to acknowledge responsibility for his actions and that the past could make legitimate demands on the present. But that present seemed to leave remarkably little space for the social conscience to operate. For Williams the past was more problematic, involving, as it did, racial guilt and corruption. His response to the crude coercions of the social world was to see them as evidence of other determinisms and seek to transmute them into tragedy.

To Erich Fromm, writing in the 1950s, modern capitalist society was an assault equally on the integrity of the individual and the social contract which sustains that individual in his relations with others. It had eroded a sense of the self and hence the notion of society as a group of autonomous selves subscribing to shared values: 'That is the way he experiences himself, not as a man, with love, fear, convictions, doubts, but as that abstraction, alienated from his real nature, which fulfils a certain function in the social system. His sense of value depends upon his success: on whether he can sell himself favourably...If the individual fails in a profitable investment of himself, he feels that *he* is a failure; if he succeeds, *he* is a success.[3] No wonder he regarded Miller's *Death of a Salesman* as an exemplary text. For Willy Loman's problem is precisely that he has internalised these values. Much the same is true of the figures in the early plays of Edward Albee – the third of the triumvirate who dominated the post-war American theatre. And Tennessee Williams's characters are so often destroyed because they offer love in a world characterised by impotence and sterility. And both Miller and Albee would also have agreed with Fromm's contention that 'man can fulfil himself only if he remains in touch with the fundamental facts of his existence, if he can experience the exaltation of love and solidarity, as well as the tragic facts of his aloneness and of the fragmentary character of his existence' – as they would with his conviction that drama is itself a primary attempt to 'get in touch with the essence of reality by artistic creation'.[4]

But if alienation erodes a sense of the real and breeds a mode of conformity as an apparent solution to the problems of isolation, it also creates a sense of guilt, nebulous, unrelated, as Fromm again has pointed out, to any sense of a religious sanction but prompted by a sense of inadequacy, an acknowledgement of that very failure of community and organic relationship which is itself the essence of alienation. And it would be hard to think of a writer who has made this theme more central to his work than Arthur Miller, though the notion of a private betrayal to be expiated by art is also clearly visible in Williams's *The Glass Menagerie*. Albee, on the other hand, is less interested in guilt than responsibility (though Miller has claimed much the same about his own work). In the early part of his career he seemed concerned with identifying the means whereby the individual can terminate his self-imposed exclusion and resist the process which otherwise erodes will, identity and imagination, and thereby destroys the basis for moral action. But both Miller and Albee unite in their assumption that alienation is a product of decisions taken, action deferred, myths endorsed, a freedom denied, rather than a simple consequence of capitalism.

While Williams retained his central theme of the romantic in an unromantic world, a theme derived in part from D. H. Lawrence whom he greatly admired, he largely turned away from a direct concern with social structures, seeing them simply as images of the facticity which threatened the necessary fictions of his characters. Increasingly he described those desperate attempts to hold the world at bay with alcohol, illusion, and fragile sexuality which, as he indicates in his *Memoirs,* came to characterise his own life. Miller, on the other hand, after writing two plays which seemed to admit of no wholly satisfactory response to public and private betrayals – *All My Sons* and *Death of a Salesman* – was stung into a defence of liberal values by the political persecutions of the 1950s. Both *The Crucible* and *A View from the Bridge* were responses to what Miller saw as the collapse of individual integrity and life under the assaults of the social system; they were assertions of the need to play socially responsible roles. Willy Loman never knew who he was or what the connection between himself and his society could be. John Proctor, in *The Crucible*, takes on total responsibility for himself and for his world. But more profound questions lie behind the immediate issues of political coercion and moral instability.

At the heart of Miller's work, partly concealed and only inadequately expressed in the early plays but fully articulated in the later ones, is a concern with guilt, a guilt directly related to his experience as a Jew who had survived the Holocaust, and as an individual who had discovered his own potential for betrayal. The apparent clarity of the clash between the free individual and a politically malevolent system had merely served to conceal the subtlety of a problem which had become increasingly central to his work, and which he perceived as having metaphysical rather than social origins. Now he tended to see the pieties of his 1930s plays as a form of sentimentality.

Tennessee Williams is hardly immune to charges of sentimentality. But in his best work the note of self-pity, which is never entirely absent, is contained by a rigorous honesty about the desperate self-deceptions practised by his characters and the fundamental evasions which may be implied by art. His broken figures appeal, partly because they are victims of history – the lies of the old South no longer being able to sustain the individual in a world whose pragmatics have no place for the fragile spirit – and partly because they hint at a spiritual yearning which Williams sees as being extinguished by the processes of life no less than by those of society. In other words, the social and the metaphysical meet in Williams's work as they do in Miller's.

His protagonists in the major plays are close kin to those other 1950s romantics, the Beats, restlessly moving on, afraid of stasis and extolling a love which is curiously androgynous. His plays are highly charged. They deal in violence, in sexual tensions, in violations of the body and spirit. His South is another country, elemental, crudely manichean, suggestive, in a sense, of a kind of Freudian war between body and mind. On occasion he was capable of a genuine poetry, and if he was equally capable of a reduction of experience to simplistic symbol he could also, in a play like *The Glass Menagerie,* demonstrate a fine control of language and image, a precisely sustained tension between the poetic sensibility and a prosaic setting which still makes that deceptively simple play one of the best works to have come out of the American theatre.

Though he, too, often failed to maintain the tension in his work, and was capable of permitting a destructive slide into sentimentality – the simplistic ironies of *The Rose Tattoo* doing nothing to prevent this – Williams at his best was from the beginning a genuinely original voice in a way that Miller, so heavily dominated by Ibsen, seemed at first not to be. Yet both remained desperately committed to the idea of an identifiable and functioning moral self, and as a consequence their doubts about individual and social coherences tended to be deflected into style. For Beckett the public and private are mutually interpenetrated with absurdity; for Miller and Williams the erosion of private space and the consequent social collapse are born out of a failure of courage and imagination on a private and public level. Needing to believe in the integrity of a resistant self they shift the threat of collapse onto the form of the play (*Death of a Salesman* and *Camino Real*) or onto a dramatic symbol which must stand for that collapse (the unicorn in *The Glass Menagerie*, the dried-up fountain in *Camino Real*, the concentration camp in *After the Fall*). But both men at times recognised the ambiguous nature of their own craft, late in their career acknowledging the potentially hermetic and deceptive nature of art – Miller with *The Archbishop's Ceiling* and Williams with *Out Cry*.

The American theatre is eclectic. It lacks stylistic consistency. And in a way its energy derives precisely from its refusal to accept conventional restraints. O'Neill writes, on occasion, interminable and, indeed, unstageable works in a wide variety of styles; Williams, in *Camino Real*, invades the audience and deliberately projects experience to extremes, exposing the generative power of sexuality and elaborating images to the point at which they assume a threatening literalness (as in *Suddenly Last Summer*). Miller opens up the mind, allowing a neurotically deluded self to recreate the past, to flow with a freedom which potentially denies stylistic unity as it does temporal logic. To Williams, indeed, there was a special virtue in the theatre's capacity to sustain conflicting pressures, to dissolve the literal in search of animating principles. And he saw the stylistic tension of many of his plays as expressive of the moral and even spiritual tension which is their subject. As he said in the note to *The Glass Menagerie*:

> The straight realistic play with its genuine frigidaire and authentic ice cubes, its characters that speak exactly as its audience speaks, corresponds to the academic landscape and has the same virtue of a photographic likeness. Everyone should know nowadays the unimportance of the photographic in art; that truth, life, or reality, is an organic thing which the poetic imagination can represent or suggest in essence only through transformation, through changing into other forms than those which merely present appearances.

6

'These remarks', he added,

> are not meant as a preface only to this particular play. They have to do with
> a conception of a new plastic theatre which must take the place of the
> exhausted theatre of realistic conventions if the theatre is to resume vitality
> as a part of our culture.[5]

Clearly in making such a statement he was ignoring a number of
developments in the American and European theatre over the previous thirty
years. But his main point of reference was the Broadway play which clung
to realism for reasons only partly to do with a consistent social and aesthetic
position. Both Miller and Williams regarded themselves as experimenters.
It is true that their fundamental impulse was mimetic; the 'continuous
present' of _Death of a Salesman_ being designed to present a mind in a state
of collapse, and the expressionistic devices of _Camino Real_ the distorting
power of a prosaic world. But they were concerned to develop a theatrical
style which reflected their desire to dissolve a confident realism and to trace
the social and psychological origins of cultural anxiety. And his notion of
a plastic theatre was not without its value, for the American theatre, at its
best, has proved remarkably malleable. In particular, it has charged the
apparently naturalistic setting with a metaphysical rather than simply a social
significance. Writers like Wilder, O'Neill, Eliot, Miller and Albee have not
merely stretched the surface fabric until opacity becomes translucence,
revealing thereby a social and psychological mechanism; they have attempted
to forge powerful dramatic metaphors out of a setting which stands both
as a threat to fragile identity and the defining boundary of the world in which
their characters must move. O'Neill's strictures against a naturalism which
simply held the family Kodak up to ill nature reflected his desire to penetrate
behind the private and public masks, but it was equally an assertion about
the nature of reality and the role of art. The world which their characters
inhabit is not simply given; it is also in large part invented by them, as
memory redesigns their lives and the imagination resists the pressures of the
real. From the very beginning, then, their work has in part been reflexive;
it has been concerned with the tension between the apparently substantial
nature of historical, economic and social realities, and the individual's
necessity to transform those supposed realities.

At times O'Neill, Miller, Williams and even Albee all seem to have
believed that this process of transformation was a literal one, involving
political action, reform, the restoration of a natural and manifest justice. They
have all written plays which either directly or indirectly insist on the need
to change the world in such a way as to accommodate the needs of the
individual or the mass. But by degrees they shifted their ground and saw
this process as a continuing effort by the imagination to resist the apparently
implacable. Thus their work becomes reflexive to the degree that their subject

becomes the process of imaginative reshaping which is in essence the one in which they are themselves engaged. The inhabitants of Harry Hope's bar (in *The Iceman Cometh*), Blanche Dubois (in *A Streetcar Named Desire*), Willy Loman (in *Death of a Salesman*), George and Martha (in *Who's Afraid of Virginia Woolf?*) are all engaged in recreating the world. They all confront, consciously or unconsciously, the paradox that while this process is possibly a necessary act of rebellion, a resistance which is perhaps not without its heroism, it is also potentially destructive. The cost of indulging the imagination may be the loss of a grasp on the moral world. The act of rebellion may also be an act of betrayal and desertion. The need to project a world in which the self plays a central role, and there is a natural consonance between that self and its setting, may ultimately be the source of irony. For Beckett it was wholly so. For the American playwright the issue was never that clear. Beckett simply accepted the paradox which made his own work further evidence of a reductive irony. The coherences of his own plays were inevitably self-mocking. For O'Neill, as for Miller and Williams, and, to some degree, Albee, the tension is sustained. For the most part the self-doubt of the writer is implicit, though real enough. But in the later works it tends to surface more directly. It is there to some degree in *Long Day's Journey Into Night*; it is there very clearly in Tennessee Williams's *Out Cry* and in Edward Albee's *Box*. And it is there in Miller's confessional *After the Fall* and *The Archbishop's Ceiling*. These are all writers who have chosen to foreground style because they are all writers whose plays concern characters who display the writer's defence against the world. Their work is in some fundamental sense about the ambiguous battle of the imagination to sustain the self. It was not for nothing that Williams's favourite Chekhov play was *The Seagull*. But it was Albee, whose first works were staged just at the moment when Miller's and Williams's careers seemed to be faltering, who made this concern with the nature of the real most central to his work.

Albee's real achievement has always lain in his control of, and sensitivity to, language, particularly at a time when Off-Broadway was in flight from the spoken word, seeing it as a tool of power and a rational restraint on the intuitive and the spontaneous. The moral fervour of the early plays and the simple distinction between illusion and the real gave way first to a complex, if not always dramatically satisfying, debate about the nature of reality, and subsequently to intelligent if at times arcane experiments with form and language. His plays no longer tend to be confidently located in time and space; the world he presents is theatrically, socially, and morally reified, as voices, detached from personal and public histories, test emotional propositions, conduct experiments in dissonance and harmony, and reveal something of the mechanisms of control which Albee seems to imply are the real source of the ethical questions with which he had begun his career. Despite his

Broadway productions Albee has remained committed to experiment, to the values and objectives of the Off-Broadway theatre from which he sprang. The very nature of these experiments implies a refusal to accept the crown as successor to Miller and Williams so eagerly thrust upon him in the early 1960s, and now as precipitately withdrawn by those anxious for the emergence of a writer who can satisfactorily bridge the gulf between Broadway and Off-Broadway. But he remains one of the most intelligent and fascinating of America's playwrights.

When he first appeared, he was seen as and, indeed, was a liberal voice recalling the individual to his moral and even spiritual responsibility. Fundamentally that remains his stance but his confidence has slowly been eroded, his sense of human potential qualified by the evidence of further decline. The verbal oratorios of the early plays, the splendid articulateness, has given way to fragmented speeches, brief snatches of language located in lengthening silences, dialogue which is little more than a series of statements, the ironies and oblique references of which mirror his sense of a loss which he sees as the central fact of modern existence. His, like Beckett's, has become an entropic art, a reflection and ironic presentation of the world which he observes and which, in *The Zoo Story* and *Who's Afraid of Virginia Woolf?*, he still believed could be saved with compassion, a liberal respect for reality, and a language which, if wilfully deceptive, could still offer hints for the restoration of harmony. That presumption has gradually been displaced by a more reified vision. And character too has collapsed. In *Tiny Alice* the characters have already become baroque creations, figures moved around with an eye to the arabesques of language and symbolic function rather than moral enquiry. Albee is here more interested in defining the contours of the real than with identifying the moral content of an assured if threatened social structure. But the allegorical dimension of that play did imply the persistence of a sense of structure, an underlying confidence in the pattern-forming power of art, though reality has already begun to dislocate, to shatter into a disturbing flux of shifting roles and competing fictions.

Even that surviving confidence has since been leached away. *Quotations from Chairman Mao Tse-Tung*, *Listening* and *Counting the Ways* show evidence of his interest in words detached from their social function, in the movement of minds no longer confidently located in time and space. *Quotations from Chairman Mao Tse-Tung* mixes time-scales as it blends the apparently fictive with the ostensibly real until the two become simply alternative fictions – systems of words and images which offer an explanation for a sense of apocalypse. Indeed the reality which he had urged on his characters with such assurance in the early plays has now splintered until the Chinese box, the interleaving of different levels and kinds of experience, the simple fact of the simultaneity and experiential equivalence of events, becomes the only model

9

which he can sustain. And so the dramatist becomes a sculptor of language, a collagist, a creator of images, a choreographer, a composer for whom character and words are found objects and the process of interaction as interesting and authentic as the ostensible but probably delusory object of that interaction. Mao exists on the same plane and at the same time as avowedly fictional characters. There is apparently no more than a simple correspondence between these experiences which are not linked by causal process but merely coexist. Albee's use of Mao is in fact a gesture of refusal. And by that I don't mean a rejection of Mao's message but a refusal to be coerced by public fictions. Albee struggles to fictionalise the public world as it attempts to fictionalise him, reducing him to number, function and role. Much the same, of course, could be said of *Slaughterhouse 5*, *V*, *Gravity's Rainbow* and *The Painted Bird* which equally imply an exact equivalence between various fictions, including the fiction which is the novel, and the society in which it exists.

But who, after all, is a greater manipulator of others, a greater plotter, than the novelist or the dramatist? Implicit in Albee's later work, as in the work of Coover, Pynchon and others, is a suspicion of art. In a sense, of course, that is a central quality of literature, certainly of American literature. What, after all, are *The Narrative of Arthur Gordon Pym*, *Moby Dick*, *The Confidence Man*, *Tender is the Night*, *The Day of the Locust*, if not confessions of the cruelly deceptive coherences implied in the act of writing? It is a dilemma which can perhaps only be adequately expressed by silence (sometimes even suicide), by the deployment of a self-destructing language whose assurances will crumble even as the book or play proceeds, or, as with Albee in *Quotations*, by the surrender of some small element of his control as author – letting the arbitrary seep into his work through spaces deliberately left open.

So, if all of Albee's characters are struggling to retain possession of a world, to imprint their own meaning on it, they are in a sense mimicking the activity of the artist as he mimics that of life. The precision with which they and he use words – they frequently correct one another's usage, try for precisely the right nuance – parody of the writer's conviction that language is indeed a net which can successfully trap experience and hence reality (though at times, it remains 'an unconscious attempt to make people aware that they must listen more carefully').

In *Counting the Ways* and *Listening*, rather as in Pinter's and Beckett's most recent work, the word 'reality' has lost all meaning. We are left with a present which is no more than the recalling of a past which may never have happened. Even the substance of the physical surroundings has shrunk to a space which offers no clue as to meaning or time. There is a chilling moral detachment in *Listening* and, to a lesser extent, in *Counting the Ways* which is reminiscent of Kosinski's *Steps* and *The Painted Bird*. For Jerzy Kosinski the natural analogue for human experience is the scientific experiment. His protagonists are often literally plotters writing scenarios for other people's lives. Albee, too, is interested in the process whereby people seek to gain control over experience, their own and that of others through their fiction-making skills.

This is in effect a drama of exhaustion – not in the sense that John Barth uses a similar phrase of a particular form of literature but to the degree that this is a theatre concerned with the entropic nature of the human machine, the defeat of the conscience, the loss of control over experience, the collapse of language and that sense of structure which it implies. Just as Pynchon's characters pursue their parodic quest for meaning through trying to track down the lexically defined but finally intangible V, or Joseph Heller's protagonist in *Something Happened* tries to sieve experience through the finer filter of his emotional responses in order to understand his situation, so Albee's characters, in his most recent plays, try to perceive their doubtful past through a language which has itself become attenuated. But, for all this, Albee will not surrender his fundamental conviction that change is possible, that some kind of intervention may be made in the logic which he identifies. Like Arthur Miller he will not relinquish his grasp on the moral world and perhaps in some respects that is a characteristic of their work and in some degree of the American dramatist. Some final redemptive possibility remains.

It would be less than generous to see Miller and Williams as facilitating the processes against which they were ostensibly in revolt but there is something of that. They both write about failed adjustments. They both run the risk of sentimentalising the misfit. The individual who cannot adjust to the new materialism is celebrated and deplored simultaneously. He or she is associated with a simpler, and, indeed, as both writers admit, even a simplistic model of society. Theirs is thus a tainted lyricism. Indeed such characters are often seen as verging on the psychotic. The fault lies not only with the system which destroys them but also with the individual who clings to myths and dreams discarded by history. Thus what is wrong with society, in Miller's view, is not that capitalism has betrayed some organic relationship between people or between the individual and his setting, but that capitalism has betrayed its own principles. So Joe Keller is attacked in *All My Sons* not as an industrialist but as a bad industrialist. Similarly, Willy Loman comes up against a brash young employer who casually discards him, but is anyway presented as a man who has betrayed his own father's capitalist principles. And, as his career advanced, Miller was prone to locate social evil in a deeply flawed human nature rather than in any system of social organisation. Accommodation to that fact becomes a moral virtue, albeit an accommodation which implies a continuous resistance to what must now be acknowledged as inevitable. Much the same is true of Williams and Albee. It is not always apparent how that can transfigure the world which menaces their characters.

In the case of Williams we are asked to celebrate the individual in a state of neurotic recoil, the person who refuses to resist the forces to which he seems to grant an implacable power. And yet the fragility of such figures, maimed, broken, destroyed in spirit and in body, ensures that our sympathy is never likely to go beyond a certain wistful regret. They are presented as ahistorical, resisting the flow of time and experience. They represent what seems a childlike response to pain, anguish and reality. Thus while we are asked to sympathise with them, to recognise the loss involved in their defeat, there is an inevitability about that defeat in which we are asked to acquiesce. A brutal or simply careless capitalism provides the context for their lives; it shapes their environment and defines and severely limits their freedom. But since that seems no more than a name for the modern there is a perverse sense in which the audience is invited to collaborate, if not in the conscious cruelty then at least in the regrettable need to lay aside dreams and to compromise on visions which are tainted by their seemingly adolescent origins or by the risk of insanity if they are persisted in in the face of a prosaic reality. There is a sense in which the man who began as a highly political playwright quickly became not merely apolitical but even anti-political as his characters were invited to retreat into personal relationships or to flee from causalities altogether. His puritan conscience survives in the high price they pay for their non-involvement but, perhaps because, professionally, he was committed to a world of fiction, he found it difficult to condemn them. Certainly his imagination for the most part found itself unequal to the task of locating them in that ongoing world of social and political exchanges to which he thereby seemed to grant some ultimate authority. In a not unfamiliar gesture he opposes the modern only by celebrating what it destroys but in doing so historicises those victims and conceals the power and logic of the forces that would crush them. He seems less concerned with pleading for a humanising of the present, for the survival of qualities and values of fundamental importance, than with regretting the passing of an age in which they had been a natural expression of human life. But to be sure, on some fundamental level, he, too, suspects that if one were willing to press the action back into the past that conflict between the material and the spiritual would always have been relevant. For the force of history is associated with a physical and material drive; the transcendent vision which justifies that history with a spiritual impulse. The war between them seems unavoidable both within the individual sensibility and, externalised, in the public world beyond. And that inevitability implies a certain level of acquiescence in the process which he seems to deplore. His protagonist—victims are not, finally, destroyed by capitalism, political corruption or a new brutalism, but by life's own internal tensions – that sacrifice of the spiritual to the material which is the motor force of history and, to Williams, as, I suspect, to Miller, the root of the tragic.

And, despite his invocations to change, Albee, too, can be accused of precisely that accommodation against which he rails so consistently. George and Martha, in *Who's Afraid of Virginia Woolf?*, in effect learn the necessity to adjust to the real. And though George speaks of the need to defend freedom and oppose what he sees as a drift towards a conformist culture this remains at the level of rhetoric. Here, as elsewhere in his work, the only available model for the society which he proposes lies in the American past. He repeatedly invokes American revolutionary principles and the virtues of a lost individualism. But since access to those principles seems to have been closed off by time he substitutes a faith in human relationship and a restored sense of community which his characters advocate but do not live by. He deplores the drift towards totalitarianism and the nullity of consensus and yet, like Miller, the reality to which he urges his characters is one of a human imperfection which explains both personal and national failure. His analysis of social collapse is so generalised, however, as to make it difficult to see precisely how the renewed commitment to which he urges his characters can operate. His rhetoric implies the possibility of change; the logic of his plays suggests a certain inevitability. And if resistance is presented as a necessary stance then the terms of that resistance have to be negotiated with a singularly unyielding reality.

Certainly if these writers are concerned with revolt the scope for radical change seems slight. But slight or not it plainly remains crucial to all three, and resistance a central theme. Their characters may be required to accommodate to the realities of time and to the diminishing space available for moral action but they ultimately refuse to capitulate to social process or the simple pragmatics of a material life. Apocalypse has become an ever more present possibility and this has exerted a pressure on character and language by no means so apparent earlier in their careers. The structures of art are themselves now thoroughly infiltrated by irony. A confident collusion between artist and audience has shown acute signs of collapse. And yet the notion of an alliance between that artist and his audience continues to be offered as a model of a social contract with some ultimate power to neutralise a destructive privatism and an equally corrosive moral conformity. When consensus disintegrated, as it did in the mid 1960s, the moral focus diffused. An anxious liberalism no longer claimed attention any more than did an apologetic bohemianism. For a brief moment the radical and the romantic anarchist seemed to have obtained some purchase on the system. Indeed the outcast, the artist and the poet now felt entirely capable of challenging the public world and deflecting the course of national policy. But

13

neither Miller nor Williams seemed to address this new concern with political action, cultural identity or sensual liberation. The sexuality of Williams's plays had seemed subversive only so long as society had been excessively puritanical. When sexual liberation became normative it was Williams who seemed the puritan. Albee's Jerry in *The Zoo Story* was more clearly a figure of the age, deploying a necessary violence and preaching a renewed community. But Albee, too, came to seem outside the central concerns of the decade as he sought his models in T. S. Eliot and generated a drama which seemed increasingly hermetic. And when the pendulum swung, in the 1970s, although their own work did reflect a growing self-consciousness and, in the case of Miller and Williams, a pull towards autobiography equally evident elsewhere in theatre, they did so with work which no longer had the kind of assurance which had once made them primary interpreters of national hopes and fears.

Nonetheless Williams, Miller and Albee all succeeded in bringing to Broadway a moral seriousness and an aesthetic sensitivity which has hardly marked that theatre over the years and which certainly can't be said to do so today when it is dominated by comedies, musicals and foreign imports. Certainly no other writers have commanded the popular and critical following which all three have achieved. There can, indeed, be little doubt that with the single exception of Eugene O'Neill theirs is the outstanding achievement of the American theatre. These were playwrights who addressed the anxieties of their age. All three have been concerned with the state of their society and with examining the fate of fundamental American myths having to do with liberal individualism, a sense of community and a utopian vision. For all three America had lost a crucial innocence. In a sense they have said of the country what Stella says of her sister, Blanche: 'You should have known her when she was a girl.' What they chiefly seem to regret is the decay of a metaphor – the metaphor which once linked history with the notion of growth and located the individual in a natural cycle which pulled him or her into harmony with the world he or she inhabited and with those who shared that fate. Like O'Neill before them they have registered some fundamental disturbance, a breaking of the natural rhythm. Their characters no longer belong, and that sense of loss, addressed through different languages and distilled into different symbols, is their theme as it has been the theme of America's major dramatists from O'Neill, through to Odets and Wilder. They lament the decline of the moral self and the slow fading of a vision but in doing so they implicitly make a case for the possibility of change and indeed see in the theatre itself a principal agent of transformation and a paradigm of the social, moral and spiritual community whose decline they regret.

1 Tennessee Williams

In 1975 Tennessee Williams published his *Memoirs*. It is an oddly shocking book, a tangle of medical emergencies, sexual adventures, and drink and drug-induced hysteria. It is the story of a crack-up which had in a sense been lifelong. Self-justification mixes with self-accusation as, like Scott Fitzgerald, Williams tries to trace the origins of personal collapse. And, increasingly, it becomes apparent that his work emerges from precisely that paranoia which had typified his life.

The reference to Fitzgerald is disturbingly apt. Both men tended to see the vocation of writer as essentially a romantic one. Both flirted with a political stance in some essential way antithetical to their pose of bohemian alienation. And it would be difficult to imagine Williams dissenting in any way from Fitzgerald's account of a personal crisis which he, too, was prone to regard as evidence for cultural collapse and, ultimately, human mortality:

> Of course all life is a process of breaking down, but the blows that do the dramatic side of the work – the big sudden blows that come, or seem to come, from outside – the ones you remember and blame things on and, in moments of weakness, tell your friends about, don't show their effect all at once. There is another sort of blow that comes from within – that you don't feel until it's too late to do anything about it, until you realize with finality that in some regard you will never be as good a man again. The first sort of breakage seems to happen quick – the second kind happens almost without your knowing it but is realized suddenly indeed.[1]

For both men one cause of that breakage was the slip into insanity of those closest to them, that and a neurotic sensitivity which was part cause and part effect. Both men became alcoholics and both not merely used their art as a desperate means of shaping their experiences into an acceptable form but also made that process their essential theme. Williams's Laura Wingfield and Blanche Dubois set out to reinvent their worlds with hardly less desperation and conviction than did Fitzgerald's Jay Gatsby and Dick Diver. For all of them it was a losing game; that is, in some respects, the essence of their romanticism. But it is the only game which is capable of animating them.

The *Memoirs* identify a conspiracy, the agents of which are sometimes his directors, actors, reviewers or lovers, but which is simply another name for the demeaning realities of human life and the dependent role of the artist. The threat of insanity, disease and death had always been close and real to

Williams, and the failure of individual plays was seen as a rejection of himself. He had always been hypersensitive to the plight of a writer whose work is an act of resistance to the very forces of materialism and prosaic literalness on whose acquiescence he must necessarily rely for his survival. His various tantrums, as he flounced out of numerous theatres during rehearsals or performances, are faithfully recorded. But the irony, of which he was all too aware, was that he had of necessity to return since his work relied on the existence of those he despised, distrusted or feared in order to come into being. He was, in other words, tied to those who were in some sense the source of his alarm and, since this is a basic theme of his work, it is perhaps scarcely surprising that he found this situation at times literally unbearable, fleeing not only out of the theatre but to hotels and apartments in Mexico, France, Italy, or whatever country had come to stand for freedom to a man who, above all, feared the commitment he so desperately needed. For much of his early life that tension was the source of a neurotic intensity which charged his work with a luminous quality. When it deepened into clinical depression and an incapacitating self-doubt the result was an artistic débâcle. The frustration is that at the very end of his life there were signs of recovery.

His apocalyptic imagination at times created a drama in which the collapse of a personal sensibility resonated on a public level. Thus, *A Streetcar Named Desire* is not only the story of a desperate woman at the end of her tether but of a culture in a state of crisis, its certainties dislocating, its myths collapsing. But at other times it led him into a lurid gothicism as he sought some correlative for a sense of private and public trauma. The lyrical impulse, so central to his early work and which there does battle with the gravitational pull of the banal and the prosaic, later devolves into a mannered sentimentality. The implicit becomes distressingly explicit as the plays discharge their energy randomly. The allusiveness of language in *The Glass Menagerie* and *A Streetcar Named Desire* gives way to the empty rhetoric and self-regarding complaints of *The Milk Train Doesn't Stop Here Any More* and *The Seven Descents of Myrtle*. His sympathy for the spiritually and materially dispossessed degrades into a coy celebration of the deviant, the emotionally incomplete and the wilfully perverse. In the early plays sexuality has a dangerous and even subversive quality; it threatens to destabilise the arrogant assertions of those who command the public world. Later, in a play like *Small Craft Warnings*, it is tainted with sentimentality and a deeply suspect desire to appeal to what was a contemporary fad for prurience. In much of his later work originality defers to parody. Many of his supposedly new works were in fact reworkings of projects which had first surfaced many years before. But none of this undermines his achievement nor, since there were indications that he was slowly feeling his way back to his earlier brilliance, can it be taken as a final account of his career whose neat and destructive symmetry was beginning to break down as he reached back into the past for the images and events which had earlier generated his best work.

Like William Faulkner, Williams created a world which was manifestly his own. His South is coterminous with but not identical to the real South (though the supposed reality of the South, composed, as it is, of fragments of myth, fiction and self-sustaining deceits, is itself suspect). It is a world on the turn, a culture caught at a moment of precarious balance. It was not for nothing that he was drawn to the work of Chekhov. And what is true of the public world is no less true of the private one, of characters who are themselves caught precisely at the moment when personal dreams and myths are under pressure and when the reality of mortality and the fact of physical decline become undeniable. The shock of that change is registered in his work in the form of a neurotic recoil. And that moment of recoil is central to his work.

If loneliness is a basic motif of the *Memoirs*, his career was in effect an attempt to people his world. The characters with which he constructed his plays were one means of filling the void if only by pluralising himself. He spent his life seeking freedom and, indeed, insisted that freedom is the primary gift and accomplishment of the writer; but he never ceased lamenting the failure of those relationships from which on occasion he himself withdrew so precipitately after the death by cancer of his lover and companion, Frank Merlo. Like the legless bird of *Orpheus Descending*, which dies when it touches the earth, he claimed the right of a solitary free existence in which he exulted, but which was plainly also the root of a terrible isolation. By his own account he often punished those who reached out to him in part at least because they represented that containment and commitment which he feared. But his need for other people was obvious. It was a paradox which he never ceased to write about and to enact, but which he never succeeded in sublimating. He died, as he feared he would, alone in a hotel room. The freedom of isolation turned out to be no kind of freedom at all.

His greatest fear was of confinement. It was a fear which he realised in the most literal of senses when he was placed in the padded cell of a mental hospital. But in a more metaphorical sense he was trapped for most of his life in the very success for which he had once struggled so strenuously. A shy man, he was forced to play the most public of roles: a writer concerned with capturing the evanescent and the lyrical, he spent his time negotiating with a world in which neither of these qualities could exert their authority.

The *Memoirs*, of course, like all autobiography, read the past through the prism of the intervening years and served the psychic and indeed the financial needs of the moment. But in summing up the life of his sister Rose, in 1975, he did at the same time offer a very self-conscious coda not only to her life but his own. 'After all', he insisted, 'high station in life is earned by the

17

gallantry with which appalling experiences are survived with grace.'[2] It was how he chose to regard himself, and it was certainly how he chose to see his central characters. Northrop Frye once said of the romance that at its most naive it is an endless form in which a central character, who never develops or changes, goes through one adventure after another until the author himself collapses. And in seeking to summarise Tennessee Williams's life and work it is tempting to apply this description not only to his plays, in which a single, fragile, vulnerable and defeated character wrestles with the fact of his, or, more often, her defeat, but also to his own life which was from beginning to end a carefully constructed piece of theatre in which collapse was not merely an ultimate fate but also a constant possibility, a sense of danger to which he frequently willed himself to submit. At times, and eventually persistently, it led to simple self-pity; but at his best he turned his own neuroses, his own hysteria, into lyricism and transformed the desperate courage of his characters into a kind of grace.

When Williams died, in an ironic accident which all too accurately summed up a quarter of a century of self-inflicted suffering (choking to death on the plastic cap of his medication following an evening of drinking), the obituaries which followed were a blend of respect and casual dismissal. Inevitably, favourable response concentrated on his first decade as a New York playwright, though the doyen of British theatre reviewers, Harold Hobson, presented a vision of that early career distorted by what had followed. Thus Williams, he suggested, had brought to the theatre 'a drunk-sodden drug-doped, self-pitying, sadistic nostalgia, particularly in his sensational "A Streetcar Named Desire"'. Indeed he compounded this by offering a travesty of that play's content, suggesting that it was the 'story of a girl of good family reduced by rape to destitution, degradation, insult and madness in New Orleans'. The obituary was plainly designed to celebrate the career of a man who was 'half aflame with poetry, half mad with distorted passion',[3] but the effect was to praise him only in so far as he had disrupted the supposed moral and aesthetic equilibrium of the English-speaking theatre, introducing a note of decadence and melodrama. For all the wilful inaccuracies of Hobson's comments, however, what does emerge from his remarks is a sense of the shock which Williams's work created – a shock dulled by time but real enough for all that.

What was new about his work was the sexual pressure behind the social surface, the distension of psychological realism to the point at which the process of invention becomes no less subject than method. His figures desperately reshape the world they inhabit, and it is the gulf between this factitious world and the one that threatens to pull them into its coercive influence which generates the anxious energy of his work – an energy the more compelling because its residue is a disturbance of the very idea of an

[handwritten: they can pass like the Sath but we are left to deal]

equable norm. His troubled protagonists are withdrawn from the stage – led towards the darkness of pure fiction (like Laura in *The Glass Menagerie* and Blanche in *A Streetcar Named Desire*) – but the world which remains (our world) has itself become instructively fragile, its contingency exposed, its characters stripped of the illusions which had formerly made them convincing actors in their own dramas, and which had charged the anarchy of their lives with shape and purpose. The naturalism apparently reinstated in the final scenes has been so thoroughly subverted that it exists only as irony, while those characters who survive the trauma of the play's action stare into a future drained of moral content. *[handwritten: guilt /anxiety /disharosk/]*

Williams brought to the American theatre a striking blend of prosaic literalness and poetic yearning, half pathos and half genuine lyricism. Early in his career the lyricism predominated; later, the pathos. But no other American playwright has created a dramatic world so distinctive, or characters so compelling in their blend of self-regarding need and desperate courage. That they choose to theatricalise themselves and their surroundings as a defence against the real places the plight of the writer himself at the centre of attention; in this sense, too, Williams was the protagonist of all of his plays. For at his best he turned to his own experience, reshaping it in an attempt to come to terms with what he freely admitted to be the pressures of a life deformed by psychic confusions. Like O'Neill, he transformed his life into art and the effect was the same for both men. His life became bad theatre; his theatre, a living memorial.

Tennessee Williams died on 25 February 1983. Though there were crucial indications of recovery of nerve on a personal level, and control and a sense of poetic self-sufficiency on an artistic one, for some twenty years he seemed to have done little more than rework ideas flung off in that brief but brilliant decade and a half between the mid 1940s and the late 1950s, when his own destructive tensions were transformed into powerful images of alienation and despair, and when his private search for self-definition was forged into a poetic rhetoric whose incompletions were an expression of the faltering language of the dispossessed. And for a while dispossession, alienation, anomie seemed the dominant tropes of the culture. For most of the last twenty or so years of his life he seemed to live out in his own life that traumatising moment which he dramatised in so many of his plays, the moment in which the central character feels the world begin to slip away, dreams to lose their conviction, love to dissolve into hard-knuckled need. There was a reason for this. The death of Frank Merlo affected him deeply. It destabilised him psychologically and artistically. And eventually what was powerful and original in his work dissolved into parody, and his life with it; where once he had written an elegy for a society in which the spiritual, the poetic and the vulnerable had deferred to simple pragmatism now the elegy was for his own lost powers.

But the achievement of those early years was undeniable and forty years on as convincing and moving as ever. No longer shocking for their subject matter his plays survive because of the honesty for which he always strived and so seldom achieved. They survive because the anxieties they express, and the social and moral dislocations they dramatise, are still felt. The struggle to escape the constraints of the prosaic, the effort to transcend mere facticity, in short to reinvent the world, arguably remains the same necessary and doomed enterprise that Williams believed it to be. In *The Great Gatsby* Fitzgerald's narrator suggests that Gatsby is his own Platonic creation. Much the same could be said of Williams whose gesture of renaming himself 'Tennessee' was merely the first step in the construction of a role which he played with total conviction. He was to be the romantic writer, afflicted with a potentially lethal illness, drawn to drink, drugs and insanity, harassed by a public world with which he must always be at odds; solitary, driven, self-destructive. His death was not merely wholly consistent with this role; it was, arguably, a result of it.

But though his final years left him at the margin of the American theatrical scene – few of his plays being greeted with enthusiasm – he was both personally and artistically more secure than he seemed. He had found a kind of personal peace and even serenity. He had come through the worst of his crack-up and begun a process of rediscovery. This was clear in *The Two Character Play*, which examined the nature of the dramatic moment and the theatricalising impulse. It was also true to a limited extent of *Vieux Carré* and *A Lovely Sunday for Creve Coeur*. In these he travelled back in time, much as O'Neill had done in his last plays, in an attempt to rediscover the passions, the evasions, the sharpness of vision and response which he had once before fashioned into art and which, with *Clothes for a Summer Hotel* and *Secret Places of the Heart*, he once again began to do. Now, however, he was able to lay claim to a sense of absolution and grace apparently unavailable earlier in his career.

Blanche Dubois in *Streetcar* confesses that she has always relied on the comfort of strangers. This was no less true of Williams himself whose own work was a curious mixture of self-revelation and concealment. The strangers are his audience invited to respond to the tortured, alienated and vulnerable figures which he places on stage. In some undeniable sense they are him, if not in the sensational sense that journalist-reviewers frequently chose to believe. His art was the communication of a pathologically shy man; his accounts of characters unable to reach one another, or even to convey a sense of the nature and profundity of their need, an expression of his own fear that his plays themselves were an imperfect communication. The poetry implicit in his work, like the over-reliance on dramatic symbols, was his attempt at an oblique contact. Regarding directness as incapable of containing the subtleties of thought and emotion at which he aimed, he turned to the allusive. It was a poet's response. And this is, finally, how he saw himself. At times he created a kind of spiritual doggerel which barely escaped its origin in self-pity, but at times he produced a deeply affecting lyricism which charged his characters and their situation with a significance which he always feared to be lacking in his own life. He was an original as few writers are. His voice was his own. And if, on occasion, it was distorted into an hysterical cry, at others it genuinely aspired to a uniquely moving aria.

At the age of five Thomas Lanier Williams caught diphtheria. It left him paralysed in both legs and with a weak constitution. Indeed later he was to express doubts about the diagnosis, tracing a heart condition back to his early illness. Though he recovered the use of his legs he was never strong afterwards, preferring the company of his sister to that of the boys at school, who regarded him as a sissy (also his father's word for him). He was, as he has said, 'a very solitary child'. By the age of ten he had read most of his grandfather's library of classics and began to write stories at the age of twelve, prompted by the success of a school essay on 'The Lady of Shalott'. He and his sister, as he later said, 'lived in our own imagination', and when the family moved from Mississippi to St Louis, Missouri, the two of them felt 'aliens'. The choice of words is instructive. It suggests that Williams's sense of alienation was partly the product of a social world unresponsive to his sensibility and partly a willed act. Like his sister, whose sanity eventually snapped, he felt in the world but not of it and the imagination was a final resort.

Family life was far from happy. His parents reminded him, in later life, of the two protagonists of Strindberg's *The Father*. She was a puritan, shocked by anything to do with sex or alcohol, while his father drank to drown his disappointments and upbraided his son for what he took to be his effeminacy. And the writing which occupied ever more of Williams's life was primary evidence for that effeminacy. His mother used to read aloud to them from Dickens; his father increasingly absented himself. The relationship seems closer to that between Morel and his wife in *Sons and Lovers* than that between Strindberg's characters. He was a travelling salesman, violent and aggressive, frequently away from the family home; she was gentle and protective. His father came from Southern cavalier stock; his mother from a New England background; and these types persist in his writing representing two poles of experience and two responses to the pressures of the private and public world. On the one hand is the Promethean figure, confident, apparently sexually secure, evading the causalities and vulnerabilities of life by keeping on the move; on the other hand is the passive, fragile self, desperately seeking in personal relationships a place to hide from the world. Williams saw both and

21

embraced both. He feared but was awed by his father; he loved but pitied his mother.

And, with the family's move from Mississippi to St Louis, Missouri, he came to feel that this was virtually an organisational principle of society:

> In the south we had never been conscious of the fact that we were economically less fortunate than others. We lived as well as anyone else. But in St. Louis we suddenly discovered that there were two kinds of people, the rich and the poor and that we belonged more to the latter...If I had been born to this situation I might not have resented it deeply. But it was forced upon my consciousness at the most sensitive age of childhood. It produced a shock and a rebellion that has grown into an inherent part of my work.[4]

His drama sustains this division, sometimes, as in his earliest work, externalised as social and even political conflict, sometimes internalised as a battle within the sensibility between will and imagination, the lure of the material and the spiritual. It operates equally at the level of fact and symbol. Hence, as Benjamin Nelson points out, in 1948 he recalled life in the family apartment in which the brutality of the squalid alley outside was to some degree neutralised by the imaginative and sensitive decoration of the apartment itself, with white furniture and a collection of glass animals.

> Those little glass animals...came to represent in my memory all the softest emotions that belong to recollections of things past. They stood for all the small and tender things that relieve the austere pattern of life and make it endurable to the sensitive. The area-way where the cats were torn to pieces was one thing – my sister's white curtains and tiny menagerie of glass were another. Somewhere between them was the world that we lived in.[5]

Somewhere between them was equally the world in which his drama was to be located, and, apart from anything else, that drama is both an attempt to reconstitute the world imaginatively and a record of such attempts by Williams's characters. Throughout his career he was haunted by a violence which could not be resisted in kind (though his early plays seemed to feel that possibility) but which could, perhaps, be controlled and accommodated by the creative mind. And this clearly had its correlative in the public world of domestic and foreign politics. While his sense of anxiety had its roots in his own psyche, he was also responding to what he saw as a fundamental shift in social and cultural values. And he was not alone in this apocalypticism. In 'The Noble Rider and the Sound of Words' Wallace Stevens too observed that:

> Reality...became violent and so remains. This much ought to be said to make it clearer that in speaking of the pressure of reality, I am thinking of life in a state of violence, not physically violent as yet for us in America, but physically violent for millions of our friends and still more millions of our

enemies and spiritually violent, it may be said, for everyone else. A possible poet must be a poet capable of resisting or evading the pressure of reality of this last degree, with the knowledge that the degree of today may become a deadlier degree tomorrow.[6]

In Williams's work that spiritual violence occasionally finds its correlative in physical violence but he is at his best when it is not converted into action. In just the same way there is a distinction to be made between his elevation of the imagination as a transforming mechanism and the manner in which he, on occasion, and in later years increasingly allowed this to degenerate into a flaccid romanticism. And this, too, is a distinction that Wallace Stevens makes:

> The imagination is one of the great human powers. The romantic belittles it. The imagination is the liberty of the mind. The romantic is a failure to make use of that liberty. It is to the imagination what sentimentality is to feeling. It is a failure of the imagination precisely as sentimentality is a failure of feeling.[7]

The problem is essentially that identified by Blake's 'Jerusalem'; to create a system or be enslaved by another man's.

Williams confessed that in his early reading he was drawn equally to the romances of Walter Scott and the more violent plays of Shakespeare – *Titus Andronicus* being a particular favourite – and it is not difficult to see how these literary influences might become braided together by someone born and raised in the South. He himself recognised 'an atmosphere of hysteria and violence' in his work but tended to see it as a product of his own fear of the fragility and danger of personal relationships, the failure of which could only precipitate pain and despair. But it is as easy to relate this atmosphere to literary and cultural influences. Loss, decline, betrayal, the distortion of a delicate sensibility in the direction of a lurid and gothic self-destructiveness are recognisable motifs of Southern writing, though it must be admitted that the strange and frightening breaking of his sister's sanity gave him a closer model for his many portraits of the individual pressed beyond the point of rational control.

The first sign that his talent might be publicly recognised came with a story called 'Can a Wife Be a Good Sport?' which won third prize in a *Smart Set* competition when he was just sixteen, and the publication of a gothic story in *Weird Tales* magazine. His favourite writers were Yeats and Rilke, while he spent much of the summer of 1924 working his way through the complete works of Chekhov. Perhaps he recognised something in Chekhov's study of a culture caught at a moment of change which reflected his own ambiguous response to Southern society. His favourite poem was Keats's Ode to a Nightingale', which appealed to his romantic spirit, not to mention his incipient hypochondria. Not untypically one of his own earliest poems was an apostrophe to death:

> Rudely you seized and broke proud Sappho's lyre,
> Barrett and Wylie went your songless way.
> You do not care what hecatomb of fire
> is split when shattering the urn of clay.
> Yet, Death, I'll pardon all you took away
> While still you spare me – glorious Millay![8]

Despite the awfulness of this early effort, his poetry did not go entirely unappreciated if the reading of an elegy at the funeral of a member of the Daughters of the American Revolution (his mother's chapter) can be taken as evidence.

homosexuality

He first became aware of his homosexuality at the age of eighteen when he went away to college, but he repressed it. In the late 1970s he was to suggest that it was this sexual repression, and the more subtle sexual tensions of his later life, that accounted for the degree to which his work was permeated with a concern for the sensual and the sexual. It was, anyway, not until he was in his late twenties that he was able to accept the full implications of his sexual identity.

When he failed his ROTC course at university, his father withdrew him and forced him to work for a while in a shoe factory where he earned sixty-five dollars a month from 1931–4. Williams was later to feel that this had been an important experience in so far as it gave him some kind of insight into the feelings of working men, but at the time he deeply resented it. He was eventually rescued by an event which continued to haunt him and which seems to have had catastrophic consequences. Returning from a movie along with his sister, he had what seems to have been a heart attack. It was an event which deepened his own sense of the fragility of life and was the cause of an almost neurotic fear which plainly invades his work. But if this was a serious event, what followed was catastrophic. His sister Rose, who had already been hospitalised twice for depression, was precipitated into a major collapse. She walked into Williams's room as he lay recovering and announced that they must die together. She was immediately committed to a mental hospital. But worse was to come. On one of her mother's visits to the hospital she announced that her school-friends were in the habit of masturbating with altar candles. The puritanical Mrs Williams was plunged into hysterics and pleaded with the doctors to do anything to stop the string of obscenities. The eventual result was a disastrous lobotomy which calmed her but ended any possibility of recovery. Though not involved in the decision, Williams himself never recovered from the sense of guilt which this inspired. And in later years he seems to have felt some connection between neurosis and creativity, feeling Rose's adjustment to 'normality' to have been purchased at the price of her imagination. It was too close to his own sense of himself as a creative artist under pressure from a prosaic world for him not to turn her experience into metaphor. The irony was that the metaphor itself became a trap, for Williams in time allowed himself to be contained and defined by this image of himself as alienated romantic.

Following his sister's operation and his own illness he retreated to his writing, producing a series of plays which addressed the public world of capital and labour rather than the private pain of his family life. It was not a decision which he could sustain for long, but at the beginning of his career he saw art as 'a kind of anarchy'. As he explained, 'Art is only anarchy in juxtaposition with organized society. It runs counter to the sort of orderliness on which organised society apparently must be based.' For all that, the anarchy was at first to be shaped by a political conviction no more clearly defined than that of Scott Fitzgerald's but nevertheless strongly felt.

Tennessee Williams's imagination, like Arthur Miller's, was dominated by the social realities of the 1930s. The melodrama of his early unpublished plays was, to a degree, that of the decade. Reality seemed to resolve itself into simple terms, and the stage offered both that direct rapport between artist and audience and that sense of a communal art which seemed to many an apt image of a necessary social action. This was a concern which survived in his later work primarily in an implicit distrust of the wealthy, a Manichean sensibility which dramatised human nature and social forces in terms of opposites, and in a melodramatic imagination which pressed experience to extremes, seeing the individual as the victim of forces beyond his or her control.

He began his career with the pieties of the age, believing that the world could be re-made by the moral sensibility, and that political change could shape an environment in which innocence could survive and the spiritually delicate be protected. These convictions were shortlived, certainly not surviving the 1930s. For him, as for many, radicalism foundered on the evidence of political betrayals and the pragmatics of war. And thus there remained only the imagination, and his position became essentially that identified by Paul Valéry when he said of poetry that it is

> productive of fiction, and note that fiction is our life. As we live, we are continually producing fictions...We live only by fictions, which are our projects, hopes, memories, regrets, etc., and we are no more than a perpetual invention...You are here, and later on you will no longer be here, and you know it. *What is not* corresponds in your mind to *what is*. That is because the power over you of *what is* produces the power in you of *what is not*; and the latter power changes into a feeling of impotence upon contact with *what is*. So we revolt against facts; we cannot admit a fact like our death.[9]

And that is the central fact to be resisted in Williams's work – a mortality which presses in the direction of absurdity, which threatens every moment of consonance, which betrays the patterned grace of youth and which ironises the relationships, the hopes and the constancies of his characters. Tennessee Williams's world is, spiritually and symbolically, always autumn. Things are on the turn. The signs of decay are there to be seen. And, as Williams himself admitted, he 'discovered writing as an escape from a world of reality in which I felt acutely uncomfortable. It immediately became my place of retreat, my cave, my refuge.'[10]

His first play was produced when he was twenty-four years old and staying with his grandfather in Memphis. 'Cairo! Shanghai! Bombay!', a comedy about two sailors on shore leave, was produced by a small summer theatre called the Rose Arbor (the production taking place on the back lawn of a Mrs Rosebrough). Williams then enrolled at Washington University and began to write plays in every spare moment, when he was not reading Chekhov, Lawrence or Hart Crane.

His second produced play was 'The Magic Tower', performed late in 1936. A slight romantic work, this gave way to the politically engaged material which he wrote for The Mummers, a 'disorderly theatre group of St. Louis, standing socially, if not also artistically, opposite to the usual Little Theatre Group'.[11] His first piece for them was a brief pacifist drama entitled 'Headlines', designed to accompany their production of Irwin Shaw's *Bury the Dead*. ('"How would you like to write something against militarism?" they had asked. "So I did."' Williams later observed.) There then followed a series of committed plays which matched not only the mood of the decade but also the enthusiasm of The Mummers.

Perhaps the most substantial of these was 'Candles to the Sun' written between 1936 and 1937. It is set in a coal-mining area and all the characters are to one degree or another victims of the company that controls every aspect of their lives. John, the son of a miner called Brom, leaves home in order to escape, but marriage and fatherhood force him to work in a New York mine where he is killed in an accident. His wife, Fern, and son, Luke, go to live with his parents. But they are equally suffering as a consequence of the Depression. The Company no longer pays wages, instead issuing scrip which can only be redeemed at the company store where goods are sold at inflated prices. Under this pressure their daughter, Star, a sixteen-year-old, leaves home.

As time passes and the mother, Hester, suffers from a fatal case of pellagra, the family survive by taking in washing. Luke, now seventeen, is introduced to Communism by a man known as Birmingham Red. As Luke says, 'It's funny about that guy. He ain't in it for what he can get out of it like everybody else seems to be. He talks about society. You know – you and me and everybody else that makes up the whole world. It's too big to understand all at once...Reds don't think it can come all at once neither. But it's worth working for just the same. It's justice – that's what he calls it – the principle of social justice.'[12]

But, under the pressure of need, Luke is forced to go down the mine where, as a consequence of another accident, Hester's surviving son is killed. Driven by sheer desperation, the men go on strike and are soon reduced to eating grass. However, the moral crisis of the play occurs when Luke steals the $300 his mother has saved in order to send him to college. He wants to give the money to his fellow workers. The choice is a stark and familiar one. The rights of the individual are contrasted with those of the group. The communist organiser faces Fern with the dilemma, seeking her sanction for what has happened:

> RED: There's fifteen hundred people in camp. Do you call them nothing?
> FERN: Only one of them's my son.
> RED: Why not the others?
> FERN: The others?[13]

The choice is precisely that posed in *The Grapes of Wrath* and *All My Sons*. What is the nature of the individual's responsibility? The needs of the community are seen as superseding those of the family. Predictably, Fern accepts this new knowledge and, though Red is himself killed by strike-breakers, the strike is itself successful. But the ironies remain. Brom works throughout the strike, his failing eyesight a patent image of his failure to perceive a central social truth. Star, having lost her lover, who dies of silicosis, goes off to Birmingham, Alabama, to be a prostitute. Luke stays in the mine. The victory is an ambiguous one. Nevertheless, it is tempting to see Luke's decision to fight for the cause rather than go on with college as Tennessee Williams's somewhat desperate attempt to deal with his own disappointment at failing to complete his university career at Washington University. Williams later explained of his relationship with The Mummers,

> The plays I gave them were bad. But the first of these plays was a smash hit. It even got rave notices out of all three papers, and there was a real demonstration on the opening night with shouts and cheers and stamping, and the pink-faced author took his first bow among the gray-faced coal miners that he had created out of an imagination never stimulated by the sight of an actual coal mine.[14]

Williams submitted the play to the Dramatists' Guild. Their reports were mixed. For one reader it was 'a terribly sincere story, reeking of loose writing and an effort to stir the emotions by cheap theatrical tricks. But the weak underpinning cannot hide the fact that the author has some well-drawn characters and some fine scenes. Story needs considerable strengthening, particularly at finish. A few loose ends can easily be developed. Whole story deserves help.' Another reader recommended its rejection on the grounds that 'the plot here is an ancient one and there is not enough new treatment to place it as being worthy of experimentation'. But for a third, 'more than most scripts which we have seen, this one deserves revision at the hands of a competent playwright'.[15]

The play was all of these things. In many respects it was indistinguishable from a dozen other protest plays. It relied on violent, though reported, action, on simplified characters and on a model of social response which left little room for ambiguity. Unsurprisingly it called for revolt. But the play's ending suggested something else – a persistence of doubt, a feeling that victory was not so easily won, that beneath the level of social action and public commitment was a sense of irony which derived from the failure of the individual to dominate his environment or to realise needs that collectivist theories could not adequately contain. It was an aspect of the play which went unremarked but which was in reality the essence of his developing interest as a playwright. For, in the figure of Luke, trapped in a world to which he is temperamentally unsuited, or of Star, driven to compensate for a meaningless present by recourse to a soulless sexuality, we have the origins of Val Xavier, of Blanche Dubois and a whole range of Williams protagonists.

His next play, 'Fugitive Kind' was described by Williams as a flop, though he insisted that 'It got one rave notice... Nevertheless it packed a considerable wallop and there are people in St. Louis who still remember it.'[16] Like 'Candles to the Sun' it also contains the germs of his later work, more especially in its sense of the social world as an implacable force invading the individual's private space. As in *The Glass Menagerie* and *A Streetcar Named Desire*, the *mise-en-scène* suggests the loss of that freedom which had once been the source of personal meaning. And so the set is described by Williams as the 'lobby of a flop-house in a large middle-western city. Outside the door is an arc-light. A large glass window admits a skyline of the city whose towers are outlined at night by a faint electric glow, so that we are always conscious of the city as a great implacable force, pressing in upon the shabby room and crowding its fugitive inhabitants back against their last wall.'[17] That is a description which in essence could be applied to a significant number of Williams's plays. His prototypical hero/heroine is precisely a fugitive trapped by the harsh pragmatics of the modern world. And the effort to deny definitional force to that reality creates, on the level of theme, a concern with romantic rebellion and, on the level of style, a pressure which erodes the authority of naturalism. So, here, as in his later work, the realistic structure of the set is susceptible of subversion as the imagination resists its own irrelevance. As he explained in his stage directions, 'when lighted the set is realistic. But during the final scenes of the play, where the mood is predominantly lyrical, the stage is darkened, the realistic details are lost – the great window, the red light on the landing and the shadowy walls make an almost expressionistic background.'

The play, produced in November and December 1937 by The Mummers, in his then home town of St Louis, Missouri, concerns a group of transients in a flop house on Christmas Eve. Terry is a petty gangster, driven to crime by desperation and by a desire to assert himself in a world which seems to conspire against him. 'I'll tell you who started it', he tells Gloria, the girl with whom he establishes a relationship, and who, as a child, had been assaulted: 'it's the ones that made a tubercular prostitute out of my mother and fixed it so's I got my education out of alleys and pool halls.' He regards himself as 'a sort of one man revolution. I haven't got any flags or ideals or stuff like that to fight for. All I got is myself an' what I need an' what I want.' He sees his criminal career as a kind of war. Revolt, indeed, is the central theme. Leo, the son of the owner, is a college student who writes pieces for his student newspaper attacking the fascists. He has been thrown out of college for his radical activities. When a group of socialites arrive with useless Christmas gifts, the transients refuse them and condescension turns to anger. Violence is clearly just below the surface in a play in which the class war is dramatised in stark form. And the plight of this group of abandoned individuals, desperately fighting for physical and spiritual survival, is linked to what Williams clearly sees as a similar struggle being waged in Spain.

But they are doomed individually just as are those fighting in the civil war. They are involved in a losing game with time and with history. As a result of the activity of an informer, Terry is shot. His conviction that 'we're fugitives, all right. But not from *justice*. We never had any justice', is vindicated by his own death, while his belief that the only real escape lies in flight – 'the best advice you ever gave anyone yet – keep moving' – is proved by his failure to take that advice.

The moral is painted by Leo who decides to start a new life with Gloria:

> They'll never catch his kind till they learn that justice doesn't come out of gun barrels – They'll never catch *us* either – Not till they tear down all the rotten old walls that they wanted to lock us up in. Look, Glory. The snow's still falling. I guess that God's still asleep. But in the morning maybe he'll wake up and see disaster. He'll hear the small boys' voices shouting the morning's news – The Criminal's Capture, the Fugitive Returned! – And maybe he'll be terribly angry at what they've done in his absence, those righteous fools that played at being God tonight and all the other nights while he's been sleeping! Or if he never wakes up – then we can play God, too, and face them out with courage and our knowledge of right and see whose masquerade turns out best in the end, theirs or ours.[17]

But the rhetoric is undercut by the fact that he, too, dies at the hands of those same anonymous forces who have taken over the world. The fugitive, by definition, must keep moving. For the problem is that commitment, compassion and a sense of communal action, which constitute the other possible reaction, require a surrender of the right to flee. Indeed Leo dies because he and Gloria return to leave a note for others to read. It is a dilemma that Williams never resolved, in play after play restaging this conflict between love and escape.

And despite the language of change, it seems clear that he again concedes an implacable force to the public world, which makes the individual's struggle for personal space at worst pathetic and at best tragic. Where Arthur Miller derived from this conflict between self and society a moral tension, where he conceded the individual's responsibility to the public world and to the moral state of his society, Williams was more inclined to see that public world as an image of a determinism that could never be successfully defeated or transformed by the impact of the moral will, but only resisted by the imagination, which becomes the primary source of romantic rebellion. It follows that the writer, the creator of fictions, becomes himself a vital part of this metaphysical resistance, while the majority of his protagonists derive their strength from their ability momentarily to sustain an imaginative world which can protect them in what is necessarily a losing game with reality.

The Williams protagonist is ill-equipped to survive in the practical world of the present. Like another Southern writer, William Faulkner, Williams, particularly in his early work, was equally repelled by a past whose public myths concealed a vacuous personal style and a brutally exploitative system, and by a present in which money and power provided the axial lines of behaviour. He was appalled by the empty style of the past, in which manners substituted for life, and by the crude rationalism of the present, in which imagination, ambiguity, and a subtle shading of response defer to the frontal assault of individuals whose brutal directness can find no space for the fragile and the sensitive. Nor was he simply claiming the rights of the id as against those of the ego. Like D. H. Lawrence, whom he admired to the point of adapting his work, he distinguished between sexuality which merely compounded the anti-human values of society (a desperate denial rather than realisation of the sensual being), and a sexuality which became itself the source of values, a private world of mutually sustained myth at a tangent to the historical world. Where Miller responded directly to historical process, seeing this as an assertion of the causality on which moral behaviour is based, Williams wished to deny history. For Miller, the past contained the clue to present behaviour. In many ways it was a present fact. Its moral authority was the source of guilt but equally of a claim exerted on the conscience. If the link with the past was cut, the chord which bound individual to individual and each individual to responsibility for his own actions would also be severed. For Williams, the past plays a different role because he sees truth as being more problematic, more generously defined; for him, as for his characters, illusions are no less true than the realities they are invented to deny. The truth of Blanche Dubois, in *A Streetcar Named Desire*, consists as much of her desperate fictions as of the moment of betrayal they are invoked to exorcise. The past has its secrets but they are not flourished as a total explanation of the present. It is true that most of his protagonists are born out of their time. They are romantics in an unromantic age. Their strength lies in their imaginative power at a time when the imagination is itself under assault by rationalism and by materialism. But it is not clear that they would ever have been in tune with the values of their society (though Arthur Miller has suggested that Blanche could have lived happily in another world and another time). What we glimpse of the past suggests otherwise.

His theme is, in essence, what Marcuse was to see as the dominant theme of the 1960s – the body's fight back against the machine. It was clear in an early work, *Me Vashya!* (1937) (originally a one-act play called 'Death is a Drummer'), an anti-war play attacking a munitions manufacturer whose mentally and physically damaged wife is momentarily rescued from despair by 'a radical, a pacifist, a young poet'. It was equally clear in 'Not About Nightingales' (1938) (written in Iowa as part of a seminar in playwriting), a play about prison conditions dedicated to the memory of four men who 'died by torture in an American prison, August 1938'. Both offered images of the constraints which he saw as crushing the spirit and the will of the individual. But the sense of containment, of social constraints, so strong in O'Neill and Miller and manifest in the stage sets of both men, takes the literal form of a prison in this play.

In 'Death is a Drummer', Sir Vashya Zontine is an arms manufacturer who bangs the drum for war. He is as sexually voracious as he is hungry for power, supplying both sides in the war which he fosters. He is, as one of the characters remarks, 'a sort of monstrous abstraction – the personification of – war and destruction or – death!'[18] This evil, however, is ultimately defeated when the wife he has mistreated shoots him dead, her own mind obsessed with the ghosts of those whose deaths can be laid at his door – not least that of her poet lover. However the poetic irony of his dying at the hands of his own wife and killed with a weapon he may well have manufactured, hardly conceals Williams's failure to engage the ambiguity involved in destroying him with an act of violence, in avenging the death of a pacifist with a bullet; 'Not About Nightingales' is hardly less crude.

In this play Eva Crane applies for the position of secretary to Boss Whalen, warden of a large island penitentiary. She is unenthusiastic but has been unemployed for six months. The warden, a sensual man, is attracted to her and gives her the job. A few days later a woman comes to visit her son, a prisoner known as Sailor Jack, only to learn, after hours of waiting, that he had gone insane and been removed to a sanatorium. Eva learns from Canary Jack, a trusty who works in the office, and who, because he is coming up for parole, is forced to act as an informer for the warden, that Sailor Jack has actually been driven mad as a consequence of being placed in the Klondike, a small, steam-heated room with little ventilation and no water.

Because of the appalling food – the warden is selling prison food for his personal profit – a hunger strike is planned. When this is put into effect the men are duly thrown into the Klondike. After thirty-six hours, Jim, a young male prisoner, persuades Eva, who by now has conveniently fallen in love with him, to give up her job and inform the newspapers. But this is prevented by the warden who confines everyone to the island for the duration of the trouble. When Jim and Eva are found together Jim is thrown into the Klondike, and Eva agrees to submit to the warden if he will approve Jim's parole.

In the Klondike Jim finds three of the men dead. Together with another prisoner he overpowers a guard and storms the warden's office, only to find that the warden has indeed forced Eva to submit. His fellow prisoner then beats the warden and throws his unconscious body out of the window into the bay, thus neatly sidestepping any moral culpability which might attach itself to Jim. But now they hear the gunboats approaching and Jim jumps through the window hoping to be able to swim to a passing pleasure boat. The troopers arrive a few moments later to find Eva still holding Jim's shoes. The ending is ambiguous but we must presume that Jim escapes.

The simplicity of the piece is apparent even from this account of its plot. It is melodramatic in its action and in its characters. The crudity of its construction is matched by the simple authority conceded to event and motivation. The rape of Eva is a threadbare device, thematically redundant and psychologically incredible. But Williams's central themes emerge strongly – the more clearly, indeed, because of the crudity of the plot. The central fear is that of being trapped. The only two solutions available are represented by the compassionate relationship with another human being (here that between Eva and Jim), or flight. Once again he is writing about the fugitive kind and Jim's salvation lies in his determination to keep moving, even if that means surrendering his relationship with Eva.

It is hard to know just how deep Williams's radicalism went. Not very, one suspects. In his first year with Continental Shoe Makers he voted for the socialist Norman Thomas but it was the last vote he ever cast. Certainly there seems little in the way of an ideological conviction in his work, and no sense of the dignity of labour. His characters, for the most part, are uninvolved in the process of money-making. They are itinerant guitar-players, would-be actors, poets, unfrocked priests, travellers and so on. The factory, the shop, the office, the mine, stand as images of constriction and oppression rather than simply locations for ideological conflict. His was not a political rejection of capitalism but a romantic's reaction against the modern. The prison cell of 'Candles to the Sun', transformed in *The Glass Menagerie* and other plays into an oppressive apartment room, is a central logic of his work. And the dash for freedom at the end of that play is equally a basic image. His sympathies are certainly with the outsider, the bohemian, the underclass, but not because they represent a revolutionary potential. It is simply that they stand for an alienation which goes beyond Marxist notions. When, years later, he expressed support for Castro it was because he was 'after all, a gentleman, and well educated'. In his *Memoirs* he was to insist, 'I am only interested in the discovery of a new social system – certainly not communist, but an enlightened form of socialism, I suppose' (p. 94). But that radicalism, lacking a political correlative, tends to be displaced into a sexual subversiveness and a celebration of the outsider. His contempt for Richard Nixon was real enough, as was his disgust with Vietnam, but these were never issues to which he felt able to address himself directly. What we do find in his work, however, is an account of the collapse of morality and morale, and his awareness of that distrust of the deviant which took public form in the shape of domestic and foreign policy but private and symbolic form in the persecution of the non-conformist. A homosexual and an artist, who was brought up in a part of the country whose myths were more sustaining than its realities, he scarcely needed economic and political theory to justify his sense of exclusion and even persecution. The psychic space allowed him in an America whose animating myths found little room for homosexuality, and whose emphasis was on the strenuous virtues of the frontiersman turned go-getting businessman, was small indeed. His characters tend to wander restlessly through America much as Williams himself had done. What they are running away from is partly the demand that they knuckle down and do a decent day's work, join in the glorious enterprise of getting rich, or settle into the bland world of reproduction and production. Partly it is a matter of trying to escape definition. But beyond that they are engaged in a losing game with time; they are reaching out for a mythological or simply illusory world in which they will be able to evade not merely the brutal representatives of power but also the more destructive world of causality and mortality. In some fundamental sense they seek to run away from themselves and the relentless passage of time. As Williams said, 'My place in society then [1947] and possibly always since then, has been in Bohemia. I love to visit the other side now and then, but on my social passport Bohemia is indelibly stamped, without regret on my part.'[19]

The early plays are not without their interest. They certainly seem to have met the needs of The Mummers, essentially an amateur group intent on challenging the social system in which each of them otherwise played his conventional role. The earnestness is apparent as is the desire for direct effect. Yet beneath the rhetoric and the melodramatic plots it is not hard to detect the beginnings of those concerns which continued to fascinate him throughout his life. And this is particularly true of a very early work, 'Hot Milk at Three in the Morning', a one-act play which he wrote in 1932 and which reads a little like a pastiche of O'Neill, but which nonetheless spells out what became a fundamental thematic paradox of his work. The protagonist of the play is a man who bitterly regrets his marriage as marking the loss of his liberty. He and his wife are reduced to brittle exchanges. She is emaciated and suffering from a breast infection. He determines to leave but when he does so the baby's cry brings him back. He is tied to his fate. The flight he is drawn to is aborted by the human ties with which he had once sought to evade his loneliness. Attached to the manuscript there is a note which suggests that the play was 'Highly Commended'. Its achievement, however, is largely one of mimicry. His talent really lay elsewhere. The tone of desperation was authentic; the determined naturalism was not, though he persisted with it in most of the plays which he wrote at Washington University, in the shoe warehouse, and then at the University of Iowa.

Williams completed his degree at Iowa in 1938 and then tried to join the WPA (Works Progress Administration) Writers' Project, firstly in Chicago and then in New Orleans, but failed to qualify. Instead he changed his name to Tennessee and supported himself by working as a waiter. He chose to change his name because he regarded Thomas Lanier Williams as more suited to 'a writer who turns out sonnet sequences to Spring', while Tennessee recalled the Williams family experience fighting Indians. Living now in New Orleans, he mixed with those on the underside of American life, much as O'Neill had done at the beginning of his career. Looking back on this time twenty years later Williams claimed to have 'found the kind of freedom I had always needed', while 'the shock of it against the puritanism of my nature has given me a subject, a theme, which I have never ceased exploiting'.[20] Given the revelations of his *Memoirs*, it is clear that by puritanism he is not referring to sexual habits but rather the conviction that pleasures must be paid for and that there is a price to be exacted for imaginative freedom and physical consolation. And that tension has, indeed, generated much of his work.

His breakthrough as a dramatist occurred when he saw an article in a newspaper referring to a play competition run by the Group Theatre in New York. Lying about his age (he was three years too old), he mailed a selection of his plays. He received a cheque for $100 from the judges, Harold Clurman,

Irwin Shaw and Molly Day Thatcher. Taken up by the agent Audrey Wood, he wrote 'Battle of Angels'. She helped him secure a Rockefeller grant with the aid of which he travelled to New York, where he attended a playwriting seminar run by John Gassner. He gave Gassner a new version of the play and he in turn recommended it for production by the Theatre Guild. It was dedicated to D. H. Lawrence 'who was while he lived the brilliant adversary of so many dark angels and who never fell, except in the treacherous flesh, the rest being flame that fought and prevailed over darkness', while one copy of the script, date-stamped 26 November 1940, carries an epigraph from Strindberg: '...I too am beginning to feel an immense need to become a savage and create a new world!'[21] It was an apt quotation for a playwright about to set out on his public career – a writer, moreover, who has always been drawn to the apocalyptic and melodramatic, as to the poetic.

A predecessor to *Orpheus Descending*, 'Battle of Angels' opened on 30 December 1940 in Boston. It was a disaster. A third-act fire in the stage store came close to asphyxiating the audience, while critics for the most part were baffled and repelled. Later, Erwin Piscator at the New School tried to turn it into a political drama about life in the South by cutting up the speeches and re-allocating them to different characters. Williams was appalled. Shocked by the collapse of his hopes, he nonetheless turned immediately to several other projects – *I Rise in Flame, Cried the Phoenix*, a play about D. H. Lawrence (he had visited Frieda Lawrence in Taos, New Mexico, in 1940), and 'Stairs to the Roof', a rather strained allegory which was to receive its only production in Pasadena, California, in 1957.

'Stairs to the Roof', described by Williams as 'A Prayer for the Wild of Heart that are kept in cages', is dedicated to the 'little wage-earners of the world not only with affection, but with profound respect and earnest prayer'. When he was half-way through writing it, the war broke out and he considered abandoning it in favour of something more 'light and frothy'. But it's hard to imagine him producing anything much more insubstantial, for though he hints at social intent ('At the bottom of our social architecture, which is now describing such perilous gyrations in mid-air, are the unimportant little Benjamin Murphys and their problems. Can it be that something is wrong among them?'[22]) in fact 'Stairs to the Roof' is little more than a whimsical equivalent of O'Neill's *The Hairy Ape*, a celebration of the human need for freedom. An expressionist drama, it tells the story of Benjamin Murphy, trapped in a dead-end job at Continental Sheetmakers, as Williams had once been similarly trapped in a shoe warehouse.

In a manner distinctly reminiscent of Elmer Rice's *The Adding Machine*, the play opens on a scene of frantic office activity, with the actors miming the mechanical movements of their work. Indeed Rice's influence extends to a divine intervention at the end of the play. Murphy longs for freedom, which he suggests was lost in the whole business of taking possession of America. As he says 'Freedom... is something my forefathers had when they marched down through Cumberland Gap with horses and women and guns to make a new world. They made it and lost it. Sold it down the river for cotton and slaves and various other commodities, sold at a profit created by cheating each other.'[23] And his image for that freedom is a stairway which he discovers leading from the office to the roof. As he tells his employer,

> there's a disease in the world, a terrible fever, and sooner or later it's got to be rooted out or the patient will die. People wouldn't be killing and trying to conquer each other unless there was something terribly, terribly wrong at the bottom of things...maybe the wrong is this: this regimentation, this gradual grinding out of the lives of the little people under the thumbs of things that are bigger than they are! People get panicky locked up in a dark cellar: they trample on each other fighting for air! Air, air, give them air![24]

It would be hard to imagine a more direct statement of Williams's position. As a response to a conviction that 'the world's cracking up' it is obviously something less than profound. And the play's style and form were clearly more appropriate to the 1920s and 1930s than to an America at war with something other than its own myths. But it was not without its original touches. Here, as in his earlier work, he was experimenting with music, introducing a singing chorus, drum rolls, parodies of Irving Berlin, guitars, and so on. And his own thematic concerns were clear. Thus, Benjamin Murphy, before leading everyone to the rooftop, releases the animals from the zoo, especially, in a gesture which said something about a continuing Lawrentian influence, a number of foxes. There, despite a speech in which Murphy calls for a reconstruction of his society based on blueprints no longer 'supplied by the old architects – the ones who put so much water in the cement that it wouldn't hold up', and in which he insists that 'we the people, are going to draw them ourselves',[25] the real essence of the play lies in his desire 'for movement...the road'. The play ends with Murphy whisked away by God to found a new world. It is an insubstantial piece, its chief interest now is in the fact that it established themes and forms which would recur in his work – the loosely structured form in particular providing a dry run for the later *Camino Real*.

These early plays clearly have major deficiencies. They reveal a writer searching for a subject and a style. Politically, they reflect the orthodoxies of radical thought without showing any evidence of his understanding the theoretical underpinning of that radicalism. Theatrically, he seems to have modelled himself on the playwrights of the 1920s and 1930s, at one moment reproducing the naturalism of an O'Neill sketch, at another the expressionism of Elmer Rice and at another the realism of a Sidney Kingsley. In another work of this period, 'Dos Ranchos', the influence was Lorca and perhaps even Yeats. But he was already something more than a simple amalgam of other writers. His central theme was as clear as was the lyricism, often now, as later, developing into a self-conscious poeticism, but equally capable of rising to genuine eloquence. He was very much feeling his way but the constant testing of forms and styles reflected a confident talent rather than an unfocussed mind. And this is as true of 'Dos Ranchos' (also entitled 'The Purification'), which is a verse play, as it is of any of his other early work. Set in the western ranch-lands of the early nineteenth century it is a Lorca-like drama of broken taboos and blood feuds. The characters are Spanish ranchers and Indians and the play takes the form of a ritualised trial which follows acts of incest and murder. The place names are derived from the country around Taos, New Mexico, where he had met Frieda Lawrence, and the presence of Lawrence is recognisable in the central significance which the play accords to sexuality. The misplaced passion, which had led to the trial, has to be purged, not merely to restore the social world but also to bring life to a country parched with drought. The symbolism is as naive and direct as in many of his later works but derives some sanction from the primitive setting. It was eventually published in *Twenty-Seven Wagons Full of Cotton* and, like his other early work, contains the tracery of images and ideas developed later. In the figure of Elena, for example, we have a hint perhaps of Laura in *The Glass Menagerie*, and thereby of his sister Rose:

> Her eyes were always
> excessively clear in the morning.
> Transparency is a bad omen
> in very young girls!
> It makes flight
> > necessary
> > > sometimes!
> You should have bought her
> > the long crystal beads that she wanted...
> Oh, I know, Mother.
> You fear that she might have desired
> to discover reflections in them
> of something much further away
> than those spring freshets she bathed in...

FATHER: He means to say
she went beyond our fences.

SON: Beyond all fences, Father.
She knew also
glaciers, intensely blue,
Valleys, brilliant with sunlight,
Lemon-yellow, terrified!
> And desolation
that stretched too widely apart
the white breast-bones of her body![26]

Rose too had gone 'beyond our fences', and had been brought back with the aid of the surgeon's knife. She was, in effect, an expression of part of Williams's own sensibility and *The Glass Menagerie* (1945) was to be his poignant and powerful testament to her plight. It was also to some degree his acknowledgement of a certain complicity, since, though he had not been there to prevent the decision which deprived her of the 'glaciers, intensely blue' and the 'long crystal beads that she wanted', he still felt responsible. It is perhaps not surprising, therefore, that in this, his first successful play, he should have chosen to define his protagonist's freedom in terms of his sister's entombment, or that guilt should be the force which leads both writer and protagonist to return to their own earlier lives. Williams did scarcely less throughout his career, himself returning to the tensions and anguish of his family life with something of the consistency, the anguish, and the effect of O'Neill.

The plight of his sister was, in fact, never far from his mind and the dilemma of his own responsibility towards her surfaces in several unpublished pieces, particularly in 'The Spinning Song', and in the play that relates most directly to *The Glass Menagerie*: 'The Front Porch Girl'. In 'The Spinning Song', a doctor discusses, with a figure called Blanche, her relationship to her mentally affected daughter:

DOCTOR: You have a right to look for something better in life than useless devotion to a sick person whose disease is a type that would keep you both withdrawn from the world as much as if this house were barred as a prison.

BLANCHE: I am responsible for her.

DOCTOR: And for your son. What of him?

BLANCHE: He will leave.[27]

In 'The Front Porch Girl', described by Williams as 'A Comedy in One Act', part of a projected series of plays to be called 'Mississippi Sketches' (and incomplete in the version to be found in the Humanities Research Center at the University of Texas), she is presented as a timid girl befriended, ultimately, by one of the lodgers in her mother's boarding house. Eventually developed into a play called 'If You Breathe, it Breaks! or Portrait of a Girl in Glass', this bears the marks of Lawrence's influence in that if the principal character is clearly modelled on his sister she also owes something to the figure of Miriam in *Sons and Lovers*, and, indeed, is actually called Miriam Wingfield (changing to Rosemary in the course of the typescript). The play, Williams explains, derives its name from the Mississippi expression a 'front porch girl', meaning 'a girl who sits hopefully, or perhaps despairingly, waiting for gentlemen who practically never drop in'. Sensitive and vulnerable Miriam detects slights, real and imagined, 'touches her hair and her throat in a

1.   Photograph of Tennessee Williams, taken in 1945.

momentary panic and starts to retreat inside the house'.[28] One of her two
brothers, meanwhile, is presented as being equally delicate, not, like Williams,
a would-be writer, but a violinist. Though Miriam, unlike Laura in *The Glass
Menagerie*, still has the courage to sit on the front porch and face her
neighbours she, too, has a glass menagerie which, as she explains to the lodger
who shows a sympathetic and understanding interest in her, is a very
conscious expression of her sense of human fragility: 'they're so − *delicate*
− they're so − easily *broken*! When you look at them sometimes it − makes
you cry!...Oh, not just for them − you understand...Not just for the little
glass objects but everything else in the world that − people break to pieces
because they're − easily broken.'[29] Described in the stage directions as a
'DELICATE, FLUTTERING WHITE MOON-MOTH', she is the prototype of Laura
and a whole succession of Williams's figures, who are so easily broken by

the world and whose gift it is to be drawn towards the very flame which will destroy them. Blanche does no less in *Streetcar* and much the same could be said of Val Xavier in *Orpheus Descending*, Alma in *Summer and Smoke*, and even Chance Wayne in *Sweet Bird of Youth*.

Williams worked on *The Glass Menagerie* (then still called 'The Gentleman Caller') on a brief six-month contract for Metro-Goldwyn-Mayer. His experience was no different from that of many other young writers taken out to Hollywood and then left to their own resources. When he presented them with the outline for the plot of an original screenplay about a young woman waiting for an admirer they were unimpressed, and his contract lapsed. He revised the script and the play was first offered to Margo Jones. She liked it so much that she saw it as potential Broadway material, and this view was confirmed by the actor–producer Eddie Dowling when shown the manuscript by Williams's agent, Audrey Wood. As Jean Gould points out, 'He not only produced it with Louis Singer, and staged it with Margo Jones, but took the part of Tom Wingfield, the son and narrator in the play.'[30] The play opened in Chicago at the Civic Theatre in December 1944. It was well received by the reviewers but poorly supported by the public, until a campaign by those reviewers eventually created an audience for it and made a transfer to Broadway possible. It finally opened there in March 1945. It was an immediate success and one in which his mother shared, for Williams signed over half the copyright to her.

The Glass Menagerie has a deceptive simplicity. Tom Wingfield, oppressed by the suffocating realities of his daily life, breaks away from his mindless job and the tensions of his life to follow his avocation as a poet while serving in the Merchant Marine. But escape is not so easy. He is obsessed with memories and the play itself is the product not only of his restless imagination but of the guilt he feels at abandoning his mother and sister. For his mother had been abandoned once before, by his father, who had also walked out on his responsibilities, this being the price of freedom. Left behind, she had dignified the relative squalor of her life with memories, real or invented, of the time when she was pursued by 'gentleman callers'. Now, she is left supporting her congenitally shy and crippled daughter, Laura, and struggling to constrain the soaring ambition and wanderlust of her son who shows signs of leaving her alone. She desperately sets herself to marry Laura off, partly out of a genuine concern and partly because Laura is a responsibility of which she wishes to rid herself. She thus evidences a strange and affecting blend of pity and cruelty. By ill-luck, however, the boy she selects is already engaged, though he, too, is not without his vulnerability. And so the world closes in on Amanda and Laura as Tom offers them up as sacrifices to his art and his freedom.

Like *Death of a Salesman*, this is 'a memory play', and as such past and present coexist. The narrator, Tom, probes into the past in an attempt to find a clue to his present, and this demands a fluidity of style that Williams came to value both as a theatrical mode and a personal strategy. As he says in the Production Notes:

> *The Glass Menagerie* can be presented with unusual freedom of convention. Because of its considerably delicate or tenuous material, atmospheric touches and subtleties of direction play a particularly important part. Expressionism and all the other unconventional techniques in drama have only one valid aim, and that is a closer approach to truth. When a play employs unconventional techniques it is not, or certainly shouldn't be, trying to escape its responsibility of dealing with reality, or interpreting experience, but is actually or should be attempting to find a closer approach, a more penetrating and vivid expression of things as they are.[31]

Williams creates a tension in the play between the constraints of the physical setting and the various imaginative strategies of the characters who recreate that world, easing its constriction and resisting its definitions. The Wingfield apartment is 'in the rear of the building, one of those vast hive-like conglomerations of cellular living-units that flower as warty growths in overcrowded urban centres of lower middle-class population and are symptomatic of the impulse of this largest and fundamentally enslaved section of American society to avoid fluidity and differentiation and to exist and function as one interfused mass of automatism.'[32] But the inhabitants of this closed world are, in essence, no more present than the father, the telephone engineer who fell in love with long distance and abandoned his family. His image dominates the room but he has long since escaped. And so, too, have those he left behind, except that what he has achieved in space they have sought in time, turning, like Amanda, to the past or, like Laura, to the timeless world of the imagination. So, too, has Tom, who, as a putative writer, perhaps scarcely needs the physical escape which leaves him with that sense of guilt that makes him reconstruct the events which constitute the play. But at the beginning of his career Williams was ready to admit to an ambiguity in the writer's ability to reshape experience. For there is a kind of stasis in a world shaped entirely by the imagination, in the fragile constructions of Laura's glass menagerie; the memories, real or invented, of Amanda's gentleman callers; the visits to the movies and even the poems written by Tom. For he, too, seeks to evade the dangerous world of human needs and the entropic nature of existence. He, too, has his glass menagerie, and in order to preserve it is as willing as his father had been to offer up human sacrifices for his freedom. As Williams says of him, he is 'A poet with a job in a warehouse. His nature is not remorseless, but to escape from a trap he has to act without pity.'[33]

The play is a work of some honesty and, indeed, irony. For his own career, of course, depended on just such a move, while the profits from this and other plays sustained his sister for life in the mental home to which the surgeon's knife and her mother's baffled compassion committed her. It would be surprising if Williams's position were anything but confused. The need for escape is clear. It is implicit in his description of the setting. The apartment, we are told, 'faces an alley and is entered by a fire escape, a structure whose name offers a touch of accidental poetic truth, for all of these huge buildings are always burning with the slow and implacable fires of human desperation'. But there is finally no escape for Tom, who has attempted 'to find in motion what was lost in space',[34] and who keeps returning to the world he thought he had escaped and which this play is now designed to exorcise. And so fluidity, which in some moods he wishes to endorse, is seen as being potentially as deceptive as stasis; the imagination as being as cruel as the real. In the real world the daily pressure of life opens up spaces between people; in the imaginative world there may be no room for others. The possible cost of peace is isolation. For those able to enter completely into that world, like Laura, there is a kind of terrifying contentment to be claimed. For those neither blessed nor cursed with that ability the result is a sense of ineradicable guilt. Amanda expresses this by a brittle, carping assault on the daughter who will never leave her and free her of a sense of responsibility she dare not voice (her daughter's infirmity is never to be mentioned, not merely out of compassion but because denial of reality is a necessary condition of life to Amanda and so many other Williams characters), and Tom by an obsessive claim on his own memories, an act of homage. And this is the special fate of Williams's protagonists. They are not simply romantics in an unromantic world. They are individuals faced with the knowledge that defeat awaits them both in the real and the imagined world, that other people are the source of their anguish but that solitude is a more perfect hell.

Williams's work accepts a fundamental determinism – social, environmental and psychological. The conspiracy, biological or economic, is a felt presence in most of his plays. The choice, in a sense, is simple. You either capitulate to it or you resist with the only available weapons – the creative imagination, or a subversive sexuality with the power to deny, if not wholly to neutralise, the pull of death. Language operates both as an agent of the conspiracy, a prosaic lodestone dragging the self into the world of money, power, routine and death, and as evidence of resistance, a poetic reshaping: but it is a different language. Thus it is that, in *The Glass Menagerie*, the gentleman caller is intent on learning public speaking as a route to power while Laura's powerlessness is symbolised by the fact that she cannot master the typewriter. Her hesitant speeches are in fact a series of withdrawals. The only language which is wholly

2.   Eddie Dowling as Tom and Julie Haydon as Laura in *The Glass Menagerie*, New
York, 1945. Designed by Jo Mielziner.

uninfected by commerce, bitterness and disillusionment is that which she employs when describing her glass menagerie, the private language in which she addresses her own inventions. And Tom, too, wishes to escape from the encasing prose of his setting into the poetry that Williams permits him in his role as narrator. It is his only resource. It is the evidence of his resistance. And this, of course, is a familiar strategy of Romanticism. The self becomes its own source of authority against an imprisoning world. But it is an inherently ambiguous refuge, as Melville knew all too well in *Moby Dick*, for the self may be a prison. This is the haunting menace of Williams's world. The desperate devices employed by his protagonists drive them further into an isolation which is itself the ultimate terror. As one of Williams's characters observes, 'We're all of us sentenced to solitary confinement inside our own skins — for life.'[35]

The earlier one-act play, 'If You Breathe, it Breaks! or Portrait of a Girl in Glass', had offered a more optimistic version of *The Glass Menagerie*. In that version Mrs Wingfield is the widow of an Episcopal clergyman, living in reduced circumstances and surviving by running a boarding house. She has two sons and a daughter, Rosemary, who is 'a rather unearthly young person. She is overly delicate like a piece of glass too finely spun in very pale, transparent colors. Her survival in a world that has too little regard for delicate things will depend entirely upon the bare possibility of her discovering somebody who is willing to stand between her and the shattering impact of experience...'[36] Her brother is equally delicate and is rejected by the army. But in this play Rosemary finds the person she is looking for, while her brother finds contentment in his music. This was not a conclusion which he allowed to stand when he revised the play.

What he celebrates in *The Glass Menagerie* is a certain courage ('the most magnificent thing in all human nature is valor — and endurance', he once remarked) and, finally, a compassion that wins out over self-interest, despair and cruelty. Thus he tells us in a stage direction at the end of the play that, 'The interior scene is played as though viewed through soundproof glass. Amanda appears to be making a comforting speech to Laura who is huddled upon the sofa. Now that we cannot hear the mother's voice, her silliness is gone and she has dignity and tragic beauty. Laura's dark hair hides her face until at the end of the speech she lifts it to smile at her mother.'[37] *The Glass Menagerie* was an attempt to lay the ghosts of his own past. It was a play which he, like his protagonist, had to write and it was not for nothing that he gave his poet his own name. It was also a play which, in its elegiac tone, dramatised his problematic relationship to the past — personal and cultural. And the past has always been a major concern of the Southern writer.

The South that Williams pictures is either disintegrating, its moral foundations having been disturbed, or being taken over by the alienated products of modern capitalism. On the one hand are the rich, cancerous, their economic power signalled, in Lawrentian manner, through sexual impotence as in *Orpheus Descencing*, or incestuous passion as in *Suddenly Last Summer* and *Sweet Bird of Youth*; on the other hand are the new, brutal proletariat, as in *A Streetcar Named Desire*, who begin by destroying a South become decadent and end, in *The Red Devil Battery Sign*, by destroying even themselves. It is a Spenglerian vision. Williams's sensibility was in an almost permanent state of recoil. The collapse of the South, though by no means unambiguous, is in some ways seen as the collapse of culture. The process is irresistible. What interests Williams is how the individual will negotiate a temporary reprieve from the progress of history and time. The uncoiling of the spring of history deconstructs the grace of youth, attenuates the urgent, authentic passions and subtle illusions with which the individual and state alike began. His characters exist in a world 'sick with neon', in which pastel shades have for the most part deferred to primary colours, the wistful music of Laura's theme (in *The Glass Menagerie*) or the Vasuviana (in *Streetcar*) being superseded by the rhythms of the dance-hall band. And that music forges a link between Miller and Williams, who both locate their characters in the same no-man's land, stranded between the real and the imagined, the spiritual and the material, a discordant present and a lyric nostalgia. Hence the flute music heard in *Death of a Salesman* is described by Miller as recalling 'grass, and trees and the horizon', a lost world of lyricism and beauty confused with sadness, while the distant music of *The Glass Menagerie* is intended by Williams as 'the lightest, most delicate music in the world and perhaps the saddest'. It is 'like circus music', heard 'not when you are on the grounds or in the immediate vicinity of the parade, but when you are at some distance and very likely thinking of something else... It expresses the surface vivacity of life with the underlying strain of innumerable and inexpressible sorrows'. 'Nostalgia', he suggests, 'is the first condition of the play',[38] as it is in a sense of all Williams's work, but it is a nostalgia for a past which he could not entirely convince himself had ever existed. Like Miller's Willy Loman, his characters find themselves hopelessly stranded in a kind of temporal and spatial void. They can relate neither to their setting nor to the times in which they find themselves living, and thus they fill that void with distorted memories of the past, or wistful dreams of a redemptive future. But they have no more connection with past or future than they do with the present. In both *The Glass Menagerie* and *Death of a Salesman* time boundaries have dissolved. The tension which holds past and present apart has gone. The imagination is the only resource, but the imagination is equally a product of paranoia; it is in some degree primary evidence of the collapse of structure.

It becomes a kind of hysterical or neurotic spasm which can no longer be controlled because there is no longer an available model of order, of social or moral imperatives, which can command respect and authority.

There is a brief essay by Tennessee Williams which does much to explain not only his sense of theatre but also his perception of the ironies of life. As with O'Neill, these ironies can generate either tragic insight or an absurdist despair, but at their heart is an implacable fear of time. For:

> it is this continual rush of time, so violent that it appears to be screaming, that deprives our actual lives of so much dignity and meaning, and it is, perhaps more than anything else, the *arrest of time* which has taken place in a completed work of art that gives to certain plays their feeling of depth and significance.[39]

Time is, indeed, the dominant fact in all of his work. The pressure of time prompts the lies and evasions which themselves become the basis for misunderstandings and despair. The undeniable reality of time drains individual actions of significance. By the same token the suspension of time in a play, or perhaps its radical foreshortening, permits the writer and his audience to abstract the individual from the obscuring random occurrences of everyday life in order to detect meaning in the heart of chaos and to give value to those lives behind by the rush of history. For Williams, if only Miller's Willy Loman could have been encountered 'outside of time', he could have prompted the concern, the kindness and even respect which was his due as an individual. Inside of time he becomes an irrelevance, a trivial cog in a machine whose relentless rhythm is alien to his own needs. The mere act of relocating him in artistic time thus becomes an assertion of values. The writer gives dignity to his characters by writing about them; he emphasises the insidious but invisible effect of time by suspending it.

This concern with time is deeply rooted in a personal neurosis about mortality which took Williams to the psychiatrist's couch and to the physician's office. But it is hardly irrelevant to his sense of a culture in which impermanence had been established as an economic and aesthetic value, and which for many people set the pace for modernity. And while admitting that passion is no less ephemeral than the facts it wishes to deny, he insists that that ephemerality 'should not be regarded as proof of its inconsequence'.[40] For the 'great and only possible dignity of man lies in his power deliberately to choose certain moral values by which to live as steadfastly as if he, too, like a character in a play, were immured against the corrupting rush of time'. So, while, 'as far as there exists any kind of empiric evidence, there is no way to beat the game of *being* against *non-being*, in which non-being is the pre-destined victor on realistic levels', it is still possible to snatch 'the eternal out of the desperately fleeting'. This is 'the great magic trick of human existence'.[41] And so the 'trick' of the artist becomes paradigmatic; the act of invention becomes crucial to survival and personal meaning, and the imagination a vital instrument of redemption. And yet, by freezing time, art mimics the death which it is designed to deny – that is the paradox at the heart of his work. For, if the imagination can generate a momentary meaning, it can also compound the forces it would neutralise. As Williams remarks, 'Fear and evasion are the two little beasts that chase each other's tails in the revolving wire-cage of our nervous world. They distract us from feeling too much about things. Time rushes towards us with its hospital tray of infinitely varied narcotics, even while it is preparing us for its inevitably fatal operation.'[42] This is the temptation to which Laura succumbs in *The Glass Menagerie*, but the alternative is equally chilling and she is unwilling to surrender her dreams for the prosaic world of the typing pool and the frightening causalities of time.

Laura's unicorn can only survive by relinquishing its horn, thereby joining the homogenised world of the horses, but Williams's characters are not free to make the choice. The imaginative perception and sexual potency which make them so vulnerable stand as images of the creative sensibility. And to that extent all Williams's plays are in effect about the plight of the writer – a special individual whose vocation demands a willed openness of spirit that makes him a natural victim of the pressure of events. It is, perhaps, for that reason that in *The Glass Menagerie* he deliberately foregrounds technique, makes his methods apparent and therefore, in a sense, his subject. Nor was Williams unaware of the irony that the act of writing, which, in the preface to *The Glass Menagerie*, he saw as an attempt to catch the organic nature of 'truth, life, or reality' by an act of imaginative transformation, is also unavoidably an escape from those objectives, a denial of their force as totally determining realities. Tom's opening speech in *The Glass Menagerie* contains an implicit attack on America. The collapse of the old world left only a sense of baffled incomprehension, while in Spain a battle was on to construct a new future. But, for all his rhetoric, it was not a battle that Tom was constitutionally fitted to join. And much the same could be said of Williams himself, whose story, in effect, this was. For he, too, after his early, directly social plays was, in effect, retreating from the battle, turning to words. By degrees he negotiated a retreat from the immediate issues of social injustice, from the need to use art as an instrument of social and moral analysis, and instead used it increasingly as a mirror in which he saw his own sense of desperation and alienation. His became a dark world which could no longer be lit up by the clear light of political commitment or an assertive moral passion, but only by the brief sparks of imagination or the reflective glow of a past which he chose to invest with an energy and radiant truth in which, in other moods, he could not bring himself to believe.

The Glass Menagerie is not narrated by a confident voice. Tom is as lost in the supposed present as he had been in the recalled past. Imagining that the suffocation of his spirit, the warping of his ideals, and the stultification of his aspirations were a product of his physical environment, he had broken free. But his freedom, like that invoked by Miller's Linda at the end of *Death of a Salesman*, is an ironic one. The space which he needed was not a physical one after all. Like Albee's Jerry, in *The Zoo Story*, he comes to realise, that all his retreat from human relationships has won him is 'solitary free passage'. If, in the words of one of Sartre's characters, 'hell is other people', he has found that hell is also isolation, so that now he is forced to people his world with memories and to acknowledge that he has stumbled on a further paradox: for his escape ties him to the past even more firmly. It creates a sense of guilt, which makes it impossible ever to evade the demands that in some way are the price of one's humanity. And so not only is Tom forced to relive the past from which he thought he had escaped, but, in *A Streetcar Named Desire*, Blanche Dubois is equally haunted by her own failure to acknowledge a human responsibility – a failure which sends her, too, on a desperate and hopeless flight.

The 'gentleman caller', invoked by Amanda to give dignity to her past and substance to Laura's future, is both 'an emissary from a world of reality' and 'a symbol' of 'the long delayed but always expected something that we live for'.[43] And as such he is indicative of the limits of the imagination. The Wingfields cannot finally make him into something which he is not, although he, too, in the form of the young Jim O'Connor, brought home by Tom as a potential husband for his sister, is trapped in the process of constructing another series of dreams, believing that mastery of public speaking will place the world at his command. He wishes to identify with what Spengler had called the 'Age of the Caesars'. For him, as for Spengler, the new spirit of the age is dominated by '*Knowledge!...Money!...Power!...*' And as such, even unknowingly, he destroys the subtle and the gentle and the maimed. But he, too, is a victim of his own dreams, slipping ever further behind in what he believes to be a crucial race for success.

Laura is a loving portrait of Williams's own sister locked up in her own inner world, her lobotomy trapping her in a permanent adolescence. It is a withdrawal from sociality for which Williams offers a gentler image, in terms of Laura's limp, an imperfection less intrusive, less totally disabling, but the play is a homage to her. Indeed, in a sense the various puns on her real name, Rose, are a writer's private acknowledgement of guilt and love. But all of Williams's characters are crippled in one sense or another – emotionally, spiritually – and out of that imperfection there comes a need which generates the illusions with which they fill their world, the art which they set up against reality. Like Laura's glass animals, however, those illusions and that art prove fragile.

For Williams, narrative itself is the origin of painful ironies. It implies causality, the unravelling of a time which can only be destructive of character and relationship. It is, in a sense, the guarantee of a final victory for death. Hence he and his characters try to stop time. They react, in a sense, against plot. In a way the narrative of their lives does not generate meaning, the meaning ascribed to those lives by history and myth generates the narrative. And as a result they wish to freeze the past and inhabit it, or they spin their own autonomous fictions and submit themselves to a logic dictated by symbol and metaphor. The virtue of the glass menagerie, for Laura, is precisely that it is inanimate. So, too, Blanche's Belle Reve, by turns the family plantation and her own system of illusions, is indestructible and unchanging so long as it can be preserved from assault by the real. Yet if that symbol is put under too great a stress then the only remaining recourse lies in flight, a fluidity of identity and event which appears to offer some kind of defence. And his characters do tend to opt for a world in which their personal outline becomes blurred. They lose definition, indeed they fear definition. Laura, her mother asserts, is 'not a cripple'. Blanche is not a sexual tramp. But if these evasions are necessary they are also destructive, for, without definition, they are without self. At the end of *The Glass Menagerie* the candles of Laura's life are snuffed out. At the end of *Streetcar* Blanche is taken off to an equally lobotomised existence. They now inhabit their fictions entirely. They are invulnerable to further assault, but their invulnerability is the mark of their destruction, of the loss of their humanity. For that is one more paradox which Williams explores in his work. To exist is to be vulnerable. In the words of one of Albee's characters, existence is pain. Narcosis is no solution in that it resolves the paradox by destroying one of its components. The problem is to find a response that permits of both form and movement. And this is equally the problem for the playwright. The solution to which both Miller and Williams were drawn was the memory play, in which the hard edge of reality could be balanced by an imaginative freedom. Constraining walls suddenly become translucent. Time, for a moment, becomes plastic, malleable; indeed it is set into reverse. In *Death of a Salesman* the surrounding apartments disappear amidst a kaleidoscope of leaves; in *A Streetcar Named Desire* the domestic squalor of the apartment is bathed suddenly in a glow produced by Blanche's silk scarf draped over a lamp, an effect which reminds her of the soft lights that illuminated her youth. In *The Glass Menagerie* candle-light abstracts the characters for a moment from an all too literal present. As Jo Mielziner, designer of the stage sets for many of Williams's plays, has remarked,

> If he had written plays in the days before the technical development of translucent and transparent scenery, I believe he would have invented it...My use of translucent and transparent scenic interior walls was not just another

trick. It was a true reflection of the contemporary playwright's interest in – and at times obsession with – the exploration of the inner man. Williams was writing not only a memory play but a play of influences that were not confined within the walls of a room.[44]

Writing to Donald Windham in 1943, Williams had complained that 'The Gentleman Caller' lacked the violence that usually excited him, but in the final version his achievement lay in the drama which he created out of stasis.

The Glass Menagerie was a considerable success. It ran for 561 performances, finally closing in August 1946 after a run of some sixteen months. It won the New York Critics' Circle Award as well as the *Catholic Monthly* and Sidney Howard Memorial awards. George Jean Nathan attributed some of its success to the play's director, Dowling, who had resisted Williams's desire to have captions projected onto a screen at the rear of the stage, and who, he suggested, had invented the scene in which Laura sits on the fire-escape and listens to the music from the dance hall, a scene which he found one of 'the most touching' in the play. But he admired Williams's work while resisting what he felt was a lack of generosity towards his collaborators. Williams's version was wholly different. He insisted that the scene in question was actually the invention of Nathan and Dowling together who concocted it over drinks in a hotel room. Not yet in a position to resist such pressures Williams himself rewrote the scene, and it was retained in the script where the most he could bring himself to say of it was that it did the play little harm. His own doubts centred around the narrations which he continued to believe detracted from the play's power.

To a degree Williams's turn from a public to a private world was itself a response to profound changes in society itself. The American poster designer E. McKnight Kauffer, in an address which he gave to the Royal Society of Arts as early as 1938, observed that,

> with the world as it is, and social values what they are, there is an almost inevitable tendency for a private world. I cannot help feeling myself that external reality has to some extent lost something of its collective significance, or perhaps it is that its significance seems less valuable and less immediate in its appeal, contrasted with the distress that social disruption on such a colossal scale as we have witnessed in our time, has created.[45]

And in a sense The Glass Menagerie and the plays which followed can be seen as a displaced response to social forces which he had earlier chosen to engage on the level of politics. In 1945, he observed:

> Today we are living in a world which is threatened by totalitarianism. The Fascist and the Communist states have thrown us into a panic of reaction. Reactionary opinion descends like a ton of bricks on the head of any artist

who speaks out against the current of prescribed ideas. We are all under wraps of one kind or another, trembling before the specter of investigating committees and even with Buchenwald in the back of our minds.[46]

His response to this, however, was no longer to confront that coercion directly or to examine it for its economic content but, 'Not to conform...the biologist will tell you that progress is the result of mutations...freaks.'[47] And so he celebrates that marginal figure, the character who finds himself, or more frequently herself, at odds with a world which is seen as threat. The tone of his essay seemed confident. In fact it was tinged with hysteria ('For God's sake let us defend ourselves against whatever is hostile to us without imitating the thing which we are afraid of!'[48]) and his characters seldom if ever prove equal to the task of resisting a coercive world. Certainly Laura is broken like her unicorn.

Writing of the American author Paul Bowles in 1950, Williams noted that he had substituted a concern with 'the fearful isolation of the individual being' for that obsession with 'group membership and purposes'[49] which had typified writers in the 1930s. A similar substitution had characterised Williams's own work. Where in the early plays he celebrated a group of people who suffered through material deprivation, now he chose to write about the solitary individual or sometimes a sad alliance of two such people. And interestingly enough he argued that this shift was necessitated by the oppressive nature of American political life: 'What choice has the artist, now, but withdrawal into the caverns of his isolated being?' It was the forces of reaction, he argued, which had created the vogue for what was assailed as decadence but which he preferred to characterise as lyricism. He, like Bowles, responded to what he called 'the extreme spiritual dislocation...of our immediate times', which he saw as the product of 'the social experience of two decades'. But, in contrast to Bowles, he suggested that life nonetheless 'achieves its highest value and significance in those rare moments – they are scarcely longer than that – when two lives are confluent, when the walls of isolation momentarily collapse between two persons'.[50] Laura knows such a moment, but it dissolves in her hands and sends her plunging back into an isolation which is all the deeper for her having glimpsed another possibility. This was to be a recurring irony in Williams's work as his imagination did battle with an increasing apocalypticism.

He was also inclined to see his own thematic concern with survival as a reflection of the political world which he had once addressed directly. For apocalypse was in the air. When he was writing *The Glass Menagerie* it was inherent in a war in which the fragile and the vulnerable were menaced by power. By 1950 he saw a more precise focus for this fear. As he wrote 'Everywhere the people seem to be waiting for the new cataclysm to strike them...they are waiting for it to happen with a feeling of fatality...

Nevertheless, the people want to survive, they want to keep on living through it, whatever it may be.'[51] And this, of course, was the primary objective of his own threatened characters. Yet what they fear is not simply or even primarily something in the social or political world for, as he insisted, 'the true sense of dread is not a reaction to anything sensible or visible or even, strictly, materially, *knowable*. But rather it's a kind of spiritual intuition of something almost too incredible and shocking to talk about, which underlies the whole so-called thing.'[52] The only name he was prepared to give to this was '*mystery*' but in fact, as his work makes clear, it is time, mortality, and a failure of love to neutralise either of these forces.

Yet as late as 1952 he was still laying claim to a social consciousness which he regarded as the distinguishing characteristic of his work. Recalling the contrast between his family's relative poverty and the affluence which surrounded them, he insisted that it 'produced a shock and a rebellion that has grown into an inherent part of my work. It was the beginning of the social consciousness which I think has marked most of my writing.'[53] Moreover, he insisted, 'I am glad that I received this bitter education for I don't think any writer has much purpose back of him unless he feels bitterly the inequities of the society he lives in.'[54] And that pressure does survive in his work but, as in *The Glass Menagerie*, transmuted into a drama in which the fragile and the vulnerable are seen to be as much victims of their own dreams as of the implacable force of the real and the unforgiving rhythms of modernity. Laura cannot adjust to a world in which she must function as a typist or trade her delicate sensibility for security. The axes of her life are different from those which locate other people, so she steps out of time into a security as intransitive as it is total.

Following the success of *The Glass Menagerie*, Williams was at one bound the public success he had always wanted to be. He was the centre of attention, pursued by reporters and taken seriously as a literary figure. Together with Donald Windham he began work on *You Touched Me!*, which was later to have a poor critical reception when it ran on Broadway. But, whatever its qualities, the striking fact was that he now had no difficulty in securing its production.

Despite the pleasure he took in his new-found success, it did – and would always – make him uneasy. As he wrote in a later essay, it had removed a valuable irritant which he saw as the source of his energy:

> The sort of life which I had previous to this popular success was one that required endurance, a life of clawing and scratching along a sheer surface and holding on tight with raw fingers to every inch of rock higher than the one caught hold of before, but it was a good life because it was the sort of life for which the human organism is created. I was not aware of how much vital

energy had gone until this struggle was removed. I was out on a level plateau with my arm still thrashing and my lungs still grabbing at air that no longer resisted. This was security at last. I sat down and looked about me and was suddenly very depressed.[55]

Behind the alarm was partly the remnants of his radicalism and partly the puritanism which for a decade he had mistaken for that radicalism. Thus he was embarrassed at finding his own luxurious life-style underwritten by those who now served him and whose lives he had celebrated in the 1930s. He had become the very thing which he had once assaulted with such confidence. But beyond that he was at risk of losing a crucial insecurity and of surrendering to the bland contentments which went with success.

The essay is not without its unintended ironies. While ostensibly disavowing his new elevated status, he is in fact staking his claim to a significance beyond mere popular success. The language implies a modesty which the rhetorical stance denies, and struggle is dignified not merely on moral but on metaphysical and ontological grounds:

> One does not escape that easily from the seduction of an effete way of life. You cannot arbitrarily say to yourself, I will now continue my life as it was before this thing. Success, happened to me. But once you fully apprehend the vacuity of a life without struggle you are equipped with the basic means of salvation. Once you know this is true, that the heart of man, his body and his brain, are forged in a white-hot furnace for the purpose of conflict (the struggle of creation) and that with the conflict removed, the man is a sword cutting daisies, that not privation but luxury is the wolf at the door and that the fangs of this wolf are all the little vanities and conceits and laxities that Success is heir to – why, then with this knowledge you are at least in a position of knowing where danger lies. You know, then, that the public Somebody you are when you 'have a name' is a function created with mirrors and that the only somebody worth being is the solitary and unseen you that existed from your first breath and which is the sum of your actions and so is constantly in a state of becoming under your own volition – and knowing these things, you can even survive the catastrophe of Success![56]

Apart from the confusion of whether essence precedes existence or existence essence the essay is characterised by an almost endearing immodesty. His personal situation is elevated to existential paradigm. But at the same time the struggle which he identifies is indeed an essential element in his work and if it does not take the form of that political struggle between capital and labour which had characterised the work which he produced for The Mummers, transmuted into an essential conflict between body and soul, reality and illusion, poetry and prose, it did come to be the essence of his drama and a distinguishing characteristic of his outstanding play, *A Streetcar Named Desire*.

When he came to ask himself the deceptively simple question, 'What is good?' his answer was a defence of the artist's role as a moral force and fierce opponent of the depredations of time:

> The obsessive interest in human affairs, plus a certain amount of compassion and moral conviction, that first made the experience of living something that must be translated into pigment or music or bodily movement or poetry or prose or anything that's dynamic and expressive – that's what's good for you if you're at all serious in your aims. William Saroyan wrote a great play on this theme that purity of heart is the one success worth having. 'In the time of your life – live!' That time is short and it doesn't return again. It is slipping away while I write this and while you read it, and the monosyllable of the clock is loss, loss, loss, unless you devote your heart to its opposition.[57]

Perhaps it was this sense of time passing inexorably away which made him apply himself to his work with an almost neurotic intensity.

Following an eye operation he left for Mexico where he could briefly relax and then work on his next two projects – one called *Summer and Smoke* and the other entitled *The Poker Night*. In Texas he met and discussed the plays with the producer Margo Jones. She felt that the former would be more suitable for her arena theatre, and accordingly he worked on it in the spring of 1946 in a rented house on Nantucket island while his guest Carson McCullers wrote her own first play, *The Member of the Wedding*. He completed the play for Margo Jones, and in the early part of 1947 rewrote *The Poker Night* during a stay with his grandfather in Key West, Florida. *Summer and Smoke* opened in Dallas in the summer of 1947 to enthusiastic reviews, and a Broadway transfer was discussed but it had to await the première of his other play, now entitled *A Streetcar Named Desire*, the script of which had been enthusiastically received by his agent Audrey Wood. The play received its première at the Barrymore Theatre in New York. Not the least reason for its success was a cast which included not only Jessica Tandy as Blanche, Kim Hunter as Stella and Karl Malden as Mitch, but also the relatively unknown but magnetic Marlon Brando as Stanley.

In an essay published in *The New York Times* four days before the opening of *A Streetcar Named Desire* Williams remarked that, 'It is only in his work that an artist can find reality and satisfaction, for the actual world is less intense than the world of his invention.'[58] This was offered as a description of the artist's attitude towards his world but it could equally be seen as the central belief of the protagonist of his new play – as it had been of the fragile Laura in *The Glass Menagerie*. The real world exists. Indeed, Williams's characters are neurotically sensitive to their surroundings. They display an almost Keatsian sensibility. The world presses on them but they react with a nervous gesture, a lie, a dream, anything that can hold the real at bay. And most

3. Marlon Brando as Stanley, Jessica Tandy as Blanche and Kim Stanley as Stella in *A Streetcar Named Desire*, directed by Elia Kazan and designed by Jo Mielziner, New York, 1947.

fragile of all is love. Thus it is that Williams chose to take a verse from Hart Crane's 'The Broken Tower' as an epigraph to what is surely his greatest play – *A Streetcar Named Desire*:

> And so it was I entered the broken world
> To trace the visionary company of love, its voice
> An instant in the wind [I know not whither hurled]
> But not for long to hold each desperate choice.

The origins of *Streetcar* are many and can be traced in the stories and sketches which preceded it. An early fragment – 'Blanche's Chair in the Moon' (written in the winter of 1944–5) – describes a woman sitting in moonlight, as in the play Blanche was to be a figure desperately shunning the light. In 'The Lady of Larkspur Lotion' he describes the situation of a Southern woman, ageing and alone, who subsists on illusions which give her life meaning. And in 'Portrait of a Madonna' a woman is taken to an asylum following an imaginary rape by a man she had loved and lost in her youth. A stranger in the present, she is drawn to a past which is part invention. What creates the particular power of *Streetcar* is that the pathos or the neurotic intensity of these figures, decadent remnants of the Old South, is exposed to the Promethean power of a Lawrentian seed-bearer – gaudy, potent, an ambiguous image of the future to which Williams dare not wholly commit himself. For if Stanley Kowalski has the vitality and sexual power of Lawrence's Mellors, he is too closely allied with the modern to compel Williams's endorsement, too lacking in tenderness to become simply a symbol of a revitalised world. Yet by the same token Blanche, as she appears in *Streetcar*, has resources of her own which make her a worthy adversary to Stanley Kowalski and which distinguish her sharply from the figures in the earlier sketches.

Two other works also bear on Williams's creation of *Streetcar*: they are 'Interior: Panic', completed in 1945–6; and 'The Spinning Song', a much longer epic melodrama, dated 1943, which has an oblique relation to *Streetcar* in that it is a play about a Southern land-owning family of the kind that eventually produced Blanche and Stella. Indeed the plantation, like that in *Streetcar*, is actually called Belle Reve, and the play's alternative title, 'The Paper Lantern', anticipates the use which he makes of that symbol in the later play. A story of the disintegration of a Southern dynasty, written in verse, it was clearly designed as a major work and, in a note written in September 1943, he explained its origin.

> The conception of this play began on my return one evening from seeing Sergei Eisenstein's film, *Alexander Nevsky*. Its pictorial drama and poetry of atmosphere, a curiously powerful blend of passion and restraint, an almost sculptural quality, had excited me very deeply and made me wonder if it were not possible to achieve something analogous to this in a poetic drama for the stage. The film of Eisenstein was immeasurably enhanced by a complete musical score by Prokofiev, which combined with picture and action so perfectly that the effects were of blood-chilling intensity. The influence of modern music and surreal art, both present in this film masterpiece, could be used as powerfully in a poetic stage play. The passionate restraint, the sculptural effect noted in the film, became the artistic tone of this play as I began to conceive it.
>
> In my dramatic writing prior to this I have always leaned too heavily on speech, nearly everything I have written for the stage has been overburdened with dialogue. In working on this new project I determined to think in more plastic or visual terms. To write sparingly but with complete lyricism, and build the play in a series of dramatic pictures. No play written in such creative terms could be naturalistic nor could it be comedy. It would have to be an epic story, as Eisenstein's film was, or a poetic tragedy. Written in verse, with a surrealist influence and a background of modern music, it would have to be independent of nearly all dramatic conventions.
>
> I realized at the outset that I was embarking on something that would make the ordinary commercial producer's hair stand on end at the mere thought

of attempting to stage. This realization is salutary in that it frees the work of any lingering instinct toward conformity and gives the poetic imagination a full license to work out its own designs. The singular thing about Eisenstein's film is that despite the popularity of its medium, the film, there is nowhere present any indication of compromise between the pure artistic concept and the popular conventions. That, I felt, was the secret of its extraordinary power, absolute fidelity to the purest single concept. And it seemed to me that after sitting on my ass for six months in Hollywood, the noblest and most cavalier act that I could perform by way of atonement was to put all popular ambitions aside and devote whatever I had in the way of energy and emotion to this extremely challenging idea, a synthesis for the stage of those artistic terms that informed the film of Eisenstein — a classic theme with broad and familiar outlines, a tragedy purified by poetry and music of modern feeling, a vividly pictorial presentation that would offer the utmost visual excitement and be informed by the rich and disturbing beauty of surrealist painting. Win, lose, or draw, the following play, the story of the disintegration of a land-owning Southern family, emerges from a desire to synthesize these elements I have noted, and anything in it of value is humbly inscribed to the Russian work that inspired it.[59]

The play is interesting in a number of respects, not least because of its experiment with music and because it is one of the few Williams plays which makes race, if not a central interest, then a central device. The two principal figures are Isabel (at various stages in the text also referred to as Blanche), the daughter of the owner of Belle Reve, and Jessie, a mulatto woman who lives in a cabin on the plantation. At the beginning of the play, as Williams's notes make clear, Jessie's convict lover is shot dead by Isabel's father, beginning a feud which is the basis of the tragedy that then unfolds. Isabel marries Paul but when she proves frigid on their wedding night he goes with Jessie, who completes her revenge by murdering Isabel's father. The play then jumps ahead showing various stages in the development of Isabel's children, Ariadne and Tom (Williams's habit of calling his characters after himself is very marked in these early plays), and the departure of the mother who, like Blanche Dubois in *Streetcar*, is afraid that time is eroding her beauty and decides that 'I will live in shadows! Nuances — half tones — subtleties and innuendos!'[60] These scenes are accompanied by orchestral music which, in particular, underscores the violent conclusion of the first act in which Isabel strikes Jessie with a slave whip when she comes into the house with Paul. Jessie snatches the whip and beats her with Paul's help. Although he is contrite afterwards, Isabel asks him to leave.

When Ariadne holds a dance at Belle Reve she is seduced by Jessie's son Luke, who 'wears the fantastic finery of Harlem' but can pass as a white man. Isabel sends for Paul, who returns, a dissipated man. He shoots Luke and carries his daughter back to Belle Reve, but is stabbed by Jessie's lover.

It is a play in the grand style. All the effects are broad. The verse is required to control the excesses of the action. It is a kind of Southern *Mourning Becomes Electra*, and this is as likely to be an origin as Eisenstein. But it does serve to locate the cultural context for *Streetcar* and to underscore the degree to which Blanche can be taken to stand as a symbol for a South destroyed by its own myths and dominated by a sense of guilt. Another fragment of a play, also called 'The Paper Lantern', and probably to have been part of the larger work, features Ariadne and her brother, now called Paul, but this time we are closer to the world of *Streetcar* as Ariadne is presented as sexually promiscuous. However, the work that relates most directly to the later success is 'Interior: Panic'.

In effect this condenses the action of *A Streetcar Named Desire* into a single act. At one stage Williams toyed with the idea of setting it in Chicago but settled for 'A SHOT-GUN COTTAGE IN A POOR SECTION OF NEW ORLEANS'. Blanche (here called Blanche Shannon – the name Gladys being crossed out) is already ensconced with her sister Grace, and her husband, Jack Kiefaber. She is in a highly neurotic state. Indeed, a fundamental difference between this play and the later one is that here he was concerned with presenting the play refracted through the sensibility of his central character. Thus, as he explained in a stage direction:

> We are seeing it through the eyes of a person in a state of panic.
> The rooms are exposed, upstage and down, divided by portieres. It is somewhat the way it might have been painted by Van Gogh in his feverish interiors, with an abnormal emphasis on strident color. Distortions and irregularities of design may be added to bring out the hysteria in this view. The white plaster walls of the interior are stained with lurid projections.
> Sounds, too, are exageratted [*sic*]...[61]

Blanche is haunted by a voice which declares her 'Unfit for her position! Unfit for her position!', and, indeed, she reveals her sexual past to her sister in great detail. But word of this past has either already leaked out, or, more likely, Blanche simply fears that it has when George (who in *Streetcar* becomes Mitch) fails to come to see her for two weeks. Indeed, when a tradesman comes to the door she transforms the banal conversation between her sister and the man into a discussion of her depravity. As Williams indicates, the conversation 'IS PART REAL AND PART IMAGINED BY BLANCHE. ONLY THE ALLUSIONS TO THE BILL AND THE MONEY ARE ACTUAL, THE REST IS AUDITORY HALLUCINATION.' In a similar way the sexual attraction between Blanche and her sister's husband, which in *Streetcar* is a potent force which eventually leads to a literal rape, is here purely an invention of Blanche's disordered mind: '...do you know why he didn't want me to marry George? Because he wanted to have intimate relations with me himself! Yes, while you're in the hospital having a baby, that is the horrible plan in the back of his mind! We'll be alone here together, only these loose portieres separating our beds. And he'll come stalking through them in his pyjamas!' However, though her growing lunacy is apparent, the play ends happily when George, described by Blanche as 'a cleft in the rock of the world that I could hide in', arrives with a bunch of flowers. Not the awkward mother's boy which Mitch was to be but 'A NICE LOOKING YOUNG MAN' who promises real escape, he constitutes a genuine hope for Blanche who may now re-enter the world of the sane.

Jack is hardly developed as a character at all. He is a vigorous and masculine figure who arrives, like Stanley, carrying a piece of meat, but he remains only a sketch. By making Blanche purely a pathological case and presenting the play largely through her eyes Williams loses the tension that is an essential component of *Streetcar*. Blanche's sexuality is described rather than enacted, her disintegration a past fact rather than a present reality. George becomes a convenience of plot rather than an object of psychological concern. The process whereby Williams moved from this one-act character study to the complexity and poetic force of *A Streetcar Named Desire* is a mark of the real achievement of that play and the speed with which his talent was developing. The real concern of 'Interior: Panic' is with the technical experiment of presenting a play whose setting and language are distorted to reflect character. Plainly here, as in 'The Spinning Song', he was concerned with testing different forms and methods. In *Streetcar* that concern is subordinated to a dominating lyricism as to a fascination with the interplay of character and setting. The paper lantern survives from the earlier play but where in that work it was offered as a patent symbol – suspended on the stage and bursting into flame as an image of the delicate and the fragile consumed by passion – in *Streetcar* it is a natural extension of Blanche's character, of her desire to evade the harsh light of reality.

A Streetcar Named Desire concerns the plight of Blanche Dubois, a middle-aged Southern spinster who comes to stay with her sister Stella, and her husband, Stanley Kowalski. The old family plantation, significantly called Belle Reve (Beautiful Dream), having been lost as a result of 'epic fornication' by the male members of the family (a patent image of the collapse of the Old South which had managed to combine a cavalier myth with a private behaviour that sanctioned immorality and violence), both sisters have fled into marriage. But while Stella had chosen passion, in the person of Stanley Kowalski, Blanche opted for what she took to be delicacy and refinement in the form of the poetic Alan Gray. But this had merely turned out to be the cover for homosexuality. Shocked and repelled by her sudden discovery of this, Blanche had publicly confronted her husband and thereby precipitated his suicide. Left alone, she had turned to a succession of sexual encounters, afraid to commit herself ever again. Determined to neutralise the fact of death, which still haunted her from her final days at Belle Reve, as from the suicide of her husband, she had pursued ever younger companions. To her, desire was the antithesis of death and her relationship with young men a defence against the destructive processes of time. Thrown out of the small Southern town where she had been a schoolteacher, she comes to her sister's house, desperate and alone. But her one hope of escape – through marriage to Mitch (a mother-dominated man who is, in a sense, a gross parody of her first husband) – is destroyed by Stanley, who thereby repays her for her attempts to ruin his own marriage. For she has indeed set herself to undermine a relationship whose honest and open physicality repels her. Ostensibly, this is because of her refined sensibility; more plausibly, it is because the natural sexuality which characterises her sister's relationship to her husband underlines the parody of sensuality which typifies her own relationships. Stanley finally destroys her through a calculated act of rape, an assault which she has in part provoked. At the end of the play, her sanity broken, she is led away to an asylum, wholly trapped in the illusions which once she had deployed as temporary refuge. Stella, meanwhile, in order to go on living with Stanley, has to accept his denial and live with a lie – but a lie which, like Ibsen's life-lies, permits life to continue.

Stanley Kowalski is a travelling salesman but he shares nothing with Willy Loman except his profession. He is a Lawrentian figure: 'Animal joy in his being is implicit in all his movements and attitudes. Since earliest manhood the center of his life has been pleasure with women, the giving and taking of it, not with weak indulgency, dependently, but with the power and pride of a richly feathered male bird among hens.'[62] He dominates existence and as such in a way commands Williams's respect, even if he represents a brutalism which frightens a writer who is drawn instinctively to the fate of those less equipped to confront the modern world. For, if he invariably identifies with that individual driven to the margin of existence and alienated from the positivist drive of his or her society, he is also fascinated by those who manage to function. If survival is a basic theme of his work it is scarcely surprising that he should have found so compelling those who seemed to be the master of their fate rather than its victim.

Williams has said of his play about Lawrence's death (*I Rise in Flame, Cried the Phoenix*) that it is about a man's pilgrimage through times inimical to human beings. This is a central theme in his work. It is certainly how Blanche Dubois chooses to dramatise her own situation in *Streetcar*. The catastrophe has happened; the centre has already collapsed. The only question remaining is how the individual will survive. The spirit is that outlined by Lawrence in the opening paragraph of *Lady Chatterley's Lover*: 'Ours is essentially a tragic age, so we refuse to take it tragically. The cataclysm has happened, we are among the ruins, we start to build up new little habitats, to have new little hopes. It is rather hard work: there is no smooth road into the future: but we go round or scramble over the obstacles. We've got to live no matter how many skies have fallen.'[63] As the Kowalskis' next-door-neighbour, Eunice, remarks, 'Life has got to go on. No matter what happens, you've got to keep on going.'[64] And the process of survival, for Blanche, involves wilful invention. Blanche is all too aware of the real. What she wishes to do is to effect some compromise, to project another world, a fictive world, and sustain it by an act of will. In that respect she is clearly close kin to the writer whose strategy she mimics. In effect she constructs her own drama, costuming herself with care, arranging the set, enacting a series of roles, developing her own scenario. Indeed, in 'The Lady of Larkspur Lotion' it had been a character called The Writer who defended the authority and rights of the imagination:

> Suppose that I, to make this nightmare bearable for as long as I must continue to be the helpless protagonist of it – suppose that I ornament, illuminate-glorify it! With dreams and fictions and fancies!...Suppose that I live in this world of pitiful fiction! What satisfaction can it give you...to tear it to pieces, to crush it – call it a *lie*?...There are no lies but the lies that are stuffed in the mouth by the hard knuckled hand of need, the cold fist of necessity.[65]

The statement stands as the credo of most of Williams's protagonists, as, indeed, it does of himself as writer. And when Blanche says, 'I don't want realism...I want. Magic!...Yes, yes, magic! I try to give that to people. I misrepresent things to them. I don't tell truth, I tell what *ought* to be the truth',[66] she is in effect defending her own dramatic constructions and, beyond that, those of Williams himself. As Jo Mielziner said of the sets which he created,

> The magic of light opened up a fluid and poetic world of story telling... Throughout the play the brooding atmosphere is like an impressionistic X-ray...This kind of designing is the most fascinating of all designing for the theatre. It deals in form that is transparent, in space that is limited but has the illusion of infinity, in light that is ever changing in quality and in color.[67]

The suspension of disbelief is not only a function of art; it is the necessary precondition of Blanche's life. What she, no less than the playwright, needs is someone who will validate her fantasies. In the words of the popular song which she sings, 'It's a Barnum and a Bailey world, just as crazy as it can be. But it wouldn't be make-believe if you believed in me.'

If in a sense Williams admired what he called the 'Prometheans', those who can survive in and dominate the reductive world of the present, he clearly could not grant them his endorsement. And while we are not obliged to accept his own description of the play as a warning that the apes are about to take over the world, Blanche's analysis of Stanley as representative of a new brutalism clearly carries something of Williams's conviction:

> Somebody growls − some creature snatches at something − the fight is on! *God*! Maybe we are a long way from being made in God's image, but...there has been *some* progress since then! In some kinds of people some tenderer feelings have had some little beginning! That we have got to make *grow*! And *cling* to, and hold as our flag! In this dark march toward whatever it is we're approaching.[68]

The statement, however, is undermined by Blanche's own casuistry, by her own complicity in death. Certainly Williams recognises that her own shallow dreams and destructive sexuality cannot constitute a real resource. Whatever her personal desperation she is a destroyer and her own neurotic lies bear little relation to the world which she invokes. But neither can Stanley's mindless sensuality offer an escape. His destruction of Blanche, a symbolic and actual rape of the vulnerable, is too calculated and cruel to offer any hope for the future which he represents. The only possible future is that constituted by Stella's child. For Stella's compassion is real. She negotiates a middle ground. Her actions are dictated by a blend of necessity and love. She alone is able to draw from Stanley momentary signs of a deeper humanity. She alone protects Blanche for as long as she is able. And Williams, who once said that the only thing left in a blighted world worth endorsing is the relationship between individuals, evidently finds some grounds for hope in Stella's power to temper the extreme, despite her blandness. Rather as Hawthorne, in *The House of the Seven Gables*, attempted to project a future in which aristocracy and proletariat blended to create a new world, Williams creates a child who, it might be thought, will offer a blend of Stanley's vitality and Stella's compassion. Blanche's destruction is inevitable. Stella has the chance to rebuild.

But in truth that future has been so compromised and so penetrated with irony that even this consolation is denied. Thus there is a patent sentimentality which Williams succeeds in holding at bay here, as elsewhere he does not. In an early draft (dated 5 April 1947) he has Stella 'elevate the child in her arms as if she were offering it to the tenderness of the sky'.[69] This is a gesture he does not permit himself in the final version, which ends with a moment of sexual reconciliation ambivalent in its blend of sensuality and moral narcosis. He similarly abandons another direct statement which is to be found in a fragment of the play in the Humanities Research Center of the University of Texas at Austin. There, in a brief sketch for a speech by Stanley, he has the character comment both on Blanche's courage and his own sexual motivation: 'You know, I admire you, Blanche. You got into a tight corner and you fought like a wild-cat to get back into the open. I was a son of a bitch to stand in your way. Protecting Mitch? Hell, I didn't care about Mitch. I wanted you for myself, is the truth of the matter. Did you know that?' It is an unsubtle statement and implies a reductive version of Stanley's character which he abandoned in the process of writing.

A considerable part of the success of *Streetcar* derived from Elia Kazan's sensitive production and the notes which he made in the process of directing it are, for the most part, perceptive, opening up crucial areas of the play. But they are not without their simplifications. Writing in August 1947, before and during the rehearsals, he reminded himself that a stylised production was necessary because of the centrality of 'Blanche's memories, inner life, emotions'.[70] But, at the same time, he recognised her as 'a social type, an emblem of a dying civilization, making its last curlicued and romantic exit'. 'In other words', he insisted to himself, 'her behaviour is *social*. Therefore find social modes! This is the source of the play's stylization and the production's style and color. Likewise Stanley's behaviour is social too. It is the basic animal cynicism of today. "Get what's coming to you! Don't waste a day! Eat, drink, get yours!" This is the basis of his stylization, of the choice of his props.'[71] The theme of the play thus becomes, 'a message from the dark interior. This little, twisted, pathetic, confused bit of light and culture puts out a cry. It is snuffed out by the crude forces of violence, insensibility and vulgarity which exist in our South – and this cry is the play.'[72] As suggested above, this over-simplifies both sides of the conflict. It is, after all, Williams's sense of deep ambiguity towards a past whose veneer of civilisation had concealed a real corruption and a suffocatingly hypocritical model of the feminine role, and a present whose social banality seems nonetheless accompanied by sexual directness untainted by a self-destructive, puritan guilt, which gives the play its tension. Kazan's notion that Blanche's vulnerability derives from the death of a tradition which offered the woman protection and a sense of social function is only part of the story. For Belle Reve was only a dream, and not all that beautiful either. The myth which Blanche does indeed cling to is as threatening to her sense of herself as the insistent realities of the present. The role offered by the Old South was social and symbolic and not personal and physical. The woman was essentially a passive creature, alternately a chaste symbol, a social icon who played her role in concealing a more anarchic and brutal reality (in this context the earlier play 'The Paper Lantern' becomes a crucial document), and a sexual convenience. But that world could never have given Blanche what she needed. As she says, 'I never was hard or self-sufficient enough...People don't see you – *men* don't – don't even admit your existence unless they are making love to you. And you've got to have your existence admitted by someone, if you're going to have someone's protection.'[73] That, the Old South of the myth could not offer. And when she tries to marry the urbane and civilised, the 'light and culture' of the South, in the form of Alan Gray, she discovers the corruption, or, at the very least, the profound deceit which lies behind the veneer of that side of the Southern past. By the same token, it is not possible to see the contemporary South into which she stumbles as distinguished only by 'the crude forces of violence, insensibility and vulgarity'. Its sexuality is specifically contrasted to that of the Old South, which is presented as either epically corrupt or effete. Its personal relationships have a kind of baffled tenderness (Mitch's relationship with Blanche and even Stanley's with Stella) which no account of the Southern past given to us in the play indicates. Blanche's problem is that she can operate in neither system. She inhabits a no-man's land. She is unable to effect even those compromises which Mitch manages, combining as she does Old South manners with new South friends – albeit there is something unconvincing about this combination which is dramatically unsettling. Just why, after all, does Stanley tolerate this lumbering mother's boy who is apparently so antithetical to his own sensibility?

When Kazan says of Blanche that she is 'better than Stella', that she is the '*only voice of light*' in the play, he ignores a crucial ambiguity. To substantiate his position he quotes Blanche's desperate assertion that

> There has been some kind of progress...Such things as art – as poetry and music – such kinds of new light have come into the world...in some kinds of people some kinds of tenderer feelings have had some little beginning that we've got to make *grow*! And cling to, and hold as our flag! In this dark march toward whatever it is we're approaching...don't...don't hang back with the brutes![74]

But her characterisation of Stanley as a brute is a function of her desire to denigrate him to her sister and also, perhaps, of her own ambiguous response to Stanley's power. Indeed, by extension, what she characterises as the brute in Stanley is another aspect of her own sensibility. She stresses poetry and music less because these are a necessary part of her experience (the only music she sings is a popular song) than because in her mind they stand in contradistinction to the sexual desire which she feels but from which she wishes to distinguish herself, and they highlight Stanley's cultural inadequacies. In other words she contains within herself those qualities which in *Summer and Smoke* Williams was to assign to different characters. It is not just that Blanche is unreconciled and unreconcilable to the world in which she finds herself; she remains unreconciled to herself. Her alienation goes deeper than a cultural revulsion. Nor is it simply, as Kazan suggests, that '*her attraction for men, is beginning to go*'[75] (he even insists that Blanche 'is like all women, dependent on a man, looking for one to hold on to' – a statement that I

64

doubt he would wish to repeat today). The fact is that what she cannot face is her mortality and the means which she chooses to mobilise against it. And, as a result, her sexuality does not for her, as it does for Stella, become an integral part of her experience and her identity. It is an aspect of herself which she cannot face. Did she perhaps not choose Alan Gray for her husband precisely because he would not force her to acknowledge her own sexuality just as her subsequent relationships have been with strangers. What she fears is consequences — to be pulled into a world of causalities, a world of time.

It is true that, as Kazan suggests, Stella has paid a price for her sanity; she has narcotised herself. But it is surely not adequate to see her only as 'Stanley's slave'.[76] In the first place, despite his self-confidence and arrogance, there is a mutual dependence. When Stella spends the night with a neighbour after he has struck her, his need for her is apparent. Proud of his male independence he nonetheless calls out for Stella (a particularly effective moment in Brando's performance). Her response is equally something more than that of someone 'buried alive' in her own flesh. Nor is she simply concerned with sustaining her relationship with Stanley — though that is fundamental. For much of the play she accepts the difficult task of negotiating between the differing needs of her sister and husband. Dramatically, however, she is required to seem passive, physically and imaginatively static, as the fulcrum between two such vital and energetic forces as Blanche and Stanley. Thus it was that Williams wrote Kazan a note complaining that, in rehearsals, Stella seemed too animated.

> It seems to me that she has too much vivacity, at times she is bouncing around in a way that suggests a co-ed on a benzedrine kick. I know it is impossible to be literal about the description 'narcotised tranquillity' but I do think there is an important value in suggesting it, in contrast to Blanche's rather feverish excitability. Blanche is the quick, light one. Stella is relatively slow and almost indolent. Blanche mentions her 'Chinese philosophy' — the way she sits with her little hands folded like a cherub in a chair, etc. I think her natural passivity is one of the things that make her acceptance of Stanley acceptable. She naturally 'gives in', lets things slide, she does not make much effort.[77]

On the other hand, and in contrast with Blanche's neurotic energy, fluttering hands and rushed speeches, or Stanley's brutal explosions of frustration, that passivity edges towards serenity. It is true, however, that her approach has no power to generate change or to sustain a mode of life. She has, perhaps, some kinship with Lena Grove in Faulkner's *Light in August* in that she sustains life and seems to have a gentling effect, but that very comparison makes clear how far she is from being merely passive. At the end of the play, of course, she has to make a radical decision. To sustain her relationship with Stanley she has to let Blanche slip away into insanity. But in doing so she opts for the future over the past, for potency over sterility. And if that also means accepting a world bereft of protective myths and cultural adornments this is a compromise which she has the strength to make. Blanche cannot and is broken.

There is much in Kazan's director's notes that is valuable and perceptive. He is, perhaps, at his most impressive in his account of Stanley. He recognises, for example, the reality of Stanley's love for Stella, draws attention to his vulnerability and reaches for his significance as a cultural sign, an image, as he sees it, of 'our National State of Cynicism',[78] of the absence of values to command his loyalty. He insists on his potential for violence, which is partly an adolescent anger (and there is something of the arrested child in Stanley) and partly the expression of a gap between his experience and something in him which he can never fully express. To Kazan *every bar in the nation is full of Stanleys ready to explode*.[79] But none of this is really compatible with his earlier remarks that he represents the 'crude forces of violence, insensibility and vulgarity', that he is a brute. His rape of Blanche, for example, is not just designed to bring her down to his own level. It is a calculated act. He is forcing the issue to its conclusion, just as he had hoped to do in informing Mitch. He is an animal at bay but then so is Blanche. He fights back; she surrenders, but her dilemma (as well as that of the decaying culture which she represents) has been the need to live with defeat. That is her fate and, in a sense, it is a fate which she has embraced as the essence of her identity. It is a familiar romantic pose, and madness, a final retreat into the self, a familiar conclusion (the image of the straitjacket haunts *Streetcar*, as it does *Suddenly Last Summer* and, in an oblique way, *The Glass Menagerie*). Stanley's dilemma is that he is locked into a logic which threatens to undermine his own self-image. He can only destroy Blanche by becoming what she has always accused him of being and at the cost of changing the only relationship which seems to matter to him. He is perplexed in the same sense that Willy Loman was to be in that he cannot understand the mechanisms of the world which he inhabits. He is not a fool. He is not without a certain wit. He is capable of tenderness. But he is ultimately baffled by the complexity of human emotions and by his dim apprehension of inadequacies in his own life and experience – inadequacies which he can only meet with a heavy-handed irony or a contempt which is never quite convincing. He destroys not only Blanche but also Mitch and he threatens the apparent equanimity of his own marriage. The final irony of the play is that he cannot quite grasp how it has all happened. Part of the pathos of the play's ending is obviously the sight of Blanche being led out on the arm of her doctor gentleman caller, but part derives from the sight of Stanley's poker night, no longer what it once had been, and Stella, separated from him by the act which was designed to eliminate the person who would have come between them. And, if the play is in part about the clash between two different models of human behaviour, it is evident that neither offers the individual access to meaning, on a private or public level, and that the crucial negotiations are those between individuals or between each individual and his or her own sense of himself. Offered a choice between decadence and brutality the audience can hardly enter into an alliance with either. What is compelling is the desperate fight which Williams's characters engage in, a fight for survival and dignity. In a sense they all lose, but for Williams that is precisely the nature of the human experience which at this stage in his career he was inclined to characterise as tragic rather than absurd. Blanche was, he insisted, 'a demonic creature' because 'the size of her feeling was too great for her to contain without the escape of madness'.[80] She is a romantic figure who, like Captain Ahab in *Moby Dick* attracts and repels.

In 1943 Williams had written to Donald Windham in praise of a necessary level of truth between individuals:

> The innermost 'you' is building his world on honesty which is the only good foundation we can find. It is the common level on which occasion[ally] 'you' and 'I' or somebody else's innermost being can momentarily meet, during the flux and torrent of our disparate parts. Without it — what a grinning desolation! Nobody can honestly blame you for anything you are. Blame or guilt is all mistaken and false...We all bob only momently above the bubbling, boiling surface of the torrent of lies and distortions we are borne along. We are submarine creatures, for beneath that surface is the world we live in, with its names and labels and its accepted ideas. And over it only is the oxygen unadulterated which we can only breathe in spasms now and again, and the only vision which is pure at all.[81]

At first sight this adolescent rhetoric seems to carry us away from the world of *Streetcar* in which the lie appears to be the precondition for survival. But in fact it touches on an ambiguity to which he constantly returns. To him the word 'truth' refers to a level of authenticity denied by the very conditions of social existence. The lies which Blanche clings to and which Stella must finally endorse are necessary gestures forced on them by the exigencies of life. He wants to believe that on some fundamental level they remain untouched by such compromises just as for a playwright the platonic clarity of his play has inevitably to be degraded by performance and yet on some level survives intact. Nor is he unaware that he is himself a creator of fiction, seeking to serve truth through lies. It was simply a paradox to be accepted. The irony is that he never could wholly accept it any more than he could the pragmatics of production. If his self-image was that of the legless bird of *Orpheus Descending* which dies if it ever touches the earth, on the other hand he was equally capable of satirising such a stance in the person of Brick in *Cat on a Hot Tin Roof* who seeks to preserve his innocence at the cost of a grasp on the real. In *Streetcar* the harsh light of the real falls on Blanche only momentarily but in that moment her true inner pathos is revealed no less to the audience than to Stanley who perhaps exorcises something in himself when he chooses to destroy her in the very sexuality which she had chosen as refuge.

A Streetcar Named Desire won both the New York Critics' Circle Award and the Pulitzer Prize. It ran for 855 performances, closing in December 1949 after two years. Yet critical reaction was not wholly favourable. Mary McCarthy in particular attacked what she saw as a tendency to overwrite, to press effects and characters to extremes so that his fictions, his 'lies...are so old and shopworn that the very truth upon which he rests them becomes garish and ugly...His work reeks of literary ambition as the apartment reeks of cheap perfume'.[82] He was, she decided, a careerist who calculated his effects in the theatre as he did his pose of alienated writer. To an English critic, Peter Fleming, Stanley was 'over simplified', a strip-cartoon figure designed to satisfy the wish-fulfilment dreams of the American male. But such views were more than balanced by Brooks Atkinson, who found the play 'almost unbearably tragic', and Joseph Wood Krutch, for whom it was 'subtle and delicate'. For John Mason Brown it was simply 'better, deeper, richer' than *The Glass Menagerie*.

A Streetcar Named Desire sealed Williams's success as a playwright. He could now afford to relax. At the age of thirty-four he had finally achieved his objective. To Mary McCarthy there was, indeed, a curious contradiction between the financial security and popular esteem which was now undeniably his and that sense of being a 'rootless, wandering writer' which he still seemed to wish to project as his public image. But in fact Williams's sense of alienation had been rooted in something far more profound than his earlier dramatic failures and the long haul towards success. And that is why some forty years as a major figure in the American theatre failed to end that sense of alienation. It is why he continued to focus on the figure of the individual whose insecurities, fears and vulnerabilities are the essence of his identity. It is also why, while revelling in his success and what it could buy in the way of a limited immunity from a sense of loss and betrayal, he remained deeply insecure in his personal affairs and apocalyptically inclined in his drama.

Indeed, immediately following the success of *Streetcar* his first instinct was to run. And run he did. He fled to Europe, where in Italy in the spring and summer of 1948 he put the finishing touches to the Broadway version of *Summer and Smoke* – a study of the conflicting demands of body and spirit.

Writing two years later Williams explained that a principal reason for the flight to Europe, in his case as in that of other American writers, was that 'America is no longer a terribly romantic part of the world, and that writers...are essentially romantic spirits – or they would not be writing.'

With the exception of New Orleans and San Francisco he regarded the 'industrial dynamism of America's city as essentially destructive and, though Hart Crane may have created some kind of 'poetic synthesis'[83] out of this dynamism, he was mindful that he had committed suicide on returning to New York from the romantic world of Mexico. Since *Summer and Smoke* was all but complete the impact of his European trip on this play is slight (the influence being clearer on the play which followed – *The Rose Tattoo*). But his precipitate flight from public success is fascinating in another respect in that it is a re-creation of the central strategy of one after another of his protagonists.

In *Summer and Smoke*, written coterminously with *Streetcar* and first performed by Margo Jones's Dallas theatre in 1947 before opening on Broadway in 1948, Williams created a Promethean figure, no longer limited by an intelligence apparently warped into simple cunning. John Buchanan represents a sexuality which is regenerative without being coercive. He is, Williams asserts in a stage direction, 'brilliantly and restlessly alive in a stagnant society'. But he is incomplete, as is Alma Winemiller, the woman he comes to love. She represents spirit as he does body, and that incompletion is the source of a potentially self-destructive energy. The world of passion is closed to Alma. As she says, she has 'looked through a telescope but never a microscope'.[84] Her eyes are focussed on the infinite; she has been blind to the human world around her. Language, for her, is a way of distorting and controlling experience. Her latinate vocabulary is a defence against the vulgar and the vital alike. She is afraid to confess her love for Buchanan for fear that its mere expression will destroy it. But the irony around which the play is constructed derives from the fact that Alma comes to be convinced of the need to complete her life by conceding the existence of a physical sexuality at precisely the same time that Buchanan learns the insufficiency of the merely physical. They pass one another in their separate developments. The problem is that Williams seems to be endorsing a state of balance to which, emotionally, he is not committed. The narrative logic of *Summer and Smoke*, as of *Streetcar* and, indeed, *The Glass Menagerie*, is the accommodated norm. Passion is balanced by spirit, spirit by passion. The emotional truth and the dramatic focus, however, reside in the neurotic, vulnerable outcast or the brutally direct and vital Promethean figure, and not in a kind of moral harmony. Neither, though, is adequate as a model of moral behaviour or a paradigm of social action. As a result, while such figures remain his principal interest and while the endings are at times poignant, they express a cultural paradox, in that survival apparently requires the acceptance of a compromise which he can propose but never dramatise.

Summer and Smoke ends ambiguously with Alma, no longer a petrified angel (like the literally stone angel which dominates the stage), establishing a relationship with a young salesman. But her direction is uncertain. She has reached the apogee of her development, opting for a physical world as Buchanan has opted for a spiritual one, but it seems that she may be about to turn into a mirror image of her young pupil's mother who picks up just such a salesman at the local railroad station.

The naive opposition which Williams proposes between body and soul, and which operates in terms of the *mise-en-scène*, is, to him, a primary tension, but it is not one which he is entirely content to synthesise, even if that seems the play's dramatic implication. The set is clearly anthropocentric. Its three areas represent soul, body and eternity. The implication seems to be the need for some kind of balance, but this is hardly validated by the ambiguity that invades the text. Here, as in *Streetcar*, he seems drawn in two mutually contradictory directions. Thus, in *Streetcar*, he had denounced Stella's state as one of 'narcotised tranquillity', but had given her a compassion and a tenacity which made her not merely a survivor but a legitimate moral focus. Meanwhile, in the person of Blanche he had offered a portrait of the poetic sensibility as destructive neurotic, though never simply that. So, here, with *Summer and Smoke*, moral sense and imaginative necessity seem to pull him in opposing directions. Alma insists that 'the secret, the principal book of existence' is 'the everlasting struggle and aspiration for more than our human limits have placed in our reach',[85] but, whatever her final fate, transcendence does not seem an immediate possibility.

To Tennessee Williams, *The Glass Menagerie*, *Streetcar* and *Summer and Smoke* constituted a natural group. As he observed in his draft for an article (included in his papers at the University of Texas), they 'formed a trio which seemed definitive of what I had to say in the form of long plays, which embodied a single theme, or legend, that of the delicate, haunted girl who first appeared as Laura, the basic theme of the over-sensitive misfit in a world that spins with blind fury. Unconsciously', he noted, 'I summed up this theme in the concluding stanza of a poem called "Lament for Moths":

> Give them, O Mother of Moths and Mother of Men,
> Strength to enter the heavy world again,
> For delicate were the moths and badly wanted
> Here in a world by mammoth figures haunted.'

The problem, as he saw it, was that it was not only his critics who saw *The Glass Menagerie* and the two plays which followed it, as a 'single burst of personal lyricism'. So did he. The challenge was 'that of finding the source of another, a second, "personal lyricism" without which writing is not organic or revealingly truthful'.[86] To his mind, he found this firstly in *The Rose Tattoo* and then in *Camino Real*. It is hard to agree.

Certainly Elia Kazan's response to *The Rose Tattoo* was to insist: 'I think you have temporarily exhausted your vein of personal lyricism, the old one, and are more concerned right now with problems of form. Later on you will find a personal vein, you must keep working and waiting.'[87] But Williams was disinclined to wait. Accordingly he went ahead with *The Rose Tattoo* while confessing that it lacked 'the personal urgency of the Southern trio'. Its virtue, however, he felt, lay in its 'vigor' and that 'affirmative sanity' which he had been 'compelled to find for myself'.[88]

There is little doubt that the power of his early work did indeed come from its personal energy. He was writing, in essence, about himself and his family. He was reflecting both a private anguish and a sense of cultural crisis. These were, as he himself later said, plays of character. Thus lyricism was partly a pose — the young writer mobilising the easy effects of nostalgia — and partly a product of his subject, the losing struggle of the sensitive spirit, who in a new, harsh, pragmatic world uses language as a form of protection. The antiquated courtesies of Amanda Wingfield, the desperate rhetoric of Blanche Dubois, the elaborate euphemisms of Alma are means of denying the reality and authority of a world too brutal to acknowledge. Though Kazan was clearly correct in suggesting that Williams had a tendency to retreat into the poetic when confronted with dramatic problems, it is equally clear that in some sense the lyric impulse and its fate lay at the heart of his early work. And, for Williams, that lyricism, that determined effort to make a prosaic world surrender some space to the poetic instinct, that effort to resist an implacable realism, was intimately connected with a tragic spirit. As he explained,

> Nothing that I have observed in the lives of artists, or anyone else, for that matter, has led me to alter or even modify my original belief that life, at best, is conditional surrender. But conditional is that half of the phrase to remember. You can and do name certain conditions in your surrender to your destroyer, time...but since I do not believe that the conditions are more important than the surrender, I am not truly a pessimist.

That was the theme of *Streetcar* and, even more completely, he suggested, of *Camino Real*. It was thus not 'the circumstances of anyone's life, but the spirit in which he endures them' which 'makes tragedy, and poetry, out of this unfathomable experience of ours'. In the draft he crosses this last phrase out, commenting, in pencil, 'Farewell, cliché.'[89]

But, for all that, it does accurately represent his sense of the connection between the lyric and the tragic impulse, as well as identifying what is clearly a central theme of his work. Thus, when he observes that the obsessive aim of the serious writer is 'to turn the noise and chaos of human experience into order and music, a mysterious order and a moving music',[90] he is not merely echoing lines given to his own Lord Byron in *Camino Real* but identifying a central commitment of his characters who, with their paper lanterns, their glass menageries, their carefully sculpted dreams and their deliberately nuanced language, are as concerned as the artist, whose function they thereby mimic, to resist the given, to reshape their memories, their experiences and their circumstances in such a way as to allow them room to breathe and to function. What they first try to find in flight, once trapped, they have to create through the imagination. But the world created by the imagination is easily destroyed (not least by dramatic critics) and, in writing about poetry in general and the work of Dylan Thomas in particular, Williams explained something of the neurotic intensity which lies behind the lyric impulse – in doing so drawing on an image which he had used in the unpublished play, 'The Paper Lantern', and which he deployed to such effect in *Streetcar*:

> It cannot exist without a kind of emotional intensity that the human organism is not meant to endure except at rare moments. The lyric poet performs his work at an emotional pitch that other people, not poets, experience or suffer only in the rapture of love or in the terror of dying, and he does it repeatedly, as continually as he can, and he seems not to care that he is building fires in a house of paper, that he is a paper lantern which is self-consuming.[91]

The image of Keats, dead at twenty-seven, Hart Crane, a suicide at thirty-two, and Dylan Thomas, dead before forty, may go some way towards explaining Williams's own neurotic fear of dying young, a thought, which, paradoxically, seems to account for some of the fury with which he committed his ideas to paper early in his career. For he saw himself as a lyric poet writing for the stage, a romantic translating human need into living symbols, and he was enough of a Puritan to believe that a price would be exacted for the creation of beauty.

And Williams was conscious that he was seen as something of an innovator in poetic drama. After all, hadn't the drama reviewer Brooks Atkinson suggested as much. Aware, as he was, of the work of Chekhov and Lorca, he must have felt somewhat uneasy about this. Certainly he had the grace to respond by locating himself only in an American tradition. But he was content to accept the accolade, granting primacy only to Carson McCullers's *The Member of the Wedding* which seemed to him to represent 'the simon pure instance of the type'. At the same time he was intent on insisting that

> the play of character is not a formless play...The dynamics of a play of character are not nearly so conspicuous as those of the play that depends on involvement of plot, but nearly always they have to exist. Change is nearly always essential and a protagonist that undergoes no change is suitable only to a one-act drama. The revelation of character progresses along the same ascending line as the involvement of plot.[92]

Having escaped the heavy plotting of several of his early efforts he took some pride in achieving success with works which he believed to be more suited to the intimate quality of arena stages, such as Margo Jones's, but which had succeeded on Broadway. However, he was now looking for a new freedom – a freedom of form but also a freedom from his own experiences which had provided the substance of his first successes.

When he went to Europe in 1948 he had been hospitalised with hepatitis and mononucleosis in a Paris hospital. In typically melodramatic fashion he wrote 'The jig is up' on the fly-leaf of his *Collected Poems of Hart Crane* and anticipated, as he did repeatedly in his life, an artistic and physical collapse. But the trip to Italy 'taught me to smile', and his conversion to 'the joy of mere existence' was set down in the form of *The Rose Tattoo*. It seemed to him that in Italy he had discovered a world in which the sense of the poetic that he associated with a fading American South still survived, but combined with a vitality which could sustain itself in the modern world. Here, he believed, were no puritan repressions. Sexuality was spontaneous, a basic and acknowledged fact of existence. The source of much of the conflict in his life and his art thus seemed to disappear. At last he had found a way of reconciling the apparent contradictions between the poetic sensibility and the substantial realities of daily life.

The Rose Tattoo (inspired by Williams's own affair with his long-term companion Frank Merlo) is an encomium to human passion, in its purity and equally in its farcical ironies. Where in *Streetcar* desire proved an ambiguous response to death, here it is offered as an effective antidote. Thus Serafina is freed of her obsession with death (in the form of the ashes of her dead husband Rosario) by a man whose sexual directness has none of the destructive overtones of Stanley Kowalski's. If death has some final victory this is a fact which is not allowed to cow the living. Originally to be entitled 'Eclipse of the Sun', it is a play about the resilience of the human spirit, the undeniable power of the will to live and the primacy of the sexual impulse. One of Williams's few comedies, it is an assertion of the sometimes reductive and sometimes ennobling power of a passion which is rekindled anew equally in individual lives and in the history of the race. Thus, Serafina Della Rose, who has remained faithful to the memory of her dead husband, is wooed and won by Alvaro Mangiacavallo – one of Williams's Lawrentian working-class characters. Brought back to life by this sudden blaze of passion, she also liberates her daughter whom she has struggled to hold back from the physical pleasures of sexuality – and the pains and disillusions which may follow. Williams once said that:

> *The Rose Tattoo* is the Dionysian element in human life, its mystery, its beauty, its significance... It is the dissatisfaction with empiric evidence that makes the

poet and mystic, for it is the lyric as well as Bacchantic impulse, and although the goat is one of its most immemorial symbols, it must not be confused with mere sexuality. The element is higher and more distilled than that. Its purest form is probably manifested by children and birds in their rhapsodic moments of flight and play...the limitless world of the dream. It is the *rosa mystica*.[93]

Or, as he said in a note accompanying what he called the 'kitchen sink draft' of the play (so called because he felt that he had thrown into it every dramatic 'implement' he could find), Rosario and Alvaro (both of whom were then to have appeared, played if possible by the same actor) 'represent the same quality in life, the Dionysian element which is like the ram's skin painted red, always possessing but only momentarily possessed, wild, cruel and tender'.[94] Interestingly his first choice for the part was Marlon Brando so that in a sense Stanley Kowalski was to return but this time symbolising the celebratory rather than the destructively anarchic dimension of Dionysus. Whatever else his trip to Italy might have done it certainly seemed to reconcile what he had earlier assumed to be a fundamental conflict between body and spirit. But the relationship between sex and poetry is no more convincingly established here than it was to be in *Period of Adjustment*, in which the consignment of two couples to bed is presented as an adequate solution to their problems. He may have set himself to celebrate a reborn and reconstructed Stanley Kowalski but he did so without any of the ironies which made that character so dynamic and dramatically effective. What he saw as lyricism is in effect little more than an attempt to make sexuality into a symbol. Neither the characters nor the action can sustain this. And when it is evident that they can't, he falls back, as he had repeatedly in his work, on dramatic symbols which are even less rooted in the play's logic. Thus roses bloom everywhere – in their names, on their chests, in their hair and scattered over the stage. Indeed, in this play, as elsewhere, such naive symbolism perhaps implies a lack of confidence on Williams's part in his ability to achieve his intentions through language, plot or character. He may, as in the introduction to *Camino Real*, insist that 'symbols are nothing but the natural speech of drama', that they appeal to the 'great vocabulary of images' which we carry 'in our conscious and unconscious minds',[95] but all too often in his work they are an alternative to action, a radical simplification of complex issues. At their most effective in *The Glass Menagerie* and *A Streetcar Named Desire*, they share with poetry an ability to condense experience and also, by implication, to evade the deceptive nature of language. At their worst, as in *Summer and Smoke*, *Camino Real* and *The Rose Tattoo*, they become a substitute for action, a nervous gesture betokening less a natural speech than an artificial focus for dramatic attention.

Serafina's flirtation with death is symbolised not only by the urn

4. Eli Wallach in *The Rose Tattoo*, directed by Daniel Mann, set designed by Boris Aronson, Broadway, 1951.

containing her husband's ashes but also by the dressmaker's dummies with which she has littered her house. As Williams commented in an essay in 1951:

> It took a long while to learn that eventually the faceless dummies must be knocked over, however elaborate their trappings. It took an almost literal unclothing, a public appearance in a wine-stained rayon slip, a fierce attack on a priest and the neighbour women, to learn that the blood of the wild young daughter was better, as a memorial, than ashes kept in a cemetery urn.[96]

The play was, then, to be a celebration of freedom and a certain subversive anarchy, and to Williams this extended to the form of the drama itself. Thus, to him, *The Rose Tattoo* was equally an expression of 'the desire of an artist to work in new forms, however awkwardly at first, to break down barriers of what he has done before and what others have done better before and after and to crash, perhaps fatally, into some area that the bell-harness and rope would like to forbid him.'[97] Yet if it was an honest attempt to move in a new direction, the crash, unfortunately, was not long in coming. His next play, *Camino Real*, claimed the right to fail, and audiences and critics alike obliged by regarding it as a failure.

He has confessed to writing the play at 'a time of desolation', at a time when he suspected that he had exhausted his own creativity. Not untypically he chose to see this as evidence of a wider crisis of confidence, offering the play 'as a spiritual purgation of that abyss of confusion and lost sense of reality that I, and those others, had somehow wandered into'.[98] A radical break with his former plays as far as style was concerned, it seems to have been a deliberate attempt by Williams to force his way through what he feared was a writer's block. He wanted to free himself from his reliance on personal experience, to create a world of the imagination which no longer tied him quite so implacably to his own past. He wrote the play first in 1948 but his agent's reaction was so negative that he abandoned it. As he later remarked, 'I am afraid that her phone call may have prevented me from making a very, very beautiful play out of *Camino Real* instead of the striking but flawed piece which it finally turned into several years later.'[99]

For Williams, freedom was both an aesthetic and a human necessity. If it is what his protagonists pursue, it is equally a necessary pre-condition for his art in so far as he wished to claim a stylistic freedom which the theatre has not always allowed itself. Indeed in a sense the factitious nature of theatre is itself an image of freedom. Its freedom from real time comes to stand for another kind of liberation. As he said of *Camino Real*, 'A convention of the play is existence out of time in a place of no specific locality. If you regard it that way, I suppose it becomes an elaborate allegory.' But if it was an allegory it was one which he suspected American audiences were likely to resist: 'A cage represents security as well as confinement to a bird that has grown used to being in it.'[100] It was for this reason that in *Camino Real* he deliberately disrupted that security by allowing the actors to spill over into the audience. The form of the play was its message. The painter in Shaw's *The Doctor's Dilemma* insists that art contains its message and that that message 'lies in the might of design, the mystery of colour, the redemption of all things by Beauty',[101] but to Williams it also lies in its dramatisation of 'light and motion'. The energy and the vitality of the theatre, its shared circumstances, its reliance on common images and experiences, is itself the antidote to that pessimism which critics have insisted typifies his work. For him 'the incontinent blaze of live theatre, a theatre meant for seeing and for feeling'[102] is in itself both a recognition of a surviving, and even in some sense triumphant, human spirit and primary evidence of it. This is the sense in which he felt in tune with D. H. Lawrence. This was the spirit in which he described Lawrence meeting his death, in *I Rise in Flame, Cried the Phoenix*. And this is why he identified, as those dramatic values which he prized most, dynamism and organicism. Those were the qualities he found in Maggie in *Cat on a Hot Tin Roof* and Val in *Orpheus Descending*, and it was the absence of these in the representatives of social and political power which makes it possible to see his work as a sustained critique of his own society and of modernity.

The radical impulse of his early work was not dead; it simply transposed itself into a drama in which the opposing forces are seen in terms of sexuality and creative energy. In his plays people are allowed a central significance which he sees them as being denied in life. Laura, Blanche and Serafina are only marginal so long as a central position is conceded to money, power and materiality. They are actually granted significance by the fact of theatre's power to arrest time. As he said:

> In a play, time is arrested in the sense of being confined. By a sort of legerdemain, events are made to remain *events*, rather than being reduced so quickly to mere *occurrences*. The audience can sit back in a comforting dusk to watch a world which is flooded with light and in which emotion and action have a dimension and dignity that they would otherwise have in real existence, if only the shattering intrusion of time could be locked out.[103]

Thus the theatre itself becomes an active force in re-instituting those very qualities which Williams saw as being excluded from modern life precisely by creating a world in which their significance is sustained. Thus, too, the theatricalising imagination of his characters, constructing the very stage sets in which they will perform their lives, is granted a central significance in his work. And this, of course, is the paradox of that work for while the process of his plays is one of ruthless exposure of truth, thematically they tend to validate the inevitable evasions and retreats of characters whose self-dramatising gestures are seen as necessary lies. The resolution of the paradox seems to lie in a belief that the activity of the imagination is itself evidence of a surviving vitality – nervous, neurotic, but real. The theatre is a correlative of that imaginative energy. As he has said, 'The colour, the grace and levitation, the structural pattern in motion, the quick interplay of live human beings, suspended like fitful lightning in a cloud, these things are the play, not words on paper, nor the thoughts and ideas of an author, those shabby things snatched off basement counters at Gimbels.'[104]

So it was, he claimed, that both he and his director, Elia Kazan, were attracted to *Camino Real* precisely because of its freedom and mobility of form, because they saw the play as 'an abstraction of the impulse to fly'. The play concerns a group of desperate people – for the most part figures from romantic literature or myth. They find themselves stranded in a desiccated town, set in a desert wasteland, where they face the imminent fact of death, objectified in the form of the two street-cleaners who collect their exhausted bodies. And there they are offered the classic Williams dilemma. Either they opt for the momentary but real consolation of love, or they set out into the barren land known as 'Terra Incognita'; love or flight. As Marguerite (the heroine of *La Dame aux camélias*) observes, 'Caged birds accept each other but flight is what they long for.'[105] Lord Byron's advice to '*Make voyages – Attempt them –* there's nothing else',[106] is then not quite the whole truth, but an ambiguity expressed in the fact that when Byron ventures out of the city he does so with several caged birds. The failure of love derives from a fear of vulnerability. As Marguerite insists: 'We have to distrust each other. It is our only defence against betrayal.'[107] And yet the fact of death makes them 'stretch out hands to each other in the dark that we can't escape from...and that's what passes for love on this terminal stretch of the road'.[108] But 'Time betrays us and we betray each other.'[109] However, to Williams this seems no more than an expression of the human condition.

> In actual existence the moments of love are succeeded by the moments of satiety and sleep. The sincere remark is followed by a cynical distrust. Truth is fragmentary, at best: we love and betray each other in not quite the same breath but in two breaths that occur in fairly close sequence. But the fact that passion occurred in *passing*, that it then declined into a more familiar sense of indifference, should not be regarded as proof of inconsequence.

This is simply the rhythm of human relationships.

In *Camino Real*, indeed, there is no judgement. Betrayal is evidence of imperfection but the love it violates is the source of a consolation which is constantly renewed. In *The Rose Tattoo* the only betrayal has been a necessary choice of the living over the dead. But this was one of the few plays in which the ironies of love were not played out – that and, perhaps, *Period of Adjustment*. The gesture at the end of *Cat on a Hot Tin Roof*, in which sexual reconciliation appears simultaneously to offer spiritual grace and material advancement, is an outward compromise which potentially threatens the paradoxes of character and the implicit social critique alike. Williams is a writer at his best when tension is palpable. When he allows it to relax the consequence is often sentimentality. This is all too evident in *Camino Real*, but there, to some degree, attention is deflected from character (which is for the most part consciously modelled on stereotype or perhaps, more generously, archetype) onto form.

Williams said of *Camino Real*: 'In that play I think I shoved open, for myself anyhow, a very heavy iron door whose resisting weight was a timidity of freedom.'[110] In a sense the 'Terra Incognita' into which Kilroy, the protagonist, moves reflects Williams's own sense of moving in a new direction, going beyond the immediate realities of his own experience, finding a setting other than the claustrophobic Southern town of his youth and a form much looser and less controlled than that of his first plays. In an article called 'Lyric Theatre: A Faith' he conceded a central role to his director, Elia Kazan, in this regard:

> Nobody knows better than Kazan that the poetry of a play is not confined to its language. Perhaps through practice, through trial and failure, I would have found this out for myself. An artist is eager to credit himself with his lessons: he should not forget to acknowledge the criticism that supplements and secures what he catches on his own hook. In our last two productions together, Kazan has moved boldly ahead of me. I have followed with fear, in his unswerving, truly courageous, aim to advance still further the plastic and dynamic kind of theatre poetry which we created on Broadway with 'A Streetcar Named Desire'. The intellectuals of the theatre, the so-called *avant-garde*, have picked fault with this almost furious translation of theatrical poetry into such strongly visual and mobile effects. Yet *Camino Real*, despite a short run, has apparently made a lasting impression, and *Cat on a Hot Tin Roof* apparently never fails to move an audience deeply, despite the fact that it assaults the attitudes, standards, and adjustments which so many of them carry into the playhouse.[111]

For Williams, the play was 'a picture of the state of the romantic nonconformist in modern society. It stresses honor and man's own sense of inner dignity which the Bohemian must reachieve after each period of degradation he is bound to run into. The romantic should have the spirit of anarchy and not let the world drag him down to his level,'[112] and Williams was clearly a romantic. Certainly he was concerned with that withdrawal from outer to inner experience which Abercrombie had seen as definitional and which he felt distinguished romanticism from realism. Indeed, in some ways that withdrawal became Williams's subject rather than his method. He was concerned with sensibilities driven to the extreme, and *Camino Real* gave ample scope for his fascination with the grotesque, with characters whose personal meaning lies in their peripheral roles. And if that equally makes him kin to the absurdists, the absurd itself is not without its deep roots in romanticism. Certainly, when Isaiah Berlin defined romanticism as the tyranny of art over life, he identified an important element in absurdist art — the sense of enacting a plot, of playing roles, of using a language already processed and conventionalised. And the paradox involved in seeking consolation for one's sense of abandonment with those who are the source of further betrayal, whose very existence indeed may heighten the irony of that existence, is now familiar from Beckett and Pinter. The sense of uncertainty, an uncertainty which must extend to the work of art itself, exists in Williams's work as it does in Beckett's or early Stoppard's. As Marguerite observes in *Camino Real*:

> What are we sure of? Not even of our existence, dear comforting friend! And whom can we ask the questions that torment us? 'What is this place?' 'Where are we?' – a fat old man who gives sly hints that only bewilder us more, a fake of a Gypsy squinting at cards and tea-leaves. What else are we offered? The never-broken procession of little events that assure us that we and strangers about us are still going on! Where? Why? And the perch that we hold is unstable! We're threatened with eviction, for this is a port of entry and departure, there are no permanent guests! And where else have we to go when we leave here?...under that ominous arch into Terra Incognita? We're lonely. We're frightened. We hear the Streetcleaners' piping not far away. So now and then, although we've wounded each other time and again – we stretch out hands to each other in the dark that we can't escape from – we huddle together for some dim-communal comfort. But this 'love' is 'unreal bloodless,' like a violet growing in a crevice in the mountain 'fertilized by the droppings of carrion birds.'[113]

And this deconstructive vision, the sense of a dislocation of logic and continuity, is a major force in Williams's work. It is a fascination with the void which is, for the most part, balanced by a faith in the redemptive power of the imagination – hence Jacques's reply to Marguerite's absurdist analysis is that 'the violets in the mountains can break the rocks *if you believe in them and allow them to grow!*'[114] Fiction becomes a defence as well as in some degree the essence of the problem.

At this stage in his career Williams was inclined to relax the tension, to see his characters, like Kerouac's Beats, reinventing America by tracing invisible paths through an urban wasteland, charging themselves and their surroundings with a significance which derived from their own transforming imaginations. And so he offers an ambiguous elegy to his outcasts, celebrating 'the poet who wandered far from his heart's green country and possibly will and possibly won't be able to find his way back',[115] and the 'last cavaliers' whose understanding and compassion is finally as redeeming and unconvincing as that of Steinbeck's outcasts in *Cannery Row* and *Sweet Thursday*.

But the absurd persists. A certain hermetic logic is established. The setting of *Camino Real*, like those of Beckett and Ionesco, is outside time. It occupies an invented space. The characters themselves come from literature or myth. Reality, then, becomes no more than a series of overlaid fictions, a collage of inventions. Love, in the play, is a convention, a literary conceit. The invasion of the audience by the actors establishes a theatricality fundamental to the play's own logic, for there are no characters, only types and archetypes, self-regarding fictions, role-players desperate to accommodate their roles to a plot which they presume to exist but for which they can find no evidence. Where Beckett's sense of reductive irony is expressed by a single tree whose spring is a mockery of fertility and growth, Williams's is contained in the symbol of a dried-up fountain. But when Williams's fountain begins to flow with water at the end of the play it is not wholly ironic. It flows for Quixote who offers the advice which is in essence that of Williams himself: '*Don't! Pity! Yourself!* The wounds of the vanity, the many offences our egos have to endure, being housed in bodies that age and hearts that grow tired, are better accepted with a tolerant smile.'[116] Endurance becomes not merely the source of further irony but a possible key to transcendence. However, it is scarcely a confident gesture, for he is repeatedly drawn towards an absurdist stance, repeatedly forced to concede the contingency of a world in which the individual is at best peripheral, resisting the pressure of experience with an imagination which cannot help but be in collusion with that which it resists. Although time is suspended, its effects seem clear on his grotesque characters. Indeed he has argued elsewhere that this is the origin of the distortion of character in his work, for the 'influence of life's destroyer, time, must be somehow worked into the context of [the play]. Perhaps it is a certain foolery, a certain distortion toward the grotesque which will solve the problem.'[117] Whether or not it solved the problem is debatable but the pressure towards the grotesque in his work seems clear.

Dramatically, *Camino Real* is less than convincing. What he saw as the freedom of its form is undercut by the coercive logic of its development. Since the characters are themselves derived from fictions they are necessarily denied the world of possibility to which the protagonist, Kilroy, aspires. And hence much of the tension is dissipated. 'Terra Incognita' represents a territory which is closed to them by definition. They are wholly known. They are not true bohemians; they are people playing at bohemianism, and for the potent sexuality of his earlier plays he substitutes an arid and passionless fantasy of relationship. These are figures without resources of their own. The lightness of touch he reached for eluded him. What was left was a somewhat heavy-handed allegory.

The play was a financial and critical failure. Williams has recalled fleeing from the party at which the reviews came in, objecting that 'They were savage about this play, which freed so much of contemporary American theater from realistic constrictions.'[118] To Williams it seemed like the culmination of a process which had started with *Summer and Smoke*. Each play had been less successful than the previous one and his attempt to break new ground had now been rejected. He reportedly considered abandoning his writing career but it is doubtful that this was more than a momentary response. Certainly he quickly turned to a number of other projects and finally presented Kazan with a new work, *Cat on a Hot Tin Roof* (1955), which proved both successful and controversial and was subsequently filmed with Elizabeth Taylor and Paul Newman playing the principal parts.

The play concerns the struggle by Margaret Pollitt (Maggie, the cat) to restore her relationship with Brick, a former football star who has turned to alcohol and become sexually insecure following the death of a male friend with whom he may have had a homosexual relationship. And beyond the renewal of the relationship Maggie wishes to make her husband into a credible heir to the estate of his dying father – Big Daddy. In this her chief rivals are Brick's brother, Gooper, and his wife Mae. Desperately sycophantic, Gooper and Mae parade their five children as pawns in their attempt to win the inheritance, in the knowledge that, though Brick is Big Daddy's favourite, the absence of any children threatens the notion of the dynasty for which he yearns. The play ends with Maggie and Brick reconciled and with their renewed sexual relationship promising and justifying the crucial inheritance. *Cat on a Hot Tin Roof* opened on 24 March 1955. It was an immediate and considerable success, temporarily stilling Williams's fears about the eclipse of his talent.

Maggie is not one of Williams's losers. She was born poor and has learned the need to fight for what she wants. She is a survivor. But it is in part these qualities that have alienated Brick, for when she had felt that his relationship with his friend Skipper had threatened her she had destroyed him. Accused by Maggie of homosexuality, Skipper tries to make love to her. His failure precipitates his suicide. There are clearly echoes here of *Streetcar* in which, of course, a public accusation of homosexuality also leads to suicide, but it is Brick and not Maggie who is disoriented by this. Wrecked by self-doubt and guilt he sets out to destroy himself, to ally himself with his friend in a kind of death. And death is a major force in the play. Besides Skipper's reported death and Brick's moral and spiritual suicide, Big Daddy, vital and dominating, is dying of cancer. But the play is also concerned with deceit in its many facets. The truth of Big Daddy's cancer is kept from him, while the play ends with Maggie's lie that she is pregnant, a lie which we are to believe will be translated into truth by Maggie and Brick as their relationship is restored.

The play is full of people who lie for one reason or another or at least refuse to acknowledge the truth. The word 'mendacity' echoes throughout. But, to Williams, it equally characterises the world in which they operate. The denial of death is fundamental, but so, too, is a refusal to acknowledge the reality and substance of human need. Hypocrisy, cant, greed and self-interest seem the governing principles of this society. Big Daddy hoards his possessions and, for most of the play's characters, life consists essentially of an attempt to gain possession of them. One of the ironies, however, and one scarcely examined by Williams, is the fact that Maggie is as involved in this process as anyone. She genuinely cares for Brick but her urgency and her energy seem to derive precisely from a refusal to let go of the inheritance which she believes to be hers by right. And she, too, is capable of lying. To Benjamin Nelson hers is 'a life-lie, told in the face of death',[119] and yet the precise distinction between those lies which generate life and those which do not is never clearly established, the more so since Maggie's lie is a desperate bid to forestall Gooper's bid for the estate. Williams's own explanation was outlined in an article in the *New York Herald Tribune* in 1957:

> I meant for the audience to discover how people erect false values by not facing what is true in their natures, by having to live a lie, and I hoped the audience would admire the heroic persistence of life and vitality; and I hoped they would feel the thwarted desire of people to reach each other through this fog, this screen of incomprehension.[120]

The irony is that the two most vital figures are Big Daddy and Maggie — the one a voracious materialist, the other determinedly upwardly mobile, eager not to be displaced from her hard-won position. Both are capable of love but in neither case is that love entirely separate from their own ambitions. Big Daddy wants to live on through Brick; Maggie wishes to consolidate her grip on the hot tin roof onto which she has clambered with such effort. It is not that this is the only source of their energy, but it is the focus of that energy.

And these two are clearly the principal focuses of the play. This fact, indeed, led Kazan to take issue with Williams's original script in which Big Daddy disappeared at the end of the second act. Williams resisted at first but eventually rewrote the concluding act so that he reappeared, albeit not to great effect. In a note published with the text of the play (which included both the original and the revised third act) he explained that Kazan had objected on three counts:

> one, he felt that Big Daddy was too vivid and important a character to disappear from the play except as an offstage cry after the second act curtain; two, he felt that the character of Brick should undergo some apparent mutation as a result of the virtual vivisection that he undergoes in his interview with his father in Act Two. Three, he felt that the character of Margaret, while he understood that I sympathized with her and liked her myself, should be, if possible, more clearly sympathetic to an audience.

Only the third suggestion appealed to him although he was convinced that he had already presented 'a very true and moving portrait of a young woman whose frustration in love and whose practicality drove her to the literal seduction of an unwilling young man'.[121] He specifically did not want Big Daddy to reappear but, wishing Kazan to direct, agreed to compromise. However, Kazan clearly seems to have been right. Though the principal speech which he is given is little more than a crude joke (introduced originally to show solidarity between Brick and Big Daddy, as the son alone joins him in laughter), a piece of bravado in the face of death, it does serve to heighten the drama of the scene in which Maggie claims to be pregnant while underscoring the degree to which she, perhaps, more than Brick, is the true counterpart and inheritor of Big Daddy.

Cat on a Hot Tin Roof bears an epigraph from a poem by Dylan Thomas whose concluding lines are 'Do not go gentle into that good night. / Rage, rage against the dying of the light.' But while Williams's work is, indeed, clearly designed as a rage against a dying light it is also an elegy both for cultural presumptions and a creative imagination threatened by the material world. Since his model of human behaviour is of an irremediable isolation, art is generally a doomed enterprise, a despairing effort at contact neutralised by the very nature of the human condition. As he explained in a crucial essay called 'Person-to-Person', the urgent need to communicate stems from a sense of abandonment, 'a lonely condition, so terrifying to think of that we usually don't'. Hence 'a personal lyricism', and the art which is an expression of that lyricism, 'is the outcry of a prisoner to prisoner from the cell in solitary confinement where each is confined for the duration of his life'. Indeed, he suggested that it was his personal shyness which originally led him to the indirect communication of drama. Thus

> we talk to each other, write and wire each other, call each other short and long distance across land and sea, clasp hands with each other at meeting and at parting, fight each other and even destroy each other because of this always somewhat thwarted effort to break through walls to each other. As a character in a play once said, 'We're all of us sentenced to solitary confinement inside our own skins.'[122]

And that constriction becomes a dominant image in his plays. The claustrophobia of the setting of *The Glass Menagerie* and *Streetcar* is clear. By contrast, in *Cat on a Hot Tin Roof* he called on the designer to create a sense of space in his set, 'to give the actors room to move about freely (to show their restlessness, their passion for breaking out).'[123] But that freedom is deceptive. For the central truth from which his characters are in flight is the knowledge that, as Big Daddy remarks, 'the human animal is a beast that dies', and 'the fact that he's dying don't give him pity for others'.[124] The rich are trying to buy everlasting life; the poor trying to acquire wealth. In Williams's world 'communication is awful hard between people'. And when that world seems open, as it did momentarily for Big Daddy, it is usually an illusion. Thus Big Daddy announces '*The sky is open! Christ, it's open again! It's open*',[125] precisely when, unbeknown to him, news of his imminent death by cancer has just been confirmed.

In the preface to *Cat on a Hot Tin Roof* Williams comments on the fact that creative work is so closely related to the personality of the writer. It is an assertion which is virtually a confession in that this play does indeed press closely to the centre of Williams's personal sensibility. It is, he suggests,

> sad and embarrassing and unattractive that those emotions that stir him deeply enough to demand expression, and to charge their expression with some measure of light and power, are nearly all rooted, however changed in their surface, in the particular and some times peculiar concerns of the artist himself, that special world, the passions and images of it that each of us weaves about him from birth to death…from the spider web of his own singular perceptions.[126]

The peculiar concern at the heart of this play is not simply the question of the individual's sexual identity, but it is that which tends to charge it with a submerged power. The ambiguity of the preface reflects that of the play. The homosexuality, which may or may not have coloured the relationship between Brick and his friend Skipper, exists as an image of suppressed truth. But it is not incidental that hidden truth should find its correlative in homosexuality; that it does so is an indication of Williams's attempt to press towards the truth which his own play urges. He is, however, left with a paradox. On the one hand he resists a simple definition of truth which too closely defines character and motive, while on the other hand he acknowledges the need to concede a reality to personal proclivities and experiences which simple denial cannot neutralise. In this respect Williams's own note on the problematic relationship between Brick and Skipper is particularly revealing:

> The fact that if it existed it has to be disavowed to 'keep face' in the world they lived in, may be at the heart of the 'mendacity' that Brick drinks to kill his disgust with. It may be the root of his collapse. Or maybe it is only a single manifestation of it, not even the most important. The bird that I hope to catch in the net of this play is not the solution of one man's psychological problem. I'm trying to catch the true quality of experience in a group of people, that cloudy, flickering, evanescent – fiercely charged! – interplay of live human beings in the thundercloud of a common crisis. Some mystery should be left in the revelation of character in a play, just as a great deal of mystery is always left in the revelation of character in life, even in one's own character to himself. This does not absolve the playwright of his duty to observe and probe as clearly and deeply as he *legitimately* can: but it should steer him away from 'pat' conclusions, facile definitions which make a play just a play not a snare for the truth of human experience.[127]

He then adds that the scene should be played 'with great concentration, with most of the power leashed but palpable in what is left unspoken'.

Williams's homosexuality is clearly a key to his personal and dramatic concerns, and it does indeed derive its special power from its unspoken quality. The word 'legitimately' has a special force for Williams, legitimacy obviously carrying both social and aesthetic implications, suggesting, in part, a socially imposed prohibition and, in part, a deliberate refusal to accept a definition which is either reductive or cannot be claimed in its complexity. He was all too aware of the mendacity forced on him by a society unwilling to validate his particular sensibility – and on people like Maggie by a social system which chose to deny poverty except as a consequence of dereliction. The sexual subversiveness of Williams's plays has its social component. By a familiar sentimentality (one equally observable in Lawrence) sensuality and sexual energy tend to be seen as class prerogatives. The rich are typified, as they are in Hemingway's *To Have and Have Not* (a novel whose title contains a conscious sexual ambiguity) or Fitzgerald's *Tender is the Night*, as impotent, incestuous and exhausted. But, then, in a country without a ruling ideology sexuality has always been seen by writers as a key to cultural presumptions – a ruling metaphor of anarchy, subversion or placid contentment.

The ambivalence in *Cat on a Hot Tin Roof* is considerable. It is an ambivalence which he saw as basic to his work. Thus in answer to the question, 'Was Brick homosexual?', he observed that

> He probably – no, I would even say quite certainly – went no further in physical expression than clasping Skipper's hand across the space between their twin beds in hotel rooms – and yet his sexual nature was not innately 'normal'...But Brick's overt sexual adjustment was, and must always remain, a heterosexual one. He will go back to Maggie for sheer animal comfort, even if she did not make him dependent on her for such creature comforts as only a devoted slave can provide. He is her dependant. As Strindberg said: 'They call it love-hatred, and it hails from the pit...'

The vast territory ruled over by Big Daddy had been accumulated by two homosexuals. For Williams this was 'a relationship which must have involved a tenderness which was uncommon'.[128] That softness lies behind the violent emotion of the play's surface. It suggests a final level of acceptance, an end equally to rebellion and to the social striving which so disrupts the lives of the characters in *Cat on a Hot Tin Roof*. And yet the process of the play is one whereby Brick's heterosexuality can be endorsed. For the truth is that Brick is himself deeply conventional. The source of his guilt, and hence the source of the pain which he seeks to control with alcohol, is that he wholly accepts the rigid and inhuman categories of his society and is deeply worried about what he fears may be his own ambivalence. The same society which rewarded him for his athletic prowess is unforgiving in its insistence on sexual propriety. Fornication can be absorbed easily into a myth of cavalier adventure; homosexuality threatens that myth. To accept society's accolades is also to accept its sexual and social dictates. Though the relationships which have surrounded him, heterosexual relationships as epitomised by that of his parents and his brother, have been charged with self-interest and resistance to common humanity, nonetheless he feels forced to concede that his own relationship with Skipper cannot have been 'normal'. Haunted by the spectre of prejudice which made him fear his own tenderness, he had denied that same friend when he was most in need. The truth which he drinks to deny is thus his complicity in the death of his friend. For when Skipper had, through the failure of his attempted adultery with Maggie, convinced himself of his own homosexuality, Brick had condemned him as implacably as the society which in his heart he despised.

Nor are these weaknesses, moral failures and even illnesses simply presented as private burdens. Big Daddy's cancer stands as an image of that of his society. It has destroyed his kidneys and he has developed uremia, which is a 'poisoning of the whole system due to the failure of the body to eliminate its poisons'.[129] Clearly this is essentially the disease from which the whole culture suffers. Its lies, its injustices, its evasions, its cruelties, have infected the body politic. The only defence, against this and the primary fact of death, is that which Big Mamma offers in the original version of the third act and which was to have formed part of the essay 'Person-To-Person' published as an introduction: 'Time goes by so fast. Nothin' can outrun it. Death commences too early – almost before you're half-acquainted with life – you meet with the other...Oh, you know we just got to love each other...'[130] And Williams attempts to neutralise sentimentality by making love an active force, by creating, in the person of Maggie, a tough version of that love. And Maggie is strong. She is tenacious and will no more surrender Brick to alcohol and death than she will her own rights to those of the avaricious Gooper. As she says at the end of the play, 'Oh, you weak people, you weak, beautiful people! – What you want is someone to – take hold of you – Gently, gently, with love!'[131] Brick's ambiguous response is thus an indication of the nature of the task rather than of its impossibility. Indeed, in the Broadway production, and under pressure from Elia Kazan, Brick's final response to Maggie's declaration of love – 'Wouldn't it be funny if that were true?' (an echo of his father's similar comment earlier in the play and hence suggestive of a destructive circularity of experience) – is excised. Indeed, Brick becomes more clearly supportive of Maggie, recognising the human need which leads to the lie about her pregnancy.

An earlier draft of the play bore an epigraph from Yeats: 'Amid a place of stone / Be secret and exult, / Because of all things know / That is most difficult.' This is precisely the kind of heroism which Williams most admires, whether the game is a winning or a losing one. It is a heroism manifested most clearly in the play by Maggie. And, in an intermediate draft for the new third act, Brick acknowledges Maggie's strength, 'If I could rise to her level, I would...be – higher...I – I am – false! Broken – Fell off the goddam roof she's been scramblin' up. Truth is something desperate, and she's got it!'[132] '*Life is a damned fire in your*...Who am I?...False! Broken – To argue with it.'[133] In this version Brick takes the initiative in having the pillow returned on the bed, confessing to a fear of his own impotence. As the play ends, he is embraced by Maggie.

Perhaps the most interesting criticism of the play was that offered by Arthur Miller in a speech he prepared for the New Dramatists' Committee in 1956–7. Emerging out of a discussion of the influences which had shaped his own work and his response to the contemporary theatre, it inevitably reflects Miller's own concerns as a writer. But it is a fascinating analysis and worth quoting at length.

> Williams has a long reach and a genuinely dramatic imagination. To me, however, his greatest value, his aesthetic valor, so to speak, lies in his very evident determination to unveil and engage the widest range of causation conceivable to him. He is constantly pressing his own limits. He creates shows, as all of us must, but he possesses the restless inconsolability with his solutions which is inevitable in a genuine writer. In my opinion, he is properly discontented with the total image some of his plays have created. And it is better that way, for when the image is complete, closed and self-contained it is usually arbitrary and false.
>
> It is no profound thing to say that a genuine work of art creates not

5. Barbara Bel Geddes, Mildred Dunnock, Madeleine Sherwood, Pat Hingle and Ben Gazzara in *Cat on a Hot Tin Roof* at the Morosco Theatre, New York, 1955. Directed by Elia Kazan and designed by Jo Mielziner.

completion, but a sustained image of things in tentative balance. What I say now is not to describe that balance as a false or illusory one, but one whose weighing containers, so to speak, are larger and greater than what has been put into them. I think, in fact, that, in *Cat on a Hot Tin Roof*, Williams in one vital respect made an assault upon his own viewpoint in an attempt to break it up and reform it on a wider circumference.

Essentially it is a play seen from the viewpoint of Brick, the son. He is a lonely young man sensitized to injustice. Around him is a world whose human figures partake in various ways of grossness, Philistinism, greed, money-lust, power-lust. And – with his mean spirited brother as an example – it is a world senselessly reproducing itself through ugly children conceived without the grace of genuine affection, and delivered not so much as children but as inheritors of great wealth and power, the new perpetuation of inequity.

In contrast, Brick conceives of his friendship with his dead friend as an idealistic, even gallant and valorous and somehow morally elevated one, a relationship in which nothing was demanded, but what was given was given unasked, beyond the realm of price, of value, even of materiality. He clings to this image as to a banner of purity to flaunt against the world, and more precisely, against the decree of nature to reproduce himself, to become in turn the father, the master of the earth, the administrator of the tainted and impure world. It is a world in whose relations – especially between the sexes – there is always the element of the transaction, of materiality.

If the play confined itself to the psychiatry of impotence it could be admired or dismissed as such. Williams' plays are never merely that, but here in addition unlike his other plays, there is a father. Not only is he the head of a family, but the very image of power, of materiality, of authority. And the problem this father is given is how he can infuse his own personality into the prostrated spirit of his son so that a hand as strong as his own will guide his fortune when he is gone – more particularly, so that his own immortality, his civilization, will be carried on.

As the play was produced, without the surface realism of living room, bedroom, walls, conventional light – in an atmosphere, instead, of poetic conflict, in a world that is eternal and not merely this world, it provided more evidence that Williams' preoccupation extends beyond the surface realities of the relationships, and beyond the psychiatric connotations of homosexuality and impotence. In every conceivable fashion there was established a goal beyond sheer behaviour. We were made to see, I believe, an ulterior pantheon of forces and a play of symbols as well as of characters.

It is well known that there was difficulty in ending this play, and I am certainly of no mind to try it. But I believe I am not alone in saying that the resolution wherein Brick finally regains potency was not understandable on the stage. But my feeling is that even if this were more comprehensibly motivated, so that the psychiatric development of the hero were persuasively completed, it in itself could not embrace the other questions raised in the play.

We are persuaded as we watch this play that the world around Brick is in fact an unworthy collection of unworthy motives and greedy actions. Brick refuses to participate in this world, but he cannot destroy it either or reform it and turns against himself. The question here, it seems to me, the ultimate question is the right of society to renew itself when it is, in fact, unworthy. There is, after all, a highly articulated struggle for material power going on here. There is literally and symbolically a world to win or a world to forsake and damn. A viewpoint is necessary, if one is to raise such a tremendous issue, a viewpoint capable of encompassing it. This is not a study in cynicism where the writer merely exposes the paradoxes of all sides and is content to end with a joke. Nor, again, is it mere psychiatry, aiming to show us how a young man reclaims his sexuality. There is a moral judgement hanging over this play which never quite comes down. A tempting analogy would be that of a Hamlet who takes up his sword and neither fights nor refuses to fight but marries an Ophelia who does not die.

Brick, despite his resignation from the race, has thrown a challenge to it which informs the whole play, a challenge which the father and the play both recognize and ignore. But if it is the central challenge of the play – as the play seems to me to emphasize – then the world must either prove its worthiness to survive, or its unworthiness must be dramatically proved, to justify Brick's refusal to renew it – or, like a Hamlet who will neither do battle nor put down his sword, it must condemn Brick to inaction and perhaps indifference to its fate.

Because of Williams' marvellous ability, I for one would be willing to listen – and perhaps to him alone – even as he pronounced ultimate doom upon the race, a race exemplified in his play by the meanest of motives. This is a foundation grand enough, deep enough and worthy of being examined remorselessly and perhaps even shaken and smashed...had the implicit challenge ripened, we should no longer be held by our curiosity or our pity for someone else, but by that error which comes when we must in truth justify our most basic assumptions. The father in this play, I think, must be forced to the wall in justification of his world and Brick must be forced to his wall in justification of his condemning that world to the ultimate biological degree. The question of society's right to insist upon its renewal when it is unworthy is a question of tragic grandeur, and those who have asked this question of the world know full well the lash of its retaliation.

Quite simply, what I am asking is that the play pursue the ultimate development of the very questions it asks. But for such a pursuit, the viewpoint of the adolescent is not enough. The father, with the best will in the world, is faced with the problem of a son he loves best refusing to accept him and his spirit. Worse yet, it is to the least worthy son that that spirit must be handed if all else fails. Above the father's and the son's individual viewpoints the third must emerge, the viewpoint, in fact, of the audience, the society, and the race. It is a viewpoint that must weigh, as I have said, the question of its own right to biological survival – and one thing more, the question of the fate of the sensitive and the just in an impure world of power. After all, ultimately someone must take charge; this is the tragic dilemma, but it is beyond the viewpoint of adolescence. Someone must administer inequity or himself destroy that world by refusing to renew it, or by doing battle against its injustice, or by declaring his indifference or his cynicism...

Again, I am not criticizing this play, but attempting to mark the outlines of its viewpoint – which is an extension of our theatre's viewpoint to its present limits. Nor is this an entirely new and unheralded idea. Be it Tolstoy, Dostoevsky, Hemingway, you or I, we are formed in this world when we are sons and daughters and the first truths we know throw us into conflict with our fathers and mothers. The struggle for mastery – for the freedom of manhood or womanhood as opposed to the servility of childhood – is the struggle not only to overthrow authority but to reconstitute it anew. The viewpoint of the adolescent is precious because it is revolutionary and insists upon justice. But in truth the parent, powerful as he appears, is not the source of injustice but its deputy.

A drama which refuses or is unable to reach beyond this façade is denying itself its inherited chance for greatness. The best of our theatre is standing tiptoe, striving to see over the shoulders of father and mother. The worst is exploiting and wallowing in the self-pity of adolescence and obsessive keyhole sexuality. The way out, as the poet has said, is always *through*. We will not find it by huddling closer to the center of the charmed circle, by developing more and more naturalism in our dialogue and our acting, that 'slice of life' reportage which is to life what an overheard rumor is to truth; nor by setting up an artificial poetic style, nor by once again shocking the householders with yet other unveilings of domestic relations and their hypocrisies. Nor will we break out by writing problem plays. There is an organic aesthetic, a tracking of impulse and causation from the individual to the world and back again which must be reconstituted. We are exhausting the realm of effects, which is the world of adolescence taken pure.

In my opinion, if our stage does not come to pierce through effects to an evaluation of the world it will contract to a lesser psychiatry and an inexpert one. We shall be confined to writing an *Oedipus* without the pestilence, an *Oedipus* whose catastrophe is private and unrelated to the survival of his people, an *Oedipus* who cannot tear out his eyes because there will be no standard by which he can judge himself; an *Oedipus*, in a word, who on learning of his incestuous marriage, instead of tearing out his eyes will merely wipe away his tears thus to declare his loneliness...

Symbolically, as though sensing that we are confined, we have removed the doors and walls and ceilings from our sets. But the knowing eye still sees them there. They may disappear and the stage will open to that symbolic stature, that realm where the father is after all not the final authority, that area where he is the son, too, that area where religions are made and the giants live, only when we see beyond parents, who are, after all, but the shadows of the gods.

A great drama is a great jurisprudence. Balance is all. It will evade us until we can once again see man as whole, until sensitivity and justice and power are utterly face to face, until authority's justifications and rebellion's too are tracked even to those heights where the breath fails, where – because the longest point of view as well as the smaller has spoken – truly the rest is silence.[134]

For Miller, unsurprisingly, it becomes quintessentially a social play. It is concerned with 'the right of society to renew itself when it is, in fact, unworthy.' Brick becomes a kind of Ibsenesque hero presenting his demand of the ideal, and the father–son relationship is seen as important less for psychological reasons than because it compresses social process into a single transaction. The son is inherently revolutionary, challenging the rights of authority, but the father is only the image of authority and not the thing itself. For him, the vital play is that in which the forces behind the masks are identified.

But *Cat on a Hot Tin Roof* is not primarily concerned with locating an alternative system of values. As Miller observes, Brick's response to experience is to idealise it, to retreat from ambiguity as he does from grossness. In a sense he wishes to freeze time, to project the adolescent world of sport and male friendship into an indefinite future. His present retreat into alcohol, his withdrawal from the sexual contract which threatens to pull him into a world of causality, is merely another version of his resort to the ideal. He is simply not a part of the world which surrounds him, a world which transforms value into price. And there is precisely a price to be put on his relationship with Maggie. It will buy him an inheritance which he does not want, and through that very utility it becomes a relationship which he cannot value. It is, indeed, for this reason that one of the changes which Kazan urged on Williams has the effect of altering the nature of Brick's character and the social consequences of his actions. Kazan suggested that, following his conversation with his father, Brick should show some alteration in his stance. The amended version has Brick joining the very world which he despised, allowing his relationship with Maggie to be cashed in for the inheritance. In one sense he seems to be rescued from his isolation: in another he sells out, betraying not just the memory of Skipper, which has to be exorcised, but also his determination not to become a part of the Pollitts' world of human barter. Williams rightly objected that, 'I felt that the moral paralysis of Brick was a root thing in his tragedy, and to show a dramatic progression would obscure the meaning of that tragedy in him.'[135]

The present resolution not merely discharges this tension, it potentially enrols Brick and Maggie, along with the Goopers, in the materiality of which the play is so distrustful. Brick's crutches, like his alcohol, are a patent symbol of his retreat from the brittle realities of experience but, thrown away, they leave him to confront those realities merely as a result of a conversation with his father and yet another appeal from his wife. Williams, here, is plainly launching an assault on mendacity, while elsewhere maintaining its necessity.

What is less clear is what truth Brick is now engaging. Is his new potency really accepted by him as an enrolment in the profit and loss of human relationships and the exercise of money and power as the successor to his father? This, I suspect, is the source of that failure of moral judgement to which Miller refers. Though I see no reason why the world should prove its worthiness or unworthiness to survive, simply in order to justify Brick's stance, it is true that the moral logic of the play seems to collide with its dramatic logic. Brick's collusion with Maggie's lie (she declares herself pregnant), and his willingness to convert the lie into reality, is a triumph for Maggie and seems a legitimate climax to the play. But it is also evidence of Brick's renewed commitment to mendacity as well as of his re-entry into the Pollitt family and the world of rapacious capitalism which it represents, and this irony is hard to sustain in the face of his apparent decision to re-embrace life. For Miller, neither Brick nor his father is ever pressed to defend a view of the world. The psychological interest drives out the social. The private betrayals are insufficiently rooted in the public ones. The problem, for him, is that Brick's refusal is never sufficiently motivated or knowing. It is a gesture incommensurate with the social question which it seems to provoke. And because he never articulates the essence of his complaint, so the representative of the world from which he recoils is never obliged to defend that world. And because sexuality becomes a central fact and image there is a risk of the play devolving into psychopathology rather than acute analysis.

But the fact is that Tennessee Williams is not Arthur Miller. The social concern is plainly there but he has an equal interest in personal psychology, in the plight of those who are not strong and the compromises which they are forced to make in order to survive. Brick does not take a conscious social stance. Like so many other Williams characters, he is in recoil from a world which fails to conform to his illusions, a world of change, of physical deterioration, of vulnerability. He tries to neutralise this by, in effect, taking himself out of time, by trying to evade causality, ambiguity and betrayal. But, on a symbolic level his attempt to run away merely results in a paralysis of will as his literal attempt to repeat his athletic past by jumping over hurdles results in a broken leg. In this sense the compromise at the end is a necessary one. The only alternative, as Laura Wingfield and Blanche Dubois found, is insanity or complete withdrawal. The fact remains, however, that this leaves him with an ambiguity which Williams was disinclined to pursue. In some fundamental sense it is less a potential homosexuality which is the heart of Brick's dilemma than his fear of life, his desire to resist a process which pulls him into the world of sexual and emotional maturity with its tensions, its profound ambivalences and its causal implications. This is, in a sense, the fundamental dilemma of the Williams protagonist.

In a speech eventually deleted from the stage version Maggie is even more explicit. The point is not that there is an overt homosexuality in Brick's relationship with Skipper, though Maggie suggests that Skipper did indeed have such impulses. It is that, like Alma in *Summer and Smoke*, they resisted involvement, or, like Val Xavier in *Orpheus Descending*, they feared corruption:

> Y'leaned on each others shoulders an' sang sad songs to the moon!...I just listened, I understood! I knew the end of the world was comin' for you two, the end of that high cloudy world, *not* stained by anything – *carnal*! or false! or ugly! – which you and Skipper had created between you like two high-minded spiders weavin' a web for just two!...Then, suddenly, all changed!...Reason? Instead of singin' sad sweet songs to the moon, you'd got together one night and made up your minds to stay *adolescents forever*.[136]

Big Daddy is clearly right when, in a speech in neither of the published versions, he asserts that 'this – *girl has life in her body, that's no lie!*'[137] (though confusingly a reference to the speech was retained in the Broadway version despite the fact that the speech itself was deleted). Though she may be lying about her pregnancy, she represents the only source of real vitality in the play, albeit a vitality touched with desperation. As she admits, in a speech again excised from the published version,

> a person who's always been a dependent learns tricks that come in to crouch gracefully at the feet of the rich and lucky and beseech their grudging favor! I'm good at that, I've done a lot of crawling, yes, I've crouched all my life at the feet of – rich relatives! – wealthy, generous friends! with the smile of a beggar, and the...claws of a cat, that's right, the claws of a cat on a tin roof, always, always! Nothin' is tougher, nothin' is fiercer, nothin' is more, more passionately determined! – not to give up.[138]

The irony is that she feels she has to fight for a grace which seems to belong to Brick by right. As she says in another speech subsequently deleted:

> he's blessed by nature with something you have to sweat for, and still can't get...it's just – bein' loved, a thing, quality in you that makes people love you!...Something that Brick has about him, a light, a light about him, a – a – natural grace about him that made him loved.[139]

But that passive quality is shown to be insufficient. It creates or sustains an incomplete sensibility which can only compound the forces around it. It is a dichotomy familiar from *Streetcar*, and here, as in that play, he implies the possibility of compromise, that compromise to be expressed through a child – there, actual, and here, projected. Yet Maggie is like Stanley only in her energy, her ability to dominate those around her. Her real strength, and the basis of the play's basic optimism, lies in her recognition of qualities and values which she does not possess, in the use of her strength not just to destroy and subordinate but to support.

94

In the same year that *Cat on a Hot Tin Roof* was playing on Broadway Williams continued to work on two other projects (while, in the summer of 1955, he embarked on a habit of washing down sleeping tablets with martinis which was to lead to a prolonged period in which drugs and alcohol became of increasing importance to him). One, an extended version of a one-act play, 'The Enemy Time', called *Sweet Bird of Youth*, was produced in Florida in 1956 but withdrawn for further work. The other was the much reworked 'Battle of Angels'. The failure of this play at the very beginning of his career had been a major psychological blow and he had continued to revise it. Under the title *Orpheus Descending* (Audrey Wood, his agent, having deleted a list of alternative titles including 'The Dismembering Furies', 'The Memory of an Orchard', 'The Fugitive Kind' and 'Something Wild') it finally opened in New York in March 1957.

Set in a dry-goods store in a small Southern town, this is another of Williams's fables about the victory of the impotent but brutal materialist over the spiritually sensitive and sexually vital. As a young woman, Lady had conducted a wild affair with David Cutrere in the arcadian setting of her father's orchard-cum-wine-garden. But when her father made the mistake of serving Negroes he was burnt out by The Mystic Crew and they were ejected from this paradise. David Cutrere then abandoned her for a society woman and Lady married Jabe Torrance, unbeknown to her one of those who had murdered her father. Now, with her husband dying, she sets out to revenge herself by recreating the wine-garden in miniature in the shop. The ritual seems complete when Val Xavier arrives, young, free, sexually vibrant. He makes her pregnant just as Cutrere had done, though she had aborted that child following his betrayal. Torrance, though, is not to be so easily cheated. He kills his wife and blames the young man, Williams's Lawrentian fox. The play ends with Xavier's screams as he is tortured with a blow-torch in an over-deliberate parody of the death of Lady's own father by fire. The only free spirit who survives is Carol Cutrere, David's sister, who is contemptuous of this closed and destructive world. But since her response is not unlike Blanche's – she has sought to purge her own sense of loneliness with a kind of corruption – there is little room for hope.

For all the play's claustrophobic setting, Williams has epic pretensions. The townsfolk are established as a kind of chorus and once again he reaches for tragic effects, but the melodrama of the action is hardly contained by a self-conscious poeticism or his attempts to provide a mythic overlay. Orpheus, turned Christ, sets out to rescue Eurydice. Classic myth and Christian iconography blend uneasily, and, as usual, he is inclined to trade the momentary passion, the brief glimpse of grace, for that transformation of the public world and the private spirit which he had once looked for.

6. Maureen Stapleton, Cliff Robertson and Graham Denton in *Orpheus Descending* at the Martin Beck Theatre, New York, 1957. Directed by Harold Clurman, set designed by Boris Aronson.

Hence Carol Cutrere's observation – 'What on earth can you do on this earth but catch at whatever comes near you, with both your hands, until your fingers are broken?'[140] – clearly has Williams's endorsement.

The central image of the play is of a bird, supposedly born without legs, which survives only so long as it continues to fly. This is Val Xavier who is destroyed because he delays his departure too long. Flight cannot be reconciled with passion, still less with compassion. Xavier is delayed by Lady and the bond between them. And this is the essential dilemma of Williams's characters. To stand still, to become involved in a relationship which appears to offer redemption, is to become vulnerable, liable to corruption and, finally, destruction. But to leave is to sacrifice the possible redemption implicit in relationship, though some of the echoes of the 1930s were not without their contemporary relevance. Thus there are remnants of the earlier Williams in the play. Carol Cutrere had once been a defender of Negro rights, even protesting over the Scottsboro case in which a number of black youths had been charged with rape by two white prostitutes. Lady's father was killed because he had served drinks to Negroes. The death of Bessie Smith is invoked and racism is presented as yet further evidence of the anti-life spirit of a world 'sick with neon'. And since the Negro is an image of this subordination of the human to the material it is plainly a sin which goes back beyond Jabe Torrance (who is close kin to Faulkner's Flem Snopes). But this social dimension is not explored. It exists as an implacable force. Its dynamics are not examined. Thus precisely why Lady, and Vee, the sheriff's wife, should be free of this taint is not clear since corruption seems endemic. Even Val has been infected. Indeed, paradoxically, it is the desire to live wholly without that corruption which is the root of a more subtle human failing in Val, as it had been in Brick. The problem then is not merely that we seem to be dealing with a definition of corruption which changes, but that the relationship between personal and public corruption is mystified rather than clarified. The play's melodrama detracts from what once seems to have been a play whose social dimension was crucial. However, even here there is something of that moral drive and subversive quality which has made his work so powerful.

Orpheus Descending recasts the South as hell. Beneath his usual concern with human desperation, with the contradictory need to seek consolation in human relationships and in flight, is his most direct denunciation of Southern bigotry. The brutal language of racism echoes through a play which dramatises a hermetic world trapped within its own myths and historically condemned by its own sexual and spiritual impotence. The dominant images are those of death and disease, while an apocalyptic fire constantly threatens. The South is dying. All signs of vitality are feared and destroyed. The wildness has been tamed. The play ends with the torture and death of the only genuinely vital character. And yet, even here, Williams offers some hint of relief from the logic which he identifies. For Carol Cutrere survives, another 'wild thing' who refuses to be cowed. Williams's figures are brittle. The strain is all but unbearable. But they fight to resist death. The implacable fact is subverted by their neurotic courage and by the power of their dreams.

The South which Williams pictures exists less as a real landscape (note, for example, the almost complete and perplexing absence of blacks except, interestingly, as a symbol of death) than as an imaginative world, a disintegrating structure which the individual must inhabit and sustain by a combination of will and imaginative economy. The clash between the Old and the New South is a common enough theme of Southern writing, but for Williams it was less a case of colliding moralities or myths than a debate about the nature of human need and the rights and limits of the imagination. In some sense his subject was always the writer, who, by definition, offers his fictions as a paradigm of order while doubting their ability to survive the onslaught of the real. In that sense Williams's plays are, in effect, metadramas – reflexive works which contemplate their own processes. And though this is clearly true, in a sense, of *The Glass Menagerie* and *A Streetcar Named Desire*, which are precisely about the effort to theatricalise the environment so that theatre becomes not an image of the real but a paradigm of it, it becomes more self-conscious in a later work, *Out Cry*. In this a post-modern doubt about the nature of reality and the fictive process itself moves to the centre of his attention as he identifies an entropic impulse infecting all structures – including his own models of artistic order. The crucial area is the boundary between fiction and the real. Indeed, the territory that interests Williams is precisely the border. It is the place where conscious and subconscious meet, where transformations occur: deep insecurities transmute into action, a sense of solitariness is discharged in language, experience shapes itself into a metaphor whose constrictions must nonetheless be resisted.

And the need to resist the force of the metaphor is a constant theme of his work and the ironic subtext of *Out Cry*. It is a process whereby event is turned into myth and actions become rituals. As such his is a reflexive art because the nature of theatre turns on just such a series of transformations, imaginative recastings of experience. In *Streetcar* Blanche is not only trapped in a world which is shrinking, economically and socially; she is the victim of her own metaphor of desire as an antidote to death. In *The Glass Menagerie* Laura is not only constitutionally vulnerable, she derives her fragility in part from the metaphor which she has elaborated and within which she now lives her life. Sebastian Venable in *Suddenly Last Summer* is, we are asked to believe, literally consumed by his metaphor of himself as victim of a voracious mankind and a terrible god. So, too, with Maggie, who actually thinks of herself as 'the cat', or Shannon, for whom the iguana is a metaphor which he allows to assume too total an authority. And to tread this border is to flirt with insanity – as Blanche, Laura, Sebastian and Shannon discover. The metaphor becomes the real. In *Out Cry* the basic underlying metaphor of Williams's work is moved deliberately into the foreground – that of theatricality itself. And there it proves implacable. Where Blanche had committed herself desperately to the necessity of a mutually supportive theatricality, in *Out Cry* that metaphor is the root of his characters' absurdity.

Williams's characters have always been self-dramatising. They see them-selves as playing roles: Southern belle, fragile soul, determined woman, unfrocked priest. They seek protection from the real in a theatricality which is the denial of causality and time. In that sense they·step outside history. After his early St Louis plays Williams never again tried to engage directly the political and social facts of his age as did Miller. Morality did not lie in accepting responsibility for the state of one's society. The performing self, indeed, became a primary strategy for denying authority to a public world which only exists as a vaguely perceived sense of menace. The difficulty is that this strategy invalidates another – that of forging relationships outside time with the power to neutralise a reductive inhumanity. And this is the fundamental conflict in Williams's work. Genuine relationships imply the need to surrender role, at least for fleeting moments, and in those moments one becomes totally vulnerable. Life, indeed, is vulnerability. For Genet, as for Williams,

> Among other things, the goal of the theatre is to take us outside the limits of what is generally referred to as 'historical' time but which is really theological. The moment the theatrical event begins, the time which will elapse no longer belongs to any calibrated calendar. It transcends the Christian era as it does the revolutionary era. Even if that time which is called 'historical' – does not disappear completely from the spectator's consciousness, another time, which each spectator lives to the full, then unfolds, and as it has neither beginning nor end, it destroys the historical conventions necessitated by social life, and at the same time destroys social conventions as well, not for the sake of just any disorder but neither for the sake of liberation – the theatrical event being suspended, outside of historical time, in its own dramatic time – it is for the sake of a vertiginous liberation.[141]

The freedom, in other words is not without a certain terror, for the vertigo which it creates derives from an awareness of a profound solitude which itself is generated by an acknowledgement of the abyss that exists beneath the surface of social life. And for Williams, no less than for Genet, that abyss is his subject. And where in his early St Louis plays he sought some political explanation for a sense of alienation, in his later work the stress that he shows as operating on the psyche is more fundamental.

Orpheus Descending which he confessed was 'overwritten' was not a success. It closed after a brief run and this, together with the death of his grandfather in 1955, and his father in 1957, sent Tennessee Williams into a deep depression. Indeed, he underwent psychoanalysis. And it was perhaps this experience which led him to write *Suddenly Last Summer*, in which he gives rather too much weight to the psychiatrist's ability to untangle neuroses from legitimate fears and to offer a rational view of experience. But the play's fascination results rather less from its psychological interest than from the degree to which it places the act of writing in the foreground.

A young psychiatrist is summoned by Violet Venable. She wishes him to operate on her niece Catherine, to perform a lobotomy which will cut out of her brain the vicious slander which she regards her as spreading about her son, Sebastian. He had been a poet who produced only a single poem a year, while travelling with his mother. When for the first time he chose to take Catherine rather than her mother he was murdered. According to Catherine he was literally eaten alive by a mob of young men whose sexual favours he had sought. The play concludes with the psychiatrist plainly recognising that it is the older woman who is mad and not Catherine.

Suddenly Last Summer is full of references to the animal world and in particular to the unending battle for survival in which one animal preys on another. The wild garden in which the play is set seems an obvious image of the primitive in man. It is a cruel world and offers Williams's most direct expression of his sense of the hostile environment and the total vulnerability of the individual which has always been at the heart of his work and which, in some sense, his writing is designed to neutralise. But in many ways *Suddenly Last Summer* raises questions about the nature of writing and the status of the imagination which he had not felt able to address before. Certainly an element of self-doubt had been present in *The Glass Menagerie* and *A Streetcar Named Desire*. The imagination had been shown to be complicit with the forms it sought to resist but this had never been seen as the source of corruption, merely as a failed strategy. But if the act of writing is an assertion of meaning, a denial of anarchy, it is also inherently ambiguous, suggesting both a positive desire to reconstruct the world and an act of evasion. In *Orpheus Descending* the sheriff's wife, Vee, paints in order to make sense out of her existence, to deny the beatings, the lynchings, the runaway convicts torn to pieces by hounds, of which she had been a primary witness. She struggles, much like Williams, to make 'some beauty out of this dark country'.[142] It is an ambivalent claim. The act of painting and writing, the imposition of a frame, to some degree seeks to transform need into reality. Art becomes reassurance, becomes in effect a lie. Hence, in *Orpheus Descending* the vision of anarchy is refracted through the lens of Williams's clear eye and confident conscience, which could not exist in the world he describes, while the structure of the play denies the moral discontinuities and the failure of aesthetic will which are its subject. Within the play, the man who tries to humanise the barren community, creating a separate world in the form of a wine-garden, with carefully cultivated fruit trees and an elaborate structure of arbours and retreats, is burned to death, as is the wild Val Xavier. But the play survives, apparently immune to the forces to which it grants such power. However, where in *Streetcar* and *Cat* the child in the womb constitutes the source of hope, albeit problematic, here the child dies with its mother. The self-doubt grows.

In *Suddenly Last Summer* the artist/writer is a more sinister figure. He compounds rather than contains the anarchic forces at large in the world. Sebastian Venable is in effect an extension of his art. He is intensely private and delicate. His perception of the world is of a grotesque battle for survival, the natural product of the imagination of a violent god. But that perception is distilled in the highly formalised shape of a poem (just as in the carefully constructed, four-scene play Williams contains his own grotesques and dramatises his own sense of the anarchic power of the subconscious and of a dominating sexuality). Admittedly, the lurid gothicism of the poet and his mother comes up against scientific rationalism and the voice of what appears to be truth in the form of a psychiatrist, but this fails to engage the paradox that in some way art is at the heart of Sebastian's inhumanity. It was not that experience was subordinated to art but that art was accepted as a paradigm. As Mrs Venable explains, 'Most people's lives – what are they but trails of debris, each day more debris, more debris, long, long trails of debris with nothing to clear it all up but, finally, death...My son, Sebastian, and I construct our days, each day, we would – carve out each day of our lives like a piece of sculpture – Yes, we left behind us a trail of days like a gallery of sculpture!'[143] The imposition of order has its advantages but it also exacts a price and that price is the exclusion of the creative flux which is actual life.

In this case Catherine is to be sacrificed to Sebastian's poetry. Her freedom is the price, and it is tempting to see in this story of a writer's achievement attained at the cost of a relative's lobotomy at least an echo of Williams's own experience and of the guilt which first surfaced in *The Glass Menagerie*. But here the doubt has extended to the process of writing itself which is seen as consuming experience and coercing it into an arbitrary and deceptive order. And Catherine's 'true story of our time and the world we live in' is, of course, the author's own fiction. Just as Catherine begins to keep a journal in which she refers to herself in the third person, so Williams dramatises his sensibilities through his characters.

Yet Sebastian is not, of course, an adequate image of Williams as a writer. His character accepts everything. He offers no resistance to the world, presenting himself as a sacrifice, compounding the cruelty of existence and of natural process by his own passivity – a passivity that becomes the source of evil. For Williams, as for Catherine, the fact that everyone is sinking, like the passengers of a sudden shipwreck, is no justification for hatred, for the attempt to use one another, which both writer and character see as typifying human relationships. Some kind of resistance is essential or one becomes a simple victim, like the young turtles destroyed by predatory birds, described in the play, or a lobotomised girl offered peace and serenity at the price of humanity. The society represented by Sebastian is literally predatory. He is another of Williams's rich characters, corrupt and corrupting, devouring other people. And consumption is a dominant image, the biological and political implications of which are made clear. Catherine runs the risk of lobotomy because of the greed of her relations. Sebastian's mother tries to bribe the doctor, offering money for his clinic, while Sebastian is literally consumed by those he has previously tried to buy with a handful of money. Metaphor collapses and becomes literal precisely because there is no longer any space between the perceiving mind and the world; there is no resistance. And that is why in his last summer Sebastian cannot write a poem. The gap necessary for metaphor has closed. The act of writing cannot help but imply a distance, a perspective, a judgement, which distinguishes the observer from the thing observed. That is its basic paradox. If the gap were genuinely to close the writer would be consumed, as is Sebastian, and as, at times, Williams himself came perilously close to being. However, beyond these concerns, it is clearly a play which addresses the question of a menacing violence – a violence which threatens the psyche – and in that sense it is simply a more lurid and literal version of a fundamental theme in his work.

Williams defended the growing melodramatic strain in his plays by referring to the public world which itself seemed to be becoming more violent. In a self-interview, published in *The Observer* (7 April 1957), he confessed that 'without planning to do so, I have followed the developing tension and anger and violence of the world and time that I live in through my own steadily increasing tension as a writer and person'. However, as the last remark makes plain he did admit to a parallel sense of hysteria in his own sensibility, confessing that his work had always been a kind of psychotherapy. He went on to say that on both levels he regarded this state of tension and violence as demanding a response, a response towards which he saw his own work as being directed:

> The crying, almost screaming, need of a great worldwide human effort to know ourselves and each other a great deal better, well enough to concede that no man has a monopoly of right or virtue anymore than any man has a corner on duplicity and evil and so forth. If people, and races and nations would start with that self-manifest truth, then I think that the world would side-step the sort of corruption which I have involuntarily chosen as the basic, allegorical theme of my plays as a whole.

Though as an individual he was necessarily implicated in the processes of deceit, somewhat surprisingly as a writer he felt detached from it, insisting that, 'I'm inclined to think that most writers, and most other artists, too, are primarily motivated in their desperate vocation by a desire to find and to separate truth from the complex of lies and evasions they live in.' It was not a conviction that is always clear in his work, the lies of art being alternately embraced as a gesture of grace and compassion and highlighted as a supreme irony. Certainly the world of 'Candles to the Sun' and 'Death is a Drummer' gave way quickly if not to a moral relativism then at least to a sense that human actions are simply expressions of necessity. Hence, in that self-interview he insisted, as Miller would not, that 'I don't believe in "guilt". I don't believe in villains or heroes – only in right or wrong ways that individuals have taken, not by choice but by necessity or by certain still-uncomprehended influences in themselves, their circumstances and their antecedents.' It is not that Miller's world devolves easily into moral absolutes (though, in the form of the Nazis, he was willing to concede the reality of pure evil), but that without personal responsibility and accountability there seemed, finally, no protection against anarchy. For Williams, guilt clearly survives – how else account for Tom's re-creation of the world of his youth in The Glass Menagerie or Blanche's self-loathing in Streetcar or, indeed, the stunning indictment of Suddenly Last Summer? – but it is not at the very centre of his work. There we find not so much the conscience as the imagination.

Like Poe's, his work is death-centred, but equally like Poe's it is fascinated with the resistant imagination. As Williams remarked, 'having always to contend with this adversary of fear, which was sometimes terror, gave a certain tendency towards an atmosphere of hysteria, and violence in my writing, an atmosphere that has existed in it since the beginning'.[144] Indeed his first published work, which appeared in 1928, was a short story in Weird Tales which culminated in the death by drowning of all the guests at a banquet. Looking back, in 1959, on a career which had stretched over a quarter of a century, he could identify only five plays which did not feature violence (being most surprised by the ready acceptance of the horrors of Suddenly Last Summer).

But he might have had greater difficulty locating any plays in which decay was not a central fact and image. His characters tend to be caught on the very verge of slipping into an asexual old age. The young are nearly always described as being about to lose their beauty. Hair is beginning to thin, taut muscles are on the point of relaxing. High ambitions and romantic dreams are already being compromised and about to be abandoned. The epigraph of Sweet Bird of Youth, from a poem by Hart Crane – 'Relentless caper for all those who step / The legend of their youth into the noon' – might have applied with equal force to all of his plays. The passage of time, the erosion of perfect form, the collapse of values, ideals, relationships, social models, love, coherence, mental stability, hope, fiction, is at the heart of his concern. 'All my life', he explained in an essay in *The New York Times* and published as a preface to *Sweet Bird of Youth*, 'I have been haunted by the obsession that to desire a thing or to love a thing intensely is to place yourself in a vulnerable position, to be a possible, if not a probable, loser of what you most want.'[145] While a terrible balance seems to be precariously maintained throughout most of his plays there inevitably comes a time when the thumb comes down securely, sending Laura into spinsterly isolation, Blanche into a sexless dementia, or Maggie into a matronly pregnancy which marks both her victory and, more ambiguously, Brick's defeat. As Chance Wayne observes in *Sweet Bird of Youth*, 'Time does it. Hardens people. Time and the world that you've lived in.'[146] Indeed, the image of decay was clearly partly socially derived. His picture of the South was akin to that drawn by Faulkner in many respects. For Faulkner, too, it was an antinomian territory, bounded on the one side by the self-deceiving myths of a bourbon golden age, which had, in effect, been the root of Southern violence and inhumanity, and on the other by a new breed of soulless businessmen, devoid of even any pretence to moral value. Insanity and violence stand as appropriate images of moral anarchy. After his initial social protest plays Williams became more interested in the dissolution of the sensibility, the flight of the sweet bird of youth, than the decay of America for which that collapse nonetheless stood as a potent image. But a certain apocalypticism remained and that was not without its social dimension, as was apparent from *A Streetcar Named Desire* through to *The Red Devil Battery Sign*. It was, to be sure, rooted in his personal neurosis, the neurosis and depression which led him to undergo analysis, but in some ways he was also responding to a cultural neurosis, a sense of lost values and the collapse of high hopes, which he witnessed in America in the 1950s. And in *Sweet Bird of Youth* the two themes come together.

Boss Finley, a white racist politician, is both primary evidence of political corruption and himself subject to the corrosive power of time. He subordinates everything to his lust for power, a lust whose sexual correlative is evident in his taking of a mistress and his unconscious desire for his own daughter. He denies his daughter the right to choose her own husband, trying to trade her off for political favours. The result is that he destroys her, though she is the image of his wife, now dead, whom he had once genuinely loved. Real cohesiveness, in terms of the individual sensibility, familial relationships, social and national values, is destroyed. Boss Finley is now sexless through age (or accused of such by his mistress); his daughter is sexless by virtue of an operation following her contraction of venereal disease from her lover and the play ends with the emasculation of that lover, Chance Wayne. In other words there is no future. It has already been destroyed. In *Cat on a Hot Tin Roof* the double bed which dominates the set is finally offered as a symbol of hope; in *Sweet Bird of Youth* it is a mark of desperation, a last retreat and, ultimately, an ironic commentary on a dying society and the defeat of the individual. The genuine resurrection of the former play becomes savagely ironic in the latter as Chance Wayne is destroyed on Easter Sunday and Boss Finley presents himself as the new god of his society – violent, vengeful, anti-human, apocalyptic. This is the god envisaged by Sebastian Venable in *Suddenly Last Summer*, a god whose consuming hatred for his creation leaves no space for life.

While *Sweet Bird of Youth* is Williams's most direct engagement with, and denunciation of, Southern racism, which he dramatises in psycho-sexual terms, it is equally an assault on American materialism. The relationship between Chance and his childhood sweetheart, Heavenly, is destroyed by her father because Chance is simply not a good enough political or economic bargain. The corruption, dramatised in sexual terms, is actually monetary. Chance's failure is much more profound than his inability to be successful as soldier or actor. His failure is that he has internalised the values of those he despises. He has agreed to judge things by their standards. And so he chooses success, the accoutrements of achievement, hoping, like Gatsby, to win what the world denies him. The result, as with Gatsby, is that beneath the charm there is corruption, a deadness which destroys first himself and then others. Chance Wayne, indeed, is close kin to a succession of golden boys in American writing, from Fitzgerald's Gatsby, through Miller's Happy Loman, to Albee's young man in *The American Dream*. They are the imperfect products of a system which values appearance over reality and the material over the spiritual. They believe in the inevitable nexus between success and sexual fulfilment. They all stand as images of what Fitzgerald felt to be a particularly American confusion. Like the sailors who first sighted the green breast of America, they thought to satisfy their spiritual yearnings by taking possession of a material world. Thus from the very beginning motives were mixed. And the sexual metaphor was an appropriate one, for America was to be both embraced and possessed. It was to be taken by force. Chance Wayne and the others glimpse beauty; they are aware of a world of mystery; they sense the significance of imagination and instinct. But they reach out for a material correlative to all this. They gradually adapt to the values of those around them, and the pressure to do this is not merely external. It is prompted by their awareness of the passage of time, the closing down of possibilities. As Chance explains, 'To change is to live... to live is to change, and not to change is to die.'[147] This disturbing truth becomes the justification for the abandonment of ideals and the loss of spiritual and moral truth.

Behind that is a more profound justification for surrender. As the heckler who pursues Boss Finley to rallies, undermining the rhetoric of the demagogue, insists, 'I believe that the silence of God, the absolute speechlessness of Him is a long, long and awful thing that the whole world is lost because of.'[148] This conviction is central to Williams's plays. It is the explanation for the absurdist thrust of much of his work but it is also a justification for that work. If God is silent then other voices must sound in other rooms. The cruelties of life must be redeemed by other means than by reference to absolute values. And the artist thus assumes a primary function. As the ageing film star, who momentarily takes refuge with Chance Wayne, remarks, 'Out of the passion and torment of my existence I have created a thing that I can unveil, a sculpture, almost heroic, that I can unveil, which is true.'[149] Her adoption of the identity of Princess Kosmonopolis is merely another such invention and her statement can stand as Williams's justification of his own art as, not for the first time, he dramatises his own plight through the person of a woman.

The truth which he chooses to present in *Sweet Bird of Youth* is one in which people, defeated by time and by the world, can nonetheless deploy what he calls 'a sort of deathbed dignity and honesty'. As he suggests in a stage direction, 'In both Chance and the Princess, we should return to the huddling-together of the lost but not with sentiment, which is false, but with whatever is truthful in the moments when people share doom, face firing squads together.'[150] And that, of course, is essentially Williams's perception of human life, no less than Beckett's. Human kind has been sentenced to death, arbitrarily and with no rights of appeal. The most that can be done is to generate a certain dignity. Despite his disavowal, this sometimes becomes the source of sentimentality in his work and sometimes devolves into something approaching Beckett's irony. But either way he is aware that his is a factitious gesture.

This implied self-doubt was to reach some kind of apogee in *Out Cry*, in which he chooses to confront the modernist process of redeeming life with art most directly, the element of self-doubt expanding to include the work itself. But, more typically, he chose to concede a certain heroism in people who finally could not escape their fate. For, although flight is a word constantly invoked by Williams and his characters, he is equally aware that there is, finally, no escape, that the individual has to face himself and the rigour of his situation. He necessarily accepts that time will eventually run out, and the evasions and strategies will collapse. Thus, as Chance recognises, time 'Gnaws away, like a rat gnaws off its own foot caught in a trap, and then, with the foot gnawed off and the rat set free, couldn't run, couldn't go, bled and died,'[151] though in an alternative ending, dated June 1958,

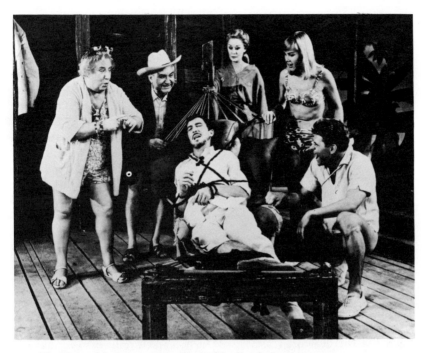

7.   *The Night of the Iguana*, 1961, directed by Frank Corsaro.

Williams has Chance driving away with the Princess and thereby dying spiritually rather than physically and apocalyptically).

The image of an animal caught in a trap is picked up in his next play, *The Night of the Iguana* (born as a short story in 1946), though here he grants a certain grace. Indeed, as his plays lurch from optimism to pessimism and back, it is as though they reflected the oscillations of his own sensibility, despair breeding hope, hope collapsing into despair. We are told that the iguana can escape only by killing itself. But, Williams does acknowledge another possible kind of release. An act of compassion is capable of freeing the iguana and despairing individuals alike. Deprived of a real god, man becomes his own deity, at times cruel, but capable of responding to the desperation of the trapped being.

Shannon is a minister of the church, provoked into a crisis of faith, and with a predilection to seduce or be seduced by the young women he encounters. Having left the church, temporarily, as he assumes, he becomes a courier for a succession of travel firms, wandering the world in search of himself and deteriorating as his youth slips away. Like the prototypical

Williams figure, he now finds himself at the end of the road, conducting tours of Mexico for a dilapidated company specialising in church groups. On the verge of a breakdown, he brings them to a bohemian hotel, the Costa Verde, set in the wild though beautiful jungle. Having scandalised the women of his party by succumbing to a young girl's infatuation, he is dismissed, being consoled alternately by a New England spinster, who is equally at the end of her tether and who is accompanying her nonagenarian grandfather (aptly named Nono Coffin), and by Maxine, the passionate proprietress of the hotel. They are all outcasts, marginal figures. As Shannon observes, they find themselves on the 'dilapidated veranda of a cheap hotel, out of season, in a country caught and destroyed in its flesh and corrupted in its spirit by its gold-hungry Conquistadors'.[152] They are, in effect, absurd figures, described by Williams as being 'like...actors in a play which is about to fold on the road, preparing gravely for a performance which may be the last one'.[153] But, for the most part, Williams lacks the rigour of Beckett. Though he confesses to the marginality of his characters, their unavoidable complicity in their own absurdity, their necessary and protective role-playing, the problematic nature of the real ('the realistic level and the fantastic level – which is the real one, really?' asks Shannon[154]), this creates a need that generates a response which he cannot bring himself to believe is wholly ironic. There is a level at which reality asserts itself. Time is real. His characters age, indeed are captured, like Shannon, on a critical fulcrum between youth and middle age, or, like Nonno, between life and death. And the presence of a group of German fascist tourists (the play is set during the Battle of Britain) offers an image of an implacable reality which makes some human response essential. They represent the threat of meaninglessness; they stand for death and assert an image of man as ineradicably violent, celebrating, as they do, the burning of England. But it is almost as if the very blackness of that world creates the necessity for a glimmer of light. For Hannah, it is precisely the 'subterranean tunnels, the...the journeys that the spooked and bedeviled people are forced to take through the...the *unlighted* sides of their natures'[155] that create the need for 'broken gates between people so they can reach each other, even if it's for one night only'.[156] The home which Hannah and Shannon and even Maxine have sought is finally 'a thing that two people have between them in which each can...live in, emotionally speaking'.[157]

The sentimentality of this position is unavoidable. His defence against this tendency in his own work lies in the clinical efficiency with which he exposes the self-deceptions of his characters, and his admission of the temporary nature of the reprieve which he grants them. Like Hannah, nothing human disgusts him, the squalid desires and pathetic gestures of his characters indicating a need felt not only by the outcasts. Nor is he unaware that the love which he proposes as a desperate strategy is itself both momentary and infected by its own absurdity. The dominant image is one of decay, of entropy. The only question is whether the individual will concede total victory to that process, or whether he can discover a momentary dignity in resistance or in a courageous confrontation with the absurd. This is the essence of the poem which the old man has been struggling to compose, a poem which is in effect a description of his own life:

> How calmly does the orange branch
> Observe the sky begin to blanch
> Without a cry, without a prayer
> With no betrayal of despair.
>
> Sometimes while night obscures the tree
> The zenith of its life will be
> Gone past forever, and from thence
> A second history will commence.
>
> A chronicle no longer gold,
> A bargaining with mist and mould,
> And finally the broken stem
> The plummeting to earth; and then
>
> An intercourse not well designed
> For beings of a golden kind
> Whose native green must arch above
> The earth's obscene, corrupting love.
>
> And still the ripe fruit and the branch
> Observe the sky begin to blanch
> Without a cry, without a prayer,
> With no betrayal of despair.
>
> O courage, could you not as well
> Select a second place to swell,
> Not only in that golden tree
> But in the frightened heart of me.[158]

Williams's protagonists are caught at the zenith or just beyond. They search for and sometimes find that courage, but the fundamental absurdity of their position is never entirely redeemed by natural process since that process is the root of their absurdity.

Williams's plays tend to be set in bars, in hotels, in apartments, in houses threatened with collapse, in temporary refuges of all kinds. He preferred to locate his characters in a kind of limbo in which causality seems momentarily suspended. They become laboratory specimens. But the threat to those characters is no longer, as once it was, external to their actions and their moral sensibilities. It is internal. They have lost their grasp on their lives and their obsessive concern, like that of their creator, is with mortality. Death is the implicit and explicit subject. And throughout the plays which he wrote in the 1960s and early 1970s he presented a series of grotesques, figures reduced to a single dominating feature. Like all his characters, they essentially inhabit separate worlds, sharing only a common desperation. But where once they had other resources, no matter how ironic, now they seem completely drained of any resistant spirit. The cry of the pure in heart seems to give way to the whine of the self-pitying. At times he sought to generalise this by presenting his plays as cultural pathology but the allegorical structure was almost invariably too heavy for the characters or the plot to bear. In *The Red Devil Battery Sign* he was to develop the allegory still further, with the world being given over to man turned ravaging beast. Indeed even his language began to collapse, devolving into pseudo-poetic rhetoric, a kind of baroque prose, or a simple expository announcement of his thematic concerns. *The Milk Train Doesn't Stop Here Any More* (1964), *The Mutilated* (1966), *Kingdom of Earth* (also known as *The Seven Descents of Myrtle*, 1968), *In the Bar of a Tokyo Hotel* (1969), *The Frosted Glass Coffin* (1970), *Confessional* (1970) and *Small Craft Warnings* (1972) all share these weaknesses and bear the imprint of the personal crisis through which he was passing at this time. The familiar elements of Williams's work remain but they now have a parodic relationship to their originals.

Thus, *The Milk Train Doesn't Stop Here Any More* dramatises the recognisable Williams situation of an older woman seeking revivification through a younger man (familiar, that is, from *Orpheus Descending*, *A Streetcar Named Desire*, *Sweet Bird of Youth* and *The Night of the Iguana*), though now it is recast as allegory, while it is hard not to read the play as in some ways the writer's own response to a growing hysteria. Christopher Flanders, a young man who visits ageing women on Italy's Divina Costura, is presented as an angel of death. He eases them through their rite of passage. But by this stage in his career it is tempting to see the figure of the fragile woman, alarmed at the prospect of death, as little more than a self-portrait by Williams. And what is true of her is no less true of the young man, a poet whose talent seems to have waned, and who is disturbed and out of touch with a contemporary sense of the real. His own account of his sense of alienation is surely not remote from Williams's own growing sense of remoteness from his audience.

> Everybody has a sense of *reality* of some kind or other, some kind of sense of being real in his, his – particular – world... And one person's sense of reality can be another person's sense of – well, of madness! – chaos!... And when one person's sense of reality, or loss of sense of reality, disturbs another one's sense of reality... he's avoided! Not welcome... Yes, you see, they hang labels, tags of false identification on people that disturb their own sense of reality too much.[159]

For Williams, concerned, as he later said, about the slow 'sinking into shadow and eclipse of so much of everything that had made my life meaningful to me', and at an increasing tendency of public and critics alike to disregard his work, this lament was plainly not without its personal dimension, though, somewhat improbably, he claimed that the play was an unmistakable attack on American imperialism. And what, in his earlier plays, had been implicit in character and action now bubbles to the surface all too explicitly in language. Thus, Mrs Goforth, approaching death, observes that: 'Sometimes I think, I suspect, that everything that we do is a way of – not thinking about it. Meaning of life, and meaning of death, too... WHAT IN HELL ARE WE DOING? Just going from one goddamn frantic distraction to another, till finally, one too many goddamn frantic distractions leads to disaster, and blackout?'[160]

Similarly, the young man obligingly identifies his symbolic function in the play, insisting that 'sooner or later, you need somebody or something to mean God to you'. He brings an all too explicit message of the necessity for acceptance in a work which discharges its energy too carelessly. We are no longer invited to 'rage against the dying of the light'. Instead we are urged to ease ourselves across a boundary which is more apparent than real, to move from one fiction into another. Thus, the play carries an epigraph from Yeats's 'Sailing to Byzantium'.

> Consume my heart away; sick with desire
> And fastened to a dying animal
> It knows not what it is; and gather me
> Into the artifice of eternity.

He seems, then, to offer his work as consolation, a fictionalising gesture which stands for that act of imaginative transcendence which is finally the only defence against death. A similar logic lies behind The Mutilated, in which two old women, at the end of their lives, eventually lay aside their animosities and agree to act out the fictions of friendship rather than face death alone. They bear the real scars of life but achieve whatever limited transcendence is possible by constructing their own world. It is fragile and contingent, but it has the power to console no matter how temporarily. Thus, one of them confesses, 'I can't imagine tomorrow'; survival is a matter of moment-to-moment self-deceit.

The potential for sentimentality (in Yeats's sense of unearned emotion) is considerable in these plays. He relies, in particular, on the immediate possibility of death to charge his works with significance, and on the various mutilations of his characters to generate sympathy for their self-regarding strategies. The tone of some at least of them is almost valedictory. They have the benignity of Shakespeare's The Tempest. That is to say the tragic is deflected into a form of low-tensile comedy. A kind of grace is bestowed but, in Williams's case, not always earned. The grotesque exists to be accommodated, not to be examined or understood as anything much more than a walking symbol of the pressure of life on the individual.

But this was not a mood he could sustain, and grace tended to give way to frustration, anger, despair, and even fear, in works like *Kingdom of Earth*, *In the Bar of a Tokyo Hotel* and *The Frosted Glass Coffin*: the first two feature the death of an artist figure, a death which bequeaths nothing to those who survive him but a brutal existence, drained of spirit and life; and the third is an absurdist reverie. Yet what seems to be an implicit defence of art in the first two plays is surely also a petulant complaint by an individual and a writer raging not merely against his own mortality but against an audience seemingly oblivious to their own brutalising existence and to the significance of the artist they have failed to cherish?

That brutality seems central to *Kingdom of Earth*, first performed in 1968 and subsequently revised for performance in 1975. Again a play about desperate people grasping at some final consolation, it has almost a parodic relationship to his earlier work. Lot, a tubercular transvestite, brings Myrtle, a one-time showgirl down on her luck, to his Mississippi Delta farmhouse. She has supposed that she had found a man of refinement who would provide her with the comfort and security she had always craved. Instead, she finds that he is dying and that she is exposed to the brutal sexual assaults of his half-brother, Chicken, who has induced Lot to sign a document ceding the farm to him on his death. In addition, the whole property is threatened by fast-rising floodwater so that all their lives are at risk.

In the course of the play Myrtle is terrified into sexual relations with Chicken, desperately anxious as she is to allay his fear that her marriage may have invalidated the document on which he pins his hope. Indeed, when Lot dies (having first put on his mother's white dress), she is forced to recognise that, grotesque as he is, Chicken may be her only hope for survival. Blanche Dubois lives again, though, in so far as Lot also becomes a parodic version of her, this time transposed into a man.

It is a brutal play. The characters are reduced to crude gestures, simple visions, mannered actions. And this reified world is presented to us as 'the kingdom of earth'. As they face the imminent arrival of the flood that may terminate their lives, they bargain with their emotional and physical qualities, trading their limited resources for survival. And this, it seems, is Williams's apocalyptic model of human existence. Lot, like Blanche, has struggled to create 'a little elegance in a corner of the earth we lived in that wasn't favorable to it'.[161] But, as ever in Williams's work, it is a losing game. In the form of Lot and Chicken he presents the two aspects of human nature that he had juxtaposed in *Summer and Smoke*. As Lot realises, Chicken is 'My opposite type'. One is spirit (ethereal, incapable of action), the other is body (cunning, with no sense of beauty or transcendence). And Williams seems to admit of no way of bridging the gap. The world of *The Rose Tattoo* has long since been left behind. His vision is essentially Manichean and this is the source of the sentimentality that always threatens his work, and which, in a play such as this, seems all but disabling. Chicken's observation that, 'life just plain don't care for the weak. Or the soft. I got to be hard. A man and his life got to be made out of the same hard stuff or one or the other will break. Because life's hard', is simply a restatement of a familiar position: 'the soft one breaks. And life is never the soft one.'[162] The play duly ends with the soft one dying and Myrtle and Chicken emerging as the only inheritors of the world.

If *Kingdom of Earth* was indeed in any sense a picture of American society, what he saw was evidently a brutalism untempered by conscience, the total destruction of a sensibility untuned to the fierce pragmatics of the moment. And the result seems to have been a despair born, perhaps, out of personal and national crisis, but transposed onto a metaphysical plane. But his romantic despair gives way to cynicism and a simplistic account of human decline. It was a period in his life in which drink and drugs created 'a deathtime' and the evidence for this in his plays seems clear. As he recognised in 'Notes After the Second Invited Audience' (1972), published as an introduction to *Small Craft Warnings*, he had failed to exercise self-discipline, and he chose to define this as 'the impulse toward self-destruction', which is 'the opposite and dark side of the will to create and flower'.[163]

In *The Frosted Glass Coffin* he seems to move more completely into Beckett territory, choosing to conclude an account of human life as an existence 'in a frosted glass coffin unburied' with a howl of despair and grief for which there is no longer any antidote. And so one of the characters 'closes his cataract-blinded eyes and opens his jaws like a fish out of water. After a few moments, a sound comes from his mouth which takes the full measure of grief.'[164] In this play, as in *I Can't Imagine Tomorrow* (whose copyright dates are 1966 and 1970), the characters lose their individuality and appear only as numbers, thereby underscoring an allegorical intent no longer located in a dense world of social and psychological reality.

I Can't Imagine Tomorrow is also an absurdist drama. It is also a pastiche of his own themes. One of the characters (called One) describes the world he inhabits like this:

> Dragon Country, the country of pain, is an uninhabitable country which is inhabited, though. Each one crossing through that huge, barren country has his own separate track to follow across it alone. If the inhabitants, the explorers of Dragon Country, looked about them, they'd see other explorers, but in this country of endured but unendurable pain each one is so absorbed, deafened, blinded by his own journey across it, he sees, he looks for, no one else crawling across it with him.[165]

The situation is essentially that of *Waiting for Godot* or *Rosencrantz and Guildenstern Are Dead*, though without the wit of either. But where Beckett's characters are trapped in an apparently unchanging world, Williams's fear change: 'If there wasn't a thing called time, the passing of time in the world we live in, we might be able to count on things staying the same, but time lives in the world with us and has a big broom and is sweeping us out of the way, whether we face it or not.'[166] They can't imagine tomorrow not because it will be indistinguishable from today but because it will be different – worse. In his next plays, however, he set himself consciously to imagine that world.

In the Bar of a Tokyo Hotel presents a series of relationships which are so fractured that even language is made to bear the impress of a certain hysteria. Sentences are fragmented; they frequently stutter to a halt. Gestures are aborted. Conversations consist of little more than incomplete remarks, and, confusingly, this applies to all the characters: to a hotel barman and an art gallery owner no less than to the neurotic, nymphomaniac wife and her dying artist husband who are the central characters. In other words, it is a principal trope of the play rather than an expression of character, and the hysteria lies in the writing rather than in the figures who are made to express it. The trauma seems to lie as much outside the text as within it. And his own plight is clearly at its heart. So, when we are told that 'Sometimes the interruption of work, especially in a new style, causes a, causes a – loss of momentum that's never recovered',[167] this sounds suspiciously like special pleading from a man whose own nervous experiments, in a play like *The Gnädiges Fräulein* (1966), had suggested a loss of direction and momentum of which he was all too aware. The later observation, that 'In the beginning, a new style of work can be stronger than you, but you learn to control it',[168] is a little too like whistling in the dark to carry conviction. And, once again, Williams seems to suggest that the human psyche is irrevocably split, that spirit and body find it impossible to inhabit the same being. Thus, as so often elsewhere in his work, he dramatises this conviction by allowing these qualities to spin off in pure form, so that the incorrigibly physical Miriam asks of her husband, 'Are we two people, Mark, or are we...Two sides of!...One! An artist inhabiting the body of a compulsive...'[169] What began in *Summer and Smoke* as a dramatic tactic has become a mere mannerism.

The play is yet another defence of the need to evade the brutal realities of experience, but by now even Williams seemed aware of the degree to which he was merely offering pieties and romantic gestures. Thus, Miriam, immediately after the death of her husband, insists:

> There's an edge, a limit to the circle of light. The circle is narrow. And protective. We have to stay inside. It's our existence and our protection...It's

our home if we have one...This well-defined circle of light is our defense against. Outside of it there's dimness that increases to darkness: never my territory...The circle of light stays with me. Until. Until can be held off but not forever eluded. You've seen how fatal it is to step out of the...If I should say that the circle of light is the approving look of God it would be romantic...[170]

Romantic, indeed. And Williams did flirt with Catholicism in the 1960s. Certainly in this play he seems to want to have his cake and eat it. The artist, by definition, is he who goes outside of the circle, who risks the dark because he has a commitment to truth. And yet he is simultaneously to be seen as the source of consolation, as generating those fictions which are offered as protection against the fact of death. It is this ambivalent quality of art that accounts for some of the ambiguities and even contradictions of his work. He wishes simultaneously to see himself as the solitary truth-teller, at odds with the world, and as the creator of those desperate lies which facilitate survival. This was no less true of his next project.

A production, in 1971, of *Confessional*, a brief play set in a beach-front bar on the California coast, led Williams to expand and reshape it into *Small Craft Warnings*, in which he acted for a few days in 1972. The favourable review of the earlier play prompted him to reach out for the success that had eluded him for so long. As he explained, having, in his own mind, just emerged from a period in which he had retreated from public view and in a sense from reality itself, he had 'an almost insatiable hunger for recognition of the fact that he [was], indeed, still alive, both as man and artist'. It was, he felt, important for him to keep writing, 'to stay active in the theatre and just staying active is sufficient for my purposes, I don't need more than the assurance that I am not prematurely counted out as an active playwright. – Like swimming and love, it's all that keeps me going.' He tried to redress an original 'bleak' ending in the hope of 'a sort of catharisis without words'.[171] It was something of a forlorn hope.

The play is in some senses a 1970s version of *Long Day's Journey Into Night*, charged with a sad sexuality, but lacking O'Neill's concern with the nature of the real, with the texture and substance of guilt, or the form and extent of responsibility. It is set in a bar which is the last refuge of an assorted group of men and women whom Williams chooses to regard as 'fragile vessels', the small craft of the title. They are threatened with life's minor squalls and major disasters. Whatever they might once have been, they are no longer: and this is symbolised ironically in the form of a large varnished sailfish suspended over the bar, a fish whose 'goggle-eyes give it a constant look of amazement', and whose wild freedom is apparent even as it is mocked by its death. They have lost the capacity for surprise. The freshness of vision has coarsened. Their actions are mechanical, their endearments drained of meaning. The most they can rise to is a sentimental gesture. More often it is a perfunctory and nervous obscenity. It is difficult not to see in this Williams's own lament about his life and his 'craft'. An explicit account of the debilitating nature of homosexual relationships by one of the characters stresses the loss of invention and spontaneity involved while the portrait of a doctor whose skill has been destroyed by liquor and who has been forced to practise on the periphery seems painfully close to Williams's own situation. With supreme irony he chose to play the role of Doc for the first five performances of the New Theatre production. The play ends with the bar-keeper allowing a hysterical and apparently disease-ridden woman to go up the stairs to his apartment. The gesture is not self-interested. It is rather the bar-keeper's acceptance of an imperfect human nature and an imperfect world. But the stairs of his apartment are a long way from those in 'Stairs to the Roof' at the beginning of Williams's career, when the world could be made over again by those who had the youth and the energy and the vision to do so. Now such people have been depleted by time and the most they seem capable of is a momentary compassionate gesture. But no sooner is it made than it is rescinded. And none of his characters can see beyond the moment or the day. He still has his travellers; one is a boy travelling on his motorbike from Iowa to Mexico, another a woman who buys sexual favours and is ready to move on in her trailer. But they have already been corrupted. Travel as they might they can never outrun time.

Small Craft Warnings has little to recommend it. Its crude nymphomaniac, cruising homosexual, inarticulate gigolo, disbarred old doctor, wise barman and understanding policeman seem to come straight from Central Casting. They have been taken down from the shelves of a theatrical supermarket. Williams believed that in some sense the play was 'very "now"' and the end 'touching'. But once he had aimed to be a great deal more than 'touching', while it is hard to see why, outside of his personal psychology, the play should be thought in any way contemporary. The overt sexuality, intentionally designed to underscore the pathos of the characters, could not in itself guarantee relevance, not least because where for Williams it emphasised human vulnerability, a contact which was necessary but in some way also degrading, its chief function and significance in the American theatre of the 1960s and early 1970s was wholly otherwise. In the work of the Living Theatre, in a play like Paul Foster's *Tom Paine* and in Off-Broadway in general such overt sexuality tended to be elevated as a symbol of freedom and communality. Far from being very 'now' *Small Craft Warnings* seemed an ironic commentary not only on such presumptions but on his own early work in which desire could take other forms than a frenetic and empty physicality. Now the dominant images are a dead baby, a failed homosexual contact, venereal disease and public sexual titillation. The final gesture is inadequate to neutralise such images and the play's principal interest lies in its anguished concern with examining and trying to come to terms with the loss of those qualities, skills and hopes that had once sustained him as a man and a writer.

By degrees the plight of the writer and the question of the nature of reality moved to the forefront of his work. Following the crisis of the 1960s, referred to by Williams as his 'stoned decade' because of his personal retreat to drink and narcotics – which were now no longer a metaphor for escapism but the primary mechanism for that escape – he engaged more directly issues always implicit in his work. Earlier in his career he had created characters who invented worlds, who chose to see existence through the rose-coloured light that escaped its cliché origin only because the force of its personal significance was communicated so powerfully. His characters turned their worlds into theatrical sets, consciously subverting a reality, the substantiality of which they conceded by their very defensiveness. It was by an act of will that the naturalistic world was reflected in sets which were never allowed to assert their naturalistic logic. Solid walls dissolved or disappeared into space, light was apt to soften, discordant sounds to reveal a hidden harmony under the impact of the transforming sensibility. But the real still existed. The debate was over the nature and extent of its authority.

By the time of *The Two Character Play* (1967), rewritten as *Out Cry* in 1971 and then rewritten again in 1973, he was ready to address a more directly ontological question. What was the nature of reality and how was it to be known? Since the process of human relationships and the assertion of identity were, as he now saw it, in some sense essentially theatrical, indeed since that social world which he had earlier perceived as an indistinct sense of menace was itself simply a series of socially endorsed fictions, in what sense were the individual fiction-making skills aberrant?

Out Cry is ostensibly set in a subterranean theatre in which a brother and sister, abandoned by their company and, in due course, by their audience (assuming it ever to have existed), enact a play in which they apparently play themselves. Yet as former mental patients, even their role as actors is suspect. Whatever their circumstances, they are trapped, in the play-within-the-play by a paralysing fear, and otherwise by the locked doors of the theatre. Abandoned and isolated, they retreat into performance, trying to generate a literal and metaphoric warmth, acting out their desperation, in the sense both of enacting and discharging their desperation. The line between fiction and reality dissolves, if it were indeed ever clear. Much of the scenery, we are told, has failed to arrive and, indeed, the fixed points which would enable clear distinctions to be made are equally missing. There is no location. No triangulation is possible. One of the characters announces that 'my watch froze to death' and describes their present setting as 'somewhere that seems like nowhere'.[172] The only realiable reality lies in the sense of abandonment, the shared plight, and the desire to create with ultimate significance. Indeed, acting and being are presented as being synonymous. It is the proof of existence. I act, therefore I exist. For Williams as for Nietzsche the ability to lie, it seems, is the source of transcendence. It is definitional.

Williams is clearly moving into the territory of Pirandello, of Stoppard's early plays and Albee's later ones. His interests here are in part those of Beckett and of Pinter (in plays such as *Old Times, No Man's Land* and *Monologue*). His sentimentality survives only in a mannered language and the self-conscious poignancy of his characters' situation. In other words it is displaced onto style. But the conceit, found in his early work, of a radically transforming vitality, a humanity pregnant with possibility affecting the social world first at the level of metaphor and subsequently at the literal level of a phoenix-like rebirth of values, defers here to a much more spare vision. The prolixity of his earlier plays is displaced by a calcified language which is no longer able to bear the weight of the muscular energy of a Maggie the Cat or a Serafina, still less the crude force of a Stanley Kowalski. Now words are used precisely, even primly, and constantly threaten to snap under the pressure of a neurotic fear. As in the plays of Albee, Pinter and Beckett, movement is reduced to a minimum – physical stasis standing as an image of constraint, as a denial of clear causality and as an assertion that the real drama operates in the mind (which reinvents the past, translates experience into meaning and imposes its own grid on experience, denying death and acting out its own necessary myth of immortality). His own penchant for symbolism is both exploited and mocked as the stage is dominated by a huge symbolic form, a monolithic figure that resists the actors' desire to dispense with it. The incompletions of the set underline the deconstructive thrust of the play which is a drama of entropy in which character, plot and language slowly disintegrate.

The play establishes several levels of 'reality'. Not only is there a play-within-the-play, with its supposed but invisible audience, but there is another posited audience addressed by one of the characters: 'Of course', observes Felice, in an opening speech, 'you realize that I'm trying to catch you and hold you with an opening monologue that has to be extended through several – rather arbitrary – transitions.'[173] The attenuations of the real become not only a strategy of the play but a basic assumption working to give a translucence to character and a neurotic hesitancy to action. For the Williams of *The Glass Menagerie* and *Streetcar* a substantial reality was needed, a hard-edged and threatening world just beyond the frame of the action, pressing hard upon character until it was forced to render up its essential meaning in the battle to sustain itself. Now that sustaining crust has dissolved. The menace is no longer external. The model of a threatening reality and a desperate world of fiction no longer holds. The menace is equally within. The real is completely problematic. The tension dissipates and with it character.

The play takes place in 'an unspecified locality' – that well known pull-in for so many playwrights of the 1970s. The characters are never seen outside the context of the theatre. Felice addresses the audience directly, asking it to 'Imagine the curtain is down.' The audience is, therefore, invited to collaborate in the process of invention, and therefore, of course, to theatricalise itself. Instead of accepting fiction as reality it is asked to accept reality as a fiction. The curtain, the interface of fiction and reality, becomes itself a fiction. The two worlds can no longer be kept apart.

The boundary remains the area which fascinates Williams but now it expands to become a total world. There are no longer any clearly definable worlds to be kept apart. Even the characters' names – Clare and Felice – support a sexual ambiguity which is rooted in more than Williams's own sensibility. The androgynous is itself an embodiment of the erosion of definition. Clare remembers little of their past except a series of frontiers on their journey from one now-forgotten place to their present indefinite situation. There is a certain desperation behind the play. In the person of an 'old, old painter...seated in *rigor mortis* before a totally blank canvas, tea kettle boiled dry',[174] he creates a figure who represents his own self-doubts but also his fear that art itself is in a state of collapse. The blank canvas stands less for pregnant possibility than a kind of stunned silence. The idea of framed experience, of order, no matter how arbitrary, can no longer be sustained. In any one moment it may be possible to suspend time but only at the cost of suspending life. And so the ironically named Felice and Clare, like Vladimir and Estragon in *Waiting for Godot*, pass the time performing familiar rituals to keep the idea of chaos at bay. Improvisation may be the sign of vitality but it is equally a threat of dissolution, and Clare is as frightened of a disruption of the pattern as Faulkner's Bengy had been in *The Sound and the Fury*. And so she fears the 'chaos of improvisation, new speeches thrown at me like stones, as if I'd been condemned to be stoned to death'.[175]

The central conceit is clearly the familiar one that life is itself a performance that we are condemned to enact. We are fated to play ourselves as Clare is told she must 'play' Clare. 'Our performance', Felice acknowledges, 'must continue. No escape.'[176] They thus play out their lives on a stage dominated by the vast dumb presence of a giant statue – a huge immovable construction with neither function nor life but whose existence creates an irony simply through the disproportion of size. As a metaphysical parable the play rests on a cliché. The literalness with which the metaphor is enacted suggests a potentially disabling banality. It is redeemed by the fact that it

119

incorporates its own critique. The neat rationalism of metaphor is itself a victim of a world reduced to fictionality and even the allegorical pattern disassembles itself in such a wholly relativistic world. Felice remarks, as many of Williams's protagonists might have done, 'I don't do lunatic things. I have to pretend there's some sanity here',[177] but in the context of the play even this can be taken as primary evidence of insanity. Both Clare and Felice fear confinement and yet in a mental hospital the latter had experienced 'the comforts, the security, the humanizing influence' of what Clare calls 'locked doors'.[178] This is the familiar Williams paradox. Confinement and insanity have their advantages. They relieve one of the terrors that come from venturing beyond the known, from crossing frontiers. But they do so through an induced narcosis. What is sacrificed is 'being aware of what's going on in our lives'.[179] However, in the context of this play that awareness is denied by the very terms of the characters' existence.

The Two Character Play becomes not merely the title of the play-within-the-play but an accurate description of the play that is their lives. Its lack of an ending is thus a natural consequence of their own desperately sustained existence. The characters rebel against 'this metaphor that you are trying to catch me in, but I refuse to be caught!'[180] But there is, of course, no choice. The echoes of the vault in which they are supposedly trapped are equally those of a reflexive art and a reflexive life. There is no external world. Art and life are part of a continuum. The elegiac note which Clare detects applies to art and life equally. Her announcement that 'I am going to find the way out'[181] is merely ironic since the only escape lies through a bullet from the gun incorporated into the play at the level of plot and symbol. The darkness beyond the dimly lit stage is the only way out, and the terror of that is greater than that of the stage itself. The theatre is a prison but so, too, is the life which it supposedly reflects but for which it is in effect a paradigm. The anguished cry with which Clare responds to her situation is the prototypical sound of her humanity but it is also the essence of Williams's theatre as he sees it. In a comment quoted on the dust-jacket, Williams has said, 'I think [it] is my most beautiful play since Streetcar, and I've never stopped working on it. I think it is a major work...it is a cri de coeur, but then all creative work, all life, in a sense, is a cri de coeur.' The play ends with the brother and sister desperately trying to sustain their invented world as the lights fade – a fading of which they are fully conscious. 'Magic is the habit of our existence', they announce together as they accept the fading of the lights 'as a death, somehow transcended'.[182] The final remark is an apt description of Williams's own conviction. It is, moreover, an assertion of faith which distinguishes his characters, finally, from those of Beckett and Pinter. They are granted, if not full knowledge, then at least full self-awareness. They recognise the ironies that constitute their world and live them out. The phoenix is no longer an appropriate image, but perhaps Sisyphus would be. No longer do his characters 'rage against the dying of the light'. They accept their situation, but part of the burden laid upon them is the unavoidable desire to transform their world, to impose pattern on chaos. And this, after all, is the essence equally of the absurd, the Sisyphean victory.

Writing in 1959 Williams confessed that for him writing itself had always been 'an escape from a world of reality in which I felt acutely uncomfortable'. Like his characters he retreated into imagination which became 'my cave, my refuge'.[183] By the time of *Out Cry* such a clear distinction between the real and the imagined no longer held. The entire set is now dramatised as simultaneously protective cave and prison. The imagination no longer presses back against a palpable reality. The mind generates its own environment. This is, if you like, a conversation between the male and female sides of Williams's sensibility. They conjoin in a neurotic fear. This is the world of Blanche Dubois after she has left the Kowalski household on the arm of the gentleman doctor and entered the mental hospital, which then becomes the setting for her theatricalising imagination.

Tennessee Williams's characters have always trodden the dangerous border between the real and the imagined, and the peculiar force of his work derives precisely from the doomed act of will with which his protagonists resist the fact of defeat or, occasionally and less believably, force a victory of sorts, a desperate compromise with time. The power of sexuality, at times therapeutic and redemptive, at times an image of determinism, gives his work its particular excitement. In his best work his over-poetic language and naive use of symbolism are kept in check by an imagination which if melodramatic is also capable of fine control. The collapse of that control, the growth of a self-pity which placed his own plight too nakedly at the centre of attention, the disintegration of his personality, eventually destroyed the honesty and perspective that enabled him to make Stanley Kowalski a worthy adversary for Blanche Dubois in *Streetcar*, and Laura's mother a compassionate friend as well as a shrill accuser of her daughter in *The Glass Menagerie*.

The confidence with which he started his career had long since drained away. In an essay in 1978 he wrote that he was convinced that no artist could 'in the least divert' government 'from a fixed course toward the slag-heap remnants of once towering cities'. He identified an 'unconscious deathwish' on the part of those in power which the artist was powerless to resist, and indeed chose to trace this back to a specific historical moment: 'civilization, at least as a long-term prospect, ceased to exist with the first nuclear blast at Hiroshima and Nagasaki'.[184] Seen thus his work becomes an account of the struggle for survival of those who find themselves living after the collapse of civilisation. But where once some temporary truce seemed possible, at this point personal crises and national decline seemed to promise nothing but extinction. He continued to assert the significance of the artist, insisting that 'I presume to insist that there must be somewhere truth to be pursued each day with words that are misunderstood and feared because they are the words of an Artist, which must always remain a word most compatible with the word Revolutionary, and so be more than a word', but the conviction had gone. 'Graceful defeat'[185] remained his objective but grace is itself a primary victim of the world which he chose to describe throughout much of the 1970s.

Then, like Arthur Miller, whose *The American Clock* was set in the 1930s that had moulded his imaginative world, Tennessee Williams returned, in the late 1970s, to the decade in which his talent had also been forged. *Vieux Carré* (1977) was set in the winter of 1938 and the spring of 1939, *A Lovely Sunday for Creve Coeur* (1979) in the St Louis of his youth and *Something Cloudy, Something Clear* (1981) in the summer of 1940.

Vieux Carré is a recreation of Williams's own time spent in New Orleans. Set in a rooming house (as *The Glass Menagerie* was to have been), it offers a portrait of a collection of misfits, killing their loneliness as best they can, a loneliness 'inborn and inbred to the bone'.[186] Nightingale is a homosexual painter dying of tuberculosis; Jane, a woman desperate for affection and dying of what seems to be leukaemia; Mrs Wire, a 'solitary old woman cared for by no one'; Sky, a young man as in love with long distance as Mrs Wingfield's husband had been in *The Glass Menagerie*. And at the centre is the Writer, discovering a homosexual identity and displaying his literary talent as one means to neutralise the 'affliction' of loneliness. Mrs Wire's comment that 'there's so much loneliness in this house that you can hear it'[187] is, indeed, an understatement, for the play presses a familiar Williams theme to the point of parody. It offers a self-portrait which, for all its recognition of a degree of cruelty in the human make-up (his observation that 'A man has got to face everything some time and call it by its true name' is a piece of gratuitous cruelty that the play rejects), is sentimental to a degree.

A Lovely Sunday for Creve Coeur concerns yet further lonely and desperate people whose fate, in the words of one of the characters from *Vieux Carré*, is to 'offer himself and not be accepted, not by anyone ever!'[188] As in so much else of Williams's work his own concerns are expressed through the sensibility of a woman. Like so much else of his work it is concerned with the compromises forced on the individual by a life which refuses to satisfy a desperate longing for human contact, or to fulfil the aspirations of those who long for a dream but exist in a harsh reality.

In *Something Cloudy, Something Clear* Williams returned to the summer of 1940 but in a sense it was a play which also looked forward to death. Set in Provincetown, it concerns August, a young writer who lives in a shack on the dunes, and who writes his first play while simultaneously making a bid for the attentions of a male dancer called Kip. But the latter is dying of a brain tumour while his friend and protector Clare is suffering from diabetes. Death is in the air and when Clare asks August how long he will continue to work he replies that he will go on until he dies of exhaustion. And so the beginning and end of Williams's career curve towards one another, the beginning implying the end, death still being resisted by desire, though now that desire is seen more clearly as the writer's passion for creation. But, then, sex and writing had always been equally potent images for one another in his work; the momentary completions, the satisfaction achieved only to be dissipated, always constituted appropriate symbols of the imperfect satisfactions of human relationships and the artistic experience alike. And yet, by the same token, these moments of consonance remained the only justification for life's continuance, for the endless struggle with determinism which seemed to him otherwise to define the nature of daily life.

As he grew older so he seemed to have been increasingly haunted by the past. His thematic concern with lost youth, loneliness, a failing public appeal and the collapse of those fictions with which people seek to neutralise an insistent reality acquired a personal relevance more acute than earlier in his career. The romantic concern with fading beauty, illness, the writer whose work is created at the cost of personal survival – always there in his work – began to seem a patent sentimentality. It smacked of self-pity. The decadence which he described and celebrated is that of the artist finding truth in appearance and even humiliation, but it is equally that of a writer whose personal neuroses invaded his work too completely.

There is a persuasive truth to the comments of his one-time collaborator and lover Donald Windham who, in 1977, wrote that:

> Hardly anyone succeeds as an artist in America without first devoting his whole being to the problems of obscurity and failure. Tennessee did this for ten years before 1945; then the tables were turned and overnight he was faced with a whole new set of problems. He controlled them remarkably well for the next five years. But a great deal of his strength must have gone into battles other than those of creation. When his emotional material began to run low, the priceless 'by-product of existence' to be in need of replenishing, and he was forced to come out of his shell of unawareness, he found himself, both by design and fate, in a totally different world from that which had enclosed him and nourished his heart before...by 1955 I believe that both he and his work were suffering from the manoeuvers he was making to protect himself and it.[189]

The early work came directly out of the tensions in his own experience. It was in a sense the public dimension of a series of private conflicts. Blanche's neurotic drive, her fear of mortality, her destructive grip on a life charged with significance by a brittle sexuality were Williams's own; but then so, too, was the implacable logic which led him to relinquish her to insanity and stasis. A cavalier sensibility and a puritan spirit coexist and the result is an oddly Manichean view of human affairs which frequently finds its correlative in terms of the *mise-en-scène*. In the persons of Laura, Blanche and Alma (in *The Glass Menagerie*, *Streetcar* and *Summer and Smoke*) he confesses to his own sense of historicity while in the very process, as a playwright, of staking his claim to contemporary attention. For a few years, perhaps a decade, these tensions seem to have addressed a similar ambivalence in the American sensibility. Certainly the political persecutions of the 1950s were in part a debate about national identity (the Un-American Activities Committee placing the definition of Americanness on the agenda) as they were equally an attempt to accommodate older models of private and public behaviour to the new realities of post-war existence. It was a society on the brink of change, uncertain as to direction and purpose. National myths were up for debate. The right of dissent – the legitimacy of marching to a different drummer – was challenged by those who regarded political and social cohesion as a virtue. And when Laura's unicorn lost its horn – stamped on by a young man on the make – it stood as an appropriate image of that new conformity which equally alarmed Arthur Miller. There is no place for Blanche in the pragmatics of the new world, except as sexual commodity. And, for many, exchange values were precisely in process of replacing human values. However, as in *Summer and Smoke*, Williams acknowledged the need to adapt. He saw the risk in his own spiritual absolutism. So, too, did Miller and many of those who fought against a new moral conformity while fully aware of the danger of their own idealism. Thus, I suggest that for a few brief years not merely did Williams's own private debates generate a drama luminous with his own psychic, sexual, social and spiritual contradictions but he also touched a nerve in the national sensibility in a way that only Miller otherwise succeeded in doing. Williams has confessed to feeling a deep chasm between himself and all other people, even deeper than the relatively ordinary ones of homosexuality and being an artist, but that condition of 'alienation' was scarcely unfamiliar in a culture in which the word was used with some abandon in the 1950s and 1960s.

In the following decades, however, his concerns seemed to exist to one side of those that commanded public attention. The urgencies of Vietnam seem to have passed him by, except for a growing apocalypticism. The special world which he wrote about now tended to seem irrelevant rather than compellingly linked to national trauma. And yet the signs of recovery were there. *Out Cry* responded to a shift in artistic concern equally apparent in the novel, while the return, in his final plays, to the experiences of his youth suggested a desire to recover the lost power and ambiguous tensions of his early career. It was just such a tactic which had unlocked O'Neill's artistic powers. Not the least of the ironies of his death was that it denied us the opportunity of seeing Williams wrestle with his own demons, though a late play – *Clothes for a Summer Hotel* (1980) – and a last screenplay – *Secret Places of the Heart* – suggest the possible direction of a career peremptorily ended by an ironic accident.

There is something rather more inevitable than ironic in the fact that Williams should turn, at the end of his career, to Scott Fitzgerald and Zelda for the subject of his play, *Clothes for a Summer Hotel* (1980). Their lives were too close, in some respects, to his own for the parallels not to be examined. In part it was a matter of the all too obvious proximity of insanity as an immediate fact and potential fate; in part it was a recognition of their shared perception of life as a losing game and art as a structure of meaning placed under constant threat.

Clothes for a Summer Hotel is set in the Highland Hospital, the asylum in which Zelda lived, and, finally, died, in a fire which swept the building in 1947. The image of a retreat which finally becomes destructive was a familiar one in Williams's work and, as *Out Cry* had implied, the origin of a self-doubt which now applied directly to his work. And this play, like *Out Cry*, places the processes of the theatre in the foreground. Thus, at the beginning of the play, one of Fitzgerald's friends – Gerald Murphy – announces its running time while Zelda's desperate fictions, which both sustain and destroy, are finally not so easily separable from the illusions of the writer who, we are pointedly told, 'creates' her. So she has to 'play' her meeting with Scott – drawn to the asylum by erroneous accounts of her recovery – as Clare and Felice had acted out their own dramas. And she accuses him of being a predator, appropriating her life for his fiction, as Mrs Venable had required the sacrifice of Catherine, in *Suddenly Last Summer*, and as Williams accused himself of the appropriation of Rose's life for his own art. Yet, for all this, the play equally stands as a justification of fiction, though now as an agent of truth and no longer simply as a tactic of survival. As the young Intern, who at times is also an incarnation of Zelda's French lover, remarks, 'Shadows of lives, tricks of light, sometimes illuminate things.'[190] This same point is, in effect, underscored by an Author's Note, ostensibly indicating the nature of Zelda's attempts to establish contact but equally a justification of his own artistic life and of the indirections but also the performatic integrity of theatre itself:

> Zelda must somehow suggest the desperate longing of the 'insane' to communicate something of the private world to those from whom they're secluded. The words are mostly blown away by the wind...but the eyes – imploring though proud – the gestures, trembling though rigid with the urgency of their huge need, must win the audience to her inescapably...the present words given her are tentative: they may or may not suffice in themselves: the presentation – performance – must.[191]

125

And yet the roles in which Williams, no less than Scott and Zelda, allowed himself to be trapped constituted an ironic distortion of this desire to communicate through the masks of performance. Thus Blanche's Belle Reve becomes the Reve Bleu of this play, the scene of Zelda's adultery, an image of betrayal rather than truth; her lover is an aviator, flight being as much his image of freedom as it was Williams's. But for him, too, that flight is a denial of some necessary contact.

Zelda is aware of the extent to which identity itself is a careful construct, a fiction elaborated partly by others and partly by social necessity. As she observes, 'I know that I must resume the part created for me. Mrs F. Scott Fitzgerald.' But, she asks, 'If he makes of me a monument with his carefully arranged words, is that my life'?[192] And yet for a writer that is essentially the dilemma – to create a factitious world which is not sealed against experience – just as in another sense it is the paradox of experience – to create a life which is not itself simply a pastiche of conventions, role-playing and self-deceit. As Zelda complains, 'All photographs are a poor likeness',[193] lacking the glow of memory. But memory is no closer to that reality, which now begins to seem an inadequate stimulus for the imagined self, which is in effect fictionalised, reconstructed, in the very process of perception. And so the stage set itself dissolves, reforms and fragments. Memory fades by turn into insanity, into realistic dialogue and into a self-conscious acknowledgement of a governing fictionality. If Zelda's (and Williams's) 'huge, cloudy symbols of a high romance' are placed under pressure, then so, too, are the supposed solidities they are taken to represent. And the erosion of that boundary threatens a final collapse into insanity or a denial of the distinction which that word implies.

Nonetheless, a modernist conviction remains, not merely as to the imagination's power to resist the real but as to its ability to vindicate an existence whose coherences are themselves ultimately threatening. Thus, Zelda suggests that 'Between the first wail of an infant and the last gasp of the dying – it's all an arranged pattern of submission to what's been prescribed for us unless we escape into madness or into acts of creation.' But invention and madness are intimately related. For if 'Romantics' will not settle for 'acceptance', then 'Liquor, madness [are] more or less the same thing', and then 'We're abandoned or we're put away, and if put away, why, then, fantasy runs riot.' And this is precisely the danger of the vertiginous path that Williams walked, for on the one hand was the pure anarchy of fantasy and on the other 'what's called real – a rock! Cold, barren. To be endured only briefly'.[194] The challenge is to sustain a 'vision' which will neither be betrayed into uncontrolled images nor earthed by a prosaic reality. And yet fictions also have their coercions. As Zelda cries out at the end of the play, addressing her husband, himself aware of his own fragile grasp on experience:

'I'm not your book! Anymore! *I can't be your book anymore!*'[195] Her only release from other people's fictions, however, lies through her own death, and, writing in 1980, just three years before his death, Williams recognised that a similar paradox applied to his own life.

There is a subtlety to *Clothes for a Summer Hotel* missing from so much of the work which he produced in the 1960s and 1970s. The elegiac tone seems to suggest the degree to which he was now able to recognise and to some extent reconcile the tensions and even contradictions in his own art and life. And the result seems to be a recovery of something of the simplicity and power of his early work as he reached back not only into the past but into the origin of his own artistic concerns.

One of Williams's last works, 'Secret Places of the Heart', a screenplay set, for the most part, in a mental hospital, seems an attempt to lay some familiar ghosts to rest. It has an elegiac tone. In a sense it brings us full circle, back to the world of *The Glass Menagerie*. It is as though we followed Laura, after the candles of her life had been snuffed out. And if that play had been a displaced account of his sister's life it is hard not to see 'Secret Places of the Heart' as an attempt both to acknowledge his own ambiguous feelings towards Rose, sequestered for more than forty years, and also to confront in himself elements of that hysteria and fear which had closed the door so implacably on her life.

Janet, former wife of Olaf Svenson, lives in St Carmine's Sanatorium, a private mental hospital run by Catholic nuns. She lives a partially narcotised existence, but there is a tenuous and fragile sense of solidarity between those who find themselves so stranded. The high point of her life is provided by her husband's visits. But he, himself, is a highly nervous man and finds the hospital frightening. It is too close to his own neurotic fears of constriction to be borne with any equanimity. He lives with another woman, Alicia, who constantly urges him to break away from his wife. The film is concerned with Olav's attempt to tell Janet that he is to move away from the area, that she will be receiving no more visits. He takes her for one last trip beyond the walls of the institution, but it is disastrous, turning her catatonic and him almost speechless.

Indeed language becomes a central theme of the play as Janet had been a speech therapist whose skills and love had given Sven access to words. It is impossible not to see the filmscript as, in some sense at least, Williams's acknowledgement of a debt to Rose. Just as in *The Glass Menagerie* he had made a connection between Tom's freedom as a writer and his sister's entombment in the St Louis apartment so now Sven's articulateness is presented as a gift of the woman trapped in this St Louis sanatorium. In both cases the two are connected by an odd blend of guilt and love, and it is hard not to feel Williams's own ambiguous response to Rose and in particular the link between her silence (social and at times literal) and his own public articulateness. The sense of panic which overcomes Sven seems very close to that which Williams himself confessed to feeling on occasion, just as Janet's fear of death mirrors his own. The filmscript does not, however, end in total despair, though her world does seem to have been effectively destroyed. Her gentleman caller will not come again but there is a level on which some final adjustment has been made which does not represent mere capitulation. At first when she returns from her disastrous trip she sits in the rocking chair which has been established earlier as a symbol of the slowing rhythms of life, a fast approaching death. She sits silent and defeated. But in the final moments of the screenplay she rises from the chair, clutching a bunch of roses (whose association with his sister's name made them an image of life throughout his work), and joins the other inmates. The final word is given to her. It is an affirmation. In reply to one of the patients who welcomes her 'hooome!' she replies, as a note indicates, resolutely, 'Yes'.[196] At the end of his life it was an acceptance of the limits of freedom, of the fact of death and of the necessity to live on the far side of despair. It was a gesture of reconciliation with what life had done to Rose and to himself. Like the name of a compassionate nurse in this final refuge, it is an act of 'Grace', and a fitting elegy for his life and his art. And if his characters are in some way at their most sincere and honest when their language fails them, this seems to emerge from a conviction, equally embraced by Harold Pinter, that the more acute an experience the less articulate its expression. And if this has clear implications for the writer for whom words are a necessary but fragile instrument, he had shown his awareness of this as early as The Glass Menagerie – as he had throughout a career in which the dramatic image was made to play a central and liberating role.

Jean Genet advocated the siting of theatres next to cemeteries. As an image this precisely captures Williams's sense both of the fact which gives birth to the self-dramatising sensibility of the individual and the public theatrical act. It is the fact of death and, even more, the neurotic fear of death, that provokes the theatrical impulse. It is not merely that vitality, the public discharge of energy, the reshaping of anarchic tendencies into satisfactory form, are counterposed to the deconstructive reality of death but that the invented self hopes to deceive death, hopes, by disguises, to evade the relentless drive of process, as the characters in Camino Real try to hide from the streetcleaners who are the agents of death. For Genet, pluralising himself, 'We will have nothing to do with politics, entertainment, morality, etc.', and if, 'in spite of ourselves, they step into the theatrical act, let them be driven out until all trace of them is gone'.[197] Williams was less rigorous. He was concerned with morality, though not with moralism, but that morality is generated by a respect for human need. It is a product of the void and a response to it. It becomes necessary not to compound the fact of that void. So that Williams was no antinomian. But unlike Miller he could imagine no abstraction to which the individual owes allegiance. Society represents only a threat, a compounding of absurdity. The only morality which he would sanction was that deriving from personal relationships. The sensibility is neurotically responsive because it must detect that human need. That the same sensitivity makes the self more vulnerable to social pressure and more acutely aware of its ultimate fate is the source of the romantic irony which pervades his work. There is, indeed, more than a little of Poe in Williams. Both men were obsessed with death to the extent that their own work was a self-conscious attempt to deny its authority and madness was an image of the delicate membrane which each believed separated the individual from knowledge of his or her own mortality.

For Genet the theatre is built on a paradox. It derives from awareness of a fact which should destroy its own premise: 'If its origin is some dazzling moment in the author's experience, it is up to him to seize the lightning and, beginning with the moment of illumination, which reveals the void, to arrange a verbal architecture – that is, grammatical and ceremonial – slyly suggesting that from this void some semblance is snatched which reveals the void.'[198] It is from this paradox that Beckett's plays derive and to some extent Williams's also, though in most of his work he chose to resolve the paradox by asserting that the imagination, operating either through its powers of self-invention or through its sympathetic understanding of the solitariness of the other, is able to create a morality which is no less real for existing outside of time. But in *Out Cry* the implacable nature of the metaphor stands exposed. The plot of life is stifled, character is dislocated and disassembled, language hollowed out. The role-playing of art and life is presented as synonymous while logical developments of theatre, from simile to metonymy to metaphor (from as if, to a slice of life, to an enactment of life), which perhaps mimics the development of the individual, moves Williams to identify a level on which art and life not merely contain their own denial but are the primary source of their own absurdity. It is not merely, as Val Xavier in *Orpheus Descending* observes, that 'We are all of us sentenced to imprisonment inside our own skins for life', but that the imagination, which is our primary bid for transcendence, is the essence of our self-torturing yearning for order and meaning. Clare and Felice perform themselves from a stage whose props contain no clue to their meaning in front of an empty auditorium. But, lacking anything else, they continue, falteringly, to repeat half-forgotten lines until the lights fade. Though he wrote subsequent plays, *Out Cry* is his valediction for the theatre not simply in the literal sense in which he lost his audience while being tied nonetheless to a craft, the

129

significance of which he had come profoundly to doubt, but to the degree that he saw his own entrapment in the endless desire to create form from the formless. Earlier he had suggested that 'the great and only possible dignity of a man lies in his power deliberately to choose certain moral values by which to live as steadfastly as if he, too, like a character in a play, were immured against the corrupting rush of time'. He spoke of 'the incontinent blaze of live theatre'[199] as a celebration of a surviving, even triumphant human spirit. But he ended his career in self-doubt, as his own fictions seemed all too directly expressive of the degenerate and self-mocking fictions of the world which he had once imagined himself to be able to transcend through the simple but transforming mechanism of the imagination.

There is a terrible, empty gregariousness about his characters. They cling to one another with a desperation which is half touching and half pathetic, the more so since they are indeed one another's hell. Cooped up, in a bid for the therapy of relationship, they are terrified by a persistent claustrophobia. Like their author they seek the comfort of strangers but those strangers merely serve to remind them of a world of causality, of competing demands and remorseless process. They detect the signs of mortality. Faces are lined, eyes are surrounded by crow's feet. They fear the light. And yet the intimacy they seek in order to neutralise their loneliness inevitably results in exposure. The real intrudes, implacable, irresistible. The glass horn snaps, the paper lantern is torn from the lamp, the instinctive and necessary lie is revealed for what it is. There is only one possible direction left for them – a journey into pure imagination and madness, an apocalyptic flame in which the self is extinguished by embracing its own image. It is a familiar romantic stance: the self is annihilated by expanding to fill the available psychic and moral space. Sometimes the apocalypse is literal, a public role performed by the cruel and selfish whose pragmatics can find no room for the deviant; sometimes it is embraced as though there were some grace to be claimed by wilfully compounding the reductivism of positivist society and biological process alike. Williams's characters go to their martyrdom in play after play, tortured and crucified for their visions which are mistaken for lies. Desperately sexual beings, the consummation which they seek is nonetheless spiritual. The body they embrace is physical enough but what they seek is seldom simply sexual satisfaction. They long for completion. They seek to close the wound opened up by their birth. They try to cheat death but more often than not find themselves holding it to them. The compassion which they seek or dispense is not merely momentary; it snares them in time, inhibits that flight, that animal-like urge to escape, which is their other basic instinct.

In his early years as he travelled around the country struggling to make enough money to finance his writing, Williams carried with him *The*

Collected Poems of Hart Crane. He must have found much which appealed to his own sensibility. In particular he must have recognised something of himself in Waldo Frank's description of the poet which appeared in the 1933 edition. For to him Crane 'began naked and brave, in a cultural chaos, the subject of inchoate forces through which he rose to utterance. Cities, machines, the warring hungers of lonely and herded men, the passions released from defeated loyalties, were ever near to overwhelm the poet.'[200] His task, as Frank saw it, was 'to bear and finally transfigure the world's impinging chaos'. Williams saw his plight as essentially the same. Though temperamentally drawn to the defeated, he was, through the very process of writing, celebrating other values. Like Maggie in *Cat on a Hot Tin Roof* he was implicitly asserting that 'my hat is still in the ring...What is the victory of a cat on a hot tin roof? – I wish I knew...Just staying on it, I guess, as long as she can...'[201] In play after play he dramatised his conviction that, in Maggie's words, 'life has got to be allowed to continue even after the *dream* of life is – all over...'[202] Indeed that was his essential subject – life as a kind of rear-guard action. He opted for neither truth nor illusion but for the need to resist. Maggie the cat uses truth; Blanche illusions. The writer meanwhile asserted the central importance of truths (Williams said that he found it painful and almost impossible to engage even in the ritual lies of personal politeness), but did so in plays which were themselves lies, factitious paradigms of social contact, illusions of order and purpose. He continued to rely on the kindness of strangers with whom he felt a momentary contact through the processes of art, but knew all too well the fragile and contingent nature of such relationships. For him, as for the characters of *Out Cry*, the stage was a world which appeared to offer a structure of meaning whose absence otherwise is the origin of personal neurosis and even hysteria. And if his confidence in that world was gradually eroded, not merely with the public decline of interest in his work but also with his own increasing sense of its arbitrary gestures and incomplete language, he was left with nowhere else to turn. Increasingly his plays became comments on one another. His characters, his language, his plots seemed to be rooted less in an experience external to the theatre than in his own earlier work. If he revisited his past it tended to be through texts, figures and images which were already transpositions of that past. Parody, pastiche and irony became his primary mode. Like the two characters in *Out Cry* he seemed to be trapped in the theatre, endlessly recreating texts rather than reaching out into an experience external to art. Blanche Dubois increasingly seemed an apt expression of Williams's own sensibility, the neurotic intensity of his inventions, the desperate fascination with transforming the past, the need to act out a public myth of sensitivity assailed by a crude materialism if not an incipient barbarism, being evident in his life and art. His *Memoirs*, indeed, with their accounts of desperate sexuality, of drink and drugs, of the artist confronted with the inevitable compromises which transfigured his dreams, constituted simply another Williams drama, a play in which the central character transforms his life into art as a means of forcing it to render up some meaning beyond mere contingency. The *Memoirs*, like his plays, offered an opportunity to move to centre stage a man whose greatest fear was that he, and the world which he valued, had long since been relegated to the past, declared irrelevant by a society disinclined to value the poet, the homosexual or the dreamer except as licensed clown.

Writing in 1955, Williams had said:

> I think my work is good in exact relation to the degree of emotional tension which is released in it. In a sense, writing of this kind (lyric?) is a losing game, for steadily life takes away from you, bit by bit, step by step, the quality of fresh involvement, new, startling reactions to experience, the emotional reservoir is only rarely replenished by some crisis...and most of the time you are just 'paying out', draining off. To offset this, to some degree, usually not enough, is the accumulation of insight and 'sophistication'. Sometimes the heart dies deliberately, to avoid further pain.[203]

Five years later he observed that 'when the work of any kind of creative worker becomes tyrannically obsessive to the point of overshadowing his life, almost taking the place of it, he is in a hazardous situation. His situation is hazardous for the simple reason that the source, the fountainhead of his work, can only be his life.'[204] This risk proved real enough in Williams's own case. The gap between his art and his life, always small, narrowed still further. For when he entered his own play, as he did by appearing in *Small Craft Warnings*, he passed through a mirror and annihilated a crucial distinction. But he had always tended to dramatise his life. Indeed he made plans to dramatise his death. A codicil to his will reportedly provided for the disposition of his body as follows: it was to be 'Sewn up in a clean white sock and dropped overboard, twelve hours north of Havana, so that my bones may rest not too far from those of Hart Crane.'[205] But then perhaps his heart had already died back there in the mid 1950s 'to avoid further pain'. In the event this injunction seems to have been dropped from his will. What did appear, apart from the seeds of future litigation, was a further reminder of his attachment to his sister for part of his estate was to go towards her maintenance and her 'customary pleasures', including her shopping trips to New York City.

In his *Memoirs* Williams asked himself, 'What is it like being a writer?' His reply was that 'it is like being free...To be free is to have achieved your life...it means to be a voyager here and there...It means the freedom of being...Most of you belong to something that offers a stabilizing influence:

a family unit, a defined social position, employment in an organization, a more secure habit of existence.'[206] But, fearing constriction above all else, Williams preferred to 'live like a gypsy. I am a fugitive', he insisted. 'No place seems tenable to me for long anymore, not even my own skin.'[207] In the end he could run no further and the personal relations on which he relied had in large part failed him. At any rate he died alone in a hotel room, a fugitive run to earth, a voyager who had found the only kind of freedom he was ever likely to secure. The legless bird had finally touched the earth and hence would never again soar above the 'Terra Incognita'.

In a poem published in his collection, *Androgyne, Mon Amour* (1977) Williams defined his territory, his subject and his method:

> My mise-en-scene is the world
> within the world,
> the greenest of all green leaves
> at the center curled.
>
> I do not forbear to call
> on demons driven
> from mortal belief by the bells
> of a proper heaven.
>
> I ferret among the used
> and exhausted lot
> from the longing not wanted because
> it was haunted and hot.
>
> I want no purpose to own me
> but only to say
> I found these secretly burning
> along the way.
>
> This girl who was lost but knew
> more places than one.
> this boy who was blind but grew
> the interior sun.[208]

Williams was that boy; his art the interior sun. And the girl? Who else but Rose and, beyond her, all those others working their way as best they can along the Camino Real.

Williams's reputation declined sharply in his later years. Undoubtedly this was in large part a fair reflection of the quality of his work which also suffered from his self-inflicted wounds. But it also said something about the culture in which he lived. Perhaps the most moving valedictory on Williams's work was that offered by one of America's best younger playwrights – David Mamet. As he observed, when Williams's 'life and view of life became less

immediately accessible, our gratitude was changed to distant reverence for
a man whom we felt obliged – if we were to continue in our happy feelings
toward him – to consider already dead'. Perhaps this was inevitable but for
Mamet there was a certain irony for Americans are, he observed, 'a kind
people living in a cruel country. We don't know how to show our love.
[But] This was the subject of his plays, the greatest dramatic poetry in the
American language. We thank him and we wish him, with love, the best
we could have done and did not. We wish him what he wishes us: the peace
that we are seeking.'[209] Despite the sentimentality which was a natural
product of the occasion Mamet accurately identifies Williams's central theme
and ultimate achievement.

2 Arthur Miller

Arthur Miller is widely regarded as the intellectual of the American theatre. He is himself baffled by the description. With its love of categories academe teaches his work under the title 'plays of ideas' as if this was in itself some kind of distinction (which, given the nature of Broadway, is not perhaps as ridiculous as it may seem). Admittedly, Miller himself has written extensively about his own work, referring freely to Greek drama, Russian literature and the work of Henrik Ibsen, and, since this is not something that American playwrights are prone to do, he came quickly to be regarded as the Adlai Stevenson of the theatre. It only needed his unlikely love-affair with Marilyn Monroe to complete the process. The truth is that the strength of his plays rests less on their intellectual force than on an emotional truth which is compelling and, in some final sense, resistant to criticism.

Although he is convinced that the essence of drama is to know more 'and not merely to spend our feelings',[1] it is finally in defence of values instinctively felt rather than learned that his characters lay down their lives. Frequently they are insufficiently in control of their own experience to understand the processes that those lives exemplify. And if this is a privilege which is available to the audience – offered lessons in causality and moral responsibility by Miller – this is not an insight to be derived from a detached consideration. It is a product of an engaged response to individuals whose symbolic function is secondary to the impact of their manifest and disturbing anxieties. It is in this sense that Miller has said that 'the theater is above all else an instrument of passion'.[2] It is in this sense, too, that until recently his work has shown a gravitational pull towards realism (and decidedly not naturalism, with its surface precision, its resistance to symbolism and its implication of hereditary and environmental determinism). Though he was happy to dislocate the presentational style of his theatre, incorporating expressionist elements and, later, more disturbingly (in After the Fall and The Creation of the World and Other Business) symbolist gestures, his central purpose was to locate the individual securely in a social, political and moral context. Thus, while the immediate pressure of his drama was to expose the emotional and psychological truths of his characters, much as a Freudian analyst might do by delving backwards into the past and sideways into sexual and social relationships, the effect of this exposure of the naked self is ultimately to lay bare the psyche of a culture. The process requires a degree of trauma. The problem perhaps is that trauma may turn into catharsis and

135

the liberal impulse become the basis of a seductive conservatism. And the temptation is there. The longing for rural simplicities is strong, the desire to reach back before corruption, and to celebrate by their absence those values placed under such strain by a modern experience of alienation and anxiety. But Miller is plainly aware of this pressure. *The Crucible* thus in part expresses a longing for a time in which moral issues seemed clear and the language of moral debate had not been ironised, but in part it constitutes a reminder that what he is examining is less history than human nature.

Miller is a playwright who has consistently sought to translate the social world into private anxieties and to trace the connection between personal fallibilities and public betrayals. Because he has chosen to write about a world of moral dilemmas and because he has always proved so sensitive to the pressure of history he has been seen as elevating himself to the position of social conscience. But this is a logical outcome of his liberal convictions. The self, in his work, exists only in relation to choices made and the results of those choices are as real as the choices themselves. He is relentless in projecting outwards into the public world the consequences of decisions which begin in the privacy of the self or the apparent security of the family, but his characters also bear the impress of national myths and social fiats. They are shaped by the world and in turn shape that world. And he has created a drama in which that resonance is a dramatic strategy and a moral fact.

Drama is a public act and Miller is more of a public character than most. As a result he has always been especially vulnerable to shifts in the national mood. In the mid 1950s, feeling no longer able to speak to an audience grown more conservative, he found himself projected into the political arena where his personal performance scarcely differed from that of his characters. Like them he clung to the integrity of his name. Like them he tried to negotiate a position in which the need to resist was not compromised by an instinctive sense of guilt. And there is in fact a clear continuity between Miller the man and Miller the dramatist. His plays are a direct expression of convictions that run deep. In a way those convictions are those of classic American liberalism; but they are also more than that. The emotional intensity in his work, amounting at times to a kind of barely controlled hysteria, which draws plays like *All My Sons*, *Death of a Salesman* and *The Crucible* towards a melodrama finally averted through the shaping discipline of language (he would often write his plays in verse before translating them into prose and indeed regretted his failure to do precisely this in *The American Clock*), suggests something more pressing and urgent than this. The answer, perhaps, lies in his Jewish identity which makes him, like Saul Bellow, resist equally the despair of the absurd and the apocalypticism of many of his contemporaries. Resistance becomes a moral duty as is an insistence on the reality and authority of the social contract. His own early belief in the perfectibility of man foundered on the fact of the Nazi death camps but this made it more than ever necessary to assert the absolute need to accept responsibility for one's actions. The room for manoeuvre was plainly diminishing. The open world of infinite possibility which he had imagined in the 1930s was gone. It is not for nothing that his plays are full of images of constriction. The range of choice facing his characters is minimal but the reality of that choice and the consequences that stem from it are vital to Miller, for what else is identity to consist of, what else can define the public world which we claim as our home?

Arthur Miller was born in Harlem in 1915 – not then what it is now. Then it was a racially mixed, largely middle-class area, though changing fairly rapidly. The Miller family, Jewish immigrants from Austria, were fairly well off, and in 1929 moved out of Manhattan and settled in Brooklyn where they weathered the Depression, though the Wall Street crash, which occurred when Miller was fourteen, destroyed the family business. The Brooklyn of Miller's youth was still largely undeveloped, though it did not remain so for long, and the set of *Death of a Salesman*, in which a rural scene slowly gives way to encroaching apartment buildings, captures a shift which he himself had experienced. In an article called 'One of the Brooklyn Villages' he described his own part of the borough, the Midwood section, 'which now has no distinguishing marks, but thirty years ago was a flat forest of great elms through which there ran the elevated Culver Line to Coney Island...children going to school could be watched from the back porch and kept in view for nearly a mile. There were streets, of course, but the few houses had well-trodden trails running out of their back door...Today everything is paved and your bedroom window is just far enough away from your neighbor to leave room to swing the screens out when the Fall comes...An invisible noose seemed to be forever closing tighter and tighter.'[3]

After leaving school Miller went to work for his father but, unable to stand the life, he tried to find another job, in doing so encountering a fierce anti-semitism. This did something to shape his social and political views and explains why it is a major, if submerged, theme of his work. Confronted with evidence of irrational prejudice, he tended to be drawn to rationalistic accounts of social process, firstly flirting with communism and then being drawn to liberalism. Faced with a denial of human interdependence, he made this a central motif of his work, from the first plays, which he wrote while working as a shipping clerk in an automobile parts warehouse, through to his major Broadway successes.

At the age of nineteen he went to the University of Michigan, beginning as a journalism major and then switching to English. It was here that he began to write in earnest and met others whose political views chimed with his own. On leaving, he joined the Federal Theatre, only to see it collapse almost immediately. Avoiding the draft because of an old leg injury, he was employed for a time in the Brooklyn Navy Yard while continuing to work on his plays. He married a fellow student from Michigan, the daughter of an insurance salesman and a Catholic. They settled in Brooklyn and lived on the income from her work in a publishing company and his own from a series of radio plays, slight efforts in which he took little pride. But, though he despised the work, familiar themes emerge even from a piece like the oddly named *The Pussycat and the Expert Plumber Who Was a Man*, in which a character observes: 'The one thing a man fears next to his death is the loss of his good name. Man is evil in his own eyes, my friends, worthless, and the only way he can find respect for himself is by getting other people to say he's a nice fellow.'⁴ This, of course, is precisely Willy Loman's problem in *Death of a Salesman*. He fails to distinguish between self-respect and popularity.

Miller's début in the theatre, *The Man Who Had All the Luck* (1944), was a profound disappointment and lost backers $55,000, but he was more successful with *Situation Normal* (1944), a series of interviews with American servicemen which emerged out of a movie project, and with *Focus*, conceived as a play but to date his only novel. It was not until *All My Sons* opened in January 1947, however, that he could begin to think of himself as a writer. It was the success of that play which created his public reputation and which secured his economic future. It was at this time and with the money from the production that he bought a farm in Roxbury, Connecticut – a small New England settlement which provides an all too appropriate setting for his celebration of liberal principles rooted equally in Lockean notions of the social contract and identifiably American ideas of political, moral and spiritual community. He still lives in Roxbury, though he has sold the house in which he wrote *Death of a Salesman* and moved to another a short distance away. When recently he chose to intervene directly in local affairs, securing the release of a man wrongfully accused of murder (his later one-act play 'Some Kind of Love Story' owing something to this experience), it was a vindication both of rational analysis and that direct involvement in the social process which underlies his personal liberalism and his sense of a recoverable American tradition. Perhaps more than any other American writer – through the determinisms of the Depression, the irrational anti-semitism of the war years and the persecutions of the McCarthy era – he has maintained the necessity for the individual to acknowledge a double responsibility to self and society which is the essence of classic liberalism, and he has remained an incorrigibly social dramatist, though *The Archbishop's Ceiling* and the two one-act plays 'Some Kind of Love Story' and 'Elegy for a Lady' represented a radical shift of direction which, nonetheless, served to remind us that plays such as *Death of a Salesman*, *The Crucible* and *After the Fall* were scarcely unconcerned with ontological questions, with the nature of the real and the power of myth. As he said in the late 1950s, looking back on his early career in the 1930s:

> O'Neill…said something in a press conference which in the context of those years seemed to be a challenge to the social preoccupations of the Thirties. He said, 'I am not interested in the relations of man to man, but of man to God.' I thought that very reactionary. Until, after repeated forays into one play of my own after another, I understood that he meant what I meant, not ideologically but dramatically speaking. I too had a religion, however unwilling I was to be so backward. A religion with no gods but with godlike powers. The power of economic crisis and political imperatives which had twisted, torn, eroded and mocked everything and everyone I laid eyes on…My standard is, to be sure, derived from my life in the Thirties. I ask of a play, first the dramatic question – What is its ultimate force? How can that force be released? Second, the human question – What is its ultimate relevancy to the survival of the race?…Society is inside of man and man is inside society, and you cannot even create a truthfully drawn psychological entity on the stage until you understand his social relations and their power to make him what he is and to prevent him being what he is not. The fish is in the water and the water is in the fish.[5]

From the beginning Arthur Miller's concern was with a baffled idealism, with the refusal of life to assume the regular pattern which seems a necessary foundation for personal and public meaning. He began his career as a writer at a moment of social, ethical and private dislocation. The Depression placed American myths no less than American realities under pressure. The apparent stability of the social world was exposed as a sham. The fixed points were shifting. And, placed under pressure, human relationships fractured, as had that between his parents. Value became price; pragmatism displaced principle. And, lacking any sustainable version of individual integrity, society became little more than systematised injustice, an enabling mechanism which validated self-interest and simple materialism. In other words, Miller observed and wrote about the process whereby an organic community collapses into a soulless society – whether it be in his Spenglerian account, *The Golden Years*, the story of the conquest of Montezuma by the brutal materialism of Cortés, or in his description of a Darwinian struggle for survival in 1930s New York ('They Too Arise').

His sensibility was forged in this pre-war America and his concern with betrayal, guilt, the collapse of moral tension, the loss of idealism, the surrender of self to process, was very much a product of a period in which the idea of implacable historical forces and a defining materialism was a ruling orthodoxy. Indeed, when he went to college Miller regarded himself as a Marxist and this may account for the confident tone of his early work. But in truth he seems to have absorbed the confidence without the ideology. For, though his work reveals a profound suspicion of materialism, a conviction that economic competition and the collapse of private and social morality are ineluctably connected, in plays like 'They Too Arise' and *All My Sons* he seemed to see the solution as lying in a kind of moral capitalism. His philosophy was rather more Emersonian than Marxist. His model had rather more to do with liberal humanism than with economic determinism. Indeed, determinism is consistently rejected except in so far as he concedes a fundamentally flawed human nature which assumes a social as well as a private dimension.

But the break-up of the social system affected Miller in another way. He has said that 'I was very profoundly affected by what I would call the disintegration of that world in which I started to write. I may have been at odds with it but I depended on it as my enemy...and when the enemy begins to change his shape, size and density, if you don't react, you're dead as an artist.'[6] Such weaknesses as are apparent in the early plays ('Honors at Dawn', 'They Too Arise', 'The Half-Bridge', *The Man Who Had All the Luck*, *All My Sons*) derive precisely from the simplified model of social action and human nature which they assume. Capitalism is seen as creating an exploitative system which denies individual identity. It creates false needs and implies that the satisfaction of those needs will resolve a longing which is in truth spiritual in origin. It substitutes role for identity and replaces individual with economic relationships. And yet in these plays he never proposes a fundamental change in the economic or political structure of his society. He merely insists that a moral basis for action should be rediscovered, that the crisis should result in a reconstituted definition of social behaviour.

For Miller the Depression was a crucial event. In his mind it was the only experience in American history, apart from the Civil War, which had affected all Americans. It convinced him of a clear causality, of the fact that 'there were concrete causes for things...that the wages of sin is death'. The leaders of society 'were either being put away in prison for malfeasance in office or were jumping out of windows, or were overnight poor people...It was a kind of millenarian moment, the return of the gods.' In the 1920s people believed that 'nothing had any consequences...There was no value, in short, economically or in anything else. It was a valueless, totally fictional world.'[7] But the events of the 1930s convinced him of the rationality of the world. What he derived from his contemplation of history was that it could be changed but not merely through the redistribution of economic power. In fact he developed a decidedly non-Marxist faith in the individual.

He has said that his Marxism 'had a stream of indeterminacy', that he 'believed that economic determinacy could be deflected', that 'once you had an image of what the process was, you could change the process', that 'history could be an agent of consciousness'.[8] As a consequence, in *All My Sons* he creates the possibility of an America purged of its corruption. No one is obliged to challenge the system; merely to reform it from within, indeed merely to be aware of the necessity for that transformation. For, looking back at his early plays, he has characterised his belief at that time as a conviction that awareness rather than judgement was the end of his work. His plays are, in effect, a continual search for an inviolable truth about human character and behaviour. And this is the sense in which his characters insist on their identities. The task is to distinguish between those elements which are external and inessential and those which are definitional. The problem is that that moment in which they shout their names out loud, to have their identity proclaimed, is, for the most part, the moment in which they are in the act of betraying that selfhood. As a character remarks in *Incident at Vichy*, 'It is the hallmark of the age – the less you exist the more important it is to make a clear impression.'[9]

'Honors at Dawn' was Miller's first play, and it won him the University of Michigan's Avery Hopwood Award (the judges including Susan Glaspell). Essentially a very 1930s product, it outlines the growing social awareness of Max Zabriskie, inadvertently caught up in a strike, who, in the course of the play, comes to understand the need for such concerted action in order to defeat the corruption and the injustice which he sees around him. Interestingly, it also tackles a subject which appears later in his work and which seemed so clearly a product of the 1950s – the question of betrayal and, more specifically, informing. In the course of the play Max, who, like Miller, has escaped into the university, discovers that his brother is in fact a paid informer working for the Administration, his job being to spy on radical students. The play ends with Max, now fully alert to the nature of his society, accepting his obligation to play a full role in trying to change that society through an action which is implied but not fully dramatised. Written in five days, it was, perhaps unavoidably, an imperfect work, while his view of the union as a possible mechanism for change underwent a radical transformation after the war. (Indeed, he subsequently wrote a bitter screenplay for Columbia Pictures which identified the corruption that affected unions as deeply as it did the companies they attacked.) However, 'Honors at Dawn' did suggest something of his concern with linking personal integrity to the wider issue of a moral society.

Miller's next play, 'The Grass Still Grows', revised as 'No Villain', also won an Avery Award. Having revised it again, as 'They Too Arise', he then sent it to the newly established Federal Theatre. The response of those who read the play for the Play Bureau was instructively mixed. For a reader called Lipschutz it was 'an exceedingly promising play, just fitted for the Anglo-Jewish Theater, since it deals with the problems of a significant strata of American Jews. There are weaknesses in dramatic structure, and the dialogue is often heavy. The play is really dramatic for all these weaknesses, and the characters are convincing, the most convincing I have found in any script coming into the Bureau for some time.' He concluded that 'it must be encouraged and accepted with recommendations for revisions'. Others were less enthusiastic. John Rinassa found it 'monotonous', objecting that it 'failed to include any drama, humor or melodrama'. The result, he found, was 'a lot of very dull talk'. Indeed, he suggested, 'it would appear that the author has taken "Awake and Sing", deleted the theatrical ingredients, and written a very lifelike but an unbearably dull play'. Fanny Malkin was even more forthright. 'The author has no knowledge, training or dramatic sense, not enough to write a play. Results: incoherence, very poor dialogue; using Jewish dialect, dreadful method of characterisation. The beginning and the end of the script ends nowhere.' She concluded her report with the terse comment that 'I reject this script, without reservations.' Nor was she alone in her dislike of Miller's script. Leo Shmeltsman found it 'a plotless, incoherent, undramatic and uninteresting piece' with 'a few lines of good humor...but juvenile and pointless dialogue'. But despite two other reports which proposed that the play 'should be given an immediate try-out', and that it 'should be done, certainly by one of the Experimental Groups' because it was 'an honest, human reflection of life and the contemporary scene',[10] the script languished, while a second one, 'The Golden Years' (1939–40), was completed after the disbandment of the Federal Theatre project and likewise remained unproduced.

'They Too Arise' is a Depression play. The reference to *Awake and Sing* was not wholly gratuitous. There is the same sense of a family struggling to sustain its dignity and its values in the face of financial collapse, the same portrait of a younger generation resisting the slow slide into pragmatism. But Miller's play is more firmly rooted in the working environment, more optimistic about the family's ability to regenerate value, to overcome the pressures originating in the external world but transformed into a destructive tracery of neurosis and guilt. The values identified in the play are not those of an enlightened Marxism but of an American idealism and a Jewish family solidarity. Though the play does not broaden that sense of social responsibility, as does *All My Sons*, it lays the foundation for Miller's insistence on the need to propose a model of human relationships which does not depend on commercial imperatives or defer to shifts in public definitions of morality.

Abe Simon is the owner of a family clothing business. Together with his son Ben he has built a successful but small business relying on a rapid turnover of stock. A second man, Arnold, is at college where he has acquired radical sympathies. When the play begins, a crisis is imminent. The badly underpaid shipping clerks threaten to strike. For a firm working on a small profit margin this could prove disastrous. When Arnold returns from college, therefore, his father sees him as potentially an extra worker who can help them over bad times. But Ben is more protective and tries to persuade his brother not to become involved while, out of loyalty to his father, failing to explain his reasons for dissuading him. Indeed both Ben and Abe recognise a certain justice in the clerks' claim but dare not concede it because of their own exposed position in an industry to which they are marginal, and which is dominated by the unscrupulous, the wealthy and the criminal. When Arnold discovers the truth he joins the strikers. His father's business collapses because the clerks prevent him from moving his merchandise and because his fellow manufacturers, with the help of strike-breakers, pre-empt his orders.

Abe is not himself unscrupulous. When the manufacturers' association is taken over by gangsters he and his sons fight them on moral grounds. While reluctantly prepared to sanction strike-breakers, provided that the majority favour this, he refuses to countenance violence on the grounds that, 'I don't think this is the way an honest man does business...it ain't the way for Jewish men to act.'[11] His son identifies a principle whereby wealth is itself the origin of corruption: 'I'm convinced that having that much money makes it impossible for you to be kind to anyone but your wife.'[12] But, like his father, he has not arrived at this conclusion through any ideological conviction. Neither man has elaborated intellectual theories but each has developed an instinctive understanding of the processes in which he is involved. This is Abe speaking:

> Do I think the poor suckers with less than five thousand dollars are angels? No. I'm not an angel. Maybe I'm a sucker but I'm no angel. But when you're way down at the bottom you sort of smell what's down there with you. You get the smell of sweat, do you know? You sort of get to know the other smaller suckers better than you would if you were way up on top with a lot of money. You know there's a much bigger distance between zero and seventy-five thousand than there is between zero and five. So when you men...the great majority of you...when you come to men like Rosen and Levy and myself, it's pretty tough...pretty *damn* tough to make us believe we have to kill boys to stay in business. Because after all, gentlemen, we aren't a hell of a lot different all around than those you want us to kill. And besides, when you win a strike that doesn't mean that we win too. It means most of the time that you get bigger and get into a better position to strangle us in the normal course of business competition, as they call it. Well I'm one of the little ones, gentlemen. I'm one of the little ones and I'm not yet ready to kill.[13]

When Abe's business collapses the future of the family lies in the balance.

The only solution which suggests itself is a marriage of convenience between Ben and the daughter of a wealthy manufacturer. A simple personal sacrifice stands to redeem their situation and it is no moral scruple which inhibits this but the discovery that it is that very manufacturer who had filled Abe's order. And here lies one of the weaknesses of the play, not merely its patent mechanisms but its confused morality. Ben's willingness to commit himself to a tactical marriage is seen as a personal sacrifice to commercial necessity. The immorality of the action remains largely unexamined. Moreover, while Arnold's honesty and his social conscience are admired, his failure of moral understanding for the most part is ignored. Miller creates a situation whose ethical ambiguities potentially go to the heart of personal and public betrayals, but then fails to engage those ambivalences with real sophistication. The American critic Tom Driver has said that Miller's problem is that he tends to see issues too early, when they take a political or social form. This deflects his attention from questions which are metaphysical in origin. And certainly, in his early work, he does lack the rigour to trace actions and attitudes to their root in conceptions of character and social behaviour not simply defined in terms of an admittedly somewhat confused ideology. Corruption lies self-evidently in a system which establishes competition not only as a natural adjunct of modern society but as a law of nature. At this stage in his career Miller seems to share Steinbeck's vaguely felt Marxism, but he responds to economic determinism with a kind of muted liberalism, a Jeffersonian model of yeoman self-sufficiency. The problem is that the change which he wishes to precipitate is a moral transformation for which, like Steinbeck, he can find no consistent ideological or historical sanction. Steinbeck chooses to deflect the debate into imagery, closing *The Grapes of Wrath* with a symbol (a young mother offers her breast to succour a starving man) for which he failed to erect a credible context and which remains a piety in so far as his own analysis allows for no mechanism which can transform the moral gesture into social fact. Much the same could be said of Miller's play, and indeed of some of his subsequent works. And this is the source of a persistent sentimentality, a moral evasion in these early plays.

Abe Simon comes to recognise the collapse of that connectiveness which is the essence of family and social life when he sees in the brutality of the commercial system a reflection of the inhumanity which has begun to invade his own life, and which had led him to ridicule and even to assault his own aged father. As he explains to his bewildered wife:

> I don't know what's gonna be Esther! Only one thing I know, one thing Esther! it's...it...it ain't right! In my life I never wanted to hurt nobody...Roth don't wanna hurt nobody...Schaft I remember on the East Side...why are they like dogs now!

Fearful that his sons will be dragged into this moral vortex, he insists:

> They ain't gonna go through what I went through in my life for nothing!
> Nothing, Esther, nothing! I wasted my life for what? They're young yet,
> Esther, they got a life to live!...I gonna see that they don't waste it like I
> did trying to get rich![14]

In other words, he has the crucial insight denied Willy Loman. But it is an
insight that lacks any practical application. Challenged by his wife to say what
his sons will do, he replies:

> I'll tell ya what they're gonna do, Esther! I'll tell ya! When I lifted that hand
> against the old man it was like some kind of a...of a thing ya can't see was
> pushing me...it was like a...Esther there was something...dirty...something
> rotten was pushing me. Esther I knew it, I knew it, I knew it! And I know
> it even better now when I see what a man like Roth's gotta do to stay where
> he is! I know it Esther and its gotta be wiped out! It doesn't stay no more!
> I don't know how, I don't know where but I gotta do it! I will not see my
> sons laughing at it the way I did till it drags them so far that they gotta hit
> an old man to stand up...we got six good arms and three good heads. We
> oughta be able to learn a lot...we can change a lot with such...with such
> equipment. A lotta changing we can do...a lotta changing.[15]

The shift from stuttering self-knowledge to full articulateness is deceptive.
The words confess uncertainty as to method; the tone and the rhythm assert
a confident transformation. But that transformation remains emotional. It
is, finally, a sleight of hand, for the world which they will re-enter, now
as labourers, had proved remarkably resistant to moral appeal. The strike has
been easily subverted. But then Miller places little faith in that. The Simon
men are not committed to joining forces with political radicalism. The
struggle to which they are committed is in essence one to restore American
idealism and perhaps also Jewish notions of moral responsibility and family
solidarity.

Abe's moral regeneration is necessarily discharged through language since
there is no action which either Miller or his characters can project as
containing those values. The act of refusal thus becomes crucial but the action
of the play has already demonstrated its inadequacy when confronted with
the blunt facts of industrial logic. Clearly the play suggests that a smaller
discrepancy between rich and poor would be desirable but offers no means
by which that may be effected.

The writer–radical, Arnold, is no better armed. Like Miller himself he can
deploy language, he can assault the system through words (he helps the
strikers draft their press releases) but the real battle lies elsewhere. Most
crucially it lies in the human heart and in a human nature which allows itself

to be contorted by economic pressures. But this was a mystery Miller as yet felt unqualified to tackle. All the play's characters are good men and women warped and betrayed by the system which they have served and which has destroyed their natural goodness. It was not a conclusion which seemed likely to survive the war but, curiously, it was not until *The Crucible* that he reconsidered this central proposition and not until *After the Fall* that he chose directly to address the question of a fundamentally flawed human nature.

'They Too Arise' (the title is clearly close to that of Odets's *Awake and Sing*) ends with Abe's assurance that not only will the world bend before his new sense of moral assurance but that his wife will accept the necessity for a fundamental change in their circumstances. Women, in Miller's plays, tend to be conservative forces and thereby to compound the distorting forces of social life. Though apparently passive, their determined materialism, their fierce sense of protectiveness and their calculated emotionalism threaten the survival of a moral being. Here it is Esther who urges her husband to capitulate, as, later, in *Death of a Salesman*, it is Linda who supports the dangerous illusions of Willy Loman, or Maggie, in *After the Fall*, who compels Quentin to allow full rein to a cruelty which, endemic in his nature, is only released at the behest of a woman desperately asserting her right to survive on her own terms. These women offer love but it is a love which is curiously dangerous to an imaginative and moral being who seeks space and freedom. If the men are poetic, the women are prosaic. They are for the most part baffled by the world, reducing it to banalities, to the level of simple necessities and reassuring certainties. They stand for continuity and sheer survival. They are protective of the family and consequently fail to engage or even to perceive a wider responsibility. They seem unassailed by doubt and thus fall outside the moral crucible which is the focus of Miller's work. For them the world is continuity.

For Miller's male characters the crucial need is to recognise that radical change is possible – not so much in the complexion of society, though that conviction lies in some baffled way at the heart of 'They Too Arise', but in the nature of one's approach to life. The crucial need is always for an identity which can be embraced with pride, defined by actions wilfully undertaken and realities confidently engaged. For his women, character is a product of role. Identity is not problematic. Abe Simon is the first of many Miller heroes for whom one's name and reputation is crucially indicative of one's character. His actions are dictated by the absolute necessity to grant full force to his moral being. 'I wanna leave you with a...with a name...with a clean name,' he insists.[16] It is the same need that drives Willy Loman, John Proctor and Eddie Carbone and which unmakes the apparently confident world of Joe Keller. That Abe Simon completes his sentence by adding the words, 'and a healthy business', is an indication of the ethical confusion which his experiences during the strike eventually purge him of.

Women, however, react rather than act. The final speech of the play proposes natural adjustment as the process of feminine response. 'Y'll see, by the time it's Sunday morning, and she sees the way I love her pickled herring, she'll forget. And the more Sundays go by, the more she'll forget, and the more she'll forget, the more she'll understand.'[17] For Miller, his female characters establish a kind of principle of continuity, a sense of the sheer succession of events, a kind of underlying historicity. They constitute the basic rhythm of life. But the male characters constitute the melody. And this, I suspect, is a potential weakness, for while such an approach does sharpen the focus on his principal characters it also inhibits a dialectic. It drives the debate within the sensibility of the protagonists. His plays become essentially interior monologues, monologues of considerable power and force, but ones in which the principle of connectiveness, the need to renew one's bonds with those around us, is ultimately unconvincing because of his failure to grant that other a similar moral perception. With the clear and potent exception of *Playing For Time*, adapted from Fania Fenelon's book, his tends to be a drama of fathers and sons. It is as though the Platonic model which he proposes would falter if it encountered an active sexuality. It does, of course, in *The Crucible*, *A View from the Bridge* and *After the Fall*, but this sexuality is seen primarily as threat. In *Playing For Time* it is virtually the only basis for an immoral barter economy, though here women are plainly at the centre of dramatic attention. Women otherwise offer only a constancy untroubled by doubt. There is no tension in most of his female characters. They are flaccid and, as a consequence, the values which they represent lack conviction and to some degree dramatic force. Miller has said of *Death of a Salesman* that love was in a race for Willy's soul. In the case of Biff, whose love/hate for his father is at the heart of his own confused sense of identity, this is an accurate enough account of a crucial struggle. In the case of Linda that love is without substance. It is a kind of background noise, diffused and unfocussed. It is real enough. It is present in the gentleness and practicality which she brings to her relationship with Willy. But it could never win any race to redeem him because of a fundamental failure of understanding that Miller seems to feel is inseparable from the feminine sensibility. Perhaps it is an American presumption. It hardly takes Leslie Fiedler to remind us of the degree to which the male American writer has physically excluded women from his work or seen the moral imagination and the definitional encounter with the real as essentially a male preserve. Women are not absent from Miller's world. Given his concern with the family it could scarcely be otherwise. Indeed, as representatives of a social system which grants the family iconic significance they have a central role to play. The problem is that as

147

conservative forces, as the guardians of a materialistic system which charges them with protecting the material interests of the men they marry or to whom they give birth, they tend to lack the tension which typifies his essentially liberal protagonists. Their symbolic role blunts the edge of their dramatic force. The boundary between them and the world is so permeable as to deny them the sharpness of identity which fixes Willy in our minds.

It is true that Elizabeth Proctor finds herself confronting the public world of Puritan New England and that she faces a moral dilemma which raises her above her own former blandness. But she is still reactive, still trying to sustain a sense of continuity and untroubled process rather than wilfully challenging that system out of a moral necessity born of a resistant self. It is John Proctor who would rather die than see his name destroyed. The same could be said of Willy Loman. It is Linda's failure to understand that, which is the final sign of her own total identification with the system which has destroyed him. And it is this male resistance which Miller chose to regard as tragic. The reckless challenge uttered by Abe Simon, Willy Loman and John Proctor is of the same kind, if not the same degree, as that proffered by Melville's Ahab and Twain's Huck Finn, but if Huck's gesture seemed as quixotic and socially unsupported as did Abe's, Twain at least had history on his side. He wrote at a time when Huck's moral assertion had gained historical sanction. Miller wrote 'They Too Arise' at the height of the Depression. Accordingly, like so many other 1930s writers, he could do no more than announce the paramount need for transformation. His own scepticism still inhibited the translation of this realisation into purely ideological terms. Arnold voices the conventional view that Russia offers a possible model, that a 'young man can be used there', and that 'under socialism large holdings of productive private property like a chain of stores would never be allowed',[18] but this never becomes a focus for the play's central argument.

Miller's next play, 'The Golden Years', written between 1939 and 1940 and, due to the collapse of the WPA (Works Progress Administration) Theatre Project, unproduced and unpublished, moves closer to addressing the more fundamental issues underlying his concern with a corrosive materialism. The play is an account of the conquest of Mexico by Cortés. Clearly the events in Europe are as powerful an influence on this play as was the Depression. By a simple but effective irony, unemployment and the virulent internecine struggles of Labour and Capital had been solved not by a renewed sense of brotherhood or a resurgent liberal humanism but by war and the consequent expansion which went with a war economy. For Miller, a Jew, there were admittedly few ambiguities about a war to defeat Hitler, but nevertheless the innocence of the 1930s, the pieties to which he had himself subscribed, could scarcely survive the realities of total war. And the collapse of those values, so recently asserted, was an implied theme of the play. So Cortés leads his troops into Mexico announcing that 'I want nothing but the brotherhood of man',[19] but plans a strategy which will abrogate that principle. He is presented as an adventurer, morally scrupulous over details but intent on imposing his will and exacting his reward. By contrast, Montezuma has a genuine vision of freedom and peace. Though trapped in a mythology which makes him offer human sacrifices and which makes him disastrously vulnerable to his invader, he still projects a world in which constraints will dissolve. 'I saw', he says, 'another world...a world where every door stood wide and unbolted in the night, where the single ear of corn grew heavy as a child, and all the brass of war, swords, and shields, were melted into rivers and the silver sea.'[20] And though the evidence mounts for a reality which would destroy the possibility of such a dream ever being realised, he hesitates to take the necessary steps to thwart Cortés. 'Let a dream depart as it came...into the SUNRISE...I cannot bring my hand to kill it yet.'[21]

The play is clearly not offered merely as an historical account; it is offered as an observation about the contemporary failure to recognise the real nature of the fascist threat and, more especially, the nature of the liberal dilemma. So, just as Montezuma is forced to recognise that 'man is still man' too late to obviate the disaster which his people will suffer, so appeasement had derived not merely from a failure to perceive correctly the political realities of the European situation but from an incapacity to recognise the potential for evil which is the other side to the coin of Montezuma's idealised dreams. However, there is another problem, a problem which he had skirted in 'They Too Arise'. For how can violence be countered? After all, to fight force with force is to destroy the dream. Thus when Cortés shouts at the god/king, Miller, in a stage direction, indicates that 'With the shout, the impact of unreasonable, relentless force hits him.'[22] The only response to this dilemma in 'They Too Arise' had seemed to lie in a faith that moral renewal, a vision of human brotherhood, could potentially negate violence. Now, three years later, that conviction has crumbled. Montezuma's dreams, his wish to believe in human perfectibility, his vision of human unity, only make him more vulnerable to assault. His one hope lies in counterforce, in recognising evil and taking steps to neutralise it before its logical treachery becomes unassailable. But again Miller evades the moral complexity that he identifies. He implies that human nature is ineluctably flawed but chooses not to investigate the nature of that flaw. He acknowledges the necessity for operating in a real world but still seeks to validate an ideal. He implicitly defends the necessity to wage war on evil but forbears to examine the implications of so doing. And in motivating Cortés with a simple desire for wealth and power he is distracted by symptoms from examining the real nature of the disease.

'The Golden Years' is an eloquent play. If it lacks the theatricality of Peter

Shaffer's *The Royal Hunt of the Sun*, it has at least as much substance, and a language no less effective for being less self-conscious. Its weakness lies in its failure to press the issues he raises to their logical conclusion. As earlier he had written out of immediate economic realities which inhibited his pressing through his own ambiguities, so now he created a play too close to the daily uncoiling of the historical spring to enable him to inspect those moral confusions pushed aside by the exigencies of war.

And he returned to the war as a context if not the theme of his next unpublished and unproduced play, 'The Half-Bridge', written between 1941 and 1943. A melodrama, with Nazi spies, villainous plots, and a man redeemed from corruption by the vulnerable innocence of a woman, it nevertheless reflected Miller's sense of an American idealism betrayed by time and by human failure. It also offered evidence for his growing, though still confused, conviction that remedial action remained possible, that the individual, and, by implication, society could still choose to arrest the spiritual decline which made war a natural product of a failure of will and imagination.

Anna Walden, who believes herself to have committed a murder, albeit in self-defence, is desperate to escape to South America. Accordingly, she goes to the docks and confronts Mark Donegal, son of a rich and talented family, who has effectively been disowned by them and become a worldly-wise, cynical mate of a merchant ship. The two are naturally drawn to one another but events are complicated by the arrival of Dr Luther, a Nazi agent, who proposes that Mark should use the ship as a raider. Mark is genuinely tempted. He is also vulnerable in that his friend, August Kruger, is a German Jew whose family is still in Germany. Accordingly he tries to persuade Anna to go ashore. She resists and he is wavering when he discovers that the real purpose of the voyage is an insurance swindle. The ship is to be scuttled by another German raider. A battle is fought and Dr Luther is killed.

The play would seem to have little to recommend it. It is certainly crudely constructed, its characters uneasy sketches and its language overblown. But his central themes emerge with clarity, and the submerged debate about American values, the nature of identity and the necessity for a reassertion of moral values establishes a counterpoint to the banalities of plot which is not without interest in the context of an examination of Miller's emerging talent.

Perhaps because of the setting, the play is at times reminiscent of O'Neill's work. There is the same desperate longing to 'belong' in a world which seems to have become suddenly inhospitable; the same sense of some paramount need for a transforming vision. As Mark laments: 'you don't know what we lost in this country. Those climbing years, the enormous men, people weren't so three-for-a-penny and the country was moving like a train, like the biggest damn thing in the world, a clean thing it seemed like, and you believed in it and you belonged, you *belonged!*' His desire is to 'find a way to do the great thing again, to feel you're steering your own life, to pull out of the mob and walk the earth like a giant again to make new roads'.[23] Mark had left the university to see what it was like to be an ironworker. He had played professional football, had learned to fly and been cashiered for flying figure-eights between the smokestacks of the power-house on Lake Michigan. But now, 'they don't fly any more, they travel by air, they put tracks in the sky...Wings were made for men who couldn't live without wings...They broke me...because the little people wanted lawyers in those planes, not artists who could land like a sparrow on the head of a nail. Yeah, they made the world a room with a view.'[24]

The only place he feels he can recapture the sense of enterprise and adventure is in Brazil, just as in *Death of a Salesman* Uncle Ben was to go to Africa. Like a Tennessee Williams character he seeks freedom through movement, but the frontier myth has collapsed. There is no longer any space. As the seductive Nazi doctor insists, 'The giants are dead in every land, the little people inherit the earth...The future time belongs not to the man in the room with a view, not to the man in the country house, but to the man who'll sail the seas and take, take what he's got the wit and daring to take.'[25] The speech is clearly offered as a justification of the totalitarian nature of the Third Reich, as an explanation of the age of the Caesars ushered in by a materialism which has eroded human values, thereby creating a vacuum which could be filled by false romanticism and a pagan brutalism. But the connection between that and the equally antinomian world of American mythology is not pursued. For F. Scott Fitzgerald the corruption had been born in the West, with romantic notions of self-invention and an aquisitiveness given the sanction of national myth. For him the callow brutality and moral reductiveness of the East were the products of a confident but morally equivocal Western ethos of physical daring, romantic self-assertion and personal and public expansionism. Something of the kind is hinted at by Miller. The language employed by Mark Donegal and Dr Luther is too similar for the reader to be unaware of the connection. But it remains largely unexamined. It is an assertion without real force precisely because it remains at the level of assertion. Indeed, as in *The Golden Years*, it becomes necessary to validate violence as the only viable response to the threat of moral anarchy, a philosophical dilemma which is conveniently skirted because the historical context in which the play was written seemed to justify the fudging of the debate. And so the specious nature of Dr Luther's argument, that the 'giant' should 'gather up the floating fragments of the world',[26] is assumed to be self-evident; Mark's conception of the world as a moral playground and of the self as the final validating principle goes largely unchallenged. Indeed, Mark is actually made the mouthpiece of a liberal conception of social values which is in many ways at odds with his own history, so that he becomes the embodiment of conflicting forces in American society. On the one hand he represents a wish to abstract the self from its defining and constraining context, a desire to find freedom in movement and space; on the other hand he also represents the recognition that moral values can only be expressed through relationships. This, of course, was essentially the paradox out of which Williams's drama emerged. Thus, if isolation constitutes freedom it also potentially represents anarchy. If civilisation implies constraint, the shackling of a free-roving spirit and imagination, it also stands as a protection against that totalitarianism of the self and that arrogant surrender of communality which he saw as lying at the heart of the European war in which America was now fully involved. And so, when Mark is asked to fake illness on board ship and thus induce other merchantmen to offer aid, thereby laying themselves open to piracy, he is implicitly asked to assault a fundamental principle of social behaviour. This, as he realises, is not simply theft; it is a wilful distortion of the social contract itself:

> When you sail a ship into port at night you know the buoys are going to be in the right place, you know the reefs are marked, the lights haven't been moved. That's...we believe that, that's civilization...and I feel the plaster falling around my head. I see dogs dragging children along the streets, a man pulling his daughter into bed, and a lie is the truth and the truth is a lie. Is that what I *mean*...is that what my life adds up to?[27]

The sentiments come unconvincingly from Mark. And, indeed, Miller clearly recognises this, for the play does not resolve itself into a simple battle between innocence and evil in which the evil is reassuringly located in the distance. He is, clearly, aware that corruption is not a national prerogative and that Mark's bewildered search for personal meaning, for a world which will resolve itself into a satisfying pattern, is as liable to result in a callous disregard for others as it is in a genuine sense of selfhood. Indeed Luther confesses that he had chosen Mark precisely because, 'the very blood of these decades has pounded through your veins.'[28] And so he becomes the apotheosis of America's restless but unfocussed yearning which can be the basis equally of cultural dynamism and an amoral drive. The failure to identify the object of that quest, the collapse of his dreams, the shrinking of his moral and physical world, only leaves him desperate to assert himself – if necessary in contradistinction to those around him.

Because of their desperate situation his collaborators are forced to consider a proposal to which they are instinctively opposed. Miller no longer makes economic deprivation primary, but it is the anger and hatred spawned by that social injustice which makes such collaboration possible. The reference to the origins of fascism in Germany seems clear enough, but Miller obviously saw this as different in degree and not kind from the American situation. For such men violence is bred from a self-hatred which is a natural product of the contempt in which they are held by others. For Mark, it is a natural product of a world without moral core, an opportunity to be 'the rider for once',[29] and not the horse.

> The poor are petty and the rich are pigs...I'm pullin' out of that now, all of it...you gotta crawl to live in this world; crawl to men...whose perspiration falls on silk, who eat the bread you make and never know your name! Well I don't crawl...and if blood spills on the water when this is done, blood never spilled for higher purpose – that at least one guy might feel as tall and straight as he was made.[30]

Against this stands only love – the sudden love of a young seaman called Carrol and the more surprising homosexual love of the ship's captain. This stands as a warning against the isolation that Mark seeks, and as a resource against the self-destructiveness which is a product of that isolation. Mark is unable to recognise anything but the grotesque nature of the captain's homosexual advance, unable to accept that the man's concern stands between him and the moral abyss. But his relationship with Anna does bring a degree of self-knowledge. He admits that 'There's no boundaries, no gauge, no rock under my feet', that sometimes he feels he is 'walking in a gas and...going to drop into a bottomless thing'. He recognises that he is afraid to reach out for anything solid, to acknowledge the attraction of the real, because 'it'll pull me down into the life I can't stand, like the rest of the millions going round and round the mill like harnessed oxen'.[31] Like so many other Miller characters he feels the need to make his mark, to imprint his name: 'I'm going to leave a special print on the face of the earth, I'm going to know that I'm more than chemicals...that I'm *Mark Donegal*, one of a kind doing a thing that even the wind will remember.'[32] Unfortunately, the bombast is not entirely the character's. Miller is reaching for a rhetoric that is more literary than apt. The language does underline the mythic dimension of the character, the kinship with self-deluding frontier heroes ('I'm walking on an orbit way over the earth, I'm taller than towers'), but it hardly carries conviction as realistic dialogue.

Mark's redemption lies in the trio of friends who eventually lure him out of his self-concern: Kruger, the refugee from Nazi Germany; the Captain, weak but consistent in his regard for Mark; Anna, whose very vulnerability is the source of her power. All three offer Mark a love which, for most of the play, he fails to recognise for what it is. All three constitute a human significance which he believes to have been destroyed. He offers an absurdist account of the world; they offer a philosophy of resistance. He sees people 'more numerous than pins' as 'the cheapest thing in the world'; Anna insists that 'it can't be that we're built for the grave'. Refusal to compound cruelty and violence, a denial of the logic which projects metaphysical absurdity from private and public inhumanity, this is the essence of her position – and the essence of these early plays. Thus Anna asserts:

> I'd rather get it like that, telling them I'm human, than to say, 'Come on, world, strike me down, I'll be obedient, I'll die like a cow!' Who should pity us if the first thing we're ready to do when there's trouble, is give up our lives? All right, the world pushes you to the grave; all right, it's hard to fight death, I know. Then the world has got to be changed, Mark! It's got to be changed so we can live, and if you've gotta die then die changing it![33]

For Miller, contemplating the fate of the Jews in Europe, the speech clearly had a profound significance. Indeed it is very close in spirit to the essay in which Saul Bellow denounced the absurdist impulse and that love-affair with apocalypticism which he saw the intellectual as having and which, to his mind, was a capitulation to despair. If it was also hollow rhetoric clearly Miller could not afford to believe it was such, for, more than any other play until *After the Fall* and *Incident at Vichy* in the mid 1960s, this work tackled the implications of Miller's Jewish identity.

The notion of ideological change, hinted at in 'They Too Arise', now disappears. The transformation required is a more fundamental one. For Mark, the evidence of human insignificance implies a personal and social worthlessness which can only be neutralised by a fiercely assertive selfhood that survives by refusing commitments beyond the self; for Anna, it implies the absolute need for compassion. And this is a conviction which eventually breaks through Mark's defences. He finally comes to feel that the restless search for meaning, the desire for a sense of completion, the need to leave an imprint on the world – to escape a numbing sense of abandonment – have their resolution not in a lust for power but in a relationship with other people. In a painful speech which provides the play's title, he observes that, 'We're built with half a bridge sticking out of our hearts, looking for the other half that fits so that we can cross over into someone else',[34] but the image was clearly an important one to Miller for he picks it up again a few moments later and it becomes the basis for a piety that links Mark's hesitant acceptance of a communality of feeling with a broader sense of the brotherhood of man. Staring into the barrel of a gun held by the Nazi doctor, he insists that 'a bridge is building, a bridge around the world where every man will walk, the Irish with the Jews, and the black with the white, stronger than any steel'.[35]

The language is entirely familiar from the 1930s, while the easy victory of the good at heart over the Nazis is a piece of patent war-time wish-fulfilment. In many ways the weakest of his early works, nonetheless it identifies the issues which continued to obsess Miller – the need for a common front against the exploiter and the totalitarian mind, the absolute necessity for granting full value to the individual, the desperate need to recognise responsibilities beyond the self, the obligation to resist reductiveness in whatever form. But it follows that the collapse of character into caricature becomes especially disabling in a play which asserts the primacy of a distinctive and responsive human nature, and that a reflexive dialogue, self-regarding in its rhetoric and its mannered poeticism, is particularly inappropriate to a play which sees language as a necessary bridge between people and experience. An apprentice work, it is a naive play. Dr Luther's evil is dramatised; it is not examined. The innocence of Anna, the captain, and August Kruger, on all but the most prosaic level, is simply assumed; it is not analysed. Mark Donegal, the principal character and the man whose transformation is the main focus of the play, exists primarily as a rhetorical device. His change is consequent on a sudden and somewhat unbelievable emotional relationship. His inner world remains closed to us. He consists primarily of a series of postures, of convictions discharged only through words. And once again the mere acknowledgement of the necessity for change is presented as a moral equivalent to that change. Indeed here the consequence is an immediate and implausible victory for the alliance which rediscovers its humanity in finding common cause against aggression. The passion is clear. The difficulty is that Miller could imagine a transformed world but he could not wholly believe in it.

Despite the attempts of the House Un-American Activities Committee, in the 1950s, to locate Miller as a radical, what one finds in his work, from the very beginning, is not so much a Marxist analysis of alienation as an insistence on liberal values, on the absolute necessity for the reassertion of an idealism eroded by financial collapse but, most crucially debilitated by a collapse of will. And though the family is seen as an agent as well as a victim of social dislocation and a disabling privatism, it is not the root cause of moral decay. He may, as in *All My Sons*, suggest, with Steinbeck, that the family is simply a microcosm of a wider community to which ultimate loyalty is owed, but he seems to remain convinced that it is a primary expression of human responsibilities, a necessary model for personal and social values. In 'They Too Arise' family bonds not only prove stronger than commercial necessities; they constitute the only real source of values in the play. Miller includes a token defence of the rights of strikers and dramatises capitalism as potentially a criminal and anti-human activity, but at the heart of the drama lies the family whose unity can neutralise a corrosive selfishness and which is capable of sustaining a view of the individual's moral universe as distinct from that implied by those for whom commercial and moral

155

necessity are coterminous. In *The Grapes of Wrath* the family has to learn to dissolve the boundary between itself and the world beyond; its function lies in its eventual transcendence. In 'They Too Arise' the family becomes a crucial barrier against moral chaos. And though that view is modified in *All My Sons*, it is clear that, for Miller, if the nature of individual responsibilities, if an adequate compromise between the needs and desires of the individual and those of other such individuals, cannot be defined within the family, then there is little likelihood of its being so in a wider community.

Miller is concerned throughout his work with the awakening of the moral conscience, and the need for a spiritual liberation. In a sense he could well have taken as the title for many of his own plays that of Clifford Odets's *Awake and Sing*, for his characters have a constant temptation to take refuge in what they assume to be an historical determinism. Cortés, in 'The Golden Years', stills his conscience by assuming that he represents a necessary and unavoidable progressive force; the clothing manufacturers in 'They Too Arise' justify their immorality on the grounds of economic necessity, as does Joe Keller in *All My Sons*. Willy Loman chooses to see himself as a simple adjunct of industrial process or, alternatively, as an embodiment of an ineluctable American myth. But, against this, Miller pitches a resistant self, a self dimly aware of other values and of a capacity for individual thought and action which determinism can only deny. That self, however, is deeply fallible. Under pressure it cracks like the cylinders in Joe Keller's aircraft engines. And that fallibility, that tendency to betray values even as they are enunciated, to blind oneself to a powerful and destructive egotism, is the source of a constant tension in his work. The guilt which characterises so many of his characters – a guilt which he chose not to engage directly until *After the Fall* – is, in effect, the product of a human nature defined by contradiction, by a persistent struggle between opposing forces. For the desperate need to leave one's mark, to assert one's identity, has a corollary in an egotistical assertion of the rights of the self, just as the desire to belong to a wider community of man seems to require a sacrifice of that selfhood. And there is, finally, no resolution available, only an acknowledgement of the nature of the contradiction. He is unable to accept Steinbeck's biological paradigm of the group animal or the underlying determinism implied by the image of the turtle in *The Grapes of Wrath*, which persists blindly in a quest imprinted on its cell structure. For Miller, the tension between self and society, between an insistence on identity and a simultaneous acknowledgement of the limitations of that identity, is the source equally of his persistent liberalism and his conception of his work as tragic. And this assertion of the equal potency of free will and determinism tends to find its correlative in the *mise-en-scène*, in his sense of the physical transition between the openness of the nineteenth-century American setting and the constraints of a twentieth-century world. The rhythm of life changes and the individual is required to adjust his personal rhythm to it. In 'They Too Arise', an immediate order for clothing turns men into machines as they frantically pack garments to meet the deadline and beat the competition. In *All My Sons* it is the necessary regularity of the production line which dictates the crucial decision to forward defective parts to the air force. The physical surroundings themselves crush the individual, limiting his freedom. In *Death of a Salesman*, the gauze curtain is painted with leaves – a memory of the natural world in which Willy feels at home. But with a shift in stage lighting this fades and the dominating apartment buildings appear, just as they had historically, standing thereby as an image of the constricted physical and moral world which Willy now inhabits.

Miller is a writer whose instinctive belief in the individual's integrity and his power to deflect apparent social determinisms is constantly coming up against an equally clear belief in the power of those determinisms. Seeing no clear mechanism whereby the moral vision can translate itself into action, he brings his characters to the point of commitment but too readily contents himself with a gesture the social extension of which is unclear. His conviction that awareness is all is finally unconvincing because of his own manifest wish to translate that hard-worn perception into social action. For if the logic of his plays denies the validity of solipsism, it denies also the force of convictions not pressed to the point of enactment. But the iconic force of that public world – dominated by the encroaching apartment buildings of *Death of a Salesman*, the mechanical shapes of 'The Hook', the courtroom of *The Crucible*, and the concentration camp of *After the Fall* and *Playing for Time* – establishes an implacable limit to free action. These images are simply not susceptible to the pressure of moral concern or an assertive individualism. The result is the uncertain compromise of a play like 'The Hook', or the simple assertion of the self-evident power of truth in a society demonstrated to be almost totally corrupt, in his adaptation of *An Enemy of the People*. The latter has a particularly ironic ending, though it is not, I think, offered as such, in that power and integrity are established as antithetical so that even reform is denied any means of effecting a change. *Death of a Salesman* has its own ambiguities. For a while implying the existence of alternative possibilities for self and society, it leaves us with a character whose crucial moment of self-perception lies in his acceptance of the fact that he is what he is.

Miller's, like Ibsen's, method rests on a presumption about an underlying rational structure to existence. The past exerts a pressure on the present because it is causally connected to it. Discontinuities are more apparent than real. As he wrote in the book which contains his notes for *Death of a Salesman*:

> Life is formless – its interconnections are concealed by lapses of time, by events occurring in separated places, by the hiatus of memory. We live in the world made by man and the past. Art suggests or makes the interconnections palpable. Form is the tension of these interconnections, man with man, man with the past and present environment. The drama at its best is a mass experience of these tensions.[36]

Art, in other words, closes the spaces opened up by time, event and memory. Thus the style of *Death of a Salesman* and *After the Fall* is less a pragmatic response to particular presentational problems than an assertion of moral continuities. The link between past and present is equally the link between an act and responsibility for that act. As Quentin observes in *After the Fall*, the primary sin of private and public life is that 'we conspired to violate the past, and the past is holy and its horrors are the holiest of all!'[37]

For Miller, as for Freud, guilt is a primary social mechanism in that it is the unconscious acknowledgement of responsibility, of a world which consists of more than fragmented experiences; it is a product of the dominance of the reality over the pleasure principle. And Miller's dramatic method in *Death of a Salesman* becomes a model of his sense of the legitimate demands of the real. As he later remarked, 'I can't say that I believe you can ascertain the real but I do believe in the obligation of trying to...To give it up is to create a kind of anarchy of the senses which believes that there are no consequences of any determinable type. It finally ends up with a kind of narcissism which makes life both boring and dangerous.' For the implication of such a stance is that 'everything is a question of taste, including the hanging of innocent people'.[38] And this was a question which he pursued further in *The Crucible* and in *After the Fall*.

Arthur Miller has written more about his work than any other American dramatist. A recent collection of his theatre essays ran to 400 pages. And these essays, while ostensibly about the nature of tragedy and the force of the dramatic, are virtually all ethical discussions. At their heart is a restless concern with the nature of man as a social animal and a relentless obsession with the moral basis for individual and social action. His characters frequently find themselves at the cutting edge of 'the devouring mechanisation of the age',[39] desperately trying to negotiate a basis for a moral life, fighting to create a space within which identity can cohere and will and imagination exert an influence apparently denied by biological and economic determinisms. It is not an unambiguous struggle, for the desire to impose order and to assert the rights of the self may as easily lead to a severing of the links between that self and the public world in which it moves, as to a valid assertion of identity. In *Incident at Vichy* this leads to the abandonment of all moral and social responsibility, to the assertion that nothing is prohibited to the will and imagination which acknowledges no obligation beyond its own absolute authority. The question thus becomes one of identifying the nature of the individual's responsibility to the other, of tracing the line between private neuroses, the disintegration of the psyche, and those social dislocations which are both a cause of personal angst and primary evidence of the collapse of the social world. Like the post-war Jewish–American novel, Miller's work becomes an examination of the basis on which the moral world can be reconstructed. Like Bellow and Malamud, he takes as his subject the need to reconstitute a model of individual action and liberal responsibility abandoned in the 1920s in favour of a romantic faith in experience, an emphasis on the self which had abstracted itself from history and declared morality to be a product of the sensibility, and in the 1930s in favour of a collectivist drive. Miller's belief in the necessity for a spiritual and moral resurgence was clear in the work which he produced in the 1930s, but the war, for him as for Bellow, clearly created a context in which the reassertion of liberal ideals became simultaneously a moral necessity and a forbidding endeavour. Character became not merely a convenience of plot; it was in many ways the subject of his work. For, if the individual was to be a moral agent, if he was to be held responsible for his actions, he had to be granted a degree of autonomy and social significance denied both by the absurdist and the Marxist, and, to many, denied by the events of a war which had not only destroyed the individual but exposed a model of human nature that seemed to permit of no confidence in the possibility of recreating an idealism not completely shot through with irony.

And the theatre was not only a mechanism for this moral renewal, it was to be a paradigm of it; a social art in which character was to be dramatised in a social context. For Miller, 'the assumption – or presumption' behind his plays was 'that life has meaning'.[40] The strategy of his plays lay in the slow unravelling of an unproblematic reality, the progressive stripping of illusions and falsehoods in a process designed to expose a truth the contours of which are presumed to be clear and unambiguous. Language is assumed to have the power both to express an inner world whose irrationalities are taken to yield to rational analysis, and paradoxically to penetrate the evasions which can equally take linguistic form. It seemed to Miller that 'the stage was as wide and free and towering and laughingly inventive as the human mind itself'.[41] And this became more than a metaphor, as in plays like *Death of a Salesman* and *After the Fall* the stage was indeed coterminous with the mind of the principal character. The character's perception of truth might result from the pressure of experience but for the most part that process was to be validated and its meaning extended by the analytic mind – Chris Keller insisting on the connection between private guilt and public responsibility in *All My Sons*, Biff offering a redundant statement of his father's errors in *Death of a Salesman*, the lawyer observing and analysing events in *A View from the Bridge*, and Quentin, in *After the Fall*, struggling to understand the meaning of his experience. It is one of the ironies of Miller's work, however, that his plays draw their power from an emotional truth to which the audience responds rather than a rational process to which the mind must assent – hence Miller's baffled response to the tears which he observed at the end of *Death of a Salesman*. His plays are confessional, not in the manner of confessional poetry (that is they do not derive from Miller's life and experience), but in the sense that their *process* is one of confession, of self-revelation, exposure of resisted truths.

The dominant mood is one of loss – loss of respect, of love, of direction, of sociality. His protagonists long to close the various gaps in their lives, the spaces which separate them from the world in which they wish for an honoured place, which divide their lyrical dreams from their practical realities, which separate them from those they had once loved and would again if betrayal and guilt and a yearning for some kind of socially endorsed significance did not weigh on them like the past which they believe so implacable. The distance between themselves and their youth, and the related distance between the ideals which have had to bend before necessity or which did bend before a selfishness which is offered as a central truth of their lives, becomes the basis for a disabling irony. It is a gulf which, in the early play, 'The Half-Bridge', he believed could be spanned by a simple confession of love, an act of grace suddenly manifested by the human heart, and which, thirty years later, in *After the Fall*, he believed could be spanned only with the greatest difficulty and with full knowledge of the momentary nature of a redeeming consonance. Unlike O'Neill, Williams and Albee, he has never flirted with despair. His work is avowedly anti-apocalyptic. At times it is unconvincing for precisely that reason. His analysis of the collapse of the self and the decay of communality is acute; his response to that, less so. Too much is expected of a gesture, a moment of self-knowledge, a re-dedication to a failing cause. For all his insistence on the public dimension of his plays he creates characters who are most interesting and compelling, indeed most heroic, when they face only themselves. They value the good opinion of others but they live and die finally because the one good opinion which they need in order to survive is their own.

In a way all of his plays are like internal monologues. Opposing views of the world, of the self and of morality, are allowed to argue. In Willy's case, as in the case of Quentin, it literally takes place inside his head. But even Eddie Carbone, in *A View from the Bridge*, is drawn in two opposing directions, as is John Proctor. It is not truly a dialectical method, however. The thumb is securely on the scale. There is a moral and an immoral course. The process of the play lies in recognising the necessity to embrace the moral, and Miller is in fact a moralist. But he did not always see himself in this light.

For Frederic Henry, in *A Farewell to Arms*, words like 'honour' and 'dignity' and 'sacrifice' had lost their meaning. Only facts retained authority; only experience was real. A decade later, under the pressures of a different kind of war, Hemingway reversed his position, and the model he invoked was, ultimately, a liberal one. And this is clearly also at the heart of Miller's work. Joe Keller, in *All My Sons*, has to learn that the 'consequences of actions are as real as the actions themselves',[42] and that the individual has to concede a responsibility for the state of his world. It is in fact an assertion that the moral world remains intact and that the demands of personal responsibility for the state of one's society – demands which had been at the heart of nineteenth-century American writing – remain real and operative. The force of the past, obviously so strong in his work, is in part an expression of his nostalgia for the simplicity of the past and in part an insistence on causality as the basis for morality. But if the pressure of the past implies accountability it also implies a determinism which must be challenged. However, we can, he suggests, transcend our history if we cannot deny it. Hence, for Willy Loman the past is the source of his guilt but it is also the burden of his responsibility. If he were only able to accept that he might be able thereby to liberate himself. For Biff, on the other hand, it is the dead weight of false dreams and betrayed ideals which he must refuse.

This is not to say that his plays are ponderous moral parables. Despite his assertion that 'the end of drama is the creation of a higher consciousness and not merely an attack upon the audience's nerves and feelings',[43] his real skill lies in turning abstract issues into human dilemmas and in establishing the lyrical as itself a value. It is for his characters that he will be remembered, people struggling, with such honesty as they can muster, to make sense out of their lives and to leave some mark of their existence on a world coldly oblivious to human need and implacable in the face of personal anguish. That their personal battles with guilt and their own moral failings touched so directly on tensions and anxieties in the culture made those battles seem exemplary gestures, but in some important respect they transcend the moment. It isn't hard to see Willy Loman as a product of post-war materialism or John Proctor as a response to the anti-Communist hysteria of the 1950s. But their anguish goes deeper than such causes and their struggles to justify themselves in their own eyes touch on an area of experience which is restricted to no individual, to no society and no time.

On the evening of 8 October 1941, Miller asked himself in his notebook, 'But why, why are you a revolutionary?' His reply was 'Because the truth is revolutionary and the truth I will live by!' It hardly needed the exclamation marks to underline the self-conscious rhetoric. But as an unproduced playwright, who had by now written a number of perfectly adequate plays, he felt the need to determine his direction as a writer. And so he continued,

> Tonight, after nearly four years of indecision and torment, after passing through the terminal gamut of bourgeois aspiration and bourgeois frustration and fear, I have that world behind [me]. And with it all I have written and all I have tried to write and failed to finish. The last two works never completed themselves, for at last the mind has exhausted its memories and is left to feed only upon itself. Mark Donegal, the 'I' that would devour the world and not enter it, David [Frieber] also died for lack of connection and the consciousness of course [not, of course, in the final version of *The Man Who Had All the Luck* where David Frieber was to appear]. Why should I continue to feign ignorance...Why try to make heroes of the Damned and the pathetic. They strive for nothing but the scene that has passed. The hero today fights to the Death for that which is to come. And now, in my strength, so do I.[44]

It was a curious piece of posturing, obviously arising out of a profound sense of unease about his life and his work. The truth was that he was never a revolutionary and has never written a play which proposes anything more radical than the restoration of American liberal principles, while his greatest play was to concern a man who was precisely one of the damned and the pathetic striving for a scene that had passed. And though his characters tend to die defending a sense of dignity, that dignity is not always rooted in the real. The future which they thereby struggle to assure is either ironic (as with Willy Loman and Eddie Carbone) or an attempt to reclaim the moral resources of the past. If his protagonists fight to the death for what is to come, it is never with the revolutionary's desire to transform the social world but merely with a desire to discover the mechanism whereby it may legitimately be claimed and inherited. Chris Keller, in *All My Sons*, does not assault capitalism; he merely wishes to be able to endorse it without guilt. Biff Loman, in *Death of a Salesman*, eventually understands the inadequacy of his father's dreams. It never occurs to him to transform the public world. At most he will retreat from it into the rural past of America which had equally been a part of his father's dreams – a lyricism constantly undermined by a more pragmatic undertow. So, too, John Proctor, in *The Crucible*, dies affirming values momentarily set aside by authority. He never sets out to challenge the fact of that authority or the world view which that authority represents. Indeed, when Sartre, ahistorically, tried to transform the events in Salem into a revolutionary model, Miller stridently objected. Likewise, Quentin's doubts, in *After the Fall*, despite the concerned language in which they are expressed, never really extend to the social world in which men suffer and die. The process of the play is one whereby the individual must learn to adjust to the implacable realities of human behaviour, pitching against a blank determinism that human compassion, that equally ineluctable urge to connect, which is the only available resource for protagonists who are damned but need not be pathetic.

In 'The Half-Bridge' Miller was clearly not only thinking of the plight of the Jews. What was at stake was a definition of human freedom. To concede absurdity was to surrender the very principles on which a moral indictment of fascism could be based. If submission was to some degree a stratagem which had proved historically attractive it was, to Miller's eyes, a suicidal compounding of evil. Just as it had proved a facile and self-destructive solution to the threat offered to the European powers by Hitler, so it was for the threatened Jew and, indeed, for any individual confronting the dark side of human nature. And this was the conviction at the heart of his only novel, *Focus*, which, apart from anything else, is an account of a personal acceptance of the need to take a stand. The issue concerned may be a public one – anti-semitism – but the urge towards commitment is a consequence of a personal necessity, the need to value oneself more highly than the public world would seem to allow.

Lawrence Newman is a personnel manager of a large business enterprise which refuses to hire Jews. Throughout his time with the company Newman has never questioned the policy, having simply internalised the prejudices which underpin it. Now, however, the purely arbitrary nature of anti-semitism is dramatised by the fact that he himself becomes the object of persecution. Having been forced to acquire spectacles because of failing eyesight (the evidence for which being, in the eyes of his employers, his appointment of a Jewish secretary), he finds that his appearance is dramatically changed. He looks Jewish. As a consequence he is removed from the front office and feels obliged to resign, confident that he will be able to find employment elsewhere. But, instead, he finds himself not only a pariah as far as employers are concerned but also in the eyes of his neighbours. His marriage to a woman who is similarly mistaken for a Jew merely exacerbates his situation. At her behest he tries to secure immunity by embracing their prejudices, but is rejected. Assaulted by a group of right-wing thugs he finds himself inspired by the resistance of his Jewish neighbour. And though his wife, who had previously worked for an anti-semitic organisation, manages to convince his persecutors of his real identity, Newman now refuses this escape. When questioned by a policeman he no longer challenges the man's assumption about his Jewish identity. He accepts the brotherhood which he had earlier denied. If persecution has made him a Jew, it has also convinced him both of the immorality of prejudice and of the need to confront and defeat it.

Although the America which Miller describes is shown as being deeply anti-semitic, his objective would seem to be less an assault on American values and the injustices of his own country than on a human failing which transcends national boundaries. The evil of the holocaust was clear and palpable; the spiritual debilitation of persecutor and persecuted was more subtle. Persecution, he suggests, requires not merely a persecutor but also those willing to accept their role as victims. In the American context that carries some conviction; in the context of the European camps it is less plausible. For Miller, the core of the novel lies in a story which the Jewish trader, Mr Finklestein, remembers his Polish father telling him. It concerns a baronial estate, cut off from the rest of the country, in which the peasants had been kept in ignorance of the emancipation proclamation. Goaded by an overseer they kill him and then, when waiting patiently for a replacement, are attacked by other overseers. Their spontaneous act is thus transformed into a rebellion. The serfs then sack the baron's house, removing large amounts of paper money which they believe to be miniature portraits of the king. On his return the baron discovers the theft and calls upon a Jewish pedlar, Itzik, to enter the estate and sell his goods for the stolen cash. Itzik realises that this is simply a device for the baron to recover his wealth and an excuse to initiate a pogrom, since once the stolen money is discovered in the house of a Jew it will justify a retributive campaign. But, knowing this, Itzik feels that there is no alternative. Accordingly, he does as he is told, and in the subsequent attack his family are brutally killed and he himself is driven insane. For Finklestein's father the story is a parable of the ineluctable nature of fate, of the need to accept the given, to acknowledge not merely the reality but the inevitability of prejudice and its consequences. For Finklestein himself, however, the moral is very different. He sees the story as showing that 'Itzik should never have allowed himself to accept a role that was not his, a role that the baron had created for him.'[45] The pogrom was inevitable; its outcome was not. Itzik, he believes, should have fought and should not have allowed himself to cheat the peasants so as to appease the baron. Finklestein insists on his own innocence and refuses to act as though he were guilty. And this is essentially the lesson which Newman learns, while the emphasis on the individual's need to accept full responsibility for his own actions, to delineate an identity which is the consequence of choices made rather than myths accepted, is a theme which runs throughout Miller's work.

In a sense the book is close in spirit to Kafka's The Trial. There is the same sense of the irrationality and the arbitrariness of persecution; the same conviction that the individual conspires in his own defeat. But, for Miller, this determinism, social or metaphysical, can be resisted. It is possible to cut a vector across a line which is only seemingly predetermined. At the heart of this book, as of most of his work, is a liberal conviction that identity exists to the side of social role, that the path to truth lies through self-knowledge, and that society should be an aggregation of free individuals respecting one another's individuality rather than a homogenous group of people clinging to conformist ideas as a way of investing empty lives with a meaning external to those lives. Lawrence Newman paints his shutters in the same shade of green as those of his neighbours as he tries to adjust his ideas and values to theirs. The effect is a loss of selfhood and self-respect, the acceptance of a coercive orthodoxy. His only moment of peace comes when he breaks free of such coercions and, by accepting his role as Jew, denies the accuracy and the relevance of such definitions – when, in other words, he realises that they were all his sons and brothers. And it is exactly these themes which are taken up in his first produced work for the stage, *The Man Who Had All the Luck*, given just four performances at the Forest Theatre in November 1944, and in *All My Sons*, produced in November 1947.

The Man Who Had All the Luck is an assertion of the individual's control of his own fate. David Frieber, a self-trained mechanic, seems successful at everything he attempts. Even when he proves incapable of diagnosing the fault in a local landowner's car, a new mechanic strolls into his workshop and does it for him, thereby landing him a major contract which is the source of his ensuing prosperity. However, the event also reveals a weakness in his character as he conceals the help he has been given by the new mechanic.

Frieber is essentially passive and though he is terrified of inhabiting an irrational world he submits himself to the simple flow of events. Wishing to marry Hester Falk but unwilling to challenge her father, who is bitterly opposed to the match, he is relieved of the dilemma by a fortuitous fatal accident. And so his successful life continues, apparently an unbroken succession of fortunate events. Even his ostensible sterility is ended with the birth of a child. But the sheer consistency of his good fortune breeds a deep-seated fear. He becomes convinced that such luck must be paid for, that there is a natural balance in the world which requires some price to be paid, some sacrifice to be made. Eventually he offers a substantial hostage to fate by wildly over-investing in mink-breeding. The venture is doubly threatened by a sudden and potentially disastrous hailstorm and by poisoned feed. At this crucial moment his wife intervenes and insists that he should allow the animals to die, for only thus will he cease living in fear. By assuming responsibility for the deaths himself he will be acknowledging his own ability to act and accepting responsibility for his own actions.

The play is a warning against an obsessiveness which takes the individual out of relationship with those around him. Thus a subplot tells the cautionary tale of a young boy whose father has trained him to be a baseball pitcher.

So determined has he been to produce a perfect sportsman that he insists that he sacrifice everything to this, abandoning his schoolwork and spending the winter in the basement pitching at a target. The result is a technically perfect player, with no applied intelligence; one who is unable to deal with the complexities of a situation in which his fellow players prove humanly predictable. But the play is more than this. It is, most importantly, a liberal homily on the individual's ultimate need to accept responsibility for his own actions.

David wishes to sustain an image of a world in which everything is ordered. 'I want it to be...just the way it ought to be, the way it...happened.'[46] He believes that there has to be some fundamental justice built into the framework of existence because 'if people don't receive according to what they deserve inside them we're living in a madhouse'.[47] And this, indeed, is the fundamental terror, that, as the new mechanic Gus avers, 'there is no justice in the world'. For Gus, this fear provokes a necessary humanism, a compassion which conquers self-interest; for David, it is the root of a fatally disturbing despair. Thus his own success becomes the basis of a growing alarm. Knowing that he receives more than he deserves he is forced to concede the fact of that disproportion and thereby the reality of injustice. This, in turn, breeds an overpowering sense of guilt, a desire to join the rest of humanity through suffering. But even this is an attempt to sustain the idea of a fundamental justice. Thus when a friend tells him of his wife's death at the age of nineteen, he insists, 'There must've been a reason. If you'd had the right doctors...' And when that same friend voices his own sense of the numbing absurdity of existence − 'What's it all for, what's it all about? You struggle, you plan, you work, for what? They'll wipe my name off my mail box like I never lived' − he can only reply, 'I don't want to hear any more of that, you understand me?'[48] But the simple truth is that he has seen the capriciousness of fate at work and has simply struggled to integrate it into his sense of cosmic order. And he has done so at the expense of acknowledging any real control over his life and any responsibility to those who surround him. Miller's point is not that, in the words of one of the play's characters, 'man is a jellyfish laying on the beach. A wave comes along and pulls him back into the sea, and he floats a while on a million currents he can't even feel, and he's back on the beach again never knowing why',[49] but that, deprived of metaphysical purpose, undetermined by any but the most obvious biological functions, the individual's duty is to assume responsibility for a world which he makes or invents rather than inherits or simply inhabits. Thus David's disburdening himself of his possessions is a refusal of responsibility which is ultimately dysfunctional. As Gus, the mechanic, observes, 'if you came once in a while and worked in your shop, and fired some of the help around here and laboured again in your own fields, maybe they would be "like mink"! These things are you. You generated them.'[50] David has to learn that to accept that 'everything can happen... anything at any time! The most terrible things',[51] does not imply that 'you'd have to bow your head and say, "Amen", it was right that it happened'; that while 'the world is made that way as if a law was written in the sky somewhere', and 'Nobody escapes',[52] this places the greater burden on the individual who must refuse to compound a metaphysical absurdity which provides the context but not the total definition of human life. It is a conviction that runs through all of his work but it gained especial force from the war.

All My Sons is ostensibly a play about morality. Joe Keller, a war-time manufacturer of aircraft engines, had been charged with supplying defective equipment which led to the death of twenty-one pilots. At the trial, however, he had denied responsibility, allowing his timid partner to take the blame. Having been exonerated, he has successfully re-established his business and though his neighbours still believe him to be guilty they have apparently accepted him back into their social life. But relief at his acquittal is tempered by grief at the loss of his son, himself a pilot, reported missing, presumed dead.

At the time of the play, some three years later, that son's fiancée, Ann (daughter of Joe Keller's business partner), arrives to become engaged to the dead boy's brother, Chris Keller. This provokes a crisis for his mother, since she has refused to accept the fact of her son's death and has seen Ann's fail-ure to marry as evidence of her similar faith in his survival. The planned marriage, therefore involves laying the ghost of the dead son. But, more significantly, acceptance of her son's death also forces her to acknowledge a connection between that event and what she knows to be her husband's guilt. The situation is compounded when Ann's brother George arrives to confront Joe with that guilt. And though he fails to wring a confession from Joe the imminent marriage does. For Chris's mother plays her final card in order to prevent the marriage which will signal the end of her hope. She reveals her husband's guilt to her son. But she and her husband are finally defeated by a letter which Ann now reveals, a letter in which the missing son had announced his intention of committing suicide because of his father's actions. Stunned into accepting responsibility for his actions, Joe Keller shoots himself, bequeathing a kind of freedom to his son, who will accept no other inheritance.

On the surface the play is an extension of earlier themes. It is an assertion of the need for the individual to accept full responsibility for his actions, to acknowledge the reality of a world in which the idea of brotherhood is an active principle rather than a simple piety. It is an assault on a materialism which is seen as being at odds with human values, on a capitalist drive for profits which is inimical to the elaboration of an ethic based on the primacy of human life and the necessity to acknowledge a social contract. Indeed Joe Keller defends himself by insisting that his own values are those of the world in which he moves. As he asks, rhetorically, 'Who worked for nothing in that war? When they work for nothing, I'll work for nothing. Did they ship a gun or a truck outa Detroit before they got their price? Is that clear? It's dollars and cents, nickels and dimes; war and peace, it's nickels and dimes, what's clear? Half the goddamn country is gotta go if I go.'[53] And his son is forced to acknowledge this, lamenting that 'This is the land of the great big dogs, you don't love a man here, you eat him! That's the principle; the only one we live by – it just happened to kill a few people this time, that's all. The world's that way, how can I take it out on him?'[54] Yet he still continues to press his demand of the ideal until his father can no longer live with his guilt and his suddenly intensified sense of loneliness. And this is the basis of the play's submerged theme – a concern with guilt as a principal mechanism of human behaviour, and with self-interest as a spectre behind the mask of idealism.

Clearly *All My Sons* rests very squarely on Ibsen's work, and in particular on *The Wild Duck*. This also had taken as its subject two businessmen, one of whom had allowed the weaker partner to go to prison for a fraud which

8.   *All My Sons*, directed by Elia Kazan in 1947. Stage design by Mordecai Gorelik.

he had himself condoned and probably initiated. He, like Joe Keller, had thrived as a consequence and, despite suspicions, won his way back into public regard. His son's suspicions cast a pall over his success and over his own imminent marriage which he hopes will finally expunge the memory of his first wife who had rightly accused him of betraying her. But Ibsen's emphasis is less on the relationship between father and son than it is on the nature of a supposed idealism itself. The son, Gregers Werle, is seized with what a benign doctor, Relling, calls 'acute rectitudinal fever'. He wishes to destroy all illusions in the belief that truth has a transcendent value, and that it provides the only basis for human life, but that idealism is seen to be an uneasy compound of guilt and naivety. In denying people their illusions he denies them also their life. And the consequence is the death of a young girl. But the play is by no means simply a defence of what Ibsen called 'life-lies' and O'Neill 'pipe dreams'. Certain illusions are patently destructive, as is Gregers's belief in his own innocence and his consequent assurance about the virtue of truth. Blind to his own self-deception, he becomes a huckster for truth at the expense of human values. In a world whose physical and moral boundaries are shrinking (the natural world has shrunk for the Ekdals to a simulated woodland recreated in their attic), those values become the crucial defence against material and physical constriction.

In Miller's play, too, there is an intricate tracery of self-justification. Most crucially, Chris's idealism conceals a compulsive need to justify his own silence, the suppression of his own doubts. The fact that he has refused to allow his father to add his name to that of the family firm is indicative of his own suspicions. Yet he has continued to draw money from the company. To accuse his father is, ultimately, to affirm his own innocence. So, too, his desire to force his mother to acknowledge his brother's death is less a consequence of his belief in the necessity for truth than a product of his desire to marry that brother's fiancée. Like so many of Miller's characters, his actions are dictated by his desire to 'build something',[55] even at the expense of others. Thus, his own repressed self-doubts about his involvement with business lead him to convince his doctor neighbour that he should abandon his practice for research. As a consequence the man leaves his wife for a while only to return with a brooding sense of dissatisfaction.

But Chris is not the only character whose actions are dictated by guilt. Joe Keller himself offers to help his partner and his son, as Ibsen's Werle had done in *The Wild Duck*. His wife struggles to maintain the fiction that her son is alive rather than admit to her husband's guilt and acknowledge her own status as a beneficiary of that crime. And, more crucially, Ann herself finally insists on showing both Joe and his wife their son's letter, partly in order to facilitate her own marriage and partly to purge her own sense of guilt. For she, like her brother, whose own concern with pressing the cause of justice is not remote from his own shame, has not visited or corresponded with her father since his imprisonment. To Joe Keller's appeal to 'see it human' they all react in some fundamental way out of a need to justify themselves. The play is thus concerned with an egotism much more basic than that displayed by a materialistic society. This fact is identified but not examined. His characters move in a world of failed dreams; they are betrayed by time and event, desperately bending the world to accommodate their need for meaning and companionship. They see themselves as victims and struggle to find happiness and purpose in adapting themselves to the given. But Miller leaves us with only a series of paradoxes which are dramatised but not analysed. For in suggesting that all actions are rooted in self-concern he comes close to destroying the moral values which elsewhere he wishes to invoke. Morality is at one moment seen as external to individuals, who, deeply flawed, can scarcely elaborate a system of ethics which could only be an expression of that fallibility; at other times it is seen as being defined precisely in terms of the internal needs of those individuals, and hence subject to human imperfection. Morality as absolute; morality as relative.

The immorality of Joe Keller in forwarding defective goods is manifest, but his accusers can invoke no moral system by which to indict him, not because he inhabits a society in which such pragmatism is a norm but because there is no one in the play who can level the accusation without confessing to his or her own self-interest. It was a dilemma to which he would return in *After the Fall*, but in *All My Sons* not only does he not have an answer to the moral dilemma which he has created, he does not even seem fully aware of the nature of the problem which he has posed. For, if idealism and demands for justice must necessarily be flawed, on what grounds can any accusation be legitimately levelled? On the other hand, Chris's belief in human responsibility, reflected in the play's title and Joe Keller's final and dramatically crucial realisation that the pilots whom he indirectly killed were 'all my sons', was born less out of this latter confession than out of an event in his own past, the loss of virtually all the members of his company during the war: 'I got an idea – watching them go down. Everything was being destroyed, see, but it seemed to me that one new thing was made. A kind of responsibility. Man for man.'[56] But there is a suggestion that this too derives from guilt – the guilt of the survivor, for 'They didn't die; they killed themselves for each other. I mean that exactly; a little more selfish and they'd've been here today.' His survival thus becomes tinged with a suggestion of selfishness which is compounded by his subsequent financial security. 'I felt wrong to be alive, to open the bank-book, to drive the new car, to see the new refrigerator.'[57] However the connection between idealism and guilt which he proposes is simply assumed; it is not traced to its origin in a model of human nature. In the earlier plays the impulse to transform the self and society had a purity denied here. Of course the war itself offers a potential explanation but the nature of the transformation which he implicitly proposes is not scrutinised. Some thirty years later Miller admitted to the significance of this submerged theme and to his fascination with the guilt of the idealist, but insisted that the sheer pressures of the moment, the immediate context of the war, made it impossible for this to break surface. Indeed he saw a similar logic behind the success, several decades after its first performance, of the Israeli production. The issue of war profiteering was simply too powerful in such an environment to permit more subtle and more disturbing questions to coalesce.

Both *The Wild Duck* and *All My Sons* end with a pistol shot. Gregers Werle remains undeflected from his destructive idealism; the dead girl's father seems likely to lapse back into his self-deceiving torpor. Only the doctor remains clear-sighted, aware of the constant battle between the real and the ideal. In *All My Sons* we are left with an irony which is worrying because Miller remains equivocal in his commitment to it. Thus a second before his father's suicide, Chris, who has precipitated that suicide, announces that 'You can be better! Once and for all you can know there's a universe of people outside and you're responsible to it.'[58] In one sense this is clearly the moral of the play, but when the pistol shot rings out it is equally plain that his insistence on the moral has killed his father. When asked by his mother whether he was trying to kill his father with the truth, he had replied, 'What was Larry to you? A stone that fell into the water? It's not enough for him to be sorry. Larry didn't kill himself to make you and Dad sorry.' But seconds later, with his father dead, he says, 'Mother, I didn't mean to.'[59] The equivocation is not merely Chris's, it is equally Miller's whose title announces *All My Sons* but whose play proposes an unbridgeable gulf between people and undercuts the very moral necessities he identifies. That contradiction could have become the basis for a more profound play. That it did not was perhaps an indication that the problem remained for him an intractable one until *After the Fall* in 1964, by which time he was clearer as to his view of human fallibility, personal betrayal and a continued commitment to the ideal, and less destabilised by the moral exigencies generated by the war.

All My Sons poses a further problem. It implies a critique of society and yet in effect identifies no way in which that society can be transformed. As Miller himself confessed more than thirty years later, 'The argument that the Marxists had quite rightly, with that play, was that the son who brings down the wrath of the moral god, remains inside the system which has created this immorality. That's perfectly true. However, I believed then that with a sufficient amount of rigorousness those crimes could be resisted.'[60] It was a conviction which remained at the level of rhetoric. It never transformed itself into social action or dramatic effect. But Miller was less concerned with challenging the structure of American society than with revivifying a moribund liberalism, a capitalism purged only of its more evident rapacity.

All My Sons is a classically well-made play. With its concealed letters and hidden truths suddenly flourished at moments of dramatic effect, it recalls an earlier theatre. Its success plainly owed something to its topicality. Its melodramatic flavour reflected a public predilection for moral absolutes. Its resentments were those of the community at large who suspected, rightly enough, that profit rather than national interest had motivated many of those who risked capital rather than their lives. And, if there was, at another level, a profound ambiguity about the motives of those who flourished truth as a banner of their innocence, this had rather more to do with the play's literary origins in Ibsen than Miller's conscious concern with dissecting a certain failure at the heart of the liberal impulse. It is true that this would become increasingly important, but now the times seemed to demand some act of reconciliation, while the play's form, the very neatness of its construction, seemed to close the spaces against ambiguity, to deny that very moral incompletion which later became a principal subject of a writer for whom the social, the economic and the political increasingly seemed no more than symptoms of an imperfect human nature drawn equally to the delusive satisfactions of the self and the genuine transcendence of love.

For all its contemporary relevance, *All My Sons* was essentially a product of the 1930s. Its emphasis on human brotherhood, its thematic innocence and dramatic simplicities have rather more to do with the moral certainties and confident principles of pre-war and war-time America than the anxieties and existential dilemmas of the late 1940s and 1950s − a world of increasing material prosperity but of growing domestic and foreign paranoia. The success of Communism abroad and fear of its subversive policies at home destabilised the political consensus and implicitly initiated a debate about those very American qualities and values which were presumably at stake. And, with the collapse of a consensus created originally by the economic necessities of the 1930s and the political requirements of war, individuals and groups felt themselves increasingly alienated. The assault on New Deal liberals, the barely concealed anti-semitism of many of the attacks on supposed subversives, the distrust of intellectuals (associated in the minds of HUAC investigators, right-wing politicians and a number of industrialists, with a betrayal of American values) created a condition in which a writer like Miller was bound to find himself increasingly at odds with the model of America which that implied. The first evidence for this, apart from his novel, was *Death of a Salesman*, which placed the whole question of American values at the centre of his attention. And subsequently came *The Crucible*, which challenged head-on the corrupting influence of those who would enforce their own model of national purpose and personal morality on others.

All My Sons ran for 328 performances. The New York Drama Critics passed over O'Neill's *The Iceman Cometh* and awarded it their Circle Award. The movie rights were purchased by Hollywood, the film starring Burt Lancaster and Edward G. Robinson. Offered the opportunity to write the screenplay, Miller declined, choosing instead to begin work on a play which he called *Plenty Good Times* which was to be a 'love story of working people in an industrial city'. When this began to lead nowhere he turned to another project which eventually emerged as his most famous play – a classic of the American theatre ← *Death of a Salesman.* As he has explained, after *All My Sons* he

> wanted to do a lyrical piece, because most of the plays I'd written...were not of that kind. So that *Death of a Salesman* was a more romantic, even nostalgic piece, apart from its social analysis, than I'd ever done on the stage, although it is nostalgia with some irony. It's an attempt to remake the West...in the middle of office buildings. But the feeling, the emotions of nostalgia, of simplicity, are very strong in that play.[61]

The origins of Miller's best-known play lie in a brief short story which he wrote at the age of seventeen and which his mother rediscovered at the time of its first production. Called 'In Memoriam', it is based on Miller's own experience with a Jewish salesman when he was working for his father for a few months after graduating from high school. The story is concerned with a single day during which the young narrator accompanies the salesman, carrying some of his samples for him (in this case, coats). The man is old and tired and has to humble himself by asking his young companion for the car fare. The salesman sells nothing and is mistreated by the buyers. The story ends with his reported death and the narrator's sentimental response. In fact, Miller observes in a note scrawled on the manuscript, the man had thrown himself in front of a subway train.

Clearly the experience and the story do contain the seeds of the later play. As the narrator observes of the old man,

> His was a salesmans [*sic*] profession, if one may call such dignified slavery a profession, and he tried to interest himself in his work. But he never became entirely moulded into the pot of that business. His emotions were displayed at the wrong times always and he never quite knew when to laugh. Perhaps if I may say so he never was complete. He had lost something vital. There was an air of quiet solitude, of cryptic wondering about both he and his name.

He is described as looking out of place in clothes which seemed to have been chosen by someone else and with a name which seemed not wholly to belong to him. 'His last name was Schoenzeit, the first I never learned, but it had to be Alfred. He always seemed to need that name.' His growing desperation is apparent in his whole manner. 'I knew that he felt as though his life was ended, that he was merely being pushed by outside forces. And though his body went on as before his soul inside had crumpled and broken beyond repair.'[62]

However, it is instructive to note the differences. Unlike the salesman Willy was to be located firmly in the context of his family life while Miller was concerned to project his illusions and frustrations onto a national level. He became both a vital character and a patent symbol. And unlike the protagonist of the short story Willy was not Jewish. Indeed, Mary McCarthy was later to attack the play as a story about Jewish characters in which their Jewish identities had been suppressed. Miller has denied this, pointing out that when the touring company, quite coincidentally, was found to consist entirely of Irish actors, including Mary McCarthy's brother, it was greeted by two Boston newspapers as an Irish drama.

Death of a Salesman – the story of an ageing salesman, baffled by a lifetime of failure in a society which apparently values only success – has proved one of the most powerful and affecting plays in American theatrical history. The confusions and dreams of a single individual on the verge of psychological collapse were made to embody the collapse of national myths of personal transformation and social possibility. Miller's achievement lay in his ability to distil in the person of Willy Loman the anxieties of a culture which had exchanged an existential world of physical and moral possibility for the determinisms of modern commercial and industrial life – the country for the city. The dislocations of Willy's private life – discontinuities which open up spaces in familial relationships no less than in memory and experience – are equally those of a society chasing the chimera of material success as a substitute for spiritual fulfilment. All the characters in the play feel a need which they can articulate only in terms of the rhetoric of a society which has itself lost touch with its youthful ideals. Aware of a profound sense of insufficiency they seek to remedy or at least to neutralise it in the public world of consumerism and status. For the most part they are blind to the consolation and even transcendence available through personal relationships. The love which they feel for one another is real enough. To some degree it shapes their actions and determines their desperate strategies, which are none the less real for their failure to be realised. But it fails to hold them back from the fate in which they wilfully conspire. And this is the basis of the irony which slowly erodes their confidence and their hopes.

And yet the play's success in virtually all societies in the four decades following its first performance shows that it is something more than a dramatisation of the American dream, its corruptions and coercions. Willy

9.   Mildred Dunnock, Lee J. Cobb, Arthur Kennedy and Cameron Mitchell in *Death of a Salesman*, directed by Elia Kazan, designed by Jo Mielziner, at the Morosco Theatre, New York, 1949.

proved an international figure, as appealing and recognisable to a Chinese audience in 1983 as it had been to an American one in 1949. Willy's dreams are too recognisable, his blindness to the reality and necessity of a proffered love too familiar, for his plight not to demand the attention for which his wife calls. Like most plays it perhaps has its flaws but the human reality of Willy Loman is such that few works have provoked the shock of recognition which has greeted and continues to greet Willy's anguished debate with himself and with the world in which he has never felt at home.

Willy betrays himself and others. Desperate to sustain his self-esteem he has an affair with another woman, buying her attention with a gift of stockings while his wife sits at home mending her own. And when his son, Biff, catches them together he believes that the moment of disillusionment links them together in a more profound way than had the love which he felt but which he could never adequately express. Biff's 'failure' thus becomes a living reproach which fuses love and guilt together in such a way as to threaten the spontaneity and integrity of his responses. Increasingly anxious to justify his life and expiate what he sees as his responsibility for his son's wilful self-annihilation, he plans a suicide which will create the

175

fortune that his life could never accumulate. The proceeds of his insurance policy will thus stand as a justification of his dreams while offering some kind of belated restitution to the wife and son he had betrayed. Desperate for love they are to be offered cash. The irony of Willy's life is that he has accepted other people's estimations of his value. He has the power to construct himself as he has the skill to fashion wood but he cannot bring himself to believe in the worth of a sensibility so constructed and a life forged out of nothing more substantial than an honest perception of the real. The play is Miller's requiem for a country which, no less than Willy, had all the wrong dreams as it is a gesture of absolution towards those who allow themselves to be too fully known. Though in a sense it is a story of defeat, its very lyricism implies the persistence of other possibilities and of a relationship with language, experience and the physical world which goes beyond the terrible banality and threatening pragmatism of a dream tainted at source. Willy is a kind of Everyman. Miller may have taken care to root him in a specific social and historical world but that specificity is raised to another level by the authenticity with which he reproduces the tangled emotions and diffuse longings of those who translate into the language of national myth what has its origin in more fundamental necessities. Willy Loman lives and dies in an attempt to sustain a sense of personal dignity and meaning. Yet if that is a struggle which has its correlative in terms of American notions of self-fulfilment and social status it is equally a battle waged by everyone who tries to locate a sense of significant purpose in a life which seems to consist of little more than a series of contingent events. And if that in turn seems in some final sense a losing game then a certain dignity is perhaps to be derived from the courage with which it is conducted and the poetry which can on occasion be forged out of the prose of experience.

Death of a Salesman is built around the relationship between Willy and his son, Biff. In his notebook Miller wrote himself a memo: '*Discover*... The link between Biff's work views and his anti W feelings... How it happens that W's life is in Biff's hands – aside from Biff succeeding. There is W's guilt to Biff in re: The Woman... There is Biff's disdain for W's character, his false aims, his fictions, and these Biff cannot finally give up or alter.'[63] Here, as elsewhere in Miller's work, the relationship between father and son is a crucial one because it focusses the question of inherited values and assumptions, it dramatises deferred hopes and ideals, it becomes a microcosm of the debate between the generations, of the shift from a world still rooted in a simpler rural past to one in which that past exists simply as myth. It highlights the contrast between youthful aspirations and subsequent compromises and frustrations. It presents the submerged psychological tension which complicates the clear line of social action and personal morality. The family, so much an icon of American mythology, becomes the appropriate prism through which to view that mythology. The son's identity depends on creating a boundary between himself and his father, on perceiving himself outside the axial lines which had defined the father's world.

Biff and Willy's relationship is bedevilled by guilt. Willy feels guilty because he feels responsible for Biff's failure. Having discovered Willy with a woman in a Boston hotel room, he had refused to retake a mathematics examination, thereby abandoning his chance of reaching university and his access to a better career. But Biff equally feels guilty because he recognises a responsibility which he cannot fulfil, the responsibility to redeem Willy's empty life. In a telling speech, included in the notebook but excluded from the published and performed versions, Biff outlines his feelings explicitly.

> Willy – see? – I love you Willy. I've met ten or twelve Willys and you're only one of them. – I don't care what you do. I don't care if you live or die. You think I'm mad at you because of the Woman, don't you. I am, but I'm madder because you bitched up my life, *because* I can't tear you out of my heart, because *I keep trying* to make good, *do something* for you, to *succeed for you*.[64]

If Biff loves Willy he also plainly hates him. Like the other characters he is composed of contradictions. Indeed, in his notes, Miller saw the conflict in Biff between his hatred for Willy and his own desire for success in New York as crucial to an understanding of the play as he did 'the combination of guilt (of failure), hate, and love – all in conflict' that Willy hopes to resolve 'by "accomplishing" a 20,000 dollar death'.[65] Indeed, the ironies of the play flow out of contradiction in *Death of a Salesman*, much as they do in another sense in *Waiting for Godot*. Action is immediately aborted, assertions withdrawn, hopes negated. Thus Willy complains of Biff that 'the trouble is he's lazy', only to reverse himself a few seconds later. 'There's one thing about Biff – he's not lazy.'[66] Happy asserts that money holds no interest for him and that he would be happy with a free life in the West, only to ask immediately, 'The only thing is – what can you make out there?'[67] The response to Biff's 'Let's go' is the same as that proffered in *Waiting for Godot*. They do not move. And so Happy regards himself as an idealist while taking 100-dollar bribes, Biff as rejecting a material life while stealing from his employer. For Willy, constant contradiction is a linguistic reflection of the collapse of rational control, but, more fundamentally, for all the Loman men it is indicative of a basic contradiction between their aspirations and the reality of their lives, between their setting and the essence of their dreams. They are denied peace because the philosophy on which they have built their lives involves competition, a restless pursuit of success, a desire to register a material achievement which they can conceive only in financial terms because they have neither the language nor the capacity to assess its significance in any other way. Hence Biff, who tries to retrace the steps of his father into the past and the West, is unable to accept a simple sense of harmony with his surroundings as adequate to the definition of success which his father has instilled in him, though that harmony is precisely what his father longs to achieve. As Biff explains to his brother,

> This farm I work on, it's spring there now, see? And they've got about fifteen new colts. There's nothing more inspiring or — beautiful than the sight of a mare and a new colt. And it's cool there now, see? Texas is cool now and it's spring. And whenever spring comes to where I am, I suddenly get the feeling, my God, I'm not getting anywhere! What the hell am I doing, playing around with horses, twenty-eight dollars a week! I'm thirty-five years old, I oughta be makin' my fortune. That's when I come running home. And now, I got here, and I don't know what to do with myself.[68]

And so the lyricism, which is a powerful and crucial dimension of the play, defers to materialism, to a pragmatism which disrupts an incipient harmony and opens up a gap between Biff and his setting which, once closed, would not only offer him a simpler relationship between himself and the natural world but also still the conflict between his sensibility and his actions. He is, however, held back not only by the surviving dream of material success, a dream which he might be able to abandon, but also by the guilt which he feels towards Willy. He continues to feel responsible to a man who has warped his life but to whom his fate is ineluctably joined. In Miller's earliest draft the point is even more explicit:

> w: ...What do you want to be?
> b: I want just to settle down and be somebody! Just a guy working in a store, or digging earth, or anything...
> w: Then do it, do it.
> b: You won't let me do it.
> w: Me? When did I control you?
> b: You do control me. I've stood in the most beautiful scenery in the world and cried in misery. I've galloped elegant horses and suddenly wanted to kill myself because I was letting you down. I want you to let me go, you understand. I want you to stop dreaming big dreams about me, and expecting anything great of me. I'm manual labor, Pop; one way or the other I'm a tramp, that's all. Can you make your peace with that...? I ask one thing. I want to be happy.
> w: To enjoy yourself is not ambition. A tramp has that. Ambition is *things*. A man must want *things, things*.[69]

In the final version these perceptions no longer need to surface in language. Biff and Willy remain bewildered for most of the play, unable to analyse the pressures at work on them, unable in particular to confess to the guilt, the love and the hate that connect and divide them. Willy's concern with things, meanwhile, is evident in his fascination with his refrigerator and his car but, most significantly, in his acquiescence in his own reduction to inanimate article to be marketed on appearance and image.

In his first stage direction Miller insists on Willy's 'massive dreams and little cruelties', but in truth the play is concerned with suggesting that the adjectives might be legitimately reversed. And Biff, like his father, is still trying to buy love. As Miller wrote of the scene in the restaurant in which Biff and Happy abandon their father, 'Biff left out of guilt, pity, an inability to offer himself to W.' He recognises that Willy's desire that he should succeed is, in part at least, evidence of his love and, as Miller reminded himself, Biff 'still wants that evidence of W's love. Still does not want to be abandoned by him.' However, it is a love which threatens to destroy him, since it expresses itself in a desire on Willy's part to bequeath his son the thing he values most of all – his dream. The drama of the play emerges from the fact that Biff now gradually recognises the necessity for this abandonment. Indeed he has returned home with an intention not that remote from that of Chris Keller or Gregers Werle. 'He has returned home', Miller insists in his notes, 'resolved to disillusion W forever, to set him upon a new path, and thus release himself from responsibility for W and what he knows is going to happen to him – or half fears will.' There is the same passion for truth which springs from guilt and self-interest as had characterised the protagonists of *All My Sons* and *The Wild Duck*. But now Miller seems to recognise the necessity for this break with illusion. For here, it is finally not truth which kills, as it had been in *All My Sons*; it is a continued commitment to illusion. Biff breaks free; Willy does not. In his own eyes his death accomplishes the success that had evaded him in life, and, more importantly, it finally purges him of the guilt that he has felt for what he takes to be his son's failure. Since Biff had abandoned his potential career after finding Willy with another woman, Willy had thereafter felt responsible for his son's failure. And this is the principal tension of the play. In order for Biff to survive he has to release himself from his father and the values which he promulgates; in order for Willy to survive he has to cling to Biff and the conviction that material success is still possible. Thus guilt becomes the principal mechanism of human relationships. As Miller notes, 'Biff's conflict is that to tell the truth would be to diminish himself in his own eyes. To admit his fault. His confusion, then, is not didactic, or restricted to Willy' elucidation of salvation, but towards a surgical break which, he knows in his heart, W could never accept. His motive, then, is to destroy W, free himself.' In the final version it is not so clear. He is intent to save Willy's life as well as his own. His motivation is less obvious, his concern for his father largely genuine. And yet, of course, in saving Willy he will be freeing himself, so that the self apparently lies behind all actions.

This was certainly to be the conclusion that Miller reached in *After the Fall*, but here that conclusion is masked by a social drama. For the fault does not only lie in the individual; it also patently lies in self-interest systematised into capitalism. Willy Loman is thrown on the scrap heap by his employer after thirty-six years, and, though Miller has objected that in the persons of his next-door neighbours, Charley and Bernard, he has created two characters who retain their humanity, it is Charley who advises Willy that human concerns can play no role in business. When Willy objects that he had actually selected his employer's first name when he was born, Charley replies, 'when you gonna realize that them things don't mean anything? You named him Howard, but you can't sell that. The only thing you got in this world is what you can sell. And the funny thing.is that you're a salesman and you don't know that.'[70] It is Charley who boasts that his son's success had been a consequence of his own lack of concern, announcing that, 'My salvation is that I never took an interest in anything'.[71] And, though his own compassionate treatment of Willy would seem at odds with this, the system of which he is the most admirable representative can clearly accommodate itself to individual acts of charity provided that these don't threaten its structure. The fact is that Charley underwrites the system that destroys Willy. Bernard, a successful lawyer, makes too brief an appearance to know whether his affability towards Willy goes any deeper than appearance. His success is certainly a consequence of hard work but the question of the human value of that success, central to the play's theme, goes largely unexamined. After all, elsewhere in the play Miller seems to be posing the question as to whether material success bears any relationship to basic human needs, but in the person of Bernard he seems to suggest the possibility of having one's cake and eating it.

Biff and Willy feel a profound if unfocussed sense of dissatisfaction with their lives. Beneath the monotony of daily survival is a yearning spirit, a perception of some kind of spiritual need which they can only express through material correlatives or through stuttering encomiums to beauty or belonging. One of the problems of the play, indeed, derives from the fact that their lack of success actually confuses spiritual with financial failure. The more significant question is whether material success would have blunted or indeed even satisfied that need and, though this might have brought Miller perilously close to cliché, his portrait of Bernard – moral, hard-working, successful, attractive – is perhaps in danger of validating the dreams which Willy had had for Biff. Willy had, admittedly, regarded such success as an inevitable product of life in America and had taught Biff to take what he could not earn, and yet in some way the adequacy of that success is not challenged in Bernard's case. Indeed he seems to represent the apparently untroubled serenity which is the reward of honest toil. Indeed, it was not until *After the Fall* that he chose to question the adequacy of that portrait, taking as his protagonist a lawyer whose success, like that of Bernard, is marked by his appealing a case before the Supreme Court. Then he was to query the value of success even when it is the product of effort and application. Uncle Ben might be a portrait of a Horatio Alger figure, stumbling over wealth, but Bernard is in many ways an idealised figure. The danger is that he is not only a model for Willy of what his sons might have become; he also becomes a model for Miller.

The dice are loaded against Willy. In the original notes he was literally to have been a little man. Miller chose to transform that into an obesity apparent in the text but ignored when Lee J. Cobb was cast for the central role: 'I'm fat. I'm very – foolish to look at, Linda...as I was going in to see the buyer I heard him say something about – walrus. And I – I cracked him right across the face.'[72] Even allowing for the exaggeration of self-pity, this offers a clue to his failure as a salesman. His misfortune was that he chose a career in which appearance was everything, at a time and in a country in which appearance was primary. As Biff was to have said in an early draft, and as is apparent but not voiced in precisely these words in the final version, 'The pity of it is, that he was happy only on certain Sundays, with a warm sun on his back, and a trowel in his hand, some good wet cement, and something to build. That's who he really was.'[73] As a salesman he has always to dissemble, to smile, to put up a front. He is an actor who has increasingly lost his audience. His life is a falsehood. But perhaps there is a certain naivety in the assumption, no less Miller's than that of one of his characters, Charley, that the situation is fundamentally different for others, for his contrast of the life of the salesman with that of a man who can 'tell you the law' seems to be justified by the character of Bernard. The real force of the play suggests otherwise. For Miller implies that Willy had the wrong dreams, not simply that his methods of fulfilling those dreams were wrong. With Eugene O'Neill he seems to suggest that Willy's mistake was to imagine that he could gain possession of his soul through gaining possession of the world. In that respect he was paradigmatic. Charley and Bernard are successful and humane, but they, too, live a life whose intimacies seem lacking. Where is the love between them? The problem is that the light is never swung in their direction and thus it is possible to see in them a vindication of the material success which they represent.

Biff's anger at his father derives partly from Willy's weakness and helplessness, partly from his bitterness, but partly also from his love for him, a love which won't cut Biff loose from his own sense of guilt. To absolve his father would be to admit to his own weakness and culpability. As Miller wrote in his notebook,

> Biff's conflict is that to tell the truth would be to diminish himself in his own eyes. To admit to his own fault. The truth is that though W did overbuild B's ego, and then betrayed him, Biff feels guilt in his vengeance on W knowing

that he also is incompetent. Through this confession of his having *used* W's betrayal, W sees his basic love, and is resolved to suicide.[74]

Again the final version of the play deflects this confession into action, intensifying the force by refraining from discharging its energy through words. Thus Biff, having denounced his father and admitted to his own inability to command more than a dollar an hour, breaks down in tears, 'holding on to Willy, who dumbly fumbles for Biff's face'.[75] And love, which Miller has said was in a race for Willy's soul, becomes the very mechanism which pulls Willy towards his death. Thus Linda, whose love for Willy has revealed itself in an encouragement of his dreams combined with a practical capacity which has enabled him to sustain his illusions in the face of reality, proves finally to be deadly. Her actions are motivated by a compassionate concern but there is a clear connection between her refusal to challenge those illusions and his death. Nor is she free of responsibility for the warped values of her children. She is simply too passive a force. Her culpability lies in her acquiescence, which is simultaneously an expression of her love. In her own way she is as obsessive as Willy. She has reduced her own life to a single focus – Willy. And so she tells Biff to leave home and completely ignores Happy's announcement of his impending marriage. Doubtless she recognises it for the self-deceiving gesture which it is, but she seems to feel no obligation towards her sons. Though she is never swept up in Willy's dreams she refuses to judge them. Her almost complete failure to understand Willy, as opposed to sympathise with and admire him, is thus finally a sign of the inadequacy of that love. It is not strong enough to make demands, to wrestle Willy away from his illusions.

Once to have been called 'The Inside of His Head', *Death of a Salesman* is a memory play. The past we see is as it is recalled by Willy Loman, as he tries to track down the moment when things began to go wrong. And not the least of Miller's achievements lay in the originality of the staging through which he created a theatrical correlative for Willy's tortured mind. The action had to move easily between past and present. The realistic texture of Willy's environment was crucial but so were the distortions created by his memory, the fragments of the past through which he sorted with increasing desperation. The result was a blend of realism and expressionism which dramatised personal psychology in the context of social change. In a sense the environment – the trees and open spaces of the real or remembered past, the oppressive constrictions of an urban environment – is a principal character in the play and a primary achievement of Miller, his director Elia Kazan, and his designer Jo Mielziner. Instantaneous shifts of scene were achieved through the ingenuity of Mielziner who, in one scene, contrived a small elevator to enable the actors playing Biff and Happy to move directly from a bedroom in the 'past' to a kitchen in the present. Writing in the introduction to his *Collected Plays* Miller has confessed to standing 'squarely in conventional realism', but has equally insisted that where necessary he has 'tried to expand it with an imposition of various forms in order to speak more directly, even more abruptly and nakedly of what has moved me behind the visible façades of life'.[76] The experiments are perhaps seldom radical since until later in his career he was too concerned with establishing the social context and implications of his plays to stray too far from a form which gives physical expression to the wider world. He is fully aware that the innovative power of realism has long since been blunted but he has always been drawn to find some way to relate the private anguish of his characters to the environment which presses upon them and which in part they themselves shape and deform. His resistance to the total determinism of naturalism, however, is in a sense symbolised by his reaction against the totally realistic set and it would not be unreasonable to see the incomplete walls and insubstantial props as evidence of his belief in change and even transcendence.

In *Death of a Salesman* the production style was necessitated by the need to create a 'continuous present'. In allowing past and present to collapse towards one another Miller was able to trace causalities and hence identify the possibility of change. However, it was also necessitated by his desire to represent the psychological state of a man whose inner and outer life are in a state of collapse, and it was precisely the fact of Willy's disintegrating mind, of his literal inability to sustain temporal or spatial boundaries, which suggests a pathological state apparently inimical to the tragic status claimed for the play and at odds with a reading that would make it simply a critique of American values. Eric Bentley even suggested that in so far as it is a tragedy this potentially destroys the social play as the social play destroys the tragedy, Willy being either the victim of his own flawed character or of society, but scarcely both. Such a stance, however, seems to ignore the degree to which tragedy seldom if ever acknowledges an impermeable membrane between the self and its setting, projecting psychological disruptions outwards into the social world and vice versa. However, talk of tragedy was ill-advised. Willy never really shows any evidence of self-knowledge or awareness of the reality of the situation in which he is involved. His dreams, described by Miller as massive, are in reality petty and sustained by sacrificing not only himself but those around him. In fact it is Biff, and not Willy, who provides the moral, though scarcely the theatrical, focus of the play. He does acquire self-knowledge and develops as a character through understanding the mechanism by which he has suffered and of which he has been a primary agent. As I have argued elsewhere,[77] so long as Biff and Happy are regarded as expressions of Willy's own mind – the one representing a vaguely perceived spiritual need, the other a sexual and material drive – such a split between the dramatic and moral focus is insignificant. Once granted genuine autonomy, however, Biff's moral development merely underlines Willy's inappropriateness as a tragic hero. This is not a weakness in the play, however, but simply an indication that it is not best approached by trying to force it into a category of merely pedagogic significance.

Willy Loman's life is rooted in America's past. His earliest memory was of sitting under a wagon in South Dakota. His father had made and sold flutes as they travelled through what was still, just, frontier territory. And this remains the world of his aspirations, a natural world in which he can create things with his hands, in which his identity is forged by his own actions rather than imposed by a job which sends him wandering through New England cities selling things he has not made himself and which therefore have no organic connection with his sense of himself. But the past had not been wholly idyllic. Familial betrayal had existed even then. His father had abandoned the family for Alaska, presumably to make his fortune there. His brother Ben had left home when Willy was a very small child with the intention of finding their father but, in fact, wandering off into an Africa part real and part myth. Willy was thus born into a world in transition, a world in which the pressure of the material was already unmaking the pastoral myth as the cities were encroaching on the rural nature of nineteenth-century America.

So Willy's house, once situated in open fields, the location dramatised in the original production by a transparent gauze curtain covered with leaves which becomes apparent to the audience when Willy is recalling that pastoral past, is now surrounded by apartment houses. And the lyrical echo of his father's flute recalling 'grass and trees and the horizon'[78] is now superseded for Willy by the sound of cars and the noise of building. In visual terms the contrast is that between the blue light of the sky, a light which falls on the house, and what Miller, in a stage direction, calls the 'angry glow of orange' from the surrounding buildings. Willy has lost the space which he needs for his dreams to assume any reality, for his identity to resist the impress of a public world which recognises only role. Forced at moments to concede his own failure, his own inability to mould himself into an acceptable form, he has to fall back on his sons to fulfil the dreams which he himself has failed to realise. Deprived of love when young, offered only a model of acquisitive self-interest, he blindly passes on the same destructive lesson to his sons, unaware of the substantiality of the love which he is offered and which was a recognition of that very identity which he had sought in the external world. In the words of Linda's sad cliché he is indeed 'a little boat looking for a harbour', but he is living on borrowed time. Suicide is a logical projection of his many failures. Just as his insurance payments are overdue and he is relying on the period of grace, so he is inhabiting a personal period of grace prior to an inevitable termination. In fact, in his notebook, Miller toyed with the idea of using 'A Period of Grace' as a title for the play. Willy, who has built his life on the conviction that 'it's not what you do...It's who you know and the smile on your face',[79] is left without meaning or direction when he can no longer smile, when he no longer commands respect or recognition. He survives but without a sense of himself. His sons are his only chance to succeed by proxy, the only mark he has left on a world resistant to his charm and his human needs alike.

But there is an ambiguity to the play's conclusion. Biff has acquired a crucial insight into himself. Presumably the striving is over, and he can now accept that simple harmony with the natural world which had always foundered on his persistent need for a material success which would appease his father and free him from his guilt. Certainly that is the only real value which has been identified – a lyricism strongly contrasted with the diminished world of urban America. He can return West to the one place where he was really happy. The problem is that on the one hand his flight to the West had originally also been a flight from responsibility, and on the other it is an ahistorical move. Like Huck Finn at the end of Twain's novel, he is lighting out for the territory ahead of the rest. But the rest will inevitably follow, and Miller admitted as much a few years later when, in *The Misfits*, the beautiful mare and its colt are rounded up by trucks and turned into dog food. Biff Loman has become Gay, an ageing cowboy as bewildered by the collapse of his world as Willy Loman had been. And so Biff, who at the end of *Death of a Salesman* has supposedly learned the lesson which Willy could not, seems to be committed to the old mistake of seeking in movement and in space what he should perhaps have sought in relationship. Indeed, when Miller returned to the stage in 1964, after a nine-year silence, it was with a play in which grace is the reward of suffering, and meaning the result of a love constantly renewed in the face of acknowledged imperfection. Like Steinbeck in *The Grapes of Wrath* he ends with a piety whose emotional force is undeniable but whose social utility is more problematic because he can conceive of no mechanism whereby Biff's moment of epiphany can be translated into social action. And that equivocation hangs suspended in the air, inhibiting the sense of completion towards which the play has seemed to move and projecting forward into all our futures a dilemma not so easily resolved by a moment of insight, by a seemingly purposeful action or by an articulate statement of intent. History has moved on and Miller's characters in *Death of a Salesman* seem close kin finally to Scott Fitzgerald's in *The Great Gatsby*. Corrupted by dreams which simultaneously denied them access to the potential redemption of human connectiveness, they had reached out for some substitute for the meaning which continued to elude them. They sought it mostly in an endlessly deferred future, a green light which beckoned them on towards a mythical world of romance and affluence. But at the end of the novel the narrator tries to find it in the past, a rural world where the dream was first born and where the corruption first started. Biff does much the same here, for the world of rural simplicity to which he will now presumably return had provided the context for his grandfather's desertion of Willy. It was also where Uncle Ben began his mythic climb to wealth and power, having abandoned his search for his lost father. The frontier bred the disease. And if it also represents a natural world of pure process then even that is under pressure. Like the land surrounding the Loman home it will presumably itself one day make way for the city and its cruelties. And so Biff, like Nick Carraway, seems poised for a deeply ambiguous and even ironic journey. So that if Willy, like Gatsby, believed in the green light, 'the orgastic future that year by year recedes before us', a future which 'eluded us then, but that's no matter – tomorrow we will run faster, stretch out our arms further...And one fine morning', he and Biff alike are also, perhaps, no more nor less than 'boats against the current, borne back ceaselessly into the past'.[80]

Death of a Salesman ran for 742 performances, won the Antoinette Perry Award, the New York Drama Critics' Circle Award and the Pulitzer Prize. Beyond that, it is undoubtedly one of the finest plays ever written by an American.

A somewhat similar equivocation to that observable at the end of *Death of a Salesman* is evident in another of Miller's unpublished and unproduced works, 'The Hook'. Written, as Miller suggests, 'about 1951', this 'play for the screen' about the Brooklyn waterfront was to have been produced by Columbia Pictures, but the project collapsed when pressure was brought to bear on Miller to make changes in his script. The 'play' deals with the connection between supposed labour leaders and gangsters. In the context of the Korean War this seemed too dangerous an area to enter so that Columbia asked Miller to change the labour leaders into Communists, thereby 'Americanizing' the story. The request was naive, perhaps deliberately so, since in the late 1940s Miller had signed a number of documents defending the rights of Communists, a fact subsequently brought to his attention when he was called before the House Un-American Activities Committee in 1956. Indeed, in the early 1950s he continued to protest the obsession with Communism which he saw as creating a dangerously conformist mood inimical to creativity.

The screenplay itself is melodramatic but it focussed on a dilemma which was not purely abstract for Miller. It raised the question of whether a constituency still remained for liberal ideals or whether the collapse of what he chose to regard as moral integrity was total. By extension the question was whether an audience for his work still existed in an America no longer so receptive to the niceties of the liberal conscience.

The play concerns the efforts of a dockyard worker, Marty, to earn an honest living in a corrupt system. Because the employers and union officials are in league with one another and, in turn, with the invisible uptown gangsters who really determine the nature of affairs, the men are unable to seek redress for their grievances. Neither is there any way to go outside the system since the police are an integral part of it. Hence, when his gang boss is killed trying to maintain the work rate insisted upon by his avaricious employer, Marty decides to leave the waterfront.

First, he tries to work in a factory but abandons it after two hours, unable to tolerate the suffocating conditions. Then, somewhat frightened and a little ashamed, he becomes a bookie and as such feeds off the despair of his friends. But the law begins to close in on him and, partly drawn back to the camaraderie of the docks and partly disgusted by the fact that union officials have begun to sell union cards, he rejoins and challenges the attempt to swindle the men out of part of their wages. When he calls a strike he finds the other men are afraid to support him. But at a meeting at which he is supposed to lose his union card more than 300 men turn up to confront the union officials and their gangster friends. He is nonetheless suspended for three months and as a result is forced to steal to survive. When he sees his son steal as well, however, he is provoked to challenge the leadership and runs for president of his local branch.

Despite attacks by racketeers, he survives the campaign and even persuades a local gangster, who, in true Miller fashion, insists that 'I wan' my good name', to apologise for assaulting one of his supporters. When the election is held the incumbent president unnecessarily stuffs the ballot box — unnecessarily, because when the box is opened it is discovered that even Marty's own supporters have voted for the corrupt leader, believing that if Marty were to be elected the uptown gangsters and union officials would simply cut off the whole branch and deprive them of work. They do insist that Marty be made a union delegate, but it is clear that he will simply be absorbed by the system which he has failed to beat. Yet he is overcome with gratitude and pride, believing the men to have shown genuine solidarity. The film closes on a shot of the gangsters watching the retreating men. As one of Marty's supporters suggests, only a complete change of the whole system will secure them justice.

Once again Miller offers no mechanism for this change. The need for human solidarity is propounded. He creates a genuinely idealistic figure, not flawed this time by a destructive guilt and self-interest, but he can perceive no process whereby that idealism can operate. The play implies the need for a total revolution, for a social transformation, but his central figure has no ideological perception and no real understanding of the largely invisible forces which he challenges. His articulateness will simply be absorbed by the system, a fear which Miller the playwright must have felt, more especially as the persecutions of the 1950s moved to some kind of personal climax.

Challenged by the system, threatened to his core, Marty insists that 'I'm gonna live like a man. I'm gonna fight for my rights. They knock me down, I'm gonna take two down with me. I'm gonna be an example, so the men shall know there's a guy around here he ain't scared to open his mouth.'[81] Addressing the local branch, he insists that 'I was born in Italy! I lived in Fascism! This is Fascism! We gotta bring America down on the waterfront.'[82] The rhetoric is there and clearly has the force of Miller's commitment behind it. The ambiguous ending, then, indicates Miller's bafflement. Marty's sense of achievement seems vindicated by the less than believable statement of one of the gangsters that democracy is on the rise, but there is no evidence for this except in the sentimental logic of his characters. However, the events of the play resist this sentimentality and come close to turning it into irony. Without power, truth becomes ineffectual.

Nor was it a subject that Miller could leave alone. If Ibsen had been a strong influence on *All My Sons*, he now chose to adapt *An Enemy of the People*, which went right to the heart of the question of an individual's will and ability to challenge the assumptions of his own society. Indeed, one of the play's characters asks precisely the question raised in 'The Hook', 'without power, what good is the truth?'[83] Again he dramatises the plight of a man who must decide whether his responsibility is owed first to his family or to the wider world; whether the truth, indeed, is an absolute necessity.

The play is not one of Ibsen's subtler works. It rests uneasily on characters allowed no inner tensions; it proposes a society not merely hypocritical and time-serving but willing to expose its hypocrisies and to articulate its self-interest. The naivety of its central character, Dr Stockmann, is matched by the simple cynicism of the supposedly liberal–radical reformers and the entrenched conservatives alike. The battle between self-interest and public good, between painful truths and public lies, is waged unambiguously. All motives are allowed to bubble to the surface. Miller's version is more muted. In Ibsen's play his attacks on the plebeian spirit go far beyond even his own convictions as his rhetoric outstrips his purpose. In Miller's play he is more controlled, more ready with plausible arguments and as a consequence he is more unequivocally the moral focus of the play. Not surprisingly the references to America in the original play are expanded in such a way as to indicate its immediate relevance to the American situation, while a number of arguments in favour of the suppression of free speech and the individual conscience are added. Once again there is a character who insists, 'I want my good name', at the very moment when he is betraying his integrity.

For Miller the play had a clear and immediate political relevance. As he said in an introduction to the play, 'its central theme is, in my opinion, the central theme of our social life today. Simply it is the question of whether the democratic vision of the truth ought to be a source of guilt at a time when the mass of men condemn it as a dangerous and devilish lie.'[84] And the use of the word 'devilish' is interesting in view of the fact that he later claimed to have begun writing *The Crucible* as early as 1948. For obvious reasons Miller removed from the play the note of intellectual hubris, the celebrations of the will and its urge to power and dominance which he feared would be mistakenly perceived as fascistic, but curiously, by way of justification, he cited a crucial line in Ibsen's play which he himself removed from his own version: 'There is no established truth that can remain true for more than seventeen, eighteen, or at most twenty years.'[85] Its removal is instructive for it suggests a relativism to which Miller was instinctively opposed.

In many ways it was especially appropriate that Miller should choose to adapt Ibsen's *An Enemy of the People*. It was a natural transition between *All My Sons* and *The Crucible*. In the former he was propounding the necessity of acknowledging one's responsibility to the public world, the fact that self and family are not the limits of responsibility; in the latter he asserts the need to resist the demands of society when these assault the integrity of the self, when, in the name of social unity and a conformity of views, authority seeks to purge itself of those whose independence constitutes a threat to publicly defined notions of order.

As he said of Ibsen's play, it has an enduring theme 'because there never was, nor will there ever be an organized society able to countenance calmly the individual who insists that he is right while the vast majority is absolutely wrong'.[86] So that, as he saw friends and colleagues harassed by the House Un-American Activities Committee, and as he detected a national mood which had little tolerance either for former radicals or his own brand of liberal humanism, *An Enemy of the People* seemed extraordinarily contemporary in its concerns. Certainly he himself felt at odds with his own society and was increasingly alarmed at the witch-hunt which gathered pace with the rise of the junior senator from Wisconsin, Joseph McCarthy, whose career, like those of certain Puritan divines three centuries or so before, was based on his supposed skills in detecting demonic threats to the state.

And there was, precisely, a religious air to the political persecutions of the late 1940s and early 1950s. Thus, Miller was struck by the fact that:

> the political, objective, knowledgeable campaign of the far Right was capable of creating not only a terror, but a new subjective reality, a veritable mystique, which was gradually assuming even a holy resonance...There was a new religiosity in the air...I saw forming a kind of interior mechanism of confession and forgiveness of sins which until now had not been rightly categorized as sins. New sins were being created monthly. It was very odd how quickly these were accepted into the new orthodoxy, quite as though they had been there since the beginning of time. Above all, above all horrors,

I saw accepted the notion that conscience was no longer a private matter but one of state administration. I saw men handing conscience to other men and thanking other men for the opportunities of doing so.[87]

The Salem witch trials, which he had previously intended turning into a play, but which had baffled him because he could find no key to what he called their 'inexplicable darkness', suddenly came into clearer focus. He visited Salem and studied such records as are available.

The House Un-American Activities Committee, first established in 1938 (in part to investigate the activities of the German–American Bund), was revived after the war and moved into prominence following the uncovering of a number of Soviet spies, real and imaginary. When the Soviet Union exploded its first atomic bomb it was assumed that only treachery could account for its success. The loss of China to the Communists in 1948 fed a growing sense of hysteria. Increasingly people were called before the Committee and asked to admit to a radical past. The favourite targets were those figures whose public visibility guaranteed maximum publicity to those politicians who had begun to realise the mileage to be derived from a vigorous defence of an ill-defined but potent Americanism – that is, they tended to be State Department officials and members of the entertainment profession. In other words, the persecution came very close to home as far as Miller was concerned.

In May 1952, while Miller was still working on the first draft of The Crucible, Clifford Odets was summoned by the Committee. He had been a major influence on Miller's work; now he confessed to having been a Communist in the 1930s and identified friends from the Group Theatre as party members. The best-known radical playwright of the pre-war era now recanted, though, like many others, he tried to distinguish between party dogma and liberal principle. But the persecution and the betrayal came still closer to Miller. Among those named by Odets was a man who had already been called before the Committee – Elia Kazan, the director of Death of a Salesman. Kazan's co-operation was well-nigh complete. He accepted the demonic significance that the Committee ascribed to Communism and asserted his belief that 'any American who is in possession of...the facts about Communism...has the obligation to make them known'.[88] He, too, named names, as did Lee J. Cobb, who had created the part of Willy Loman, when he, too, was summoned by the Committee in June 1953.

The Crucible is set at a time when society was showing signs of dislocating. Back in England a revolution had taken place which for a time had displaced the king, the elect of God. In America the ordered Puritan community was ringed around by an unsubjugated natural world concealing Indians who fitted all too neatly into the iconography of the Church. Threatened from without, they felt obliged to insist on the absolute nature of religious authority. And so persecution was born out of fear, out of a desire to identify and eliminate subversive forces on the assumption that since any failure of will and purpose could not be a product of their own ideological stance it must necessarily be evidence of the demonic. The parallel between the situation in 1690s Salem and 1950s America was lost on no one and Miller chose to underscore it, though with some tact, in the description of the historical circumstances which appears at the beginning of the first act. For, having observed of the Puritans that 'They believed that they held in their steady hands the candle that would light the world', he adds that 'We have inherited this belief, and it has helped and hurt us'.[89] And in identifying the elements of repressed guilt, simple vindictiveness and opportunism involved in the witch-hunt he proposes that 'one can only pity them all, just as we shall be pitied some day'. At the time of writing, he observed,

> only England has held back before the temptation of contemporary diabolism. In the countries of the Communist ideology, all resistance of any import is linked to the totally malign capitalist succubi, and in America any man who is not reactionary in his views is open to the charge of alliance with the Red hell. Political opposition, thereby, is given an inhuman overlay which then justifies the abrogation of all normally applied customs of civilized intercourse. A political policy is equated with moral right, and opposition to it with diabolical malevolence.[90]

The Crucible was a play whose ironies intensified as Miller found himself hauled before the House Un-American Activities Committee and asked to name names.

> MR ARENS: Tell us, if you please, sir, about those meetings with the Communist party writers which you said you attended in New York City... Can you tell us who was there when you walked into the room?
>
> MR MILLER: Mr. Chairman, I understand the philosophy behind this question and I want you to understand mine. When I say this, I want you to understand that I am not protecting the Communists or the Communist Party. I am trying to, and I will, protect my sense of myself. I could not use the name of another person and bring trouble on him... I take the responsibility for everything I have ever done, but I cannot take responsibility for another human being.[91]

It was an exchange that must have sounded remarkably familiar to Miller. Indeed it was a virtual paraphrase of that between Proctor and Deputy-Governor Danforth.

> PROCTOR: I speak my own sins; I cannot judge another. I have no tongue for it... You will not use me! I am not Sarah Good or Tituba,

> I am John Proctor!...I have three children – how may I teach
> them to walk like men in the world, and I sold my friends...Tell
> them I confessed myself; say Proctor broke his knees and wept
> like a woman; say what you will but my name cannot –
>
> DANFORTH: [*with suspicion*] It is the same, is it not? If I report it or you sign
> it?
>
> PROCTOR: [*he knows it is insane*] No, it is not the same! What others say and
> what I sign to is not the same!...Because it is my name! Because
> I cannot have another in my life![92]

The irony is that the second quotation predates the first by three years. Called before the House Un-American Activities Committee in June 1956 Miller found himself in the position of his own protagonist and, like Proctor's, his performance was by no means wholly unambiguous but the sticking point was the same. For a writer obsessed with the need for the individual to lay claim to a moral identity, to be able to invest his name with meaning and proclaim it with pride, the very formulation of the request to 'name names' was likely to prove unacceptable. For a writer whose concern had been with elaborating the individual's responsibility to other individuals and for the shape and direction of his society, demands that he should betray that responsibility were likely to prove critical. For Miller, as earlier for Proctor, it was a test that he did not fail. He was cited for contempt and received a thirty-day suspended sentence and a $500 fine. Though exonerated by the courts in 1958 he, like Proctor, had discovered by then that confession and repentance were not enough to guarantee the good grace of the persecutor; the real price required was betrayal. And this became a basic theme of his work for more than a decade as, in a broader sense, it had been from the beginning of his career. Indeed his break with Elia Kazan, who had directed two of his plays, was in large part occasioned by Kazan's decision to name names – a decision which is in part justified by Kazan and his fellow informer, Budd Schulberg, in their 1954 film *On the Waterfront* (though Kazan insists that it was 'aimed at something more universal'), and openly denounced by Miller in *After the Fall*.

The critic Eric Bentley attacked the implied analogy between the Salem of 1692 and the America of the 1950s on the grounds that the witches were a figment of the collective imagination while the Communists were real. Miller himself later observed that

> *The Crucible* appeared to some as a misreading of the problem, at best a 'naivete', or at worst a specious and even sinister attempt to whitewash the guilt of the Communists with the noble heroism of those in 1692 who had rather be hung than confess to non-existent crimes...The truth is...the playwriting part of me was drawn to what I felt was a tragic process underlying the political manifestation...When irrational terror takes to itself

the fiat of moral goodness somebody has to die. I thought that in terms of this process the witch-hunts had something to say to the anti-Communist hysteria. No man lives who has not got a panic button and when it is pressed by the clean white hand of moral duty, a certain murderous train is set in motion.[93]

Earlier, in an article in *The New York Times* in 1958, Miller had said,

It is not any more an attempt to cure witch hunts than *Salesman* is a plea for the improvement of conditions for travelling men, *All My Sons* a plea for better inspection of airplane parts.... *The Crucible* is, internally, *Salesman's* blood brother. It is examining... the conflict between a man's raw deeds and his conception of himself; the question of whether conscience is in fact an organic part of the human being, and what happens when it is handed over not merely to the state or the mores of the time but to one's friend or wife.[94]

When Jean-Paul Sartre adapted *The Crucible* for the cinema, as *Les Sorcières*, he concluded his script with a spontaneous rising of the common people of Salem against a corrupt authority. For Miller its force lay elsewhere. As he said of Sartre's version,

I thought it was Marxist in the worst sense. I thought that anybody who had the least sensitivity to history would be embarrassed by it... But he was also imposing a simplistic class analysis on the play. In other words he showed the witch hunt as being devised by the upper class against the lower class. Well, for God's sake probably 30% of the victims were people of property... Rebecca Nurse was one of the biggest landholders in the whole area.[95]

Miller was not concerned with the conflict between classes but with a public challenge to the priviate conscience, though it must be admitted that in an early draft of the play he makes it plain that when the accusations extend to the wife of the Reverend Hale, and, more importantly, Lady Phipps, the Governor's wife, Danforth intervened, 'turned to the girls and said, "You are mistaken, children. Now let me hear nothing more of Lady Phipps nor Mister Hales' good wife. The Devil cannot have reached so high."'[96] And there was perhaps also another more profound concern. Behind the anti-Communist fervour of the mid 1950s there were other ghosts, other evidences of the demonic, which perhaps played their part in prompting a play which is in effect an enquiry into the plight of the individual threatened by the perverse logic of the irrational and confronted with what Miller could call by no other name but evil. For, though it was to be a decade before Miller chose to tackle head-on the issues raised by the war, the events in Salem – the irrational persecution of a group denied all possibility of self-defence, and the deliberate creation of scapegoats – were not without their relevance to the war-time persecution of the Jews. The failure to challenge manifest evil and the moral assurance which is a product of being untainted by suspicion were equally a product of the organised hysteria of Nazi persecution.

Then, too, careers were built on an alleged expertise in identifying the demonic. The apparatus of persecution, the demands for betrayal, the challenge to one's identity and moral being, were in essence the same.

The Crucible concerns a supposed outbreak of witchcraft in Salem in 1692. A group of girls play at summoning up devils with Tituba, a black servant. One of their number, the daughter of the Reverend Parris, suffers what is apparently a catatonic reaction. When the Reverend Hale is summoned to test for witchcraft, Tituba is encouraged to confess and to implicate others in order to save herself. In the ensuing hysteria the girls find that their best defence lies in accusation. This finally reaches out to include the saintly but emotionally cold Elizabeth Proctor, named by her husband's former mistress, Abigail Williams. Proctor himself, guilty, frustrated, constitutionally independent, is forced to go into court and try to expose the girls' conspiracy by revealing his adultery. His attempt to discredit Abigail flounders, however, when she accuses him of being an agent of the devil and Elizabeth is caught out in a lie. Condemned to death, he is offered his life if he will confess and thus validate the court. That he is able to resist this is the evidence and source of his dignity. It is also presented as a social act, an acknowledgement of the obligation which he has to others.

Miller was clearly interested in the question of authority and the need to define oneself in terms of opposition to that authority, but equally clearly, despite his early espousal of Marxism, he did not look for a solution so much in communal action as in the assumption of a total responsibility for one's actions, in the restoration of the significance of the individual. For, to him, the power of authority ultimately derives from the individual's willing acquiescence in the idea of his own insignificance. He had come to feel that the 'steady and methodical inculcation into humanity of the idea of man's worthlessness − until redeemed'[97] was the basis of all power, religious and political. It was a power which could only be broken by reasserting that significance. Thus Proctor announces, 'I like not the smell of this "authority"',[98] believing by that that it is possible for the individual to abstract himself from the world in which that authority has power. The process of the play, however, proves otherwise; it constitutes a moral education in the nature of power, the central significance of guilt, and, almost paradoxically, the possibility of rational analysis. Even confronted with an outbreak of irrational behaviour, Miller seeks, not wholly successfully, to impose a rational explanation. For to concede a place to the truly arbitrary and to acknowledge the authority of mystery and unmotivated action is to conceive of a world in which no moral demand can be made and no responsibility assigned. Hence, Abigail informs against Elizabeth Proctor out of jealousy, as all the girls accuse others in order to secure their own freedom. The other accusers are motivated by guilt. One of the principal changes that

Miller made in dramatising the events was to raise the age of the children, thereby injecting a sexual motivation into their actions and providing an explanation for Proctor's equivocation. The sexual component, which Miller probably correctly identifies as a vital element in Puritan repressions and the consequent explosions of Dionysian rituals, becomes the fulcrum of the play. It is a dramatic strategy which is not without its distracting force, but Miller clearly sees in sexual betrayal an image of the egotism which is at the root of human cruelties and the collapse of communal values (in contrast to the element of sacrifice and selflessness evident in genuine love).

And yet he does posit the existence of an evil which exists almost in pure form. For this he offers no explanation. For all his closeness to McCarthyism and his full awareness of the atrocities of the holocaust there persisted an area of experience which resisted analysis. Thus the judges remain virtually unexamined, while the minor, though crucial figures (Parris and Hale) are presented as being motivated by considerations of career and self-importance. The principal figures, in terms of authority, Deputy-Governor Danforth and Judge Hathorne, are presented only in externals. So, though the injection of the sexual component provides a clear line of motivation for the accusers and the source of a vital sense of guilt, it does little to penetrate the evil which really fascinated him. That evil becomes simply an implacable force against which the individual defines himself. It is the bland face of administrative efficiency for which questions of moral truth are irrelevant. Indeed, later he was to regret not making Danforth more completely committed to evil:

> I was wrong in mitigating the evil of this man and the judges he represents. Instead, I would perfect his evil to its utmost and make an open issue, a thematic consideration of it in the play. I believe now, as I did not conceive then, that there are people dedicated to evil in the world; that without their perverse example we should not know the good. Evil is not a mistake but a fact in itself...a dedication to evil, not mistaking it for good but knowing it as evil and loving it as evil, is possible in human beings who appear agreeable and normal. I think now that one of the hidden weaknesses of our whole approach to dramatic psychology is our inability to face this fact.[99]

It was, perhaps, a conviction having rather more to do with the painful truths of the holocaust than the realities of Puritan New England, though Miller has insisted that he found no mitigation from the unredeemed and absolute 'dedication to evil' displayed by the judges. But Miller had seen much the same force operating in the Greek theatre. Thus *Oedipus* was concerned with 'the irony of authority seeking evil outside of itself when evil is right in it, in the authority'. The problem, as he explained, was that 'I couldn't find a space, so to speak, around that evil, a space on which to stand'.[100] The fact is that Miller seems content to register the opacity of that force. Thus

Danforth is portrayed as naive, while Hathorne's intransigent blood-lust provides only a constant background rhythm to the drama which is played out in his court. There is little in the play that suggests where the blood-lust derives from. He does not propose a model of human nature which offers to explain their central role, as that of the other characters is rationalised by material or sexual jealousies and compounded by a desire to sustain one's own innocence by accusing others. Though there clearly comes a time when they must realise their own complicity in the events, and hence become the more implacable in order to conceal their sense of guilt, Miller never really explains the force which makes them such rigorous persecutors in the first place and this, I suspect, is not unconnected with the difficulty he has in establishing the precise nature of the religious fervour of late seventeenth-century New England. John Proctor's sensibility is too close to our own not to make his judgements seem the touchstone by which to convict the prosecutors of judicious tyranny.

The parallel with McCarthy is plainly, in certain crucial respects, misleading, for the judges are not best understood as cynical manipulators of public fears, deliberate falsifiers of information, totally careless of people's fate in the way that McCarthy undoubtedly was. They were captured by a myth to which most of the community would have subscribed. Their fault lay in their continued prosecution of a case which was slowly revealed to be false, in their permitting their early honest error to be extended and compounded. For a modern audience the fraud is liable to seem patent. Even Joseph Wood Krutch objected that 'whereas witchcraft was pure delusion, subversion is a reality',[101] an observation which is historically misleading but an accurate reflection of a central problem which confronts Miller. For the people of Salem, believers in witches and subscribers to the myth which made the girls' accusations so plausible, it was only as the circle widened that disbelief strengthened into something close to revolt. McCarthy could point to real traitors as well as to those whose own disaffection with their radical past made them vulnerable to accusation and susceptible to a potentially disabling guilt. But Tituba makes a poor Klaus Fuchs. On the other hand, Miller does succeed in finding a correlative for that moral and political guilt which made so many of those called before the House Un-American Activities Committee not merely vulnerable but almost complicit in their own destruction. Here that guilt takes sexual form but its crucial component is a similar sense of self-betrayal which leads Proctor, no less than many of those, in the 1950s, accused of offences for which in their heads they condemned themselves, to seek absolution either through confession or action. Proctor's room for manœuvre, however, is reduced not merely by the reality of public hysteria but by the fact of his own past errors.

For the physical constrictions of *Death of a Salesman*, *The Crucible* substitutes a sense of moral constriction. As Miller wrote in his notebook,

'There must be a counter-party. Proctor, and others – who feel hemmed-in, surrounded.'[102] The space which has to be created is one in which identity can coalesce, and the individual assert the possibility of action and moral authority. For Miller, the play was not to be simply a social drama. He was still reaching for the tragic. As he wrote in his notebook, 'A difficulty – This hanging must be "tragic" – i.e. must [be] result of an opportunity not grasped when it should have been – due to flaw.'[103] Plainly, where Sartre was looking for an image of social revolt, Miller was interested primarily in the creation of bourgeois tragedy, in the battle of an individual not only, or even primarily, with a world external to the self but with a personal fallibility and, beyond that, a deeply flawed human nature.

He knew early on that guilt was once again a central mechanism but was unsure at first as to how it would operate, hence his note: 'Proctor – guilt stays his hand. Against what action?'[104] The play was to be about Proctor. In another note, underlined for emphasis, he wrote *It has got to be basically Proctor's story*',[105] and guilt was to be a central mechanism behind his actions, as, on a broader scale, it was to be behind the whole fanatical witch-hunt. 'The important thing', he wrote in his notebook, was 'the process by which a man, feeling guilt for A, sees himself as guilty of B, and thus belies himself, – accommodates his credo to believe in what he knows is not true.'[106] The process which interests him is clearly the one of self-betrayal. Hence he sketches out a plan whereby Proctor would have retreated from his early opposition to the Reverend Parris and the witch-hunters, seeking safety in sustaining his opposition on a private rather than a public basis. Hence, while things 'are still theoretical, it is a question of "principle", of "honor" etc, – public good'. Proctor is 'a *leader* among them, however unwilling'. But, as he then sketched it out, it was later to become clear 'that he is backtracking in re: outspoken action'.[107] The parallel between this description of Proctor and Miller's own subsequent path in the mid 1950s is uncanny and suggests that the play came out of a profound sense of self-doubt.

Writing later in the introduction to the *Collected Plays*, Miller saw the distinction between his concern with guilt in *The Crucible* and that in his earlier work as lying in his new sense that guilt creates the conditions for self-betrayal, that it is the cause of a critical vulnerability. There was an attempt, he explained 'to move beyond the discovery and unveiling of the hero's guilt, a guilt that kills the personality'.

> I had grown increasingly conscious of this theme in my past work, and aware too that it was no longer enough for me to build a play, as it were, upon the revelation of guilt, and to rely solely upon a fate which exacts payment from the culpable man. Now guilt appeared to me no longer the bedrock beneath which the probe could not penetrate. I saw it now as a betrayer, as possibly the most real of our illusions, but nevertheless a quality of mind capable of being overthrown.[108]

The trouble with this, of course, is that it is not Joe Keller's guilt which betrays him but his illegal and immoral act. And his guilt is no illusion. It has the power and even the moral authority to take his life. In John Proctor's case the guilt seems more illusory because it is tangential to the principal action. His adultery is an offence against social mores (backed here of course by religious sanction), but the moral affront at the centre of the play is against natural justice. It is not guilt that takes Proctor into the courtroom but it is arguably a combination of guilt and moral probity that enables him to go to his death. And in so far as guilt is an acknowledgement of a social responsibility it is not illusory. There are in fact two different forms of guilt in the play – one destructive, one creative. It is not wholly a betrayer. But either way it remains central.

The Crucible is built on a rhythm of assertion and denial, statement and retraction. Hence, Mary Warren is first an accuser, then confesses the truth and then retracts her confession. The Reverend Hale is at first a fierce prosecutor and then a desperate defender. Elizabeth Proctor at first privately insists on her husband's moral culpability and then publicly asserts his probity; Giles first accuses his wife and then retracts; Proctor first signs the confession and then tears it up. Human nature is apparently equivocal by definition. Only evil remains consistent. That equivocation, that tension between the ideal and the practical, an obsessive self-concern and a genuine selflessness, is itself definitional. It is presented as the source of guilt and moral action alike. It is also the root of an informing irony in human affairs. Hence, Miller noted that 'Could be a wonderful scene if [Proctor] approaches Hale, thinking H a hunter, and speaks to him as though he is trying to accommodate himself to the trend. Then H reveals he believes the convicted better people than the confessors, and P changes.'[109] The irony survives into the text, though in a more subtle form. In his notes he had supposed the possibility of pushing that irony more strongly, having Proctor convince Hale that there was indeed some cause for the witch-hunt and having Hale despise Proctor. But it would not have been a credible reversal. In the final version of the play guilt works on both men.

The final version of The Crucible indeed represents a considerable advance on the 'Untitled Play' that he had completed in September 1952. In that the character of Abigail Williams had been announced early in a stage direction: 'There is an endless capacity to dissemble in her; the Devil made her soul, God her face.' She stretches 'the cloth of her gown against her body',[110] flourishes a charm and intones a demonic chant designed to lure Proctor to her. Her adulterous relationship with him is known to the other girls, thus potentially reducing the impact of Proctor's own courtroom confession, a dramatic high point which is actually missing from this early version. The sexual corruption of the girls, indeed, is taken to considerable lengths, Mercy Lewis being presented as a sexual adventurer, while Mary Warren, Proctor's servant, also lusts after her employer. And yet in a scene not included in the final play, in which Proctor and Abigail meet alone in the wood, another and somewhat contradictory version of Abigail is offered – a version at odds with Miller's own initial description of her but fascinating in its portrait of an individual genuinely self-deceived, a person who would condemn the world in order to assert her own innocence.

> Oh, John, I have grown deep as a well; there are dark wisdoms in my soul I cannot even speak. But this I can tell you: all my life I felt a cramping cloud around my head; the world and I were hidden from each other – I was so ignorant! – When the women called me loose because the wind lifted my skirts up; shook a thousand fingers at me when a boy would call beneath my window – I would believe them and think myself an evil girl, and weep...And then...the fire came...I think of it always as a red, red fire, where we burned together, you and I. And out of it I walked, all new, and my ignorance was burned away. And I saw the truth as a December tree; those good and Godly women all hypocrites! Walking like saints to church, running to feed the sick and sit with the dying, and all the while pussed with envy for me; hateful they are and murderous, and oh so full of lies! And I cried out the truth, and God made men listen, and I will scrub the world clear for Him...Oh, John, I will make you such a wife when the world is white again![111]

It is a complexity which is sacrificed to consistency in the final version in which Abigail becomes little more than a calculating and cruel figure. Touching on a theme that has fascinated Miller from *All My Sons* through to *After the Fall*, this is one of the few deletions that diminishes the work. The principal change lies in the addition of the scene in which Proctor accuses Abigail before the court and is inadvertently betrayed by his wife. The only reference to the event in the earlier draft lies in Rebecca Nurse's observation that he had confessed only to retract his confession immediately. Such a reference to off-stage action constituted an ineffective device while the confession and retraction were anyway repeated in the play's final scene. The published version, which focusses the drama on the courtroom itself, is plainly superior in that it represents a crucial moment for all the characters. Abigail's credibility is threatened as is that of the whole witch-hunt. Elizabeth is faced with the choice of sustaining her principles or, as she thinks, supporting her husband. Proctor is forced to expose his private self in a public arena. It is a pivotal scene, and one which testifies to Miller's ability to wed moral enquiry to dramatic effect.

The Crucible was not particularly well received. It did win the Antoinette Perry and Donaldson awards and ran for a quite respectable 197 performances, but critics were divided and the public not altogether responsive to the play's overt concern with morality. But this was precisely what had attracted Miller to the seventeenth century. In contrast to a pragmatic society in which the open discussion of moral principle was shunned, the delight of Salem was that it was

> 'morally' vocal. People then avowed principles, sought to live by them and die by them. Issues of faith, conduct, society, pervaded their private lives in a conscious way. They needed but to disapprove to act. I was drawn to this subject because the historical moment seemed to give me the poetic right to create people of higher self-awareness than the contemporary scene affords.[112]

It is, however, that 'poetic right' which tempts him towards a rhetoric which brings the play at moments close to melodrama. Not the least of his accomplishments, therefore, is to retain control of the inflated language which he permits to his characters and to turn moral debate into powerful drama. When Miller applied for a passport in order to attend the Belgian première of the play it was refused. Tennessee Williams immediately wrote to the State Department:

> Dear Sirs:
> I feel obliged to tell you how shocked I am by the news that Arthur Miller, a fellow playwright, has been refused a passport to attend the opening of a play of his in Brussels. I know only the circumstances of the case that have been reported in the papers, but since I have been spending summers abroad since 1948, I am in a position to tell you that Mr. Miller and his work occupy the very highest criticism and popular position in the esteem of Western Europe, and this action can only serve to implement the Communist propaganda, which holds that our country is persecuting its finest artists and renouncing the principles of freedom on which our ancestors founded it.
> I would like to add that there is nothing in Arthur Miller's work, or my personal acquaintance with him, that suggests to me the possibility that he is helpful or sympathetic to the Communist or any other subversive cause. I have seen all his theatrical works. Not one of them contains anything but the most profound human sympathy and nobility of spirit that the American theatre has shown in our time and perhaps in any time before. He is one man that I could never suspect of telling a lie, and he has categorically stated that he has *not* supported Communism or been a Communist.
> I don't think you have properly estimated the enormous injury that an action of this kind can do our country, even in the minds of those who are still prejudiced in our favor in Western Europe.
> Yours respectfully,[113]

It was a brave gesture from a writer whose own past convictions and personal predilections made him vulnerable to attack in turn but the very wording of the letter makes plain precisely that erosion of fundamental freedom which Miller had attacked in his play. The issue becomes not the right of the Committee to conduct its persecutions but the honesty or otherwise of Miller.

This was precisely the irony of Proctor's position. Finally, dignity lies less in honest denial than total resistance, the more especially when the accusers seek to turn their victim from principal into agent. Neither Proctor nor his creator turned informer, but as a playwright Miller became increasingly fascinated with the impulse to inform, an impulse to which many of those he most admired eventually succumbed.

In the middle of Miller's notebook on *Death of a Salesman* he states his intention of writing 'the Italian play', noting the case of 'X., who ratted on the two immigrants'. He then reminded himself that 'The secret of the Greek drama is the vendetta, the family ties incomprehensible to Englishmen and Americans. But not to Jews. Much that has been interpreted in lofty terms, fate, religion, etc., is only blood and the tribal survival within the family. Red Hook is full of Greek tragedies.'[114]

A View from the Bridge, set in Red Hook, is his attempt at such a tragedy as well as his portrait of the informer, motivated, he suggests, by a compound of jealousy and guilt. Eddie Carbone, an Italian-American longshoreman, lives with his wife and niece, Catherine. His protective attitude towards that niece is not entirely free of a sexual desire which he can never acknowledge. But the situation is exacerbated by the arrival of two illegal immigrants, Marco and Rodolpho. When the latter forms a relationship with Catherine, Carbone does his best to destroy it, threatened in a way which he can barely understand. When everything else fails he calls the immigration department and turns informer. Challenged by Marco, he fights to uphold his name but is killed. While true to the original incident, which Miller had been told by a longshoreman, it was, however, consciously and ironically, false to the America of the mid 1950s, for it was not the informer but the man who refused to inform who found himself the social pariah. Indeed, in some senses *A View from the Bridge* offered a direct reversal of the situation described in *An Enemy of the People*. Stockmann finds himself reviled because he places truth and social well-being before self; Eddie Carbone is despised because he betrays that social bond out of a solipsistic desire to affirm his selfhood, to dominate his circumstances. Carbone is afraid of time and process. Refusing to recognise an aberrant impulse in himself he projects it onto others. The mechanism is thus the same as that which operates in *The Crucible*. The accuser denounces in others the sin which he suspects in himself.

Despite its power, the play lacks the weight of tragedy while Miller's concern with the betrayer threatens to lead to a disregard for those he betrays. Wife and niece's lover exist as dramatic statements rather than as complex individuals themselves, confused as to motivation and action. They have no inner life. Once again, though, his concern is with a moral failure, a failure to recognise normal human bonds. And, once again, sexual betrayal is at the heart of things. For Miller it clearly has an exemplary role. But the effect is to drain the act of its social meaning. Treachery which is a consequence of innate weakness, of an impulse which never rises into the rational world, can hardly become a component of Miller's moral dialectic. And Carbone's lack of control over his instincts is more absolute than Proctor's or Willy Loman's. For Proctor, it was one pole of a world rigidly constructed around the concrete war between good and evil. Surrender to irrationalism was a powerful attraction for a man uneasily located in a society which transforms morality into moralism, one for which charity and love are simple pieties and in which the effusion of passion is regarded as ethically and aesthetically reprobate. But for Eddie Carbone the world is otherwise. Certainly he denounces passion primarily because it is an image of the anarchy which he fears in his own being, but that passion is in his case literally misdirected. It is not simple adultery to which he is tempted, but a symbolic incest, since he acts as Catherine's father. He is anarchy incarnate. All his actions spill out of a central madness. And it is that madness which to some degree nullifies his force as a tragic hero and threatens his significance as social commentary. The play becomes less an analysis of the informer than a study of the madman, obsessive, self-destructive and destructive of others.

Like *The Crucible*, it was apparently conceived before the events which gave it its special social relevance, but it lacks what gave that play its particular force; it lacks self-conscious characters confronted with moral choices which are real because the alternatives which they face are equally available. Hence John Proctor had both challenged the authority of the church and submitted himself to it; both offered himself as putative leader and reneged on that offer. Thus, when presented with that choice again, complicated now by moral failings of a personal kind whose force he had acknowledged even while compounding them, and by the fact that the stakes are now his wife's and his own life as well as the lives of others, the options are real and have the force of past action behind them. For Eddie Carbone there is no choice. In terms of the character we are shown, he has no freedom of action. He is trapped in a moral system which is in fact no more than an aspect of his sexual compulsions. His actions certainly have no cultural or social function. He is pulled outside the society of man by an action which is not willed and therefore not inspected and has no social force. What he does in informing on two illegal immigrants who are also his wife's cousins, not to mention one of them being his niece's lover, is not illegal; it is simply presented as being immoral. And the authority for that view – which in a real social situation might actually be a fit subject for debate – lies in his own denunciation of such acts. But that denunciation has no force or application in his own case, for where there is no freedom there is no choice – where there is no choice there can be no culpability. It is not only a principle of natural law but a cause of fundamental significance to Miller's own moral view. Guilt cannot accrue by virtue of one's simple existence. That, after all, was too close to the position adopted by those for whom the Jew – placed in a position in which social action was severely circumscribed by law and prejudice – was forced to surrender his freedom of action and become guilty simply by enacting that determinism. It was the very position he had argued against in *Focus*. In *A View from the Bridge*, the loss of freedom, the presentation of action as simple pathology, not only undermines his moral point, it also erodes the play's theatrical potency. Once again it was to be a question to which he would return in *After the Fall*.

Miller's original version of the play, which was staged in September 1955, was a one-act verse drama deliberately pared down to essentials. As he explained:

> I saw the characters purely in terms of action...they are a kind of people who, when inactive, have no new significant definition as people. The form of the play, finally, had a special attraction for me because once the decision was made to tell it without an excess line, the play took a harder, more objective shape. In effect, the form announces in the first moments of the play that only that will be told which is cogent, and that this story is the only part of Eddie Carbone's life worth our notice and therefore no effort will be made to draw in elements of his life that are beneath these, the most tense and meaningful of his hours.[115]

There seems a curious edge of contempt in Miller's description of his characters, a contempt at odds with his concern for the unique qualities of the self in its encounter with experience. His tragic aspirations seem to lead him to an external view of figures whose characters are subordinated to dramatic role.

Following a disappointing run, Miller reworked it for its London production. Much of the verse was refashioned as prose, the play became a two-act drama and character was rendered more densely. The effect was to root Carbone more securely in his setting, to move the play away from myth and towards a more substantial reality. But for all that it remains one of the less convincing of Miller's works. He himself thought that the changes which he had made did something to meet such objections. It is hard to agree. He explained the alterations, arguing that they led to a greater sympathy for his characters:

> Perhaps the two most important were an altered attitude toward Eddie Carbone, the hero, and toward the two women in his life. I had originally conceived Eddie as a phenomenon, a rather awesome fact of existence, and I had kept a certain distance from involvement in his self-justification. Consequently, he had appeared as a kind of biological sport, and to a degree a repelling figure not quite admissible into the human family. In revising the

play it became possible to accept for myself the implication I had sought to make clear in the original version, which was that however one might dislike this man, who does all sorts of frightful things, he possesses and exemplifies the wondrous and humane fact that he too can be driven to what in the last analysis is a sacrifice of himself for his conception, however misguided, of right, dignity and justice. In reversing it I found it possible to move beyond contemplation of the man as a phenomenon into an acceptance for dramatic purposes of his aims themselves.[116]

This, Miller felt, had the effect of freeing the women characters, Eddie's wife and niece, so that they could become more than simple observers. It also 'modified its original friezelike character'[117] and the play, to Miller's mind, moved closer to realism and became more engaged, more open to passion. But his retention of Alfieri as narrator works against this, framing the action as a conscious fable. Miller liked the more realistic setting which the play's London director, Peter Brook, contrived, but that realism sits uneasily with the myth-like qualities with which he had worked to invest Eddie Carbone.

It is a play about passion which is curiously drained of passion. Like so many other of Miller's plays it is concerned with the implicit contract between people which proscribes betrayal, as it is with the individual's desperate need to maintain his own good opinion of himself. But in making Eddie Carbone a victim of passion which he can neither articulate nor acknowledge he deprives him of some ultimate responsibility for his own actions. It is not that betrayal is rooted in self-interest, although viewed objectively it is. It is that he acts under a compulsion which alienates him from himself. He watches his own betrayal with a kind of detached horror but feels unable to intervene. The lawyer/narrator Alfieri is the god to whom he turns for absolution but in another sense he is simply an objectification of his own tortured conscience. Unable to act, he wishes to see himself as the unwilling victim of the gods. It is a central irony of the play that in some sense Miller concedes this consolation by closing off Eddie's own self-perception on all but the subconscious level. And when he confronts Marco that self-deception, which is not willed but an expression of the degree to which his own motives have always been closed to him, brings him to the brink of madness. In defence of his honour he destroys the meaning of honour not merely in the sense that he is guilty of dishonourable actions but to the extent that Miller presents as psychopathology what might more appropriately have been seen as a tragic flaw. Eddie creates a fiction which will relieve him of responsibility but it is not a conscious invention. The play becomes in effect a psychological study of an individual who displaces his sexual passion into a concern with honour and family responsibility. In effect he resists the very analysis which is the basis of Miller's own dramatic strategy; that is he refuses to allow his motives to be stripped bare; he resists the process

whereby his life is to be reduced to a simple passion. And if that is precisely
the nature of the tragic dilemma it is nonetheless oddly at a tangent to Miller's
own liberal theme, which is concerned to celebrate possibility, a freedom of
action and thought at variance with the character of Carbone.

A *View from the Bridge* seems oddly external to Miller, and his decision
to introduce a narrator through whom we see the events seems a natural
objectification of this fact. It does convey something of that effect of a modern
fable which he was anxious to achieve but it also withdraws our commitment.
The play's virtues and vices are closely related. In a sense, the framing of
the action is a deliberate strategy which has the effect of setting the events
off as a legend, an exemplary tale, a tragic fiction, but it also subordinates
character to tragic function and removes the action to a plane on which the
logic of action seems, ironically, to have less to do with personal psychology
than narrative necessity. Of course Eddie Carbone's dignity is that, unlike
Alfieri, he will not settle for half. He offers total commitment in an age in
which compromise is the order of the day. But it is a commitment to passion
unregulated by morality. And there is a difference between the two versions
of the play in this respect. The earlier verse drama emphasises the elemental
power of the irrational side of the human animal, balanced in some respect
by the rationality of Alfieri. The latter turns the play more in the direction
of moral analysis. But in neither is there final conviction in so far as passion
– by its nature intense, unsusceptible of analysis – is presented, for the most
part, only as perverse (the love-affair between Catherine and Rodolpho is
curiously passionless), while rationality is curiously impotent. For Alfieri,
Eddie's distinction is that he allows himself to be wholly known and yet this,
of course, is in no way willed. In so far as we glimpse his motive and
commitment it is because we are allowed a perspective denied to the
character. As a result it is hard to know what value to grant to the moral
drama enacted before us. Is it simply that, like Willy Loman, he had all the
wrong dreams and threw his life, his name and his passions behind a perverse
phantom, or are we called upon to admire a man who breaks the code of
his society in the name of some transcendent value whose authority is no
less because it cannot be called by its proper name? Arguably, Eddie sacrifices
his honour in order to save his honour. If his betrayal can be seen as being
spawned by self-interest, it is possible to see it also as stemming from a desire
to sustain the notion of innocence. Seen in this way he doesn't betray
Rodolpho in order to gain Catherine for himself but to preserve her purity.
If he is a rebel, it is not against a social code but the whole natural process
which pulls the individual into an adult world in which betrayal, corruption
and pride are the other side of maturity, sexual fulfilment and honour. His
dignity and irony alike thus stem from his struggle to sustain a model of
the world which is doomed to collapse. He becomes a kind of Dick Diver

(in *Tender is the Night*), deeply self-interested, but in a sense unable to stare into the darkness of his own motives because he is too busy trying to save others from a similar fate. In effect Eddie and Diver are linked by a willed collaboration in the anarchy that they seek to resist – an anarchy symbolised in Freudian terms by suggestions of incest. And yet both Miller and Fitzgerald clearly feel a certain admiration for someone who is willing to commit his whole being to sustain a fictional world in which the idea of innocence is preserved in the very midst of corruption.

Not the least of the ironies of the play is that Eddie Carbone's sin is to do his civic duty. Rodolpho is a law-breaker. But not for one moment does this seem of importance. Indeed Miller's social convictions are if anything expressed indirectly by his assumption that honour and justice are matters which exist at a tangent to the public world of law and civic responsibility. Values fundamentally derive from the need to respect oneself and others. The problem is that respect may be interpreted in different ways. Eddie's self-respect may be no more than pride or self-interest. But viewed differently it is, perhaps, rooted in his need to sustain a view of the world commensurate with his fantasies and dreams. If society has no right to generate prescriptive values, and if the self is deeply suspect, where are values born? It is a problem which *A View from the Bridge* raises but does not resolve.

Part of Eddie's problem is to have outlived his time, to be living at the wrong moment. His grand act, which would be an offence at any time, is nonetheless stripped of its grandeur and its glorious futility by its setting, a slum on the seaward side of the Brooklyn Bridge, described by Miller as 'the gullet of New York'. Miller, too, is not without his own nostagia for a world in which something more than pragmatism and the daily urgencies of urban survival demand attention. His desire to create modern tragedies betokens as much, as does the pull of history in his work, implicit not simply in the historical setting of *The Crucible* but also in the longing for America's past which sounds, like Willy Loman's father's flute, through many of his plays. In a sense, his characters are as much destroyed by time as are Tennessee Williams's. They certainly all yearn for a past in which there had still been space – literal and metaphorical – for the moral conscience to function and, for a moment, perhaps a kind of adolescence, in which it was not necessary to acknowledge the reality and disabling pervasiveness of corruption. Yet as Miller seems to imply throughout his work, that very nostalgia might be the root of corruption. For, in play after play, the longing for innocence is not merely a symptom of its loss but the beginnings of an implacable evil. It is simply that it fails to break surface as an issue until *After the Fall* which, written, perhaps, to declare his innocence, turned into a confession of personal and social guilt.

A View from the Bridge appeared with *A Memory of Two Mondays*, which was itself a slight work related to its companion piece only by its use of verse. It was, in fact, often Miller's habit to write speeches in his notebooks in verse. Indeed it is this which in part explains his economy of language. But both of the plays in his double bill moved between verse and prose, two forms which correspond with Miller's dualism – his sense of human nature as a compromise or, more strictly, a sustained tension between spiritual yearning and physical enervation, between dream and prosaic reality. In *A View from the Bridge* Alfieri's lyrical invocations to human nature, his detached view of the unfolding of a naturally determined process, is close, perhaps too close, in spirit to that of Thornton Wilder's stage manager in *Our Town*. In *A Memory of Two Mondays*, the verse highlights a sense of nostalgia which has always been strong in Miller's work and which, in *Death of a Salesman*, constituted a real, if deceptive, source of value. Here, however, it relates only to a vaguely perceived sense of camaraderie ostensibly balanced by a realistic assertion of the need to subordinate human sensibilities to the exigencies of life. A minor work, *A Memory of Two Mondays* was a return to the world which Miller had known some ten years earlier.

Neither *The Crucible* nor *A View from the Bridge* was particularly successful with the public. *An Enemy of the People* was even less so, closing after thirty-six performances. Miller found himself increasingly at odds with his society. 'From where I stood', he has recently said, 'the country was going exactly one hundred and eighty degrees in the opposite direction. I didn't feel I had anything to say to these people. I really felt that I might as well be living in Zambia. I had absolutely no connection with these people any more.'[118] Asked whether he was, in effect, the figure in his film *The Misfits*, who sees the things he believes in being destroyed, he replied:

> Yes, I didn't see it that directly at the time, but yes... It's not that it was difficult to relate; it was totally impossible. I felt that if they succeeded it would be a disaster for America and for the world... There was no way to communicate and indeed we didn't communicate and I was left high and dry. Theater is a very public thing. You're not writing a poem for some small magazine.[119]

Also he was confronted with a theatre structure which offered little outlet for drama beyond the Broadway theatre with which he was ethically and aesthetically at odds. He had, he explained,

> a sense that the whole thing wasn't worth the candle. Also the sense that the time had gotten away from me, that I didn't really understand or sympathize with what was going on here... It all became rather pointless... I wrote a lot of stuff and tore it up... If I had had any kind of company of actors... an active theater... I probably would have written and completed a lot of stuff.[120]

And it was, indeed, the emergence of Lincoln Center, rather than a fundamental shift in the mood of the American public, which eventually brought him back to the theatre after a nine-year silence. His despair of the Broadway audience might have been mitigated had he felt that he had any general support, but he felt that 'I had been backed into a corner, really...I didn't know who I was talking to.'[121] *The Misfits* showed him the possibility of appealing to a wider public, breaking through the barrier which he had felt growing around him. A comment on his alienation, it nonetheless played a role in terminating it. And he anyway detected a shift in American values. When President John F. Kennedy was elected, Miller was one of a clutch of writers, artists and scientists invited to his inauguration, though since his previous visits to Washington had been occasioned by subpoenas from the House Un-American Activities Committee, he was none too sure he could bring himself to go there without a lawyer. As he remarked, 'I would naturally like to imagine that we are at the end of a period. To be perfectly blunt about it, I should call it the decade when America really got its brains knocked out. Indeed, I do not regard it as mere accident that the American Legion has recently taken to clubbing rabbits to death in wire enclosures. They have temporarily run out of intellectuals.' Now, at least, it was possible that 'a man capable of speaking and writing a complete English sentence will not for that reason alone be barred from public office'.[122] At last there was a return of confidence, but other more profound anxieties were about to surface in his work.

The basic theme of America's major dramatists is the effort to survive in times inimical to man. Virtually all their protagonists cling to human values apparently superseded by material ones. The rhythm of life has changed along with its purpose. Nostalgia is an active but an ironic force. It highlights the disproportion, the sense of loss, the fact of betrayal, which are the dominant moods of Miller's work, as of O'Neill's, Williams's and Albee's. Memory becomes the source of absurdity in that it recalls dreams which failed to be actualised, hopes which were never realised, a youth which has been eroded by time. And yet some final determination survives – a need for the poetic, a desperate urgency to estimate one's personal value at full weight, to make an assessment of oneself apart from the pragmatics of the public world. Hence the need to remake the world, either, as was the case in the 1930s and again, briefly, in the 1960s by transforming its social and political priorities or, more often, by constructing pipe dreams, illusions and fantasies which can sustain the self in its battle with the world. In the 1930s, there was for a while some expectation that those visions could be translated into social fact, that social coercions were just that and were hence susceptible of transformation. The self pressed back against fact and against idea. That was the mood of Miller's and Williams's earliest plays (in Williams's case primarily the unpublished plays) as it was of Albee's. O'Neill was always more deeply touched by a sense of the irremediable, though even he flirted with the notion of revolt. But by degrees that confidence began to disappear. Increasingly these writers began to locate social imperfection in character and then in human nature. The battle with imperfection became internalised, not simply in translating social and political dislocations into pathology but in establishing a model of human behaviour which was in some sense Calvinist. Imperfection becomes definitional. Social and political evils are thus seen as less a moral hiatus, a deviation from manifest principles of ethical behaviour and human well-being, than inevitable eruptions on a public scale of a corruption designed into individual behaviour. Materialism, capitalism, the assertion of the apparent primacy of the external world, are no longer seen as the primary causes of moral collapse; they are presented as the consequence of it. At the heart of the public as of the private world is the self's obsessive need to survive and to establish its significance. Beneath the public betrayals is a private betrayal, an obsession with declaring a personal innocence, if need be at the cost of announcing the irremediable guilt of the rest of the world. Where in the earlier works there was a self whose integrity was assumed or at least in some degree recoverable, this deferred, in the work of Miller and Albee in particular, to a vision of a self whose world became progressively less assured because the nature of the self itself was in process of radical redefinition. For Albee, this led directly to the ontological debates of the work which came after *Who's Afraid of Virginia Woolf?*; for Miller, it led, inevitably perhaps, to *After the Fall*, a play in which he tried to face the principal evidence for the inadequacy of his own liberal ideology, a play which was to tackle some of the issues raised but never really confronted by his earlier work. Thus *All My Sons* had appealed for an acknowledgement of a human unity and concern essentially denied by the character who voiced that appeal; Biff Loman committed himself to a new life which was not merely ahistorically located both in space and time (the frontier world of his father's youth) but at odds with a social world and an economic environment in which a celebration of the mere fact of being and an acceptance of one's status as an imperfect being does nothing to guarantee either fulfilment or survival. In *The Crucible*, Proctor, forced to the point of commitment, was able, finally, to achieve selfhood through willing the sacrifice of that selfhood; but betrayal was equally a powerful compulsion for him as for others, and that is less convincingly examined. By bending history Miller proposes sexual hysteria as an explanation but is clearly dissatisfied with that. The compulsion goes deeper. In proposing a motive composed of an amalgam of jealousy, guilt and vindictiveness he comes closer to presenting a convincing picture but why these characteristics assumed public form in the person of Abigail Williams while others are totally immune, and even precisely what words like good and evil mean in terms of human nature, he is less sure of. *After the Fall*, with which Miller returned to the American theatre in 1964, was his attempt to track these issues to their source; it was his effort to relate personal and public betrayals, to account for those failures of private and social morality of which the manifest evidence were the Depression, the holocaust and the persecutions of 1950s America. In *All My Sons* he dramatised the fatal consequence of truth and deception alike but never acknowledged the moral paradox which he had uncovered. In *After the Fall* he forces himself to confront it: 'the truth, after all, may merely be murderous...Then how do you live? A workable lie?'[123] His own view had itself darkened over the years. This was in part a function of his shifting perspective and in part an expression of his growing sense that the moral world was disintegrating – not because morality was an absolute assaulted from without but because it was a consequence of a constantly renewed battle with imperfection which was in process of being abandoned through a failure of morale. His earlier confident vision of the coherences of the social world had collapsed. Society itself had 'lost its definition'. His early plays had dramatised this without explaining it. *After the Fall* was, finally, to deal with this. The gulf, which he has confessed to feeling, between himself and his audience, became paradigmatic of a more fundamental rift. It began to symbolise for him a failure of community. The House Un-American Activities Committee and, in retrospect and most spectacularly, the concentration camp, had provided evidence for the attenuation and even collapse of that sense of human connectiveness which had provided both the context and the subject of his art. Hence, in *After the Fall* he dramatises the plight of a man who suddenly realises that 'some unseen web of connection between people is simply not there. And I always relied on it, somehow.'[124]

His own conviction, a product of the 1970s rather than the 1940s and 1950s, that 'all history is fundamentally a fiction' does battle with an obligation to try to ascertain the real. 'I think the effort is necessary even though one is doomed to misapprehend reality.'[125] So, too, his belief that the moral world is collapsing breeds in him a conviction that 'the struggle is necessary', for 'when the struggle is up we're all up for grabs...we've got to grapple with it somehow'.[126] For if social values do not hold, it becomes necessary to reconstruct them. The presumption on which the play rests is that the truth can only be reached with a certain courage and honesty. This is the principle behind his dramatic strategy no less than a central article of faith.

Miller has insisted on the difference between European and American experience, which he suggests goes some way towards explaining the gulf between his own work and that of a writer like Beckett. And yet the same Jewish experience which he claims as the source of a philosophical resilience in his own work is equally capable of generating a profoundly disturbing sense of despair. *After the Fall* was his attempt to resolve this conflict, to track public and private failure to their root in human character, to discover the basis on which human life can continue after the holocaust has revealed the extent of human depravity, the degree to which human complexity has ostensibly been nullified. It is the account of a man who suddenly realises that he inhabits a world in which justice, rational conduct and moral behaviour have no ultimate sanction, in which the self is cut adrift in an antinomian world with the need to find some justification for survival, some function and identity. Miller, like his protagonist faced with the evidence of deceit and brutality, is concerned with locating the remaining scope for confidence. As he has said, 'The European playwrights...can tell me that it's hopeless, and by and large it is. But it's not 100 per cent hopeless, is all I'm about to tell you.'[127]

Quentin, the central figure in *After the Fall*, is in a way a portrait of Bernard in *Death of a Salesman*, a successful lawyer who has pleaded a case before the Supreme Court, but now suddenly transfixed by an awareness of the irrelevance of that success to his central needs. For beneath the veneer of social success is a sense of human failure which is the source of a potentially disabling guilt. On the verge of remarrying he feels the need to come to terms not only with his own former marital failures but with the implications of a human nature for which betrayal is a natural mode and the self the prism through which all experience is viewed. Having himself been called before the House Un-American Activities Committee and having urged an idealistic course of action on a colleague who subsequently committed suicide, he is made suddenly aware of the complex nature of moral responsibility and the suspect nature of idealistic demands (as in *All My Sons* Chris Keller had not been), and recognises social evil as a projection of private failure. And since the woman he is to marry had lost relatives in the concentration camp which he, too, as an American, had avoided, he is forced to examine this, too, as further and potentially overwhelming evidence of a failure of human values. The whole action of the play takes place in 'the mind, thought and memory of Quentin', and as a consequence the lines which connect these apparently disparate experiences can be dramatised immediately and directly, the image of the concentration camp coexisting with evidence of the petty deceits of daily life. Miller seems to have been at work on the play as early as 1959, at least there is a fragment of a play which seems to contain elements of what later became *After the Fall* and *The Price* in one of Miller's notebooks dating from that time. Certainly he anticipates there the device of a story being told to a silent psychoanalyst and includes a character called Quentin. In the final form of the play Quentin delves into his private and public self, spilling out his experiences to the hidden psychiatrist who is an expression of his conscience.

And as his mind traces backwards through time in an attempt to track down the origin of the betrayals for which he finds all too much evidence, he comes to feel that it lies in a determination to sustain one's own self-image. To accuse others is to affirm one's own innocence. Since responsibility implies guilt, responsibility is willingly denied. Thus, by degrees, Quentin comes to feel that a claim to innocence is neither desirable nor possible. It is not only an implicit accusation levelled at others; it is an assertion of non-involvement. For Miller this, as his title suggests, is a world seen after the Fall. Since public cruelties have the same root as private ones there can be no innocence and since, as Nathaniel Hawthorne implied, a shared guilt may imply a shared perception, it may prove an avenue to a form of grace resting on compassion. Human nature is imperfect. Like the idiot child, of whom Holga, Quentin's wife-to-be, dreams, it simply has to be embraced. But imperfection does not validate despair or the simple surrender of all values. It necessitates the constant renewal of a love which, though flawed, is presented as the only resource with which the gulf opened up by that imperfection may be bridged.

For Quentin, as for Miller, there had always been 'some saving grace. Socialism once, then love.'[128] For Miller, of course, that had been the position implied in 'They Too Arise' and Death of a Salesman respectively. Now, however, 'some final hope is gone that always saved before the end'.[129] The fact that in the concentration camp you could be killed 'for no reason', the fact that 'they don't even ask your name', destroyed even that dignity which John Proctor had been able to claim. The real terror of the camp was that you died anonymously, that this was a death which destroyed tragedy. It was thus a direct challenge to Miller's liberal philosophy and to a theatrical strategy which placed the self and its struggle with determinism at the heart of his concern. Illusioned or not, his characters had tended to focus the meaning of their lives onto their names, which they shouted out – with despair, exultance, pride or pathos. But here, number is substituted for name and individuality literally rendered down. And yet the process of the play is designed to restore to the individual a sense of control, to reassert a notion of moral responsibility. The absolution of war-time, with its pantheon of heroes and villains, located meaning in an external world. To be committed to the fight was to derive meaning from that struggle. Quentin's problem is that he lives in a more complex time in which such necessities have disappeared and there is no external validation of behaviour or identity. His survival seems to have laid a responsibility on him which he cannot believe himself to be fulfilling, for the deceits and self-concern of his life seem to make him an accomplice of those forces manifest in the fact of the camps. And all around him he sees evidence of the cruelty and the fiercely destructive egotism of virtually all of his friends. Lou, a university professor, had wilfully distorted the truth about conditions in the Soviet Union in a book written in the 1930s and is now publicly

10.   Elia Kazan and Arthur Miller preparing *After the Fall*.

assaulted for ineptitude by his wife. Mickey, another friend and apparently
a portrait of Miller's own director, Elia Kazan, betrays his former associates
to the House Un-American Activities Committee. (By a curious irony Kazan,
a character in the play, actually directed it for Lincoln Center, a situation
which Miller understandably described as 'weird'.) Maggie, Miller's
denials notwithstanding, seems plainly based on Marilyn Monroe and is presented as a self-regarding neurotic, wilfully wounding those who love her.
No one, except possibly Holga, the woman whom he plans to marry, is
exempt. The problem is that this assertion of a Calvinist moral fallibility,
albeit eventually balanced by a will to neutralise this with compassion, his
view of human relationships as struggles for power, as expressions of an
irremediable self-concern, leaves little room for the elaboration of a moral
system which can distinguish the concentration camp guard from his victim.
If we are all guilty we are all in some sense innocent and the basis for
accusation, for the erection even of a contingent set of values by which to
indict the criminal, is destroyed. Values, as he himself, in a different context,
confessed, then become a matter of aesthetics.

The notion that the concentration camp is simply individual fallibility writ
large, that there is a direct and demonstrable connection between the mother

213

who sends the maid out with her son, while she takes the rest of the family to the seaside, and the fundamental abrogation of human responsibility involved in genocide is too simplistic. The disproportion is simply too great. Miller's response to this criticism was to say: 'you've got to begin somewhere. Otherwise the larger social evil becomes simply something spinning in space. It has no human root at all, which is a very common thing to believe.'[130] It is not a wholly adequate reaction.

Though *After the Fall* tries to tackle fundamental issues directly and with some honesty, it is a play which generates its own sentimentalities. Holga is a still point in the storm. She has won her way through to a state of grace as a consequence of suffering, a fact which suggests a redemptive quality in experience which is essentially denied by the rest of the play, except in so far as Quentin, too, lays claim to a similar peace of mind. And though Quentin's experience is presented as paradigmatic he proves remarkably immune to the incubus of treachery. His self-doubt, his spiritual crisis, posits a failure of moral being which never really reaches the point of action. He confesses to feeling relieved when the man he was to defend, at the risk of his own career, commits suicide. He confesses, that is, to a failure of love. And yet, for the most part, he is a model of a rational, understanding and compassionate being. In the face of extreme provocation from Maggie he remains calm. His guilt appears something of an indulgence, an invention which will unite him with the victims and which will, as a consequence, relieve him of a more fundamental guilt, namely that of the survivor. And this, more fundamental issue, though hinted at by Miller, never moves to the centre of his attention. It is invoked as a justification for Quentin's introspection but is implicitly at odds with the idea of a natural depravity which is pressed with equal force. Indeed knowledge of that depravity is, for Miller, the key to transcendence. He no longer believes, as once he did, that evil is the product of a particular economic or political system; he certainly cannot subscribe to the notion of national guilt, since Holga is the moral catalyst of the play. What he substitutes is Quentin's conviction that to acknowledge that 'we meet unblessed; not in some garden of wax fruit and painted trees, that lie of Eden, but after, after the Fall, after many, many deaths'. This is already to have taken the crucial step. For to acknowledge that 'the wish to kill is never killed' enables one 'with some gift of courage' to 'look into its face when it appears, and with a stroke of love – as to an idiot in the house – forgive it; again and again...forever?'[131] The question mark is purely rhetorical. The speech is clearly the spine of the play. The problem is that it occurs in the context of his relationship with Holga. Indeed she stands waiting for him as the speech is delivered. The effect is a curious and distracting ambiguity. Eros and Agape become confused. Indeed, unless love is to be granted some active social constituent, Miller would seem to

11. *After the Fall* in 1964 at the ANTA Washington Square Theatre where it was staged for the Lincoln Center Repertory Company, with Jason Robards Jr and Barbara Loden. Directed by Elia Kazan.

be propounding a simple quietistic response, a surrender to determinism at odds with the play's equal appeal for personal responsibility.

And Miller's control of language seems to desert him. The profundity of the subject seems to generate a linguistic solemnity ('if there is love, it must be limitless; a love not even of persons but blind, blind to insult, blind to the spear in the flesh, like justice blind').[132] Though plainly not a realistic play, and though Miller is trying to squeeze a metaphysical significance out of experience, the effect is a kind of pretentiousness, a solemn moralising which is a substitute for enacted truths. Unless, that is, Quentin is implicitly being accused of voiding in language what should have been discharged in action and that is always a temptation for Quentin, a lawyer, as it had been for Miller, a writer.

Many felt uneasy with the play. In his book *Naming Names* Victor Navasky quotes an anonymous member of the company as saying:

> I couldn't believe what was going on. Gadge [Kazan] in his own really paranoid way thought he was the hero of this play – not that he ever asked Arthur. He thought it was about him, not Marilyn. He and Jason [Robards Jr] had a big battle about that long naming names speech. That's when Jason vanished – went off on a week's binge and they couldn't find him. It was a bitter, dark, and terrifying fight they had over that speech.
>
> At first Miller thought Kazan understood his play – then he thought Kazan used Barbara Loden (Maggie) to take it away from the central issue. I mean, he looked at things sexually instead of intellectually – he made her play it in a see-through dress – and that was a road to escape.

The problem with Arthur is that he *was* an 'informer'. He was informing. Gadge kind of had one over him because he was really 'naming' Marilyn and the rest of them. The invasion of privacy is what made it so sick.[133]

The radical writer Albert Metz, who had featured as a constant point of reference in the HUAC trials and who was one of the original Hollywood Ten called as witnesses in 1947, wrote that 'In *After the Fall* he gives to the informer as complete a justification as he gives to the man upon whom he informs and whose career he ruined. And I was told that Kazan paused in rehearsals and said proudly, "That man is me".'[134] Miller had embraced Kazan and absolved him. But he was concerned with absolution of himself no less than others (he has said that to have opposed Kazan as director would have been to perpetuate a blacklist), and his revelation of private anguish did indeed seem to many like a piece of special pleading, a naming of names to preserve his own innocence. But the theme of the play denied the very innocence to which he seemed to be laying claim. The myth of the McCarthy period had cast him in the role of hero and Kazan that of villain. It was a simplification which he was not, finally, content to perpetuate. The man who had written *All My Sons* was not likely to accept a model of human motives and actions which denied an essential ambiguity and concealed a talent for betrayal which he had long felt to be a basic human trait. *After the Fall* may be a piece of self-justification but it is also a play which attempts to confess to that impulse and to discover a means of surviving if not transcending it. It is, I think, a remarkably sincere, if not wholly successful, attempt to pull together private and public acts of treachery in an effort to understand the terrible facts of modern history and to acknowledge a culpability which links us all. Finally, neither Victor Navasky nor Albert Metz have touched the core of a play which does not so much justify the informer as expose the motives and mechanisms of betrayal. And, if it seems to leave Quentin more sinned against than sinning, it is necessary to recall that we see the world purely through his eyes. The play thus becomes primary evidence of that very self-justifying impulse which he imagines himself to have understood and purged, an irony of which Miller is fully aware. As he has said:

> when Quentin goes to the concentration camp, he can very well understand the people who helped build it, the plumbers, the masons, all those people saying, 'Well, really, what has it to do with me, I'm building a building?'... They had to know what they were building. And the interiors: they had operating tables which were built of stone with drains to let the blood out, and what they were doing was pulling and knocking people's teeth out. And yet the race, the human race, cannot face its culpability, its responsibility. We do it here all the time. We cop out. Now it's an extraordinarily difficult thing and maybe it's impossible finally, but I think the commitment has to be made.[135]

After the Fall is the first of Miller's plays to address itself directly to the nature of the Jewish experience. It was followed by *Incident at Vichy* and *The Price* which were the first of his published plays to include manifestly Jewish characters. Interviewed in 1978 and asked why this concern should suddenly become apparent in the mid 1960s rather than directly after the war (*Focus* had been the only one of his published works to deal with this issue) he replied that,

> I became far more aware of what Jewishness meant to me. I quite honestly hadn't any such sensation earlier on. It probably was suppressed by the fact that we lived in a country with a lot of anti-semitism, in the forties, the thirties, too. And what that does to somebody is to suppress his identity in a way. Neither my father nor mother could speak Yiddish...I kind of dug it out of myself...I think the establishment of a new Jewish state probably meant a lot to me. It meant the establishment of an identity that I would never live to have.[136]

His attendance at the Auschwitz trials in Frankfurt was to some degree accidental. While in Europe he read a newspaper account of the trials and simply went out of a wish to see a Nazi, having not knowingly done so before; but he also went because he wished to 'look into the darkness'.

Incident at Vichy, which received its première eleven months after *After the Fall*, was in some ways an extension of the argument presented in that play and in part an evasion of it. The action is set in 'a place of detention' in Vichy France, in 1942. It is a kind of ante-room to hell in that those who find themselves there are suspected of being Jews, or, in one case, a gypsy. They are there to be sorted, therefore, into the 'innocent' and the 'guilty'; the former being given a white pass which is the emblem of their racial purity, the latter being sent on towards their death. As they wait they discuss the reason for their arrest – an inherently ironic discussion since reason plays no part in their plight. Indeed their vulnerability lies precisely in the urgency with which they look for an assured rationality. Hence they look for meaning where there is only the brutal fact of prejudice and *real-politik*. To that degree and to that degree only they acquiesce in their fate through a failure of imagination. They are simply unable to conceive of the fate which awaits them. At times, indeed, the play hints at a fascination with the role of the imagination which the pressure of its moral concern finally inhibits. Thus an artist complains of those who are forever looking for meaning in his work rather than experiencing its simple truth. But the sheer force of the immediate and the specific deflects such concerns. Debates about human nature, guilt and responsibility, all occur in the context of a threat too precise to permit generalisation without moral evasion.

And this exerts a similar pressure on character. Although Miller is interested in stereotype as subject and dramatises the attempt of accuser and accused alike to make an old Jew and a gypsy conform to type, he himself could be accused of a similar fault. Gathered in the room are a Communist, a gypsy, an old Jew, an aristocrat, an artist, a psychologist, a German officer repelled by his work, and an SS man enthusiastic for his. The Communist talks about Communism, the artist about art, the psychologist about psychology and so on. They are hardly conceived outside their roles. While the play argues against a process which encourages people to see themselves and others as symbols, it simultaneously uses just such a process as its theatrical strategy. Reductivism is not merely the subject of the play it is also its methodology.

The play is an extension of *After the Fall* in that it argues for a view of human nature that makes the concentration camp a logical extension of human behaviour, rather than an aberration. The self, it seems, always asserts its absolute rights even at the expense of others. Hence the German officer who despises his job nevertheless carries it out for fear of the consequences to himself. Those gathered in the room are determined to plead their 'innocence', to demonstrate their racial purity, even though this involves a process which condemns others. But it is a denial of *After the Fall* in that, in the person of an Austrian prince, it dramatises a figure whose greatest sin is naivety and an unwillingness to conceive of the evil which he suspects. It presents a character who is able to make a clear and decisive act of self-sacrifice. The paradox of the earlier play lies in the fact that it undermined the basis for moral action. All men were guilty; some were more guilty than others. This is a view represented in *Incident at Vichy* by the psychologist, Leduc, who asserts that 'I am only angry that I should have been born before the day when man has accepted his own nature; that he is *not* reasonable, that he is full of murder, that his ideals are only the little tax he pays for the right to hate and kill with a clear conscience.' For Von Berg, the Prince, however, 'There are ideals... There are people who would find it easier to die than stain one finger with this murder. They exist. I swear it to you. People for whom everything is *not* permitted, foolish people and ineffectual, but they do exist and will not dishonour their tradition.'[137] And this is a position which he vindicates by sacrificing his own life. He gives his pass to Leduc and thus voluntarily joins the condemned. He thereby also vindicates his own belief that the individual is the linchpin of history and the key to moral values. While Miller, through Leduc, insists that 'each man has his Jew; it is the other. And the Jews have their Jews',[138] that every man shares complicity because it is his human birthright, in the person of Von Berg he creates a man who resists that knowledge and acts out of moral necessity. For Leduc, he has simply translated his guilt into responsibility, but the evidence for Von Berg's complicity is slender; it is an abstract notion of culpability too comprehensive in its scope, too reductive in its implications,

12.   *Incident at Vichy*, 1964, with Joseph Wiseman as Leduc, Hal Holbrook and Ivor
       Lewis.

to command belief. His action is thus not merely a challenge to the German major who stares incredulously at Von Berg: it is a challenge to the determinism outlined in *After the Fall*. In that play the only hope lay in a losing struggle with a deeply flawed human nature – a tragic transcendence; in *Incident at Vichy*, forced to dramatise the evil of the SS professor, he is forced also to concede degrees of culpability, establishing a spectrum which even permits an idealism not inevitably touched with irony. So the tragic transcendence defers to a simple assertion of a resistant moral sense.

The play may avoid one paradox but it raises another. For a writer, the failure of art to deflect the evil of the Nazis, indeed in some degree its complicity in that evil, gives cause for concern. The sheer power of fact defeats the imagination. Hence the efforts of Manceau, an actor, to 'create one's own reality in this world'[139] founder on the banal authority of social action. And yet the play itself clearly operates on wholly other assumptions. It is a contradiction which goes to the heart of Miller's own beliefs. He has repeatedly spoken of the ineffectualness of art, of its inability to deflect social process. However, the whole of his creative life has been based not only on the necessity of exposing hidden truths but finally on the moral utility of so doing. Perhaps in some fundamental sense that is the essential nature of art.

13.   *Incident at Vichy*, 1964.

In many ways Arthur Miller's next play, *The Price*, seems to mark a return to the world of Joe Keller and Willy Loman. Indeed there are notes among Miller's papers at the University of Texas which suggest that he was working on an early version of the play a decade and more earlier. Once again, it appears, we are invited to witness the struggles of a man who has 'the wrong dreams', and who embraces too completely the ethics of a society intent on success at any price. but in the twenty years since *Death of a Salesman* Miller has become aware of more fundamental influences than those exerted by Horatio Alger Jr, and while he continues to expose the vacuity of the

American dream he is more concerned with probing the nature of human freedom than with exposing the social charade. *The Price*, therefore, owes more to *After the Fall* and *Incident at Vichy* than to *All My Sons* and *Death of a Salesman*, though its humour suggests that by this stage in his career he has successfully reconciled himself to some of the more painful realities which he had identified in those plays. The line between *Incident at Vichy* and *The Price*, indeed, is disturbingly direct. Miller has said that he is fascinated by the Nazi era because it constituted a turning-point in man's perception of human nature. The war and the Nazi occupation of Europe produced not merely 'a chilling of the soul by the technological apparatus' but also 'the obstruction of the individual's capacity for choosing, or erosion of what used to be thought of as an autonomous personality'.[140] While this was carried to its extreme by the Nazi regime, however, Miller sees his contemporary society as 'struggling with the same incubus'.[141] Indeed, in a sense, as Miller has suggested, *Incident at Vichy* itself is 'about tomorrow morning',[142] and *The Price*, in turn, about man's continued surrender of identity and submission to a false concept of human nature.

As in *Death of a Salesman* and *After the Fall* we are at a point in time when the main characters are made suddenly aware of the futility of their lives thus far. For Willy Loman it had been an imperfect perception – a dull sense of insufficiency and failure. For Quentin it was a sudden realisation that his life had been dedicated only to self-interest. In *The Price* the crisis emerges from a meeting between two brothers. Both men are at a crucial stage in their own lives. Victor, a frustrated and bitterly disappointed policeman, looks back over his life and sees no meaning and no hope for his remaining years. He is poised. He lacks the courage to retire because this means that he will be forced to acknowledge his failure to create anything worthwhile through his career. Likewise he lacks the will to start again – to change a destiny which he has already rationalised away as the consequence of the economic determinism of the 1930s. His brother, Walter, is in a similar position. Although a highly successful surgeon who has made money by sacrificing his vocation to simple greed, he can find no purpose or meaning behind his frenzied pursuit of wealth and fame. His personal life is in ruins, his professional integrity compromised. But after a serious nervous breakdown he feels at long last that he has begun to understand himself and, as the play progresses, it becomes apparent that he is determined to put this new, imperfect, knowledge into practice. For the first time he feels genuinely alive to the possibilities of a life built on something more substantial than mutual recrimination and obsessive guilt. Seized with a naive excitement he struggles against his old nature and fights to explain his new perception to his brother.

The play is set in the attic of a Manhattan brownstone house. With the building about to be torn down, Victor and his wife, Esther, arrive to negotiate the sale of his father's furniture. The room is as it has been for sixteen years, since the time, that is, of his father's death. The sight of his former home and the various reminders of his youth provide an appropriate background for the revelations of the past which now follow.

We soon learn that Victor's marriage is breaking up. His wife is embittered by his failure and contemptuous of his weakness. Rather than face the reality of her position she resorts to alcohol and when her husband discovers an old fencing foil the mock thrusts that he makes are a weary re-enactment of their antagonisms.

Into this tense situation there intrudes the figure of the furniture dealer – 89-year-old Solomon. Dragged out of retirement, he grudgingly admits to satisfaction that he should be working again for only then does he regain a sense of purpose in his life. Thus when he resists Walter's attempts to take the business away from him he is literally fighting for his survival. Solomon's role is to act as a chorus, but not merely that; he is also a moral arbiter

14.   Kate Reid, David Burns, Arthur Kennedy and Pat Hingle in *The Price*, 1968.

between Walter's seemingly callous realism and Victor's apparent good nature.

Walter, having avoided his brother for many years, is conscious of the importance of their present meeting. But the bitterness which has long existed between them quickly wells to the surface and in the course of the accusations and confessions which follow we gradually discover the truth about a past which both of them had embroidered to suit their own purposes. At the end of the play each brother is finally left 'touching the structure of his life'.[143]

Tennessee Williams has said of American businessmen, 'Disappointed in their longing for other things, such as tenderness, they turn to the pursuit of wealth because that is more obtainable in the world'.[144] This 'reverse sublimation' clearly characterises the protagonists of The Price. Shocked by the failure of love and bewildered by the treachery and cruelty of human relationships, they retreat into illusion. Victor adopts the role of victim while Esther turns to the bottle. Walter substitutes the ethos of business for genuine human relationships. Even Victor, like Willy Loman before him, embraces the cynical competitive ethic of a commercial society. Having failed himself, his main hope rests in having produced 'a terrific boy', but his proud boast that 'nobody's ever going to take that guy' exposes the true nature of his values. Trapped in an illusory world, none of them have been able to discover or create any meaning. But Walter, like Quentin before him, is suddenly forced to re-examine his life and to test the presumptions on which his actions have been based. What he now understands and tries to convey to his brother is that human failure can be traced not to some indefinable hostility in the universe or to the destructiveness of a particular social system but to the failure of individuals to recognise the paramount importance of some kind of genuine human relationship. The misery of their own family life, for example, was not a sign that 'there was no mercy in the world', but rather that there was 'no love in this house. There was nothing but a straight financial arrangement.'[145] The mother had blamed the father for destroying her musical career; the father had watched while his son unnecessarily sacrificed his future for him. Thus, rather than make his father confess that he had adequate financial resources of his own, Victor unquestioningly accepts the cancellation of his college plans, and the collapse of any career which could make him a rival to his brother. Victor has refused to face this particular reality by creating an elaborate fantasy, but has forced himself to sacrifice sixteen years of his life in order to give substance to this illusion. But Walter now insists on the need to face the real world with courage and determination, and when Esther asks, 'But who...can ever face that?' he replies, 'You have to'.[146] Like Quentin before him he finally comes to feel that only when the individual is prepared to confront reality and to cease defending himself by indicting others does he really take his destiny into his own hands. In his own words, 'I don't look high and low for some betrayal any more; my days belong to me now.'[147]

The Swedish dramatist, Peter Weiss, has talked of the urgent need for 'getting over' a concern with the 'guilt laden, doomed and damned bourgeoisie'.[148] While his own Marxist leanings make this primarily an apology for a more clearly political drama, his rejection of bourgeois 'problem plays' puts him in line with the mainstream of modern drama. To many critics, Arthur Miller has long been the exception to this development, remaining obsessed with precisely that 'guilt laden' bourgeoisie rejected by Weiss. Nevertheless, there is evidence that with his more recent work Miller too has come to concern himself with more fundamental aspects of the human condition. He has turned his attention from the symptoms to the disease itself.

In an article written in 1960, Tom Driver could say with some justice that Miller lacked 'that metaphysical inquisitiveness which would take him to the bottom of the problems he encounters'. Miller's chief fault, according to Driver, lay in the fact that he tended to see the issues 'too soon...in their preliminary form of social or even moral debate', and not 'in terms of dramatic events that disturb the audience's idea of basic truth, which is the foundation for its moral attitudes'.[149] Driver overstates the case but there is a sense in which Miller has not been ready, in several of his earlier plays, to trace moral and social failures to their source in human character. But with *After the Fall* and then with *The Price* he has probed not only behind the bland façade of success but also behind the social and psychological rationalisations of earlier plays. Now he identifies an existential ethic, asserting the imperfection of human nature but insisting on man's responsibility for his own fate. Earlier he had said, 'The great weight of evidence is upon the helplessness of man. The great bulk of the weight of evidence is that we are not in command.' But significantly, even then, he felt constrained to add that 'we surely have much more command than anybody, including Macbeth's Witches, could ever dream of and somehow a form has to be devised which will account for this. Otherwise the drama is doomed to repeating and repeating *ad nauseam* the same pattern of striving, disillusion and defeat.'[150] However, in spite of this panegyric in favour of man's power to act, few playgoers can have seen much evidence of this in Willy Loman's sure progress towards death or even in Biff's belated and untested declarations of faith in a realistic future. Even *The Crucible* proved only that men could be brave in the face of their fate, not that they could do much to avoid unjustified persecution. To recant or to remain obdurate was still to be subject to circumstances not of one's own making. It is only with his most recent work that Miller has been able to reconcile man's freedom to act with the determining factors of his own nature.

Both Miller and Peter Weiss attended the Auschwitz trials. They went, separately, as Jews who had escaped the persecution and agony of the Nazi onslaught. Weiss's family had escaped from Germany during the so-called *Kristallnacht*. They lived out the war in Sweden where Weiss still works, writing in his native language. Miller spent the war years in America, safe from any threat of invasion and thus direct persecution, and remote from the incomprehensible brutality of Nazi terror. With the end of the war he was left to face a number of paradoxes and his attempt to resolve them is the story of his development as a writer.

As a Jew who had survived and indeed suffered little inconvenience, he felt an ill-defined sense of guilt. This guilt appears throughout his work in a sublimated form. Only with *After the Fall* do we discover the real source of this guilt as Quentin confesses to feeling the 'guilt of the survivor'. To be a Jew and to have survived is to be inexplicably favoured and hence to be a hostage to the past. This play, then, resolved many of the problems that had vexed Miller throughout his writing career. It served to exorcise his personal sense of guilt, but, more significantly, provided evidence that he had finally evolved a consistent concept of the relation between human freedom and human limitations. In a sense *The Price* could scarcely have been written before *After the Fall* had successfully laid some of Miller's more persistent personal ghosts. Only now could he create a character such as Solomon; only now could he maintain the tension between determinism and freedom with conscious and subtle control and yet finally permit a synthesis which retains conviction.

In *The Price* we are presented with several characters who are made suddenly aware of their direct responsibility for their own actions and of their freedom of action – a demonstration, perhaps, of his earlier comment that 'The only thing worth doing today in the theatre...is to synthesize the subjective drives of the human being with what is now demonstrably the case, namely that by an act of will man can and has changed the world.'[151] If Victor, the unsuccessful policeman, offers little proof of man's power to transform his surroundings this is because he refuses to acknowledge his own freedom of action. He conspires to create his own irrelevance and as such becomes a depressingly apt image for what Miller sees as a nerveless and deluded society. Indeed Miller would agree with the Swiss dramatist, Friedrich Dürrenmatt when he says that, 'True representatives of our world are missing; the tragic heroes are nameless. Any small-time crook, petty government official or policeman better represents our world than a senator or a president.'[152] Miller has no need to claim tragic proportions for Victor, as he had earlier for Willy Loman. In an essay written after *Death of a Salesman* he had defined his understanding of tragedy. It was, he insisted, a quality which exalted the 'thrust for freedom' and which 'automatically demonstrates the indestructible will of man to attain his freedom'. As a description of his earlier play this was inappropriate enough; here it is simply an ironical comment on Victor's failure to recognise his own freedom of action. Unlike Miller's own conception of the tragic hero he does 'remain passive in the face of...a challenge to his dignity'.[153] He tries to justify his failure by reference to personal and social necessity, but under Walter's ruthless questioning it soon becomes apparent that his failure was entirely his own responsibility. He denies his freedom rather than accept the price that goes with it.

The paramount need to accept the consequences of one's actions; the need to 'take one's life in one's hands',[154] as Holga had put it in *After the Fall*, is underlined in *The Price* by Solomon. At eighty-nine he had thought his life finished until contacted by Victor. Now, faced with the prospect of disposing of the furniture, he seems to get a new lease on life. He is suddenly aware that there are 'more possibilities'. This, indeed, is the very heart of the play. Victor has been living his life as though there were no alternatives. He is trapped, in Saul Bellow's words, in a perpetual state of 'becoming' rather than 'being'. Like Quentin, he has been mortgaging the present to the future. In *After the Fall*, Quentin had finally come to realise this, confessing of his personal future that, 'I've been carrying it around all my life, like a vase that must never be dropped.'[155] In *The Price*, it is Victor's wife, Esther, who points out that 'all these years we've been saying, once we get the pension we're going to start to live...It's like pushing against a door for twenty-five years and suddenly it opens...and we stand there...everything's always about-to-be.'[156] The furniture itself, stored for sixteen years in a single room and left untouched, is in many ways an appropriate image for Victor himself. When Solomon says of the furniture that its main drawback lies in the fact that it has 'no more possibilities', the comment could obviously apply equally well to Victor's own self-image. But even after the need for some kind of positive action has been demonstrated both by Solomon and Walter he is still unwilling to concede the truth of Esther's comment that, 'You can't go on blaming everything on...the system or God knows what else! You're free and you can't make a move.'[157]

The two brothers in *The Price* represent profoundly different approaches to life – approaches which not only coexist in the world but which constitute the basis of most individual lives. This is the significance of Walter's remark that 'we're brothers. It was only two seemingly different roads out of the same trap. It's almost as though...we're like two halves of the same guy. As though we can't quite move ahead – alone.'[158] The qualities of the two brothers are ambiguously presented. At first sight it appears to be simply a contrast between heroic self-sacrifice and callous self-interest. But beneath this public face is what Pirandello used to call the 'naked figures'. This apparent reversal of moral force is evidence of Miller's wish to penetrate to 'the pantheon of forces and values which must lie behind the realistic surfaces of life'.[159] Victor is revealed as a weak and irresolute individual, unwilling to concede responsibility for his own life and consciously avoiding painful realities by retreating into illusion. Walter, on the other hand, is a man who, like Biff, has gradually come to understand the inconsequence of wealth and success and who now tries to pass on his insight to others. He recognises the need to acknowledge the reality of human weakness and to accept responsibility for one's own actions.

When Edward Albee presented a similar contrast between those who lived in a fantasy world and those who insisted on the primacy of reality, in *Who's Afraid of Virginia Woolf?*, he suggested that illusion, far from destroying man's loneliness merely exacerbated it. Only when George and Martha have ritualistically destroyed their illusions does real contact beween them become a possibility. The same is essentially true here. As Walter points out, 'It is all an illusion and if you could walk through it we could meet.'[160] To Albee, this conflict between illusion and reality has a political and moral dimension, for continued refusal to acknowledge reality is as lethal on a national and international scale as it is for the significantly named George and Martha. This further dimension is a significant part of Miller's play too, for in a production note he insists that, 'As the world now operates the qualities of both brothers are necessary to it.' But while accepting their necessity in the world 'as it now operates' he admits that 'their respective psychologies and moral values conflict at the heart of the social dilemma'.[161] This conflict is not simply defined by the individual brothers in some kind of moral polarity. If Walter has a clearer understanding of reality and the need to accept responsibility for one's actions he lacks Victor's moral sensitivity. Yet the struggle is to find an interpretation of existence which depends neither on a naive endorsement of human perfectibility nor a cynical pose of alienation. The real problem lies in acknowledging human imperfection and the inadequacy of society, and yet continuing to place one's faith in human potential. In the words of the wise Solomon, 'it's not that you can't believe nothing, that's not so hard – it's that you've still got to believe it. *That's hard*. And if you can't do that...you're a dead man.'[162] As a piece of moral philosophy this is no different in kind from Quentin's final perception, in *After the Fall*, that it is perhaps enough to know that 'we meet unblessed; not in some garden of wax fruit and painted trees, that lie of Eden, but after, after the Fall'.[163] To accept imperfection in individuals and in society is not to capitulate before despair. Rather it is the first stage in the reconstruction of meaning and purpose. But there is a price to pay for such a revaluation. It means granting the death of innocence; it necessitates the acceptance of responsibility for one's actions. However, the price for ignoring the challenge is even greater. It involves the destruction of human relationships and the erosion of identity – a price paid by both Victor and Walter. At the end of the play, however, purged of all illusions and forced to face the reality of their lives, they have at least a chance to recreate not only themselves but also the society which they in part represent. In this way the social element of Miller's work is traced to its origin in the nature of individual experience and the essence of human experience.

Like the earlier *After the Fall*, *The Price* has a further intriguing dimension in that it offers an insight into Miller's sense of his own role as a successful playwright. Günter Grass has said that 'art is uncompromising and life is full of compromises', adding that 'To bring them together is a near impossibility, and that is what I am trying to do.'[164] Miller's attempts to reconcile art and reality have reached some kind of climax in his recent work, just as the personality of the artist has progressively become a matter of central concern to him. For many critics the autobiographical nature of *After the Fall* was crass and unwelcome, and while too many disregard the play's genuine virtues there can be little doubt that it is an intensely personal document, commenting not merely on the vicissitudes of his private affairs but also on the problems of the writer. When Quentin confesses, 'I felt I was merely in the service of my own success',[165] this can be seen as not merely the complaint of a lawyer suddenly made aware of the inadequacy of his life but also as the comment of a playwright desperately reassessing the nature of his personal and artistic career. The advocate, indeed, is an appropriate image for the writer, but so too is the surgeon. It comes as no surprise, therefore, to find that *The Price*, like *After the Fall*, has an equally personal dimension; a parallel which is enforced when Walter accuses himself of becoming 'a kind of instrument...that cuts money out of people and fame out of the world'.[166]

The parallel between the surgeon and the writer is apt enough. For both are concerned with penetrating beneath the surface in order, as one of Albee's characters has put it, to get down to 'the bone, the marrow'. Both are trying to discover the true nature of a disease which manifests itself in external symptoms. This is the implication of Miller's remark: 'I am trying to account as best I can for the realistic surface of life.'[167] Both playwright and surgeon are also faced with a choice of motives. Do they act from personal ambition or from an objective integrity? The question, as we saw in *After the Fall*, has long haunted Miller. When Walter admits that he has been trying to 'pull off the impossible. Shame the competition',[168] one is even reminded of Hemingway's fisherman, in *The Old Man and the Sea*, whose suffering symbolised the writer's own anguish and whose attempt to achieve more than others was the cause both of his unique success and of his apparent failure. Yet Miller acknowledges a doubt which never seems to have troubled the self-assured Hemingway. For, like his surgeon protagonist, he fears that 'In dead centre, directing my hands' is none other than 'my ambition – for thirty years'. The craft has become subordinate to ambition and wealth. In Walter's words, 'I wanted to be tops – I ended in a swamp of success and bankbooks.'[169]

Miller's own dissatisfaction with his Broadway success is well known. *After the Fall* was first produced for Lincoln Center because, as he himself put it, 'the first order of business in this theatre is to open the theatre to a wider audience, an audience of students, of people who are not totally oriented to the most vacant kind of entertainment'.[170] While he could scarcely classify his own work in these terms he is aware that for many critics and writers Broadway success is taken as evidence of inconsequence. While he has not shown the attraction for Off-Broadway productions of his work that Tennessee Williams evidenced, it is clear from his own comments that he feels somewhat uneasy about a success built on an audience which is 'totally strange to the aims and the preoccupations of the artists'.[171] Success, like failure, then, has its price.

On reading Jerzy Kosinski's *The Painted Bird*, Miller wrote a letter to the author. 'The surrealistic quality of [the novel] is a powerful blow on my mind', he wrote, 'because it is so carefully kept within the margins of probability and fact.' He continued: 'To me, the Nazi experience is the key one of this century – they merely carried to the final extreme what otherwise lies within so-called normal social existence and normal man. You have made the normality of it all apparent, and this is a very important and difficult thing to have done.'[172] He responded to Kosinski's work because he, too, had struggled to dramatise the normality of what he did not hesitate to call evil. Indeed, in many ways, that has always been Miller's subject. It simply took him several decades to recognise it. It focussed finally and most completely in *Playing for Time*, a television film based on Fania Fenelon's experience as a member of the wo:..en's orchestra in the Auschwitz–Birkenau concentration camp.

Fania Fenelon, a half-Jewish Parisian nightclub singer, is arrested and transported to Auschwitz where her life is saved only by virtue of her musical talents. She, and other prisoners, are required to form an orchestra which will entertain the camp staff and provide an accompaniment to the daily ritual of work and genocide. And though in a stage direction Miller refers to Dr Mengele, the motorious camp doctor, as a 'monster', a crucial moment in the text occurs when Fania asserts his human identity. The fact that the camp personnel can both kill and admire music is not a paradox. It is, in a sense, because they are human that they do both. As Fania remarks of a woman guard, 'What disgusts me is that a woman so beautiful can do what she is doing...Don't try to make her ugly, Esther...she's beautiful and human.

We are the same species. And that is what's so hopeless about this whole thing.'[173] It is for this reason that she can accept none of the consolations offered to her. Neither the prospect of a homeland in Palestine for the Jews nor the hope of a post-war Communist state, clung to like so many talismans by some of the other inmates, can mean anything to her because, as she insists, 'we know a little something about the human race that we didn't know before. And it's not good news.'[174] It is for this reason that the Nazis' love of her music is some 'ultimate horror', for, on the one hand, she is forced to accept that there is nothing incompatible between total cruelty and love of art, and on the other, it deprives her of her only consolation – namely her own innocence. Indeed to survive at all is to become aware of one's own capacity for betrayal. Thus she eagerly seeks to take over when the orchestra's conductor is murdered, knowing that to ingratiate herself with those in control is the only way to survive. And yet the guilt which she feels is, paradoxically, the only available source of grace; it is the basis of a distinction which Miller was never quite able to make in *After the Fall*. It is the fact that she feels guilty which is the basis of whatever redeeming power the play identifies, for the fact is that those who perpetrate the crimes will survive the war and 'everyone around you will be innocent, from one end of Europe to the other'.[175] And so the guilt which features in all of his work, as a burden tying the individual to others, the past to the present, the act to its consequences, is presented here as evidence for the survival of values, for the persistence of some part of the human spirit which does not resign to a pure antinomianism. Thus, although in a sense there is justice in the complaint levelled at the principal character as a collaborator, that she is 'on the side of the executioners', her justification of existence lies in two directions. Firstly, it resides in the surviving moral sense which creates her sense of guilt and which makes the prisoners capable of honouring two deaths among many in the camp because they recognise the bravery and the love which prompted them. And, secondly, it lies in her determination to remember and eventually to record the events which she has seen and experienced, and in which she feels complicity.

And it is not hard to see Miller's own justification for his art in this play. For though *Playing for Time* ends as the camera pulls back from a reunion of three of the prisoners, including Fania, in 1980, so that for the viewer 'we resume the normality of life and the irony of it...the life that continues and continues',[176] the fact of Fania's book and Miller's play represents some kind of transcendence and, above all, some justification for survival. For the fact that there are those who feel the need to justify their lives is evidence of the fact that a full picture of human potential has to take account of this moral drive as it does of the temptations of cruelty and betrayal.

The achievement of *Playing for Time* is that for the most part it avoids sentimentality; indeed, it sees sentimentality, particularly among the German characters, as an evasion of human commitment. The principal characters – Fania Fenelon and the conductor, Alma – are ambiguous figures. Their strengths are, to some degree, their weaknesses. The single-minded drive to survive is intimately connected to moments of surrender and even betrayal. But it is not primarily a play about heroism, and, while concentrating on a small group of prisoners, Miller makes a conscious attempt to convey the sheer scale of the disaster:

> From time to time, one or more of the secondary characters will emerge in the foreground of the story in order to keep alive and vivid the sense that the 'background group' is made of individuals. If the film is to approach even an indication of the vastness of the human disaster involved, the minor characters will have to be kept dramatically alive even in shots where they are only seen and don't have lines.[177]

Inevitably, on the television screen the attempt to approach an epic effect fails. However, more than either of the other two plays with which Miller attempted to tackle the experience of the camps, Playing for Time dramatises not merely the horrors which have quite clearly haunted his imagination for more than forty years but also the problem of justifying to himself his survival as a Jew and as a writer condemned to continue after the death of his own early optimism and after the extinction of a certain kind of hope. To survive the camps is to inherit an obligation. In this play both Fania Fenelon and Arthur Miller seek to discharge that obligation.

But the concern with complicity, with the need to acknowledge kinship with the persecutor, was not purely a product of these late plays. It is true that in After the Fall, Incident at Vichy and Playing for Time he was attempting to confront an imperfect human nature, to confess to a disturbing failure of moral vision which seems as much a birthright as the necessity to transcend such a painful truth. But in fact it had been implicit in much of his earlier work, except that then he had been unable or unwilling to track such evidence to its origin. Hence the moral equivocation of Chris in All My Sons, Biff in Death of a Salesman and John Proctor in The Crucible exists as fact but not really as a matter of central dramatic concern. There is, indeed, a speech which he delivered in 1956 in which he spells out the direction of his thought and which focusses, interestingly enough, on his own sense of dissatisfaction with another play that attempted to confront an aspect of the holocaust – The Diary of Anne Frank. Confessing to the power of the work he nonetheless objected that:

> with all its truth the play lacks the kind of spread vision, the over-vision beyond its characters and their problems which could have illuminated not merely the cruelty of Nazism but something even more terrible... What was necessary in this play to break the hold of reassurance upon the audience, and to make

it match the truth of life, was that we should see the bestiality in our own hearts, so that we should know how we are brothers not only to these victims but to the Nazis, so that the ultimate terror of our lives should be faced – namely our own sadism, our own ability to obey orders from above, our own fear of standing firm on humane principle against the obscene power of the mass organization. Another dimension was waiting to be opened up behind this play, a dimension covered with our own sores, a dimension revealing us to ourselves. Once this dimension had been unveiled we could not have watched in the subtly perverse comfort of pathos; our terror would no longer be for those others but for ourselves, once that part of ourselves which covertly conspires with destruction was made known. Then, for one thing, tragedy would have been possible, for the issue would not have been why the Nazis were so cruel, but why human beings – ourselves, us – are so cruel. The pathetic is the refusal or inability to discover and face ultimate relevancy for the race; it is therefore a shield against ultimate dramatic effect.[178]

In part he was describing the concerns of *The Crucible*, written just three years earlier, and, indeed, as previously suggested the events of the holocaust are perhaps more relevant to that play than is conventionally supposed. But the faults of John Proctor, of his wife Elizabeth, and of the townsfolk Rebecca Nurse and Giles Corey are simply disproportionate to that evil which he posits in their judges to make the connection convincing. And while much the same is true of the later work betrayal is presented in a context in which more than personal dignity and self-respect are at stake. On the other hand the very clarity of analysis in the later plays, the concern with exposing in language and action a complicity which relates the individual to his persecutors, discharges the dramatic tension which is sustained in the earlier works. Granted too clear an insight into their own actions and motives his characters tend to become less compelling as individuals as they become more convincing as exemplars. Their emotional truth is sacrificed to their allegorical utility. The fate of Willy Loman and John Proctor matter in a way that that of Quentin and Von Berg do not. John Proctor has a self-conscious awareness denied to Willy Loman but he still sees experience in terms of his own desperate need to sustain a self-image commensurate with his aspirations. The characters in his later plays tend to see themselves in terms of history and metaphysics. Miller may be concerned with the relationship between human nature and the private and public acts of the individual. It is dramatically unconvincing, however, when his characters do likewise. Willy Loman, denied access to his own inner being, seemingly unaware of the relationship between his own hopes, dreams and failings, is finally more believable and moving than those who, alarmingly, are all too fully aware.

Stylistically, Miller conceived of himself as an experimentalist. He had come to feel that 'realism, as a style, could seem to be a defence against the assertion of meaning'.[179] Concerned, on the one hand, with penetrating the inner world of confused motive and suppressed guilt, and, on the other, with establishing not merely a social context but also the social extension of that inner world, he created a stage setting where there could be a free-flowing continuum between the two. Social realities, in both *Death of a Salesman* and *After the Fall*, could thus at one moment be granted a hard-edged, tangible substantiality, and at the next be dissolved as the mind retreats into itself. Time dissolves because the mind which he wishes to dramatise is capable of near instantaneous temporal dislocations. Though the presumptions of realism remained strong, Miller was not drawn to any particular style. The form grew out of the play. In *A View from the Bridge* the engaged narrator was a response to what he took to be the failure of the audience to distinguish subject from theme in *The Crucible*; it was his attempt to project beyond the closed circle of Eddie Carbone's mind. Yet his experimentalism has not, perhaps, been as great as he himself imagined. The engaged narrator clearly owed something to Wilder's *Our Town* while *The Price* seems to constitute precisely that realistic drama against which he imagined himself to be in revolt. Indeed Miller's formal sense of structure was fundamentally conservative. Thus he observed, in the introduction to his *Collected Plays*, that 'A play must end, and end with a climax, and to forge a climax the forces in life, which are of infinite complexity, must be made finite and capable of a more or less succinct culmination.'[180] And this observation was made after Beckett's and Ionesco's plays had been performed. Yet, in *A Memory of Two Mondays*, he showed that he was quite capable of creating a play whose circularities come close not merely to embodying an absurdist ethic but to generating a form the ironies of which are crucially contained in the tension between character – fragile, contingent – and setting. When the windows of a grimy factory are cleaned they reveal only a whorehouse. Sober or drunk his characters occupy the same constricting and deforming environment – rising above it only to the extent that their frustrated and inarticulate dreams are an expression of resistance. The play is a comment on theatre no less than on life. The new light thrown on experience may simply reveal a reality more sordid than that perceived through daily routine; but the will to imagine may be the only remaining freedom.

Perhaps this is what Miller meant when he claimed that this play, in common with *A View from the Bridge*, demonstrates the impulse to

> present rather than represent an interpretation of reality...for a moment I was striving not to make people forget they were in a theatre, not to obliterate an awareness of form, not to forge a pretence of life, but to be abrupt, clear and explicit in setting forth fact as fact and art as art so that the sea of theatrical sentiment, which is so easily let in to drown all shape, meaning and perspective, might be held back and some hard outline of a human dilemma be allowed to rise and stand.[181]

Clearly it was in some degree a naive assumption. Wilder's narrator, his deliberate foregrounding of technique, has never acted as any kind of barrier and even Brecht's attempt at alienation in *Mother Courage* proved a consistent and, to Brecht, a disheartening failure. But his concern with theatricality and the nature of the real, always, perhaps, a submerged theme of his plays, was itself to move into the foreground in a fascinating and effective way with later plays such as *The Archbishop's Ceiling* and the two one-act plays eventually published as *Two Way Mirror*.

And Miller did see the theatre as a paradigm of human behaviour. In his introduction to the *Collected Plays* he observes that 'Determinism, whether it is based on the iron necessities of economics or on psychoanalytic theory seen as a closed circle, is a contradiction of the idea of drama itself as drama has come down to us in its fullest development. The idea of the hero, let alone the mere protagonist, is incompatible with a drama whose bounds are set in advance by the concept of an unbreakable trap.' Interestingly, while conceding that 'in sociology, psychology, psychiatry, and religion, the past half century has created an almost overwhelming documentation of man as a nearly passive creative of environment and family-created psychological drives', he observes that, 'If only from the dramatic point of view, this dictum cannot be accepted as final and "realistic".'[182] It is a curiously inverted argument which owes something to the modernist's view of art as a final resource. The imagination creates its own necessities. But all this is merely playful rhetoric, for at the heart of Miller's philosophy is a conviction that the human will is not susceptible of defeat, that within the constraining power of the psychological and social world there remains a resistant self which is undetermined and that the theatre properly celebrates that self — that 'however closely he is measured and systematically accounted for, he is more than the sum of his stimuli and is unpredictable, beyond a certain point'. And hence 'a drama, like a history, which stops at this point, the point of conditioning, is not reflecting reality'.[183] And so it becomes apparent that what is at stake is not a debate about the nature of realism but an assertion about the nature of reality.

This is nowhere more apparent than in *The Archbishop's Ceiling*, in which, for virtually the first time, his assurance about the nature of the real begins to crumble. It is a play which suggests the impact on the one hand of Watergate (in which the presence of microphones in the Oval office of the White House turned the events which transpired there into a form of theatre) and on the other of the ontological dilemma of the East European, never entirely sure whether his behaviour is observed, his conversations overheard, and his very being read as a kind of code which may be transcribed as innocence or incorrigible guilt.

The play is set in eastern Europe, in a now somewhat tatty residence which had once housed an archbishop. Adrian, an American writer, arrives to see Maya, a woman with whom he had once had an affair and who features in the new novel he is writing. His motives are tangled. Partly he is trying to test out the rumours he has heard which suggest that she and Marcus, the one time dissident writer with whom she is living, are in fact agents of the state, luring people into the house, which is electronically bugged, in order to make them betray themselves. Partly he is seeking some kind of absolution for the betrayal implied in the act of incorporating her in his art as a mere character (he has made her a character in his new novel). But the central conceit of the play is that the presence of hidden microphones does no less, while even this is merely a paradigm of social behaviour which turns everyone into an actor. As Adrian asks, 'Is it always like a performance? Like we're quoting ourselves?'[184] When Sigmund, a dissident writer friend, arrives, shattered by the seizure of the only manuscript of his new book, he underlines the point. Indicating the ceiling which may or may not conceal a microphone he insists that 'We are some sort of characters in a poem which they are writing; it is not my poem, it is their poem.'[185] And yet to resist the public fictions it becomes necessary to generate private ones. As Sigmund explains:

> ...perhaps is not exactly lying because we do not expect to deceive anyone; the professor lies to the student, the student to the professor – but each knows the other is lying. We must lie, it is our only freedom...Is like a serious play, which no one really believes that the technique is admirable. Our country is now a theatre, where no one is permitted to walk out, and everyone is obliged to applaud.[186]

When Marcus objects that this is simply a description of the whole world Sigmund insists that it is specific to his society and that as a consequence 'I believe everything but am convinced of nothing.'[187] Miller is less willing to see it as a special case and the play thus becomes simultaneously a social critique and a recognition of the factitious nature of his own work.

The 'real' is more problematic in The Archbishop's Ceiling than in any of his earlier works. There is still a reality and there are still legitimate human demands but these are less securely rooted. They are plainly not embedded in any absolute set of values. God is absent – merely another construction, another fiction. He no longer presides over His house any more than does the Archbishop over his. The new gods are the power brokers ('angels hovering overhead. Like power always with you in a room. Like God, in a way'[188]) or the creators of fiction ('You are like God...You can always create new people'[189]), artistic or political. It is power which makes the filaments glow. For Marcus, power has always resided in the collective and religion has merely been an image of that fact. Thus he asks 'When was a man ever conceivable apart from society? Unless you're looking for the angel who wrote each of our blessed names in his book of gold. The collective giveth and the collective taketh away – beyond that...was never anything but a metaphor; which now is simply a form of art.'[190] When the manuscript taken from Sigmund is arbitrarily returned the gesture has no meaning beyond the fact that it underlines the power of authority to do anything. The mysterious ways of God are thus easily translated into the mysterious ways of man. But Sigmund's moral superiority is not easily detachable from the forces which he opposes. He needs them in order to define himself. Indeed, in a sense, *The Archbishop's Ceiling* is another cry of *mea culpa* from Miller for just as each of the writers in the play is forced to acknowledge that to some degree his or her art is in the service of their own drive for power or prestige ('Always to them, in some part to them for any profit – here and everywhere in this world!'[191] and 'For your monument. For the bowing ushers in the theatre. For the power...the power to bring down everyone.'[192]) so Miller seems to be examining the roots of his own art. In *All My Sons* the moral ideal was propounded by a character whose own self-interest was patent if unexamined. Now, he examines, with some honesty, the situation of a writer whose career has to some degree been built on his stance as moral arbiter, whose fictions have been deployed in the name of truth, and whose success has not been unconnected with his assault on those whose desire to occupy centre stage is different in degree but perhaps not kind from a certain artistic hubris. It is also, perhaps, in some ways a lament that 'reality' has been so suffused with art that the two are no longer easily distinguishable if, indeed, they ever had been. As Adrian laments: 'Funny how life imitates art; the melodrama kept flattening out my characterizations. It's an interesting problem – whether it matters who anyone is or what anyone thinks, when all that counts anymore – is power.'[193].

The play ends with Sigmund deciding not to flee the country – the implied price of having his manuscript returned to him – and with the daughter of a Minister arriving who may rescue or condemn him. It is a work that addresses issues which in many ways are antecedent to those that have engaged him throughout his career. Certainly his concern with the nature of the real, his sense of the theatre as paradigm, his suggestion that social power is simply a substitute for religious authority (for which, indeed, it had perhaps always been a metaphor) raise questions which surface elsewhere in his work in a different form. The social and the psychological defer in some degree to the ontological. The world is reduced to competing fictions. And yet not quite. In some paradoxical sense Sigmund's putative gesture at the end of the play is presumed to have meaning. In some way it seems immune to the relativism which the play's logic seems to imply. The microphones may or may not exist, the characters may or may not be motivated by self-interest; betrayal, in one form or another, may typify every single character in the play (as it does) but there seems to be an irreducible commitment which retains genuine substance. One of the play's paradoxes is in the baldness of this assertion. Of course we may simply be seeing another example of self-deception, another protective fiction, another piece of bad theatre by an individual still playing a double game for the hidden listeners but the logic of his character and the play's dramatic logic seems otherwise. The problem which faces the characters is simply how they are to reconstitute a moral world when reality itself is seen as problematic and character reduced to role. And the characters in *The Archbishop's Ceiling* are flattened, just as are those in Adrian's novel. They could scarcely be otherwise. They are acting out roles imposed on them by those who create the *mise-en-scène* of their lives. Their problem is how to step outside this world of fiction. The playwright's problem is to make us care. They represent various different positions (the observer, the compromiser, the resister). In a sense they have been cast into these parts by those who remain hidden from us and them or simply by their conviction that such people exist. And that of course is the crux. Precisely what is the nature of the determinism the pressure of which they feel but of the reality of which they can never be entirely sure? What is the extent of the freedom to which they wish to lay claim? And if the world in which they move is purely factitious, if what they take for the real is mere appearance or vice versa, then how can they locate themselves, validate the relationships which they forge or justify the positions which they adopt. Their dilemma and ours is to find some basis for moral action in a world apparently composed of nothing more substantial than competing fictions.

In an odd way they are dependent for the meaning of their lives on what they believe to be the hidden presence of the secret police. It is that which gives a particular shape to their lives and a meaning to their gestures. In a paradoxical sense, then, the real terror may be that there is no one there, that they are condemned to pure contingency and that they are wholly responsible for their lives. Like Clare and Felice in Williams's *Out Cry*, they may be on a stage in an empty theatre. And behind the psychological, social and political drama there is clearly a metaphysical anxiety in the play which moves Miller closer to Beckett and Pinter than ever before. The real pressure comes from not knowing, from a sense of profound uncertainty which destabilises the foundation of action and being.

As a contemplation of the ironies of art no less than life it is a fascinating play. Miller's audiences, after all, are in a sense his hidden listeners and hence are complicit in the moral and metaphysical conundrums which the play poses. And although it is worth recalling that a number of his earlier plays had themselves been concerned with the nature and meaning of the real (from *Death of a Salesman* onwards), *The Archbishop's Ceiling* clearly marked a major new phase in his work. That it failed in performance had less to do with its intrinsic merits than with a resolutely realistic production. Played for its realism, it was in fact a work which set out to deconstruct that realism and dramatise anxieties which go far beyond a concern for psychological veracity or social analysis.

Miller was conscious of the problem of staging the play in America. As he has explained:

> I came to realize that it wasn't just America; I think it's anywhere. This is the essence of *The Archbishop's Ceiling* which is about Czechoslovakia. People aren't aware really of what the situation is. I don't know what will ever make them aware of it in a country like that, but that isn't what the play depends on anyway. The play would depend, if it were articulated properly, on a kind of awareness that the State is in the wrong, the great power is in the wrong.

But, beyond this, the play engaged a level of ontological and metaphysical concern which seems to have got lost in production. Certainly this was the dimension which Miller himself chose to stress. As one of the play's characters observes:

> 'You know, it's just like God...You don't know whether he's there or not, and so you'd better speak as though he were there.' But they rebel against it, then they are not sure whether they are being simply stupid. I mean, what's the point of rebelling against something that isn't there and so it makes a kind of comedy of this disaster. Well, I think I did not succeed in making the terms of this disaster as clear as I might, because, you see, while we bug and have bugged everything and everybody forever, it's not in the consciousness of the American people. One doesn't go around thinking of being bugged. It's not a social play in that sense. It's really a play about reality.[194]

And, as he insisted, if you don't know whom you address, 'You don't know who you are.' It is in this sense that the play is both a new departure and a continuation of his concern with the nature and form of reality.

And in November 1982, two new one-act plays were performed at the Long Wharf Theatre in New Haven which confirmed this new direction in his work. Once again they had a less than satisfactory production which tended to stress a realism at odds with their intent. *Some Kind of Love Story* and *Elegy for a Lady* were not so much the five-finger exercises in psychological realism that they appeared to be as further examinations of the nature of the real. Ideal companion pieces – one being a powerful dramatisation of a psychosis which is as much that of a culture as of the individual who bears its marks, the other a lyrical, elegaic tone poem which forms and dissolves like a memory, possibly true, possible the purest fiction – they combine to create a double vision of a reality to be distrusted but accepted. Indeed when the plays were published in an acting edition Miller added an Author's Note which stressed precisely this dimension:

> The stories and characters of this pair of plays are unrelated to one another but in different ways both works are passionate voyages through the masks of illusion to an ultimate reality. In *Some Kind of Love Story* it is social reality and the corruption of justice which a delusionary woman both conceals and unveils. The search in *Elegy for a Lady* is for the shape and meaning of a sexual relationship that is being brought to a close by a lover's probable death. In both the unreal is an agony to be striven against and, at the same time, accepted as life's condition.[195]

Some Kind of Love Story concerns an attempt by a detective to arrive at the facts about a murder committed some five years earlier. Convinced that an innocent man is in jail he continues to try to extract the truth from Angela, a call girl, who is terrified to the point of psychosis. Indeed, whenever he seems to be getting close to the truth she reverts to one of a series of alternative personalities. At one time the two had been lovers but now what links them is primarily the crime to which she may be the key, the apparent truth which she constantly promises to reveal. But it is precisely her failure to realise this promise which keeps their relationship alive. His problem is how to derive the truth from someone who seems literally insane; hers is how to convince him that she is not paranoid in her fears of retribution. By degrees, however, he seems to succeed in extracting the information he needs. She reveals a conspiracy which involves both the police and a local prosecutor but continues to hint at further revelations if he will not desert her, and refuses him the evidence which he needs. On the one hand Miller seems to imply that with corruption at the heart of things the real is dangerously irrecoverable ('I've got to stop looking for some red tag that says "Real" on it', says the detective. 'I think that somewhere way upstream the corruption is poisoning the water and making us a little crazy....'), and on the other hand he seems to destabilise the very idea of reality. All that remains is a plausible fiction. As the detective remarks, 'If it's real for me then that's the last question I can ask.'[196]

In *Elegy for a Lady* reality becomes even more problematic. The play begins with a man, who appears in a single beam of light. Slowly elements of what seems to be a boutique emerge, almost as if they were being summoned into being by his mind, as perhaps they are, for the shop 'consists of its elements without the walls, the fragments seeming to be suspended in space'. But just as he is discovered staring 'as though lost in thought...deep into himself', so, too, is the woman, the Proprietress, who stands motionless 'in passive thought',[197] and who perhaps creates the man who now engages her in conversation. He asks for something appropriate to a dying woman and, though they speak, seemingly, of a third person, when she replies it is 'With helpless personal involvement'.[198] And as the play proceeds so the clues appear to build up. Thus the man describes the shop's proprietress as having 'her coloring' and being 'just about her age', while she replies with a 'throaty, almost vulgar laugh' of a kind which we are told characterises the dying woman. The detached nature of the exchanges implies a lack of intimacy between them but this is precisely what the proprietress accuses the man of having brought to his relationship with the woman, observing that a point is reached in such a relationship when 'it begins to be an effort to keep it uncommitted'.[199] By degrees they begin to address one another in the role of the man and the dying woman but it is unclear as to whether these are roles which they are adopting for the occasion or whether they are the two figures in question. We seem close to the world of Pinter's *Old Times* or *Silence*. Even memory seems insecure. Neither can remember when they first met nor, as it turns out, can the man even be certain as to the progress of the woman's disease, or even her location. Perhaps a clue lies in the proprietress's remark of the dying woman that doubtless 'She tends to objectify her situation... Sees herself... From a distance... She's had to control because she's alone.'[200] Like Pinter's *Monologue* what we see may be no more than the projection of a single mind. Certainly *Elegy for a Lady* ends with the darkness flooding back and the man 'facing front, staring'. But in the world of the play there is no certainty. Everything is, indeed, a fiction. In the last resort all plays are peopled by the solitary imagination of their writers who invent for a myriad of reasons, many of which are irrecoverable. In a sense they may do so as an act of resistance against mortality but equally they may do so as a celebration of possibility. In a sense both *Death of a Salesman* and *After the Fall* take place within the minds of their protagonists, so that the nature of the real has always been an implicit concern of his work. *The Crucible* was, apart from anything else, a debate over who should have the power to define the real. These plays, then, can be traced to a concern evident throughout his career. But now this has become a major theme in some essential way antecedent to questions of public and private morality but ineluctably linked to them as to more profound questions having to do with our existence in a world of fictions, our own and those of others.

For Miller, the Depression was a central experience. Not only had it shaped his own imagination and defined the terms of his own engagement with American values, but it was one of the few experiences genuinely shared by the American people as a whole. It provided the subject matter for his early unproduced and unpublished work; it prompted the political sympathies which, twenty years later, brought him before the House Un-American

Activities Committee and, together with the events of the Second World War, it seems to have convinced him, on the one hand, of the fragility of personal identity and the social contract and, on the other, of the necessity to reaffirm the substance and significance of that identity and that contract. And if betrayal became a constant theme of his work, then it operated on a public no less than a private level. For the Miller who grew up in the 1930s the process of disillusionment, which is perhaps a natural part of the rites of passage from adolescence to maturity, coincided with a stripping of masks at a national level.

This also is essentially the process behind *The American Clock*, first produced at the Harold Clurman Theatre in New York City before opening at the Biltmore Theatre on 20 November 1980. Set in the 1930s and 1940s, it is an attempt to turn back 'the American Clock...in search of those feelings that once ruled our lives and were stolen from us all by time'.[201] It is a familiar process in Miller's plays. The present contains the past while that past contains the clue to present behaviour. And *The American Clock* continues Miller's attempts to psychoanalyse America, to trace the origins of trauma. As he said in a speech to the Dramatists' Committee in 1956–7,

> I used long ago to keep a book in which I would talk to myself. One of the aphorisms I wrote was, 'The structure of a play is always the story of how the birds came home to roost.' The hidden will be unveiled; the inner laws of reality will announce themselves; I was defining my impression of 1929 as well as dramatic structure.[202]

The play in some senses comes full circle back to those early works submitted to the WPA in so far as it identifies in capitalism itself the source of a terrifying amorality. But where in those early plays he had been inclined to dramatise his capitalists as simple crooks and knowing exploiters of labour, now he is inclined to show them as baffled men, for the most part decent and without malice. They are as profoundly betrayed as those they have pulled along in their wake. The ideological certainty has disappeared. He offers brief portraits of petty officials anxious to capitalise on the situation but, for the most part, he seems concerned with offering a portrait of an America bewildered by the collapse of the dream.

A central figure, Lee, a young boy who seems to reflect something of Miller's own experiences of the Depression, is allowed to offer an analysis which would not have been remote from Miller's own at the time: 'I keep trying to find the holes in Marxism but I can't. I just read an article where the salaries of twelve executives in the tobacco business was more than thirty thousand tobacco farmers made. That's what has happened – the workers never made enough to buy back what they produced. The boom of the Twenties was a gigantic fake. The rich have simply looted the people.'[203]

But the prediction with which he concludes this analysis – 'There is going to be a revolution' – deliberately undermines an analysis which, though reflecting accurately enough the instinctive radicalism of many at the time, remains at the level of rhetoric in the play as it did in the America of the 1930s.

The American Clock is in some respects a curious play. In a sense it is a pastiche of the attitudes and even the style of 1930s drama. In the original production some thirty-five parts were played by fifteen actors. These parts included financiers, farmers, a shoe-shine man, a prostitute, a seaman, and so on. In other words, it is a play which has epic pretensions, trying in some way to capture the mood of an entire society. But onto this is grafted, not entirely successfully, the story of a single family – the Baums. The collapse of their upper-middle-class life is offered as in some sense a paradigm of the disintegration of a central American myth – the prosperous immigrant family. Yet for all its offer to demythologise, to expose the fundamental betrayal of American values which he believes to have occurred in the 1920s and 1930s, it is a portrait which is still tainted with a certain residual nostalgia. The scenes that attempt to explore the poverty and need in the country at large remain, for the most part, at the level of assertion, brief agit-prop sketches which involve dispossession sales, and the feeding of a starving man with the milk from a baby's bottle (a less risqué version of the concluding scene of Steinbeck's *The Grapes of Wrath*). Those which concentrate on the Baum family show a group of people largely rising above their difficulties, displaying a resilience which seems not to be wholly unconnected with their apparent class superiority. There is, too, a certain smugness about the son's final speech which seems rooted less in his sensibility than in Miller's own liberal convictions. Thus, he observes that the Great Depression went down with the fleet at Pearl Harbour, 'and with it, too, our resigned toleration of pointless suffering. Much was clarified by that blast.'[204] And, though he expresses uncertainty as to the reality of his mother's conviction 'that the world was meant to be better', he confesses that 'whenever I think of her...I always end up – with this headful of life!' The play ends with his mother at the piano uttering the single word, 'Sing', as the stage directions indicate that 'bright light flashes over the cloud-covered continent in the background'.[205] The end, in other words, directly mimics the conclusion of so many 1930s plays, most especially those of Clifford Odets. And it is difficult to resist the conclusion that *The American Clock* is Miller's attempt to pay his debt to the past.

It is the play which he never succeeded in getting produced in the 1930s, except that now he brings to it a kind of benediction which it is difficult to accept. Miller never wrote a play about Vietnam or the America so at odds with itself in the 1970s, unless it be *The Archbishop's Ceiling* which could

15. Joan Copeland and John Randolph in *The American Clock* at the Biltmore Theatre, New York, 1980.

perhaps be regarded as a response to the confusions and ambiguities of Watergate transposed to an East European setting. Instead, after his painful contemplation of the lessons of the war and the persecutions which followed it, he chooses to opt for nostalgia. *The American Clock* seems to have leapt back over such ambiguities to an era of clear issues in which character was unproblematic and rhetoric operated outside of the ironies which seem increasingly to have defined the nature of American experience. It is a hybrid play in several respects. It comes late in his career and has the air of a final gesture in its attempt at reconciliation, in its effort to lay the ghosts of the past and in the note of indulgent hope with which it concludes. Like Shakespeare's *The Tempest* it appears to offer a grace of sorts, to retreat some way from the extremes of human cruelty and self-betrayal, the moments of courage, of guilt, of anger and occasional despair which his plays forged into such potent images of a mid-twentieth-century world.

From the beginning of his career Arthur Miller has seen the individual being as deeply flawed but capable of resisting the fact of that imperfection. In one sense he is a kind of reluctant Calvinist, believing in original sin but wishing to deny the determinism which that implies. In another sense he is a Freudian, seeing guilt as a basic mechanism of human behaviour. In yet another he is a confusing and confused blend of romantic radical and classic liberal, balancing the demands of the self against those of the group, seeing social behaviour as an expression of a fallible human nature, and announcing simultaneously the dignity, opacity and irreducible truth of personal identity

243

and the human responsibilities which potentially render that identity suspect. In Miller's work nothing exists in pure form. Everywhere is division, tension without dialectic. Society becomes both a necessary protection against an imperfect human nature and an expression of it. The self is seen as the key to moral integrity and the source of a destructive egotism. And that is at the heart of a paradox which he could never satisfactorily resolve. For the will to pursue truth, to propound brotherhood, to propose a mutually supportive society of individuals constantly founders on his conviction of an ineradicable selfishness. The freedom which is required if moral principles are ever to be realised is denied by his acknowledgement of the implacable nature of history and human character. Time has an authority and defining power which makes it difficult to concede radical change. Ibsen, dominated by the past, can, when he chooses, slam the door on that past. He can conceive the individual as cutting a vector across the social world. For Miller that past cannot be so easily denied, except in his very first plays which positively glow with a belief in the transformation of the self and society. But in the post-war plays, with the possible exception of *All My Sons* (and even here the ideal is stained with guilt and self-interest), no Miller protagonist believes, as does Ibsen's Stockmann, that the individual can successfully challenge history and the public world. They all grant its implacable nature and try to win what battles they may within its contours. Miller wishes to believe in certain fundamental moral truths. Ibsen is less sure. Miller's decision to omit Stockmann's claim, that 'There is no established truth that can remain true for more than seventeen, eighteen at most twenty years',[206] is crucial. For Miller, if that were accepted as an adequate description of reality, the moral axes of his world would collapse.

And this is why he has tended to regard his work as tragic. The crucial victory won by his characters is a private one. The struggle is to sustain one's integrity in what is accepted as a determined world. The problem is that in the early plays the rhetoric in fact suggests otherwise. It proposes the possibility of transforming society. It announces the need for a complete transformation of the social system in such a way that the individual conscience will be able to operate but can propose no way in which that transformation can be effected.

Miller's central theme is the problem of relating one's deeds to one's conception of oneself. The echoic insistence on identity, the endlessly repeated demands to sustain one's name in the face of flux and in the teeth of personal betrayal, suggests a Platonic sense of self which must be maintained. It is the correlative of that idealism, of spiritual fulfilment, which even the least articulate of his protagonists requires in order to continue living. But that absolute need to insist on one's innocence repeatedly finds itself in conflict with an imperfect human nature and a deterministic world. It is a tension which Biff Loman and John Proctor recognise, in *Death of a Salesman* and *The Crucible* respectively, and from which they derive a true sense of being. It is a tension which Willy Loman and Eddie Carbone, in *Death of a Salesman* and *A View from the Bridge*, refuse to acknowledge. As a consequence they remain locked inside their own illusions, condemned to the inner solitariness which is the result of a failure of self-knowledge. With the later plays that innocence is seen as a fantasy and the need to insist on its reality the root of human cruelty.

Miller identifies his persistent assertion of the necessity to struggle with determining realities as rooted in both his Jewish and American identity. He has said that the Jewish element is important not only in his own work but in that of a number of American writers, because the Jew cannot afford to flirt with apocalypse, cannot 'exult in disaster, because the elimination of the Jew is a credible proposition, it is one with an historical reality to it'. Consequently, 'the grip on life, the demand that life continue, is very close to the surface'.[207] And this, he sees, as equally strong in America. His work, in one form or another, is thus a search for the basis on which life may be continued, on which imperfection may be accepted as an undeniable but not disabling truth.

In recent years Miller's reputation has been somewhat eclipsed. He no longer seems to address the immediate moral problems of the age as once he did. Perhaps this is because, as Susan Sontag remarked in her essay 'Going to the Theatre, etc.', 'We still tend to choose our images of virtue from among our victims', but 'in just a few short years the old liberalism, whose archetypal figure was the Jew, has been challenged by the new militancy, whose hero is the Negro'.[208] Certainly in the 1960s and early 1970s what seemed the passive acceptance at the heart of *After the Fall* and *The Price*, and even, in a sense, of *Incident at Vichy* was at odds with the new orthodoxy. Certainly it is also true that Miller never really challenged the essential premises of his society in such a way as to suggest the necessity for or the possibility of radical change. He seemed only to advocate a kind of moralised capitalism, a return to the liberal virtues of a pre-urban New England. But he was never really a political radical. His chief struggle as an artist and as a public figure was to reinvest the individual with a moral responsibility apparently stripped from him by economic determinism and the forces of history. He believed and believes still in the social contract. But he has seen it abrogated too frequently and too profoundly to believe it to be anything but fragile and contingent. The purpose and process of his plays has thus been to locate the individual in a social context which goes some way to explain but never wholly to define his or her identity. The dominant image of his plays is of that individual in relationship to family and society, and if from the very beginning he felt that betrayal was a natural compulsion he has also continued to insist that there is a counterforce which seeks to heal the wounds, to find the meaning of the self beyond the self. If the space available for action is ever diminishing, as the city closes in on the individual and the walls of the prison cell cast their shadow, in the darkness there remains a crucial spirit of resistance. And the heart of that resistance is the imagination, which is still capable of projecting itself into the place and the sensibility of the other. And since that is the method of drama the theatre itself becomes both an image and an example of this process.

As he said in a speech made in the late 1950s:

> You can't understand anything unless you understand its relationship to its context. That much, for good [or] ill, the Great Depression taught me. It made me impatient with anything, including art, which pretends that it can exist for its own sake and still be of any importance. A thing becomes beautiful to me as it becomes internally and externally organic. It becomes beautiful because it removes some of my helplessness before the chaos of experience. I think one of the reasons I became a playwright was that in dramatic form everything must be gently organic, deeply organized, articulated from a living center.[209]

Art becomes a principal means of exposing a hidden process and hence the basis of a reassurance about the nature of experience. Outside the pure blank face of evil, which remains inscrutable to him, all experience, public and private, was available for examination and could be explained and understood by means of rational analysis. It was a lesson which he felt himself to have learned from Freud no less than Marx, from liberal philosophy no less than from writers like Dostoevsky and Ibsen. As he said of the latter:

> I connected with Ibsen not because he wrote about problems, but because he was illuminating process...From his work, read again and again with new wonders cropping up each time, as well as through Dostoevsky's, I came to an idea of what a writer was supposed to be. These two issued the license, so to speak, the only legitimate one I could conceive, for presuming to write at all. One had the right to write because other people needed news of the inner world, and if they went too long without such news they would go mad with the chaos of their lives. With the greatest of presumption I conceived that the great writer was the destroyer of chaos, a man privy to the councils of the hidden gods who administer the hidden laws that bind us all and destroy us if we do not know them. And chaos, for one thing, was life lived oblivious of history.
>
> As time went on, a lot of time, it became clear to me that I was not only reporting to others but to myself first and foremost. I wrote not only to find a way into the world but to hold it away from me so that it would not devour me.[210]

There is a fragment of a play in one of Miller's notebooks at the University of Texas in which a writer looks back over his life. It is so close to his own experience as to suggest that it is a self-portrait. It certainly describes a process which is reflected in his plays from the earliest work through to the deeper anxieties and insecurities of the work that he produced in the 1960s and 1970s:

> Sometimes I think it's only that I'm suffering because socialism collapsed as an ideal. Sometimes it seems as though we had a peculiar advantage, growing up in the Depression. As bad as it got there was always a kind of promise in the air – people seemed on the way to being good. We were supposed to be such hard-headed materialists, now I think we were really the last of a long line of romantics. Everybody could be saved if only society were just and prosperous. It didn't matter how good or bad a person was – only what he believed. There's no belief any more.[211]

As he said in 1979, the moral world has been under increasing pressure throughout his work:

> but I've been struggling with it, you see. Anyway, I think the struggle is necessary. When the struggle is given up (and it is really given up in totalitarian places) then we're all up for grabs and I'm not ready to give up...You've got to grapple with this somehow. It seems insane to say this, and maybe I've lived here too long in this district, in New England, but I believe there is an appeal to people left. You have to work at it but you can make it, and this is a democracy here, you see. I'm not so sure I would feel this way if I lived in the middle of New York City where I was born, you see? But this is as real as that, isn't it? I mean, this is taking place. This is not a delusion in my mind. See, these people here in their blundering, in our blundering, sometimes completely mistaken way, once they get a glimmer of some path, can make it happen within certain tenets but they are very broad tenets...My effect, my energy, my aesthetic lies in finding the chain of moral being in the world...somehow.[212]

The theatre is a crucial mechanism in this search. After the production of *All My Sons* it seemed to him that the stage itself was 'as wide and free and towering and laughingly inventive as the human mind itself'.[213] And if that sense of freedom has been attenuated, if that sense of physical and moral space has been drastically curtailed, the imagination still survives. The social act which is both a necessary precondition for theatre and the basis of its method is itself an assertion of value. It is a model of that sense of human community which has been threatened but not, in Miller's eyes, destroyed by a fallible human nature and the history to which that human nature has given birth. To Miller, the imagination is a value and the theatre a testament to the human need to understand, to communicate and to create a reality which we can inhabit with dignity and hope.

In the introduction to his *Collected Plays*, Miller insisted that determinism, whether it was based on the 'iron necessities' of economics or psychoanalytic theory, 'is a contradiction of the idea of drama itself', because it leaves out of account 'an innate value, an innate will [which] does in fact posit itself as real not alone because it is devoutly to be wished, but because, however closely he is measured and systematically accounted for, he is more than the sum of his stimuli and is unpredictable beyond a certain point'.[214] To him, drama exists precisely to show this moment of transcendence, to attempt to explore the nexus between determinism and free will. And while his confidence has undoubtedly leached away over the years his own summary of his work can still stand. His plays, he insisted, were all ultimately dedicated to the faith that, just as a play is more than the sum of its parts, 'we are made and yet we are more than what made us'.[215]

No other American dramatist has so directly engaged the anxieties and fears, the myths and dreams, of a people desperate to believe in a freedom for which they see ever less evidence. No other American writer has so successfully touched a nerve of the national consciousness. But Miller is claimed with equal avidity by the international community. The Crucible was seen by the Chinese as immediately relevant to a Cultural Revolution in which youth had exacted its revenge on an adult world. Death of a Salesman has been hailed in countries where the profession itself is unknown. Miller may have been moved to write by specific circumstances but the plays which resulted transcended those circumstances as they did national boundaries. He is, above all, a writer whose art and example have dignified the theatre which for him has always been a realm of possibility, a paradigm of that tension between the given and the created within which we all move and have our being.

3 Edward Albee

If Edward Albee had not existed he would most certainly have been invented. When he emerged in 1959 the theatre was in its usual state of crisis, but it was a crisis which seemed deeper and more irremediable than usual. Arthur Miller had apparently withdrawn from the public realm, appalled by the political persecutions and public conservatism of the decade. Tennessee Williams, after fifteen years in the New York theatre and nearly a quarter of a century as a playwright, had begun to succumb to personal problems and was, indeed, to produce very little of note throughout the 1960s and 1970s. O'Neill was dead – finally and undeniably. Even the posthumous mining of his last work, which had breathed a kind of artificial life into an otherwise comatose American theatre, had come to an end. America desperately needed a new playwright but the economics of Broadway were such that the financial risks were too great to take a chance on untried talent. However, by great good chance Albee chose as the moment for his dramatic début precisely a time when the financial vicissitudes and theatrical conservatism of Broadway theatre had prompted the emergence of a new experimental theatre. And the drama critics of the major papers were, for virtually the first time, driven by the same mood of desperation to venture beyond the comfortable but huge theatres of the Great White Way to the smaller and often not at all theatre-like spaces which were called Off-Broadway.

And so, as the Eisenhower years gave way to the Kennedy era there were three heirs apparent: Jack Gelber, whose apparently realist play *The Connection* was bringing considerable attention to the Living Theatre, the more so since it seemed to have overtones of a fashionable European influence; Jack Richardson, whose *The Prodigal* suggested the possibility of a renewed interest in ritual, and Albee. The laurels finally went to Albee not so much because of *The Zoo Story*, powerful though it was – *The Connection*, after all, was no less impressive – but because he alone proved successful in transferring his talents to Broadway. And so, by an instructive paradox, Off-Broadway received its greatest fillip from the Broadway success of one of its products. Though he himself parodied his new status as the great white hope of the American theatre in a brief play called *Fam and Yam*, about the encounter between a *Famous American* playwright and a *Young American* playwright, he played his new role to the hilt. His, after all, was a classic American story of the twentieth century: from riches to riches in a single generation.

Albee was an adopted child. If he wasn't actually born with a silver spoon in his mouth, one was duly inserted two weeks later when he was taken into the home of a multi-millionaire, Reed Albee, and his domineering wife, Frances. Reed had inherited a chain of theatres established by his father, Edward Franklin Albee II, and he now repaid his debt by naming his adopted child Edward Franklin Albee III. Symmetry before originality. At one stage the family controlled some seventy vaudeville theatres and had an interest in 300 more but they wisely sold out to RKO before the bottom dropped out of the business (often literally as old vaudeville houses turned over to strip-tease).

Edward Franklin Albee III was thus a pampered child. He had private tutors and could command a reasonable array of servants. He wanted for nothing and responded in the only way possible for someone cruelly inflicted with complete absence of want. He grew to dislike his parents. Family life was not happy. His mother was twenty-three years younger and almost a foot taller than her husband and this seems to have inspired gratitude and fear in almost equal quantities. She, surely, was the basis for the many portraits of domineering and threatening women in his plays and his father for the effete and cowed men. The only relative who seems to have inspired anything but adolescent scorn was his grandmother, to whom *The Sandbox* is somewhat ambiguously dedicated and who is plainly celebrated in *The American Dream*. Throughout his work the generation which seems to inspire the most disdain is that of his parents. That particular generation is repeatedly accused of a failure of nerve and love, of a capitulation to the pursuit of wealth, prestige and power, while the one that preceded it is seen as humane, and sensible of an obligation beyond the accumulation of goods. This is presented as a social analysis rooted in history but it might equally be seen as a displaced reaction to his own family experience.

It is certainly very tempting to see in Albee's upbringing the origin of a number of his themes. Surrounded with material goods but perhaps deprived of love he turned into an educational rebel as later he would become a social critic creating a series of dramatic parables about the loss of love and the ironic triumph of the pragmatic. In the person of his grandmother he found someone who loved him – but she represented another time and another set of values remote from that of a family who wintered in Florida and Arizona and travelled around in Rolls Royces. He associated her with an America unspoiled by wealth and with values derived from an authentic American myth of frontier individualism and liberal commitment rather than the debased myth of Horatio Alger Jr. She was then, in a sense, the origin of that thread of sentimentality which runs through much of his work as he implies the existence of, but forbears to identify or examine, a prelapsarian America in which private humanity generated public harmony. Later he was inclined to ironise such a conviction and, indeed, to extend that irony to the whole notion of a presumed world of order and grace destroyed by human imperfection. But in his first plays he required a time and a place to use as a point of contrast. He needed somewhere to stand. And in the person of Grandma Cotta he found a representative of that time and place. As he later said, 'I could communicate with her...She was at the end of it and I was at the beginning. So both of us were outside the ring.'[1]

Albee's poor home situation was undoubtedly a factor in his disastrous educational record. He was expelled from two schools and one university – the kind of record which in England would have won him a seat in the Cabinet. In 1940, at the age of eleven, he went to Lawrenceville, a boarding-school in New Jersey, but failed four of his five courses and was expelled for poor academic work. His mother then arranged for him to be sent to the Valley Forge Military Academy where she believed he would be inculcated with the need for discipline – a quality she found lacking in him, and for the absence of which she implicitly blamed her husband. Unimpressed by an institution which claimed as its function the preservation of America, he succeeded in getting himself dismissed in less than a year, leaving the preservation of America to people with shorter hair and more discipline than himself, and moved on to Choate School. Though this, too, was very much an institution for the wealthy (its former pupils include Adlai Stevenson and John F. Kennedy), for the first time he seems to have found himself in a sympathetic environment – which is to say one which did not regard a young man who wanted to be a poet, or, alternatively, a novelist or a playwright, incorrigibly undisciplined and effeminate. Accordingly he began to write, producing poems, short stories, a novel (called *The Flesh of Unbelievers* and over 500 pages long) and a play. Indeed when one of his poems, called 'Eighteen', appeared in a Texas literary magazine he could begin to fantasise about a career as a writer.

His poetry was unimpressive, adolescent in precisely the way that one would expect an adolescent's poetry to be. But it is not without interest in relation to his later work. In particular he seems to have been concerned with challenging the right of the artist to project a personal despair onto a metaphysical plane. This was the essence of a poem called 'Nihilist', which he published in *The Choate Literary Magazine* in 1946, and which also shows a respect for established values which in any other culture might seem conservative but which, in an American context, might perhaps just as reasonably be seen as liberal (in the sense that Gunnar Myrdal once remarked that 'America is conservative. But the principles conserved are liberal.').

> Upon this pedestal of self he strikes
> The pose of studied carelessness, or plays
> The role with Judas-like humility,

Of priest confession to his following
With Santayanian finesse he spikes
Existing principles, old, trusted ways,
And offers in their place sterility
Of soul and thought; these are his plundering.
What causes him to mouth the purple grape
Of life experience, then spit the seeds
Back at the world? His shouting at the skys,
His quarreling with God will not escape
The judgements of his work. His shout recedes
His pedestal collapses and he dies.[2]

His play, *Schism*, published in *The Choate Literary Magazine* in May 1946, when he was just eighteen years old, seems heavily influenced by O'Neill. It concerns the attempt of a young man, Michael Joyce, to persuade a girl, Alice Monahan, to leave her family and run away with him. He is, in effect, the nihilist of the above poem. Disillusioned with the Catholic church he infects Alice with his own cynicism as he offers her his love. He persuades her to run away with him, although to do so is to desert her dying grandmother! When Michael confronts the old woman, she tries to prevent the affair but in struggling out of her wheelchair she collapses. He conceals her in an adjoining room and the two young people leave together, Alice knowing nothing of the incident. As a result, their expressed belief, that 'We're not wrong...we're just searching for happiness',[3] becomes heavily ironic.

It scarcely takes the clue of the saintly grandmother to locate Albee's sympathies here. The inhumanities of the Catholic church are accommodated to the personal cruelties of the young man. Both are condemned for their failure to engage the human. Nothing can be constructed on illusion. The Catholic church 'restricts free thinking or unregulated action',[4] but offers an after-life of justice and harmony. Michael Joyce dominates and coerces Alice Monahan but identifies 'a golden future' of material well-being. The price in both cases is the eclipse of the free spirit and the erosion of genuine human sympathy.

It is not hard to see behind this moral tale the pressure of Albee's personal life. His mother's obsession with discipline, the family's material well-being but emotional and spiritual aridity, all find their correlative in this play, as does the existence of an old woman who stands aside from and represents a judgement on the world in which she finds herself. *Schism* is melodramatic and its language inflated, though scarcely more so than O'Neill's early work. In a sense, the writer allows as little freedom and humanity to his characters as do those whom the play accuses. But it is possible to detect the beginnings of a dramatic talent here, while the concern with moral responsibility and with the coercive myths of religion and personal relationships was one which would recur later in his career.

In 1946, Albee left Choate for Trinity College in Hartford, Connecticut, where he is still remembered, not least by a professor of history called George who is locally assumed to be at least in part the model for the protagonist of *Who's Afraid of Virginia Woolf?* But he failed to graduate, and at the age of nineteen began writing continuity material for music programmes on WNYC radio. And music had always been an important element in his life. An early dream was to be a concert pianist (a dream which foundered on his inability to play the piano), and he still spends many hours listening to records, insisting that the composition of his plays owes a considerable amount to musical rhythms and structure. After a year at home he left to live in an apartment in Greenwich Village. Despite a small inheritance he worked in a series of menial jobs, including a spell as a Western Union messenger (where he knew the Crazy Billy referred to in *Who's Afraid of Virginia Woolf?*). At that time Greenwich Village was the centre of New York artistic life; it was a bohemian and cosmopolitan area, as it had been when O'Neill lived there at the beginning of his career. But when the middle class began to move in a couple of decades later Albee left and now maintains an office and home on the top two floors of an old warehouse in lower Manhattan as well as a home in Montauk. Denouncing America's excessive materialism is not without its material advantages. No wonder irony is his strong suit.

Albee himself has fostered a myth that, apart from his youthful effort, *The Zoo Story* was his first play, that he burst upon the scene fully-formed, a playwright who had just discovered his vocation. In fact, like Miller and Williams, he had a pre-history, having written plays for a decade before his public début.

And these early works, including *Schism*, are remarkably consistent in their theme. They are all concerned in some way with identifying the need for compassion, the necessity of relinquishing a destructive egotism and corrosive materialism for a redemption which can only lie in human relationships. In 'The City of People' (1949) a domineering father deliberately crushes his son's spirit and inhibits his sexual maturity. Though sexually aggressive himself, hiring secretaries for their sexual favours, he preaches self-denial and withdrawal from the distractions of the world. An emotional totalitarian, he manipulates the lives of those around him, insisting on the virtue of isolation from the corrupting communality of the city. The narrative logic is clear. The son has to learn the absolute necessity for breaking out of his isolation. He has to run the risk of human contact or remain an emotional cripple, as he is already a physical one. Though his father observes that the only distraction for the inhabitants of the city is death, the truth of that

253

absurdity makes the need for human contact the more desperate. The son has to learn to rejoin the city of people.

Essentially the same theme is picked up again in an untitled play (probably 'In a Quiet Room') written in the same year – in which a man, shocked into withdrawal by the collapse of his personal world, is urged by a friend to relinquish his solitary condition – and in the fragmentary play, 'The Invalid' (1952), in which the need to participate in the world is urged as the only way to operate within history, the only way to enter a moral world in which judgement is both possible and necessary. The world, as one of the characters observes, is on the brink of destruction, but the possibility of participation remains. Participation thus becomes a necessity equally for the individual and for that society which is beginning to fall apart for lack of moral purpose and direction.

Among these early unpublished and unproduced plays one can also find two that address directly an area of experience which many critics have insisted exists in a suppressed form in his later works – homosexuality. While suggestions that *Who's Afraid of Virginia Woolf?* was originally written for four men (a canard easily disproved by reference to the manuscripts held at Lincoln Center) are manifestly absurd, and while the familiar language of the lawyer and butler in *Tiny Alice* has more to do with theatrical than homosexual argot (Albee specifically denouncing a San Francisco production that implied otherwise), there is perhaps some justice in the suggestion that a part of Albee's power as a playwright derives from experiences which are never allowed to surface clearly in language, from images of human contact charged with a subversive frisson, a covert consciousness that some social interdict is being challenged. For Albee, in his early plays, like Tennessee Williams, sexuality is an available and powerful symbol of the absolute need to escape the self and to evade an egotism which is the source alike of personal betrayal and social injustice. And his sense of the coercive nature of the social world, portrayed in a work like *The American Dream* as specifically undermining sexual identity, is perhaps explicable in terms of his personal predilection. But it is only in the early, unpublished plays, there, and in another unpublished work – a two-act play (dated 1982–3) called 'Finding the Sun' – that the issue is tackled directly.

'Ye Watchers and Ye Lonely Ones' (1951) is a brief play in three scenes which ostensibly addresses itself to the plight of the homosexual. A young boy inducts his friend into the possibility of making money through selling one's services to homosexuals. Meanwhile, in a nearby bar, two homosexual men are ending an affair. It is a painful break, and when one of them goes out he encounters the boys. One of these, unable to go through with it, runs away; the other, more cynical, stays, contemptuous both of his friend and of the man he thinks himself to be exploiting. He is blind equally to the man's genuine distress and the destruction of his friend's innocence. Human relationships are reduced, as in many of Albee's subsequent plays, to the level of simple material gain. Thus, individuals, like the society which they inhabit and which they constitute, are held together not by freely acknowledged emotional and moral bonds, but by money. Love threatens to become simply a form of currency. In this play that love takes a specifically homosexual form, but the theme is a more general one. It is that human relations should exist outside the cash nexus, and that the sometimes brutal realities of sexual need conceal a more fundamental urge for human contact.

Much the same point is made in 'An End to Summer' (n.d.) which also presents the sexual impulse as an image of the human desire to break out of isolation. The play is set in Mrs Dana's rambling summer-guest home in Nantucket. Ann and Jayson are to be married but have an unsatisfactory sexual relationship. Jayson, indeed, has an affair with Margaret, who is married to a 64-year-old man and feels equally frustrated. Ann's brother is a homosexual and has a relationship with another man. Albee planned to introduce a murder into this already tangled plot and it is hardly surprising that after forty pages he decided to abandon it.

The broader political implications of his work, visible, for instance, in *Who's Afraid of Virginia Woolf?* and *Quotations from Chairman Mao Tse-Tung*, as well as, implicitly, in many of his other plays, crystallise in his opera, 'The Ice Age' (n.d.), an allegory which comments equally on totalitarianism and on America. An ambiguous and ironic work, it dramatises the ultimate defeat of morality less by the forces of violence than by a bland contentment, a passive acceptance of an isolation which is partly imposed and partly willingly accepted. It is, perhaps, not surprising that, together with William Flanagan, he should subsequently have chosen as the subject of his only performed opera, *Bartleby*, Melville's ambiguous story of the law clerk whose denial of social connectiveness is ultimately also a denial of life (as it is also a resistance to social pressure). Perhaps, more crucially, he was concerned with the way in which Bartleby denies himself access to language. For to speak is already to enter not merely an ambiguous sphere but also a social and moral world. It is to accept vulnerability, to gain manipulative power, to admit the possibility of deception. And this becomes a major concern of Albee's work as does another theme of his early plays, namely, the necessity to reconstruct a moral existence, to recuperate the liberal virtues of an America which has betrayed its values and lost its purpose.

The scatter of plays held in the restricted collection of his work at Lincoln Center show Albee feeling his way gradually towards a subject and a language. They range from an untitled play (probably 'The Recruit'), in which five recruits discuss a dead comrade in rhyming couplets, to a 76-page verse play, 'The Making of a Saint', in which a metaphysical debate takes place in a kind of celestial railroad station (possibly influenced by Hawthorne's 'The Celestial Railroad'), and the beginning of an opera (probably to have been entitled 'Hatchet, Hatchet'). The most accomplished is 'The City of People', but none would really benefit from performance. The interest lies in the fact that for a decade before *The Zoo Story*, when according to his own accounts he still saw himself as a poet, he was in fact refining his technique and perfecting his skill as a dramatist. Not unreasonably he chose to suppress information about this work and substitute instead a version of his career which has him, at the age of thirty, sitting down at a wobbly table in his apartment at 238 West Fourth Street and writing *The Zoo Story* in three weeks. Certainly the story of the path towards eventual production has become a familiar part of American theatre history. It began with William Flanagan, a young composer with whom Albee was then living, and who collaborated with him in writing *Bartleby*:

> William Flanagan...looked at the play, liked it, and sent it to several friends of his, among them David Diamond, another American composer resident in Italy; Diamond liked the play and sent it to a friend of *his*, a Swiss actor, Pinkos Brown; Brown liked the play, made a tape recording of it, playing both its roles, which he sent on to Mrs Stefani Hunzinger, who heads the drama department of the S. Fischer Verlag, a large publishing house in Frankfurt...[5]

The play eventually received its first performance in Germany at the Schiller Theater Werkstatt in Berlin on 28 September 1959. It arrived in America four months later where it received its American première at the Provincetown Playhouse – an entirely appropriate location for the first American production for the first play by a writer who seemed a natural successor to O'Neill, and who, given the depressed state of the American theatre, appeared to offer the possibility of a dramatic renaissance. It was a tall order, but each subsequent play strengthened his claim until, with the Broadway success of *Who's Afraid of Virginia Woolf?*, he seemed to justify such predictions. That he never became what many wished to make him has left some critics with a sense of betrayal and certainly there is something paradoxical and even perhaps perverse about a playwright who wishes to claim the right both to engage in arcane experiment and to present those experiments to an audience more conservative and less supportive than most. The right to fail, which Albee claims as fundamental to the artist intent on testing his or her own limits, is precisely the right proscribed by Broadway. But this is in part the fascination of a writer who has refused, among many other things, to accept the division of the American theatrical scene, as he has rejected the alienating divisions within American society. His objective as a writer has been two-fold. As he later explained in the introduction to *Box* and *Quotations from Chairman Mao Tse-Tung*: 'A playwright – unless he is creating escapist romances (an honourable occupation, of course) – has two obligations: first, to make some statement about the condition of "man"...and, second, to make some statement about the nature of the art form with which he is working. In both instances he must attempt change.'[6]

The Zoo Story is a parable. Its two characters constitute a model of American experience as he sees it. Indeed the description of Jerry could equally be applied to his sense of an America which has become flaccid and enervated, which has lost its clarity of outline, its energy and its vision: 'What was once a trim and lightly muscled body has', we are told, 'begun to go to fat; and while he is no longer handsome, it is evident that he once was. His fall from physical grace should not suggest debauchery; he has, to come closest to it, a great weariness.'[7] On the other hand we are offered Peter, a man defined by negatives – 'neither fat nor gaunt, neither handsome nor homely'[8] – who survives by suppressing a troublesome humanity. He is in fact a cliché and the one weakness of an otherwise brilliant play lies in Albee's failure to solve a basic problem – how to invest Peter with sufficient imaginative autonomy to make his eventual transformation a real possibility and a matter of concern. As Albee has confessed, he was 'very badly underwritten'. But he insists that 'even though I did badly underwrite that character, he is not quite the clown that he was in the original version. I did sort him out a little bit.'[9]

The play consists of an encounter between the two men – Peter sitting on a bench in Central Park, anxious at all costs to avoid human contact, and Jerry, alarmingly irrational, apparently determined to provoke some response from the man he encounters. Peter is bland, the epitome of the successful businessman; Jerry has the wild-eyed intensity of a convert. The process of the play is the slow revelation of the nature of Jerry's convictions, the elaboration of a myth which he himself only seems to understand through the process of narration. He apparently glimpses where the encounter is leading him but the momentum of the new myth carries him forward regardless. He taunts Peter, assaults him and finally, in some kind of terrible blend of love and despair, forces him to take an irrevocable step, pulling him suddenly and ineluctably into the world of causality in which actions have consequences and responsibility can no longer be denied. He throws Peter a knife and kills himself on it. As Albee himself remarked in an interview some twenty years later,

> *The Zoo Story* concerns a meeting between two men: Peter, who has accommodated too much to life, to his society, to his environment, who has made too many final choices too soon; and a younger man called Jerry who in the course of the play tries to transfer a sense of all the anguish and joy of being alive to Peter. In order to accomplish this transference he must precipitate an act of extraordinary violence.

Not the absurdist account which many critics (following Martin Esslin's lead in *The Theatre of the Absurd*) assumed it to be, but an articulate assertion of the need to break out of an isolation which is socially rather than metaphysically derived, which is self-imposed rather than determined, *The Zoo Story* is concerned with Jerry's attempts to convert Peter to his new religion of man. Awakened himself to the desperate isolation of people – as typified by his own rooming-house in which people suffer their private anguish in separate rooms, like animals in a zoo denied access to other animals and hence denied both self-definition and consolation – he has come to realise that such 'solitary free passage' as they and he have won for themselves is not gain but loss. Their privatism is not the result of the absurdity of their position; it is the essence of it. He does try to bring this message to Peter; to ease, or, if necessary, to shock him out of his isolation. But Peter resists a truth that will lay obligations upon him and shake him out of a tranquil but banal existence. And since language has been drained of its real meaning, infiltrated by clichés and conventionalised to the point where it loses its ability to express truth, Jerry is forced to adopt a more oblique approach: 'sometimes', he explains, 'a person has to go a long distance out of his way to come back a short distance correctly'.[10] This is equally a description of Jerry's method and Albee's dramatic strategy – that resort to metaphor which he sees as fundamental to art. The theatre is to be a mechanism for truth. Its methods may be oblique, but it is ultimately concerned with the need to identify and embrace the real and the true – which, at this stage in his career, are not perceived or presented as being problematic.

Jerry attempts a number of strategies. When simple conversation is subverted by Peter's inability to engage language on any but the most superficial level, he resorts to parable, telling the story of his relationship with his landlady's dog, a relationship which parallels that between Peter and himself. Far from being as indifferent as the human inhabitants of his rooming-house, the dog had consistently challenged Jerry, attacking him in the lobby as he dashed for the stairs. And in order to secure his privacy Jerry had firstly tried to appease the dog and then, eventually, to kill it. Only when he has regained his isolation does he realise that what he had seen as a threat was perhaps an attempt at contact, and that the isolation to which he has returned is itself the source of his absurdity. And the dog, in a sense, stands for Jerry's landlady, a grotesque woman who pursues him and offers him a love that he cannot accept. The story is plainly a displaced account of his encounter with Peter, who now plays Jerry's role as Jerry plays that of the dog. And eventually the truth of this does penetrate Peter's mind but he refuses to acknowledge its relevance to himself, so his response is firstly to insist that he doesn't understand and then to assert: 'I DON'T WANT TO HEAR ANY MORE.'[11]

Jerry now resorts to a more desperate device to force Peter off his park bench – a bench to which he retreats in order to escape those people who are the source of his own anxieties and which thus comes to stand as an image of his self-imposed isolation. His dispossession of the bench becomes Jerry's prime objective, a symbol of his forced repatriation into the human community. Unable to convince Peter by argument or through the oblique lessons of the parable, Jerry now provokes him into defending his bench. He throws Peter a knife and then deliberately impales himself on it. The Christian overtones are clear. Like Christ, whose name his own is clearly designed to recall, his message of love has finally to be reinforced through his own sacrifice. As he dies, so he wipes the knife clean of fingerprints, as Christ had absolved those who killed him. And Peter, like the disciple who had thrice denied Christ, offers a triple affirmation as that disciple had done: 'Oh my God, my God, my God.'[12] He is now irrevocably tied to Jerry by guilt. He can never return to his isolated bench. As Albee has said,

> I suspect that he can't return to being the same person after that experience with Jerry. I can't imagine that he does. Not that he is going to become Jerry himself, but I suspect that he has been altered considerably by it. I think that he has certainly been jarred. And he is a bright enough man not to be able to retreat.[13]

The Zoo Story is constructed like a musical composition. It is built around a series of crescendos and diminuendos as Jerry makes his bid for contact. And while the sexual analogue is plainly relevant the model is more clearly a musical one. As Albee has said, 'I have an extraordinary relationship with music...I go into a sort of training before I write a play.'[14] Certainly much of the dramatic effect of the play derives from a text in which the tone of voice, the pitch, the volume and the rhythm are as carefully controlled as the dialogue itself. Albee is particularly careful with what he is apt to call the 'notation' of his plays, insisting that 'a production only proves a good play. It doesn't improve it.'[15] Nonetheless the part of Jerry remains one of the most powerful and compelling in the modern American theatre. Not an absurdist account, but an urgent plea for human contact, The Zoo Story is a blend of impressionism and realism which places considerable demands on the actor.

It is a play which combines a critique of American values with an acknowledgement of the fragility of language, but which does so in the context of that drive for communication which Albee sees as central to a reconstruction of the moral world. On one level the play invites a Marxist analysis. A commodity value has been placed on human relationships. Social alienation, after all, is a clear product of a system in which the individual has no organic control over the product of his labour and no vision of a future which can transcend the pressure of, and toward, the inanimate. But Albee's position is inherently anti-materialist and in *The Zoo Story* he proposes a revivified human relationship as lying at the core of a reconstituted society. His analysis is bleak; his conclusion less so. Indeed, it is perhaps inherently sentimental, embarrassingly close to that soft-centred romanticism to which the Beats had been drawn in the 1950s and which would re-emerge in the 1960s in the form of public rites of sexual and platonic community. The language alone, precise, tightly controlled and rhythmically structured, pulls against such an impulse, turning a banality into a closely focussed dramatic action. Jerry and Peter's embrace is ironised to a degree that would have shocked Jack Kerouac and Julian Beck alike, and which deflected some critics into discussions of Albee's homosexuality. But the blend of pain and insight implied something other than a callous resort to sensation. He was concerned with the hard, substantial thrust of the real and those who detected no more than the sexual underpinning of the image mistook the symbol for the thing itself. For Albee, love is not an abstraction any more than it is simply a momentary sexual union. It is an acknowledgement of the irremediable, a confession that there comes a point at which evasion serves no further purpose and the self concedes that its definition depends upon the existence of the other. And that mutuality makes demands upon the conscience.

The distinction between the European absurdist stance and Albee's is best described, I think, by reference to a question posed to Brecht by the Swiss dramatist Dürrenmatt, and which I have quoted elsewhere. Dürrenmatt asked Brecht whether it was possible to dramatise the modern world. His answer was 'Yes, if it can be changed'. And he in turn offered an image. He described a report of an earthquake in a Japanese newspaper. The article had carried a photograph of a devastated city with a single building still standing. Underneath was the caption: 'STEEL STOOD.'[16] Where the absurdist would tend to see the single building as an ironic commentary on the area of devastation, Albee, like Brecht, was apt to see it as the nucleus for a new city. He was not interested in denying the bleakness of the scene but in identifying the one area of possible hope, no matter how tenuous it might be. He was, in other words, a social critic, though his insistence on the reified nature of the world which he described and his strategy of deforming character and action in the service of his critique perhaps justified his own description of himself as a 'demonic' social critic. This was certainly true of his next play *The Death of Bessie Smith*, which appears to address the racial situation in the South by tackling an issue then high on the political agenda (President Kennedy's telephone call to the jailed Martin Luther King constituting one of the more dramatic moments in the 1960 presidential campaign). But over and above the level of social protest this is a play about individuals trapped in their own myths, condemned to act out their fictions to the point at which they are forced to deny their own humanity and desires.

A middle-aged white nurse, bred in the racism of the South, desperately tries to seduce a young intern. He represents her only chance of escape. But when he challenges the racist practices of the hospital she is forced to make a choice. Either she will support his rebellion and thereby allow a dangerous moral reality to intrude on her life by stepping outside those comforting and simplistic fictions of her upbringing which confer a certain dignity on her role as white Southern woman, or she will distance herself from him and thereby protect the myth by destroying her own chance of escape (a dilemma which was to recur in a different context in *Who's Afraid of Virginia Woolf?*). She opts for the systematised illusions. In fact Albee's target is not racism as such. This is merely symptomatic of a more profound malaise. As the intern observes, 'I am not concerned with politics...But I have a sense of urgency...a dislike of waste...stagnation.'[17] Apart from anything else this is an accurate enough statement of Albee's own position. Here it identifies the central thrust of a work which has all the components of social protest but which is more usefully seen as a morality play about the collapse of human values and national purpose.

Bessie Smith was a black blues-singer who died in 1937 as a result of injuries sustained in a car crash. The injuries proved fatal when she was turned away by a whites-only hospital. Albee was struck by the story when reading the notes on a record sleeve. Since the play appeared at a time when the civil rights movement was at its height there was a tendency to see it as Albee's gesture towards the cause of racial justice, but in fact it presents racism as symptom rather than as disease. For the inhumanity involved in the callous treatment of Bessie Smith is merely the logical extension of a process that goes beyond the question of prejudice.

The South of the play is indeed typified by bigotry. The nurse's father is a racist for whom the past has a mythic quality, while she herself vents her frustration on a Negro orderly. Nor is the liberal intern without his equivocations. His commitment to the loyalist cause in Spain remains at the level of language while for most of the play he defers rather too willingly to the apparatus of power. He, no less than the other characters, has his illusions – as does the Negro orderly who tolerates racial abuse in order to be accepted into the society which abuses him. But the sickness that Albee identifies in his Southern hospital goes not only beyond the literal illness which afflicts the town's mayor but also beyond a simple indictment of racism. As Albee explained, 'while the incident itself was brawling at me, and while the characters I had elected to carry the tale were wrestling it from me, I discovered I was, in fact, writing about something at the same time slightly removed from and more pertinent to what I had imagined'.[18] Beginning with the fact of racial prejudice in a small Southern town Albee broadens his canvas until the intern, looking at a sky which has turned into 'a great, red-orange-yellow sunset', observes that 'fire has enveloped half the continent' and 'The West is burning.'[19] When he himself makes a gesture, offering to treat the wounded Bessie Smith, it is already too late. She is dead. Much the same, Albee implies, is true of a culture in which people are alienated from one another and from themselves. As the nurse cries out,

> I am sick of everything in this hot, stupid, fly-ridden world. I am sick of the disparity between things as they are, and as they should be!...I am sick of talking to people on the phone...and I am sick of going to bed and I am sick of waking up...and I am tired of the truth...and I am tired of lying about the truth...I am tired of my skin...I WANT OUT![20]

The North is invoked but none of the characters go there, nor is there any suggestion that to do so would transform their alienation. When the 'great sunset blazes' at the end of the play it is an ironic gesture. It implies the apocalypse which is an inevitable consequence of a failure of humanity. The intern's belated gesture exists as the only hint of transcendence.

The Death of Bessie Smith was first produced in Germany at the Schlosspark Theater in Berlin, in April 1960. In some ways it tried to compact rather too much into a slight form, and given the social and political pressures of the moment it is perhaps hardly surprising that it was seen primarily as a timely gesture towards the battle for racial justice. Its rather more general lament over an enervated society, encysted in myth, went largely unregarded. The same could hardly be said for Albee's next play.

In his introduction to *The American Dream*, he insisted that it was 'a picture of our time', and that its aim was to transcend 'the personal and the private'. It was, he explained, 'an examination of the American Scene, an attack on the substitution of artificial for real values in our society, a condemnation of complacency, cruelty, emasculation and fatuity; it is a stand against the fiction that everything in this slipping land of ours is peachy keen'.[21] It is a play that clearly derives its technique from Ionesco, in particular from *The Bald Prima Donna*, but that technique is employed in the service of expressionistic satire. And the moral values which Albee implicitly embraces are now historically situated. The principles which he wishes to endorse are those of a presumed communal past; they are in fact those of the American revolution.

The play, first performed in January 1961, is an account of the vacuous lives and the destructive power of Mommy and Daddy. The family, an icon of the American system, is exposed as the heart of its venality and inhumanity. Thus the parents in the play systematically destroy an adopted child, being particularly sure to annihilate any sign of vitality and potency. So the new generation is destroyed in the bud, and in the person of a Young Man we are presented with a living embodiment of the American Dream, personally attractive, totally amoral and drained of all humanity. The only hope resides in the figure of Grandma, an old woman representative of older values and immune to the destructive power of Mommy and Daddy. She alone is allowed to step outside the action, to break out of the fiction which these two characters create. Albee has said that he sees the play as showing that 'both young people and old people are outside the corrupting mainstream of society', but his explanation that if the young man had not 'been adopted by that particular family he probably would have grown up all right'[22] carries no conviction. The emasculation is too complete. And so the source of values lies only in a receding past, in the person of a woman whose age is itself a sign of the tenuous nature of the hope which he proposes. Indeed in a brief play called *The Sandbox* we are actually shown her death and the final victory of Mommy and Daddy.

Mommy and Daddy, like Peter in *The Zoo Story*, are role-players. They enact the fictions offered to them by society, willingly reducing their complexity to stereotype and moving in a linguistic world constructed to deny the power of reality. Language is conventionalised to the point where it is emptied of all meaning. Death is denied. Euphemism becomes the principal linguistic tactic. And lacking a language which relates them to their own experience, they are equally unable to make contact with one another.

Though this play, together with *The Zoo Story*, was seen simply as a domestic version of Ionesco and as evidence that the theatre of the absurd had finally infected an American writer, in fact Albee resists accommodation to Martin Esslin's category. The language of his own introduction is that of the social critic and satirist who believes that change is possible. He is, he explains, taking 'a stand'. He acknowledges the existence of 'real values' and attacks 'artificial...values'.[23] His assumption, embodied in the person of Grandma, that it is possible to step outside the frame of national fiction implies the possibility of free action, though he chooses to evade the irony implicit in her apparent, but in fact simulated, transcendence of the fictional frame of the play. He is, in short, invoking the American past in order to attack the vacuity of the American present. Such a historical stance, however, would make no sense to Beckett for whom past and present are crushed into one continuous and unvarying moment. For Beckett the illusion of freedom is a central element of the absurd, an ironic birthright; for Albee the principal moral failure of his characters lies in their inability to acknowledge a freedom which is the only basis for personal identity and national purpose. The problem of *The American Dream* is that he is more successful in dramatising Mommy and Daddy and their vapid lives than he is in identifying any alternative. And in so far as those characters are simple stereotypes they are more likely to confirm an audience's sense of moral superiority than distort its sense of the real.

Nonetheless, *The American Dream*, along with *The Zoo Story* and *The Death of Bessie Smith*, proved immediately popular. They were quickly taken up by university drama groups and were widely produced. Few playwrights (other than O'Neill) can ever have acquired such a national reputation on the basis of a few one-act plays produced in such unlikely places as the Schiller Theater Berlin, the Schlosspark Theater, the Jazz Gallery (*The Sandbox*), the York Playhouse (*The American Dream*) and the White Barn, Westport, Connecticut (*Fam and Yam*). This was, however, precisely the period when Off-Broadway was coming into its own, so *The Zoo Story* was reviewed by Brooks Atkinson for *The New York Times* as well as by Robert Brustein for *The New Republic* and Harold Clurman for *The Nation*. *The Times* also covered not only *The American Dream* but also *The Sandbox* and even *Fam and Yam*. Albee's success in turn added to the growing prestige and dignity of the new movement. It was in a sense the more surprising, therefore, when he decided to turn to Broadway for the production of his first three-act play. Certainly it was against the advice of his director Alan Schneider, who had first met Albee when a television programme had brought together new young playwrights and directors for the screening of scenes from new works. Albee's contribution had in fact been part of the play which subsequently became *Who's Afraid of Virginia Woolf?* Schneider has said that no one involved, with the possible exception of Albee himself, thought the play would have anything but a short, though respectable run. Certainly Schneider, used to producing on Broadway, thought that it would stand a better chance in an Off-Broadway house. But Albee was adamant. However, locating a theatre which was willing to stage a play quite as excoriating and sexually frank as it then appeared proved difficult. Rejected by the reader for one theatre chain as 'a dull whiny play without a laugh in it', it was eventually placed at the Billy Rose Theatre. The reviews were mixed but *The New York Times*, the most crucial of all, was largely favourable. And it was the popular and critical success of this play which consolidated Albee's reputation. The first of his generation successfully to accomplish the transition from Off-Broadway to Broadway, he did so without making any concessions (outside of the play's apparent naturalism) to that audience's supposed sensibility. Twenty years later the play still holds up and has deservedly come to be regarded as one of the classics of the American stage.

Who's Afraid of Virginia Woolf? (1962) is set in a small New England college (the film version was shot at Smith College). Its single set, a womb-like living-room, stands as an image of a refusal of life by those who enact their fears and illusions within it. George is a professor of history married to the daughter of the college president. Unable to have children, they have conspired to create a fantasy child, designed to cement their relationship, to compensate for a delinquent reality. But in fact the child becomes a divisive principle, claimed as an accomplice by both George and Martha.

The occasion of the play is critical in terms of the myth which they have created, for the boy is on the verge of his twenty-first birthday. Thus, they are trapped by their own logic. If they sustain the myth they must let the boy go. At twenty-one his independence is an inevitable stage in his development, and a necessary concession to his supposed reality. Alternatively, if they refuse to allow him to reach his majority they will undermine a myth whose utility and whose conviction rests on the acceptance of a coincidence between real and fictional time. And witnessing this crisis is another couple, newly arrived at the university and already beginning the construction of their own illusions.

The play's three acts are entitled 'Fun and Games', 'Walpurgisnacht' and 'The Exorcism' (the latter being the play's original title) and this progression accurately describes both Albee's method and his theme. The humour of the early part of the play gives way to a witches' sabbath in which dangerous truths are exposed while the final act drives out the deadly fantasies and lays the ghost which George and Martha have created but by which they have been haunted. Word gives place to act, illusion to reality. Albee's own explanation of the play's title is that he derived it from a sign which he had seen in a Greenwich Village bar, and that it means, 'Who's afraid of life without false illusions?'

Ostensibly a Strindbergian drama of sexual tension, in fact the play is an elaborate metaphor for what Albee sees as the willing substitution of fantasy for reality, the destructive and dangerous infantilising of the imagination and the moral being by fear. And the apocalyptic overtones of the play are deliberately underscored. The action takes place in a township called New Carthage – a Spenglerian reference underlined by George's casual reading from *The Decline of the West*, jokingly characterised by him in an early draft of the play as 'a cowboy book'. For Spengler, there was a clear parallel to be drawn between Carthage and modern America. In both, power and money provided the principal axes for behaviour. In his cyclical view of history, both marked the age of the Caesars, the victory of money power over culture. And the consequence was a brutalism and a sterile intellectualism in which 'Children do not happen...because intelligence at the peak of intensity can no longer find any reason for their existence'.[24] And so, when George reads out the Spenglerian prophecy that 'the west must...eventually fall', he voices what is in effect a central thesis of the plot – a thesis underlined when George likens New Carthage to Gomorrah and Penguin Island (the latter being an island destroyed by its own capitalism in Anatole France's book of the same name), and when he suggests a parallel with Illyria – Shakespeare's fictional world.

The liberal values of the past have been willingly surrendered. George has compromised. Martha is in danger of moving 'bag and baggage' into her own fantasy world. The process of the play is a slow and relentless stripping of illusion, a steady move towards the moment when their myth will collapse of its own weight, when George and Martha will be left to confront reality without benefit of their fantasies or the protective articulateness which has been their main defence. The play is, indeed, as Albee has explained more than once, 'an examination of the principles of the American revolution, half tongue in cheek, but half not'.[25] George and Martha, named after the first President and his wife, embody the fate of the American dream which has moved progressively further away from the supposed liberal idealism of those revolutionary principles.

16. Uta Hagen, Arthur Hill, Melinda Dillon and George Grizzard in *Who's Afraid of Virginia Woolf?* at the Billy Rose Theatre, New York, 1962.

Nick and Honey, the young people who witness the collapse of their hosts' fantasies, are themselves a warning of the next stage of decline. Honey is hopelessly timid, afraid to have children, terrified of the real. Unwilling to confront the fact that in many ways 'consciousness is pain', she retreats into a childish dependence and, indeed, at one stage assumes the foetal position. Her husband, named, apparently, after Nikita Khruschev, lacks George's moral sensitivity. He is a totalitarian interested in power. In many ways he is close kin to the Young Man in *The American Dream*. He is conventionalised. Indeed, in an early version of the play he was simply to have been called 'Dear'. And together they have also begun to elaborate their lies. But for Albee these cannot be accurately described by Ibsen's term, 'life-lies'. They are, finally, destructive of life. And the hope of the play lies not simply in the process whereby George and Martha come to sacrifice their illusions and hence recover a genuine relationship with one another and with their surroundings, but also in the hope and perhaps the expectation that Nick and Honey will learn a vital lesson of the kind which Peter was presumed to derive from his experiences in *The Zoo Story*. Thus Albee has said of Nick that:

> it is conceivable that there might have been some humanising going on during the course of the play to him. I don't know the extent to which Nick and Honey will be able to go on with their lives. They may have to alter a bit themselves...in the play all that is suggested is that you clear away all the debris and then you decide what you are going to do. It doesn't say that everything is going to be all right at all. O'Neill suggested that you have false illusions in order to survive. The only optimistic act in *Who's Afraid of Virginia Woolf?* is to say, admit that they are false illusions and then live with them if you want and know that they are false. After all, it's an act of public exorcism.[26]

George and Martha inhabit a city of words. In recoil from reality, they laboriously construct an alternative world, lovingly elaborating their illusions in an apparently concrete language. They provide their fantasy child with an entire history, transposing a supposed genuine emotional commitment onto language which must do the work for them. They meet on a lexical battlefield. Their elaborate language games are a substitute for real contact. They are, indeed, as they explain, walking what's left of their wits. George, who has surrendered to his wife's strength and fear, who has conspired both in the creation of the child and in his own moral collapse, fights on verbally. Indeed he constantly attempts to shift affairs onto a linguistic level where he can still operate, and where, apparently, there are no consequences. But while, in one sense, to speak is to lie, in another, there is a real risk that the lexical superstructure, the crust of language, will eventually collapse of its own weight and leave them with the silence which they both fear but which may reduce them to what Pirandello once called 'naked figures'. Their verbalisation is indeed a response to their terror of a silence in which the real questions will assert themselves. Thus, though the play's humour functions in Henri Bergson's sense of intimidating through humiliation, it is a desperate humour (what Dostoevsky called 'joking between clenched teeth'[27]) which derives from a profound anxiety. George and Martha are role-players because the role offers a retreat. They perform in front of Nick and Honey. The events have a self-consciously theatrical air. Indeed, they scarcely even need that audience. Terrified of being, they play like children (there are many references to their childishness) or like actors, and 'play' becomes a central metaphor. Hence the 'Fun and Games' of the first act. But, more significantly, they are retreating from reality into fiction, into self-dramatisation. And inevitably that raises questions about the function of art, and, most crucially, the status of the play in which they are themselves dramatised.

There is, perhaps, a suggestion here of self-doubt on the part of a writer who distrusts not only the devalued language of public exchange but even his own articulateness. For if the process of both *The Zoo Story* and *Who's Afraid of Virginia Woolf?* is a slow retreat from language – a suggestion that truth is pre-linguistic, that speech is designed less to communicate than to give access to power or to articulate the need to deceive (the self and others) – then his own splendid articulateness as playwright is also suspect and profoundly ambiguous. It is the kind of perception, I suspect, which led him to value the strident metaphor implicit in expressionism (in *The American Dream* and *The Sandbox*), which persuaded him to warn of the values of indirection (in *The Zoo Story*) and which, in *Tiny Alice*, was going to press him to transpose the essence of his metaphysic from a linguistic to a symbolic mode. Later still (in *Quotations from Chairman Mao Tse-Tung*), it was to provoke an aleatory mechanism, with language being splintered into fragments, a lexical jumble designed to force the audience to recognise and re-enact the process of pattern-forming, and hence fiction-making, which lies at the heart of art and life equally, and which is the basis of an absurdity which grows out of the gulf between disorder and the persistent need for reassurance.

In *Who's Afraid of Virginia Woolf?*, however, there is nevertheless a kind of truth in language, a Freudian upsurge of the subconscious perception breaking through into the conscious world. Thus George's observation that 'Martha's a devil with language' is a joke containing an element of psychological insight. And though the humour in which George and Martha excel is certainly a protective device it is also evidence of a perception of dissidence or disproportion, of that sense of the ridiculous, of which Nick and Honey are unaware.

George is a liberal who admires diversity and who, as an historian, is aware of the principles which he and his society have abrogated. In the person of

Nick he comes up against a man who represents an undifferentiated future. But his own withdrawal from the world of present reality, symbolised by his retreat to this small university and to the study of history (he reads or at least pretends to read a history book during his wife's adulterous gestures towards Nick), suggests a complicity in this process. Beneath the humour is a serious fear of a fatal collapse of liberal individualism. As Jung had suggested in *The Plight of the Individual in Modern Society*,

> Under the influence of scientific assumptions, not only the psyche but the individual man and, indeed, all individual events whatsoever suffer a levelling down and a process of blurring that distorts the picture of reality...The goal and meaning of individual life (which is the only *real* life) no longer lies in individual development but in the policy of the state, which is thrust upon the individual from outside and consists in the execution of an abstract idea which ultimately tends to attract all life to itself. The individual is increasingly deprived of the moral decision as to how he should live his own life...[28]

This is the context in which George, somewhat curiously and apparently irrelevantly, announces his determination to defend Berlin. A rhetorical gesture designed to baffle Nick, it is, in effect, a half-joking, half-serious assertion of the need to resist the totalitarian. That had been the subject of his unpublished play *The Ice Age*, and Albee has spoken of his fascination and alarm at the apparent readiness of individuals and nations to embrace totalitarian political structures and modes of thought. And, of course, President Kennedy had made Berlin a symbol of the need to resist in his famous 'Ich bin ein Berliner!' speech earlier in 1962 (the year of the play's production). George's previous failure had lain precisely in his surrender of moral conscience, his inability to acknowledge the power of abstraction, and his denial of the lessons of history. Now he has to acknowledge his role in the creation of a society which could produce Nick. He is 'in' history, in the sense of being both in the history department and subject to the impact of time and process, but he 'is not' history, in the sense of running the history department or acknowledging his power and responsibility to deflect the course of his society and his individual fate alike. The play does presuppose a freedom which he has willingly and perversely rejected. Its process and its theme argue the necessity to re-engage that freedom which is and must be inherently ambiguous, a freedom which enables the individual to define his own nature and to establish relationships with others, but a freedom which can be seen as synonymous with abandonment and desertion. It is a freedom, moreover, which posits no transcendence. George's respect for the ageing god of the college (the president whose offer of an eventual reward has cowed him) must end. But the cost of that is to abandon the future as a compensatory mechanism; it is to inhabit the present. Buried in the play, indeed, is a metaphysical dimension which becomes more explicit in *Tiny Alice*. George and Martha are to be redeemed by the sacrifice of a son. But the gospel of love becomes a secular necessity. Vertiginous freedom has to be embraced. It is the knowledge that, in Martha's words, 'You're in a straight line...and it doesn't lead anywhere...except maybe to the grave',[29] which is the source of their terror, the ultimate reality which they would evade but must end by embracing. Denied even the vicarious survival implied by children they have to settle for the irreducible reality of an existence whose meaning has to be generated by actions taken and relationships forged.

The process of Albee's early plays tends to be a progressive stripping not only of illusions but of language. The too-ready gush of words reduces to a trickle as the characters learn to accept the reality which their articulateness is designed to deny. And the fundamental thing that they have to accept is their own mortality, the pressure of time. The denial of time is ultimately the denial of one's humanity. And so George identifies the ageless quality of the insane, who 'maintain a...firm-skinned serenity' because 'the under-use of everything leaves them quite whole'.[30] And, of course, the characters in the play are just such figures. Their baby talk, their games, their unengaged human potential, has infantilised them. Afraid of time they have become vicious Peter Pans. Nick prides himself on his detachment. George has simply compromised: 'Accommodation, malleability, adjustment...these do seem to be the order of things.'[31] Either way, moral instincts are suppressed. Euphemism becomes a central strategy and alcohol a convenient opiate. They have suffered a 'gradual...going to sleep of the brain cells'.[32] Afraid of pain, they retreat from consciousness into oblivion or myth. Hence, as George observes, 'when people can't abide things as they are, when they can't abide the present, they do one of two things...either they...either they turn to a contemplation of the past, as I have done, or they set about to... alter the future'.[33] History and science, as represented by George and Nick, become forms of evasion, rationalisations. They are fictions, ways of structuring the world and experience in such a way as to deny its contingent power. So, too, is the role-playing, the theatricality in which they indulge. And this is in part the point of the various parodies in the play, of Eugene O'Neill ('Awww, 'tis the refuge we take when the unreality of the world weighs too heavy on our tiny heads'[34]) and Tennessee Williams ('Flores para los muertos', a line from *A Streetcar Named Desire* whose original title, *The Poker Night* is also invoked by Albee), two playwrights whom Albee saw as sanctioning illusion in the face of reality. And just as Williams had been drawn to Eliot's observation that human kind 'Cannot bear very much reality', so Albee has George quote from the same poem ('Here we go round the mulberry bush'[35]) as he is about to destroy the illusions behind which he and Martha have hidden.

The play ends with a radically simplified language, with the simple cadence of monosyllabic question and answer. Language no longer comes between them. Neither does illusion. The fabric of their fiction has come apart. They are left only with one another, with relationship; they acknowledge the responsibility which they had previously evaded. Where once they had used the fantasy child as a means to accuse one another, now they accept their joint failure: '*We* couldn't [have any children].' As Albee comments in a stage direction, 'a hint of communion in this'.[36]

The question remains, however, whether they have simply been reconciled to their own weaknesses and unrealised dreams. Eliot identifies such a state when he has one of his characters in *The Cocktail Party* (a play which has continued to haunt Albee's imagination) announce

> If that is what you wish
> I can reconcile you to the human condition,
> The condition to which some who have gone as far as you
> Have succeeded in returning. They may remember
> The vision they have had, but they cease to regret it,
> Maintain themselves by the common routine[37]

But Albee, like the conspirators of Eliot's play, does not predetermine the result. Thus Julia, in *The Cocktail Party*, remarks:

> We must take the risk
> All we could do was to give them the chance.
> And now, when they are stripped naked to their souls
> And can choose, whether to put on proper costumes
> Or huddle quickly into new disguises,
> They have, for the first time, somewhere to start from.[38]

George and Martha, who once, like Eliot's character, had consoled themselves with the thought that '...we can fight each other, / Instead of each taking his corner of the cage'[39] (a thought not that remote, either, from *The Zoo Story*), now have the chance to start again, as do Nick ('My God, I think I understand') and Honey.

Like *The Zoo Story*, *Who's Afraid of Virginia Woolf?* is a protest against what Albee saw as a growing conformity, a retreat from individuality and moral responsibility. It is offered not merely as an observation about human relationships but as a Catonian warning about the collapse of value in society. It stands as an assertion of the absolute need to accept responsibility for one's actions and to close the gap between individuals, to end private and public alienation. In this, Albee is in many ways close to the conviction expressed by Jung in *The Undiscovered Self*, though without Jung's faith in a transcendent dimension. In this sense George and Martha's battles become a model of social and political battles which derive from a desire to externalise

271

and defeat qualities and tendencies inherent in the body politic. As Jung observes, 'Nothing has a more divisive and alienating effect upon society than this moral complacency and lack of responsibility...There can be no doubt that in the democracies too the great distance between man and man is much greater than is conducive to public welfare or beneficial to our psychic needs.'[40] Human relations derive precisely from human vulnerability, from 'imperfection...what is weak, helpless and in need of support'. Nor, he insists, should such observations be seen as 'superfluous sentimentalities', for 'The question of human relationship and of the inner cohesion of our society is an urgent one in view of the atomization of the pent-up mass man...the free society needs a bond of an affective nature, a principle of a kind like *caritas*, the Christian love of your neighbour.'[41] And this is precisely the value identified by Albee. The association of *caritas* with a sexually charged relationship certainly runs the risk of sentimentality but here this is largely avoided. Albee's objection to the film version, however, lay precisely in its capitulation to this cliché. The concluding scene, filmed against the dawn of a new day, made the emphasis too clear while Albee objected both to the saccharine nature of the musical score and the virtual elimination of the political element, excluded by too great an emphasis on what Elizabeth Taylor called the 'love-story' dimension. But, in fact, in an early version the play did end more positively and with a more explicit statement of the nexus between private and public terrors and consolations. George was to have remarked:

> That is, after all, the way things work...The balance...mutual respect through mutual terror?...Well, perhaps, if there is no other way, that, at least, is a way. I wish you both well; I fear for your headaches tomorrow, but...that will pass. And I would make a suggestion to the two of you: You have within you and between you...ripped out of you, maybe, and all, all for the wrong reasons, though, who cares?...a possibility. Try to...try to, in some way, establish basis for a legend: try to...learn; I don't hold out much hope for you...things being as they are...people...but, and I trust you've learned this by now, the least dishonorable failure is the only honorable goal.[42]

As a redundant summary of action and character it was deleted with some purpose and effect but it stands as a clear statement of Albee's liberal faith in the need to sustain the battle for selfhood.

For a number of critics the play's upbeat ending was seen as callous and sentimental (in Yeats's sense of provoking unearned emotion). For Diana Trilling, however, its weakness was that it posited a spiritually vacuous existence for which there was no historical explanation and no sanction in personal psychology. All it offered was a terrible kind of awareness. For Harold Clurman its chief failing was that it seemed to confirm that disease

- in the sense of morbid-mindedness – could be turned into a brilliant theatrical formula. Each, in other words, reacted against the play as though it were an absurdist account. But in fact the historiography of betrayal is spelled out with some care and the politics of despair located as a product of fear and not some metaphysical determinism. The university is chosen as a setting not out of any desire to flatter the audience (Diana Trilling suggests that 'the privileged position of Mr Albee's characters permits his audience to identify itself with a supposedly superior class in our society'[43]) nor even simply as a justification for an articulate debate over moral values, but because the university is conventionally regarded as the centre of a particular kind of freedom, as the embodiment of liberal humanist values, and hence betrayal here is the more profound and disturbing. And far from articulateness being presented as a virtue the process of the play exposes the degree to which it may be the root of a crucial act of evasion, and intelligence, drained of human purpose, a threat to survival. It is possible to see the final tableau as sentimental. Restored personal relationships are made to carry the weight of the play's allegorical meaning. But in a sense it is the very fragility of that new structure which inhibits a complete collapse into the dubious sexual metaphysics of Tennessee Williams's *The Rose Tattoo* or *Period of Adjustment*. Nothing is certain. The fear remains: what has gone is the elaborate structure of illusion. They can never simply fall into such a strategy again. Like Peter in *The Zoo Story*, if they are to revert to their old habits it must at the very least be a willed and knowing acknowledgement of defeat.

In a sense Albee's early plays read like a pastiche of Martin Buber and Erich Fromm, both popular figures in the late 1950s and early 1960s. They address the question of alienation, an alienation which is partly a product of capitalism and partly an aspect of what it was then popular to call the human condition. A classic statement of this is to be found in Erich Fromm's *The Sane Society*:

> Man is torn away from the primary union with nature, which characterizes animal existence. Having at the same time reason and imagination, he is aware of his aloneness and separateness; of his powerlessness and ignorance; of the accidentalness of his birth and of his death. He could not face this state of being for a second if he could not find new ties with his fellow man which replace the old ones, regulated by instincts. Even if all his physiological needs were satisfied, he would experience his state of aloneness and individuation as a prison from which he had to break out in order to retain his sanity...There is only one passion which satisfies man's need to unite himself with the world, and to acquire at the same time a sense of integrity and individuality, and this is love.[44]

But under the conditions of modern society men become 'atoms...little particles estranged from each other' so that 'the drive for exchange operates in the realm of interpersonal relations', and this becomes 'a symptom of the abstractification and alienation inherent in the social character of modern man'.[45] Rather than love, the solitary individual places value on the material.

For Fromm, 'The experience of love does away with the necessity of illusions',[46] and illusion is the source of a failure of moral will and political commitment. Thus he quotes approvingly the comments of the political and economic observer J. A. Schumpeter who remarked on the loss of a sense of reality which 'accounts not only for a reduced sense of responsibility but also for the absence of effective volition', which 'in turn explain the ordinary citizen's ignorance and lack of judgement in matters of domestic and foreign policy which are if anything more shocking in the case of educated people'.[47] While Albee was not concerned to enrol anyone in the cause of national or international politics *per se* in both *The Death of Bessie Smith* and *Who's Afraid of Virginia Woolf?*, he does see a lack of such commitment as evidence of a collapse of will, more especially among those intellectuals who have betrayed a central responsibility. In the early one-act plays he presents a series of alienated individuals and in *The Zoo Story* offers love, in the Fromm sense, as a means of escaping from a sense of anomie. In *Who's Afraid of Virginia Woolf?* and *A Delicate Balance* he spells out the apocalyptic alternative, the threat to the sanity of those who fail in this responsibility. But love, touted as a solution to isolation and a route to a sense of community which might translate into liberal commitment, gradually proves fragile, a demand not to be so easily realised.

Albee's plays add up to a portrait of man in the modern age and, indeed, they seem remarkably close in spirit to Karl Jaspers's observations in his book *Man in the Modern Age*, first published in 1930 but reissued in the 1950s. Jaspers was appalled by the rise of mass order and a positivism which seemed to subordinate continuity and individuality to an accommodated norm. 'The individual', he observed, 'is merged in the function. Being is objectified, for positivism would be violated if individuality remained conspicuous.'[48] It is certainly tempting to see echoes of this in *The Zoo Story* and *The American Dream* while the Young Man in the latter play seems the embodiment of Jaspers's conviction that in such an age 'Youth as the period of highest vital efficiency and of erotic exaltation becomes the desired type of life in general.'[49] And Peter, in *The Zoo Story*, blandly courteous, resistant to personal enquiry, anxious to deploy the clichés of conventional conversation as a protection against intrusion, would seem to be a perfect model of that 'universal language', drained of content and unconnected with genuine communication, which Jaspers also sees as a product of the modern age. Thus he remarks:

> Since positivism makes a general demand for simplicity that shall render things universally comprehensible, it tends towards establishing a sort of 'universal

language' for the expression of all modes of human behaviour. Not merely fashions, but rules for social intercourse, gestures, phrases, methods of conveying information, incline towards uniformity. There is now a conventional ethic of association: courteous smiles, a tranquil manner, the avoidance of haste and jostle, the adoption of a humorous attitude in strained situations, helpfulness unless the cost be unreasonable, the feeling that 'personal remarks' are in bad taste.[50]

Precisely portrayed in *The Zoo Story*, this process is pressed even further towards parody in *The American Dream*. But neither is it difficult to see elements of this description in the person of Nick in *Who's Afraid of Virginia Woolf?*, who, as a scientist, represents precisely that positivism against which Jaspers inveighed, and who is accused by George of plotting just such a dystopia as that which Jaspers identifies.

Conversely there is an element of utopianism in Albee's work, as there is in that of Miller and Williams. All three offer a critique of modernity in the name of a system which is not so much dramatised as defined by its absence. In the case of Miller and Albee it would seem to be a form of liberalism in which Freudian notions of an opposition between the interests of the individual and those of society are denied. As with most utopias the model is essentially located in the past, and this is the source of a certain irony, for they seem to wish to resist the myths of modernity with another myth, no less susceptible to irony but secure as a model precisely because it remains for the most part unexamined. What they seem to be employing in order to deplore what they see as the collapse of community, the decay of individualism and the demise of social responsibility is a kind of Jeffersonianism. But that Jeffersonianism is not inspected for its historic contradictions, for its presumptions about the privileges no less than the responsibilities of individualism, and for its reliance on the primacy of values which now we would be inclined to identify as conservative and capitalist. Tennessee Williams's utopianism is, if anything, even less securely rooted since, the ideological underpinnings once abandoned, he seems to reach for a world in which a kind of spiritual anarchism prevails, in which there is no longer a norm and in which all boundaries are dissolved, not least that between reality and illusion. In other words, on the surface there is a clear distinction between his model and that deployed by Albee and Miller, for whom a certain rationality is essential and for whom the distinction between reality and illusion is basic to both a sense of identity and a system of morality. But, given the uncertain basis of their utopianism perhaps the distinction is not quite as fundamental as it may seem.

Jaspers's own solution to a system of 'levelling down' which led only to 'the most superficial, the most trivial, and the most indifferent of human possibilities', in which the 'historical civilisations and cultures become detached from their roots, and are merged in the technico-economic world and in a vacant intellectualism' was the re-establishment of human relationships. But, faced with 'A consciousness of peril and loss as a consciousness of the radical crisis' in which reality has become 'a masquerade', the first and unavoidable step was to rediscover that reality. As he explained, 'He who wishes to find his way to the origin of the crisis must pass through the lost domain of truth, in order to revise it possessively; must traverse the domain of perplexity to reach decision concerning himself; must strip off the trappings of the masquerade, in order to disclose the genuine that lies beneath.'[51] It is hard to imagine a more precise description of the process of Albee's plays, more especially of *The Zoo Story* and *Who's Afraid of Virginia Woolf?*. Indeed it is hard to think of any of his work in which this is not both his dramatic method and his central theme. And since the process seems to be one of rediscovery, whereby the individual 'grows aware of his own being' which has been obscured by his willingness to be 'nothing but a means', the process seems necessarily historically regressive. This, of course, is why Miller and Albee seem to turn to the past. As Marcuse was to insist in the 1960s and as Albee has Jerry remark in *The Zoo Story*, sometimes it is necessary to retrace one's steps in order to find the correct path. Thus the modern situation, in Jaspers's words, 'compels man, compels every individual, to fight wittingly on behalf of his true essence. He must either maintain it or lose it according to the way in which he becomes aware of the foundation of his being in the reality of his life.'[52] And having located that reality it becomes necessary to act. So precisely does his description of the ensuing process match that which Albee's characters undergo and identify that it is worth quoting at length. For Jaspers insisted that:

> The present moment seems to be one which makes extensive claims, makes claims it is almost impossible to satisfy. Deprived of his world by the crisis, man has to reconstruct it from its beginnings with the materials and presuppositions at his disposal. There opens to him the supreme possibility of freedom, which he has to grasp even in the face of impossibility, with the alternative of sinking into a nullity....He must, through communication, establish the tie between self and self...and in default of this his life will be utterly despiritualised and become a mere function...The reality of the world cannot be evaded. Experience of the harshness of the real is the only way by which a man can come to his own self. To play an active part in the world, even though one aims at an impossible, an unattainable goal, is the necessary precondition of one's own being...Man wins destiny only through ties: not through coercive ties imposed on him as an impotent creature by great forces which lie without; but by ties freely comprehended which he makes his own. Such ties hold his life together, so that it is not frittered away but becomes the actuality of his possible existence. Then remembrance discloses to him its indelible foundations; and the future reveals to him the region wherein he

will be held accountable for what he does today... What frees us from the solitude is not the world, but the selfhood which enters into ties with others. Interlinkage of self-existent persons constitutes the invisible reality of the essential... The best gift the contemporary world can give us is this *proximity* of self-existent human beings. They are, in fact, themselves the guarantee that being exists... True nobility is not found in an isolated being. It exists in the interlinkage of independent human beings. Such are aware of their duty to discover one another, to help one another onward wherever they encounter one another, and to be ever ready for communication... Man cannot evade this situation, cannot return to forms of consciousness which are unreal because they belong to the days of the past. He might tranquillise himself in the self-forgetful pleasures of life, fancying himself to have gone back to nature in the peace of timelessness. But one day iron reality would again confront him and paralyse him.

For the individual, thrust back into his own nudity, the only option today is to make a fresh start in conjunction with the other individuals with whom he can enter into a loyal alliance.[53]

The peace of timelessness is precisely what Tennessee Williams's characters seek, as indeed it is in some degree the condition of drama whose time-scale is factitious and only analogically related to that of its audience. The problem for his characters is precisely that that timelessness is a tranquilliser inducing a spiritual equivalent of death; the problem for the theatre is the necessity of avoiding complicity in the illusions which it projects. Jaspers himself had been all too aware of this problem, recognising that one of the problems of the theatre was that it could so easily pander simply to 'the need for illusion'. And without a doubt this poses a central problem for Albee. For, while his plays patently concern themselves with exactly that process outlined by Jaspers, that is to say while they not merely urge the acknowledgement of reality but also see human relationships as an essential means of distilling and defining that reality, they are themselves factitious. They are inventions which can easily be accommodated by audiences seeking simple entertainment. Albee has been accused of just this – of pandering to the audience's desire for reassurance, of creating pre-packaged dramas which simulate a debate the conclusions of which are not merely pre-ordained but also essentially comfortable. And it would be foolish to deny that the problem exists. In a sense, no playwright is responsible for his audience, only responsible to it, but this is not in itself sufficient answer. And I suspect that there is a degree to which Albee's increasing desire to discomfort his audience, even to the extent of creating plays whose meaning is distressingly opaque and whose references are disturbingly private, may have something to do with his own awareness of the problem. But in reading his plays it is easy to forget just how challenging and disturbing some of them were in their first productions and remain even today. The apparently reassuring nature of the naturalistic set for *Who's Afraid of Virginia Woolf?* is, indeed, itself a tactic for ambushing an audience whose expectations are thereafter systematically frustrated. And despite what is, perhaps, rather too pat a conclusion to *The Zoo Story*, in which myth seals up some of the spaces left by the action, the sheer power of the play resists easy accommodation. However, it is true that his subsequent work, from *Tiny Alice* and *A Delicate Balance* through to *All Over* and *Quotations from Chairman Mao Tse-Tung*, reveals a writer not merely less confident in the human strategies which he had hinted at in his earlier work, and less sure of the willingness or ability of audiences to acknowledge or even understand the nature of those strategies, but also less willing to offer reassurance or to create plays unaffected by irony. Transcendence rooted in the real and based on vital relationships remains a primary faith, but an intensifying social experience no less than a growing doubt about the capacity of audiences to respond to his work, led to a darkening of his vision.

As the author of a highly successful Broadway play Albee was in a curious position. His reputation had been founded on experimental work performed Off-Broadway or in a Europe whose drama had clearly been a major influence on his own work. With the aid of profits derived from *Who's Afraid of Virginia Woolf?* Albee established the Edward Albee Foundation (largely, it must be said, for financial reasons). This sponsored the work of new young writers and artists. But he himself turned consistently to Broadway. Even the opacities of *Tiny Alice* were paraded before an audience more attuned to the usual Broadway fare of comedy and music. He was swiftly enrolled by the State Department as a literary ambassador (despite being attacked by *Izvestia*) and increasingly joined the college lecture-circuit making highly paid appearances. And yet while presenting play after play on Broadway he made few concessions. The result over the years has been a curious blend of respect and bafflement on the part of audiences looking for something beyond the usual banalities but ill at ease with Albee's metaphysics and his determined experimentalism. In his late fifties he is still treated as a promising writer who has unaccountably drifted off course. Admittedly *A Delicate Balance* was awarded the Pulitzer Prize previously denied to *Who's Afraid of Virginia Woolf?* when the drama committee's recommendation was rejected (one member, reportedly, objecting that it was 'a dirty play', while its assault on American mores seemed to place it outside the restrictive definitions of the Prize's original terms). But he has never repeated the popular success of his first Broadway play, works like *Tiny Alice, Seascape, Box* and *Quotations from Chairman Mao Tse-Tung* seeming deliberately provocative in their obscurity. At the same time, paradoxically, he was prepared to perform the kind of low-level surgery required of Broadway's play doctors, attempting in particular to restore some semblance of life to a musical version of Truman

Capote's *Breakfast at Tiffany's*. He also chose to adapt Giles Cooper's less than profound *Everything in the Garden*. Add to this a personal style which is highly ironic and uncompromising and you have a writer who has been alternately praised and peremptorily dismissed, a writer who, if he took care not to repeat his effects, has reiterated his thematic concerns to the point at which at times he comes close to offering parodic versions of his own early work.

But, in a way, he seems to have revelled in the apparent contradictions. Indeed his own relationship with the commercial theatre was to a degree a model of that relationship between the individual and contemporary society which became a central concern of his work. As he asked, 'What can one do in a society in which commercial success is equated with excellence? What can one do in a society in which what the public wants becomes a standard of judgement, and what is done in the large Broadway theatre is considered the standard by which the theatre as an art form should be judged in this country?' Again, speaking of the Broadway audience but with obvious relevance to his own characters, he observed that 'Most people are unwilling to suffer the experience of great joy or great sadness. They prefer the barren middle ground of nothing.'[54] Declaring that 'most of our audiences are lazy', he recognised but rejected the pressure to simplify his work, seeing American society, for all its faults, as potentially redeemable:

> I am rather thankful that I exist in a society where my work is not censored by the government but I worry sometimes about the fact that people are humbled by so much information these days, by so much reality, that they are retreating from it...I do believe that a society which is allowed the opportunity of a crisis of its own making is in a far better state than one that is not permitted this opportunity. We are nowhere near utopia anywhere on this planet but I do believe in the perfectibility of society. So I'm an optimist, I suppose. Nobody writes out of absolute despair. It's impossible. Absolute despair would silence you. For example, a number of my plays concern themselves with the fact that it would be nice if people stopped kidding themselves, realize that all those false illusions they are carrying onward are false illusions.

As he acknowledged, 'we prefer the easy to the complex'. But he still felt that 'we are one of the few societies where the complex and the questioning are allowed to co-exist with the simple and facile'.[55] That coexistence, however, proved rather more fragile than he might have imagined.

The metaphysical overtones of *Who's Afraid of Virginia Woolf?* were clear, though muted. The model of reality was a simple phenomenological one. And although George comments on the difficulty of distinguishing truth from illusion there is, finally, a truth to be acknowledged, an emotional and a factual reality. But in his next original play, *Tiny Alice* (1964), Albee tackled the question of the problematic status of the real more directly, addressing the nature of religious faith and the concept of spiritual truth.

Julian, a young lay priest, is ordered by his Cardinal to visit the ornate gothic castle of Miss Alice, a rich and apparently old recluse who wishes to make a huge donation to the church. On his arrival, however, he is offered a salutary lesson about the nature of truth and illusion as Miss Alice throws off her disguise and appears as an attractive young woman. Julian then finds himself the focus of a conspiracy by Alice and her two assistants, Butler and Lawyer, who are apparently intent on winning him away from the church. He is asked to embrace a secular deity of whom Miss Alice is merely the surrogate. He is regarded as a suitable candidate because of his own serious doubts which had led him, on one occasion, to a mental hospital; and because, as a lay priest, he is poised – not yet committed – and may be pushed over one way or another. He is, indeed, seduced by Miss Alice, but is unable to grasp her surrogate role any more than he can work out the metaphysical paradoxes involved in the presence in the castle of a smaller castle which may be either a paradigm or a replica. Eventually, unable to win him by indirection, like Jerry in *The Zoo Story* they resort to violence. But this time Julian is himself the victim as they force him to become a saint to the secular religion whose reality he has been tempted to deny.

The play was the focus for considerable critical debate, public bafflement and, eventually, scholastic pedantry, while Albee's disingenuous belief in the self-evident nature of its subject was less than convincing. And, in truth, Albee was sufficiently disturbed by the bafflement of the cast itself to offer them a gloss on the text, an explanation which is today to be found in Albee's papers at the New York Public Library:

> It will be revealed by Julian – and here you must let my dramatic instinct accomplish it – that Miss Alice is surrogate for the woman Julian thinks she is; that the true Alice, if, indeed, she exists at all, and they all believe it rather than know it, exists in the model, and that they must act on what they assume to be her wishes. Julian, in spite of what the Cardinal and the others say, will not accept what has happened to him, threatens to upset and expose the entire machinery. They shoot him. He is badly wounded, but could be saved. The others make the decision it is best to leave him to die. Butler begins to cover the furniture and all the characters make their 'abschieds', their justifications, apologies, and slow farewells. Finally, Julian is left alone. I'm not sure at this point whether or not he has been tied, arms spread, to the model. Julian begins a semi-hallucinated monologue, half to God, half to the true Alice...if she exists, if, in fact, there is a difference between her existence or non-existence and between her identity and God's. It is a long monologue, ending in Julian's Christ-like statement of having been forsaken, having forfeited his life for a falsehood. In a semi-coma, he begins to call to Alice—God, as he is dying. He begin[s] to hear a heavy breathing, see one or two lights moving, going on

and off in the model. The breathing is slow and enormous, filling the theatre. A great shadow begins to fall across the stage, the true Alice, enormous, transferable. Julian dies, accepting the existence, accepting his crucifixion. Please don't ask me here to go into the psychological justifications or philosophical fine points. It will all be clear.[56]

It was a hopeful thought. Whatever else it may have been neither actors nor critics ever found it clear.

The continuity with *Who's Afraid of Virginia Woolf?* is apparent, the metaphysical hints of that play now moving to the centre of attention in a work which poses Platonic questions about the nature of reality, which describes the processes of myth-making and which implies the need to seek consolation in the diminished world of the present and the real rather than in abstraction. But at the same time Albee has begun to move in a different direction. The realistic model of character has begun to collapse. The characters here are role-players (Butler's and Lawyer's habit of calling one another 'Darling' is a deliberate reference to theatrical hyperbole rather than sexual attraction). Indeed, as Albee has observed, 'they have assumed arbitrary levels of authority...There is absolutely no reason why in another situation Butler couldn't play Lawyer and Lawyer play Butler.'[57] The sudden transformation of Miss Alice from an old crone into a beautiful woman is not only a device reinforcing the Platonic theme but an observation about the plasticity of character itself.

And if character is placed under pressure, so, too, is language. His paratactical strategy assumes missing components, deliberate spaces left in language and experience which the individual tends to fill with myth. Julian describes an occasion on which he had injured himself and called out to his grandfather for help. When help failed to materialise he began to call for God instead. In one sense this is a description of the process whereby religious faith is born out of fear and need, the process whereby absence creates the need for existence. But it is also a description of the failure of language, which so easily loses its transitive quality. The debate with God is in essence seen as a debate with the self. Indeed the play fittingly concludes with a monologue. As I have pointed out elsewhere this is very close to Robbe-Grillet's description of conversion in an essay entitled 'Nature, Humanism, Tragedy':

> I call out. No one answers me. Instead of concluding that there is no one there...I decide to act as if someone were there, but a someone who, for one reason or another, refuses to answer. The silence that follows my outcry is hence no longer a true silence, it is now enhanced with content, with depth of meaning, with a soul – which sends me back at once to my own soul...my hope and my anguish then confer meaning on my life...My solitude...is transformed at last by my failing mind into a higher necessity, into a promise of redemption.

And Albee, like Robbe-Grillet, distrusts 'a path towards a metaphysical "beyond"', which represents 'a door closed against any realistic future'.[58] But if *Tiny Alice* is in one sense about the process whereby religious faith is born, and if its plot is concerned with an attempt to 'deprogramme' an uncertain convert, it is also about the inadequacy of language to command the real. For language is a code with elements missing, less evidence of rationality than of a desire for rationality. In other words, it is itself an example of that absurdity which derives from the need to impose order on an implacable anarchy. In a sense the theme of the play becomes the need to penetrate symbols and to deal with the thing itself. Reality is represented not by the grand castle, which is a mere illusion, but by the diminished world of the model, the stark fact of pain and death, the essential solitariness which we would rather people with shadows than see for what it is. In *Tiny Alice*, as in *Who's Afraid of Virginia Woolf?* and *The Zoo Story*, reality exists at the moment when language stops; language, indeed, is seen in some ways as the pressure which prevents an implosion of the real. But that can hardly be the final position of a writer who depends upon language and who has not chosen to follow Beckett into the realm of mime. As Albee has said, language 'is imprecise, but if you ask people to pay more attention to it, it helps. Language is both the disguise and the nakedness, written and spoken language. There is a body language and that which is not said – that is part of the language – but we communicate and fail to communicate basically by language.'[59] And yet, in *Tiny Alice* it is the inadequacy of that language which leads the conspirators to communicate so obliquely, to fall back on images, symbols, surrogates and parables. The mystery of religion begins where language ends, while the theatre itself relies on something more than verbal communication. As Albee has said 'Theatre is imprecise anyway is it not?'[60] It is indeed, and in many ways it is the problematic nature of language which fascinates him. It is both truth and lie. The trick is to tell the difference.

Tiny Alice is not designed to deny the experience from which religious belief stems. That is real enough. The elaborations contain the falsity. As Jung observed, 'The Churches stand for traditional and collective convictions which in the case of many adherents are no longer based on their own inner experience but on *unreflecting belief.*' The formalised creeds that result are 'full of impressive mythological symbolism which, if taken literally, comes into insufferable conflict with knowledge'.[61] And so the church, with its injunction to render unto Caesar, becomes an adjunct of those political forces which so coerce the individual, which deny his freedom and the reality of his experiential life. It is that perception, the suspicion that God is a projection of need, a convenient denial of the real, which had sent Julian to a mental hospital for six years. He is entirely accurate when he observes that 'my faith and my sanity...they are one and the same'.[62] For, as he explains elsewhere, a man locked in an attic room has to presuppose the existence of someone outside the room who can release him or go mad. But that solitariness is an illusion. Man may have been abandoned by God, whom he created to make sense of an otherwise contingent existence, but he does have access to those others who feel themselves similarly abandoned. Absurdity derives not from abandonment but from the conscious creation of a God who can never manifest Himself and whose non-appearance creates the sense of abandonment in the first place. The fact is that Julian is not alone, in an attic or anywhere else. He has simply accepted the denial of human consolation as the price of his religious faith. As he remarks, 'I have...given up everything to gain everything, for the sake of my faith and my peace'.[63] Thus, as a lay brother he is committed to the systematic denial of contact; he has taken an oath of chastity. Significantly, the one occasion on which he may have abrogated that oath was when he lost his faith. Denied the consolation of religion he was obliged to find it in another human being. This is in effect the sanity to which he must be won. And this is to be achieved through his marriage to Miss Alice, whose name means truth, and who is the surrogate for that truth.

It is this gap, between symbol and substance, between expression and experience, language and referent, which is at the heart of the play. As Lawyer remarks to the Cardinal, 'he worships the symbol and not the substance', to which Butler replies, 'Like everyone'.[64] The conspirators recognise that because of his potentially redemptive doubt he is 'walking on the edge of an abyss, but is balancing. Can be pushed...over, back to the asylum...Or over...to the Truth.'[65] And the truth does exist for them; it is the need to 'accept what's real'. The question is, what is meant by the real? Confronted with a choice between 'Predestination, fate...accident', Julian has chosen the conviction that 'faith is knowledge'. But his own doubts make him a candidate for a more secular belief, a diminished world which no longer relates the individual to notions of cosmic order and divine purpose but offers a more tangible if limited religion of man. As Butler insists, 'there is something. There is a *true* God.'[66] And Lawyer identifies it: 'There is an abstraction, Julian, but it cannot be understood. You cannot worship it...There is Alice...That can be understood. Only the mouse in the model. Just that...The Mouse. Believe it. Don't personify the abstraction...limit it, demean it. Only the mouse, the toy. And that does not exist...but is all that can be worshipped...accept it.'[67]

Julian, the man who withdrew to the asylum precisely because he found himself 'dedicated to the reality of things, rather than their appearance', still proves incapable of seeing through the symbol, incapable of realising that in embracing Miss Alice he is not embracing reality but only the seductive and attractive image of that reality, the Platonic shadow. Accordingly he is shot and dies in effect tied to that diminished world in the form of the castle. Abandoned by all the others, he finds himself in a similar situation to the time when his unanswered calls to his grandfather had turned into calls to God. Now, however, his call to God changes to a call to Alice.

And Platonism does seem to lie behind the play's central image. Dominating the stage is what appears to be a model of the castle in which the action takes place. Lights go on and off in the small rooms, and a fire breaks out in the 'model' just as it does in the larger castle. The problem is, which is the original? Is the small castle a model or a paradigm? In his parable of the cave Plato had presupposed a group of people chained inside a cave and able only to see the giant shadows cast on the rear wall as people and objects passed in front of a fire in the mouth of the cave. He then proposed the problem faced by one of their number, suddenly released, allowed to see the diminutive size of the real world, and then required to return to explain this new insight to those still chained within. This man is Plato's philosopher, and in effect the conspirators in Albee's play have a similar problem. The 'real' world is so much less expansive, so diminished in size and significance, that it is difficult to accept and yet this seems precisely the point that the conspirators seem determined to make. As Lawyer says to Julian, of the castle in which they are acting out their ceremony, 'it is a replica...Of that...[Pointing to the model]'.[68] Recognising the difficulty of the leap of unfaith that they require of him they provide him with a surrogate in the form of Alice. She represents that diminished world, as she does its physical and human content. Slowly Julian comes to suspect that the period which he had spent in the asylum – years of lost faith in which the immediate reality of personal relationships replaced the expansive visions of religious commitment – may actually have been the basis of the only available transcendence: 'I cannot have so misunderstood my life; I cannot have...was I sane then? Those years? My time in the asylum? WAS THAT WHEN I WAS RATIONAL? THEN?'[69]

The play seems to owe a great deal to Eliot's The Cocktail Party, and Albee has recognised as much. In that play there is also a somewhat mysterious group – called the Guardians – who intervene in people's lives at moments of crisis in order to direct them towards their individual salvation. Typically such individuals have suffered 'a loss of personality...lost touch with the person' they thought they were. One of the central characters is a lawyer who jokes of being mistaken for a butler, though he and his wife Lavinia are closer kin to George and Martha in Who's Afraid of Virginia Woolf? than to any characters in Tiny Alice. The real parallel is with Celia, a woman who comes to feel that the world she lives in 'seems all a delusion'. She, like Julian, is sent to a sanatorium because she has 'an honest mind', which is in fact the cause of her suffering. She is struck by the conviction that:

> everyone's alone − or so it seems to me
> They make noises, and think they are talking to each other;
> And I'm sure that they don't[70]

She projects the existence of something outside of herself to which she must atone because the alternative is a sense of abandonment too forbidding to be borne:

> Like a child who has wandered into a forest
> Playing with an imaginary playmate
> And suddenly discovers he is only a child
> Lost in a forest, wanting to go home.[71]

When the leader of the Guardians suggests, much as Albee has done in many of his plays, that

> Compassion may be already a clue
> Towards finding your own way out of the forest[72]

she objects:

> But even if I find my way out of the forest
> I shall be left with the inconsolable memory
> Of the treasure I went into the forest to find
> And never found, and which was not there
> And perhaps is not anywhere? But if not any where,
> Why do I feel guilty at not having found it?[73]

And this is the problem equally for Julian (whose, name, incidentally, is perhaps an echo of that of one of the Guardians in Eliot's play − Julia). His sense of guilt and his pursuit of a transcendent vision leave him incapable of seeing compassion as a way out of the forest. He, like Celia, is asked to choose between being reconciled to 'the human condition' or pursuing transcendence to the point of death. Here Eliot and Albee part company, since for Eliot there is substance to religious transcendence and though

> Both ways avoid the final desolation
> Of solitude in the phantasmal world
> Of imagination, shuffling memories and desires.[74]

Celia chooses to be 'transhumanised'. Her decision is celebrated with a ritual, a champagne libation is drunk, as it is later in the play when one of the other characters acknowledges the alternative path, a perception which is rescued from its banality precisely by the ritual:

> I think that every moment is a fresh beginning;
> And Julia, that life is only keeping on;
> And somehow, the two ideas seem to fit together.[75]

Celia is crucified, having joined a religious order. Julian is apparently converted to a more secular faith. Certainly the conspirators in that play also drink a champagne libation, but he dies in a rather more ambiguous frame of mind.

According to the reviewer Henry Hewes, Irene Worth, who played Miss Alice in the original production, believed that the play

> urges us to stop using religion as armor to protect ourselves from the abstraction which is God (or Tiny Alice). Since the infinity of the universe cannot be defined or expressed, Julian has the choice of being a surrogate (remaining alive with Miss Alice), or 'finding the centre of the sun' (dying in the presence of Miss Alice), or going back to the asylum.[76]

Albee, himself, argued that he was less concerned with attacking the church than with stressing the evil uses to which it could be put and the reality of its authority as a power structure. But he was ready to admit to certain weaknesses in the play, confessing, 'I expected the audience to be able to become deeply concerned with Julian's predicament. If it cannot, something is wrong.'[77] A psychiatrist writing in the *Saturday Review* commented on the final scene, identifying echoes of 'Freud's queries about whether all religious dogma stems from man's unwillingness to accept mortality, to recognise the rapacious cruelty of nature, or to sacrifice some of his libidinous gratifications for the help he needs from his fellow men'. But it is a curiously passionless debate. And, while it might be claimed that the audience's bafflement merely mirrors that of his protagonist, the detachment of the play is curiously at odds with its theme. In a discussion with John Gielgud, Albee asked himself the question, 'Is *Tiny Alice* meant to be intentionally confusing?' His reply was less than convincing: 'I wonder if I meant it to be intentionally confusing. Maybe I meant it to be something a little different from confusing — provocative, perhaps, rather than confusing.'[78]

It is scarcely surprising that the play created such bafflement, nor is it without its logical contradictions. A warning against the personification of the abstraction, it nonetheless adopts precisely this process as its central strategy. An indictment of semantic and moral evasion, it employs a prose style which is itself oblique and creates baroque characters who are too fragile to sustain a thematic commitment to the real. Though the play concedes a role to mystery, its own opacity in performance (Albee, himself, in an author's note, accepts that it 'is less opaque in reading than it would be in any single viewing' while contradictorily asserting that 'the play is quite clear') is at times a wilful obfuscation rather than a subtle projection of the unknowable. Certainly neither the play's director nor John Gielgud, who somewhat surprisingly, given his age, was engaged to play the role of Julian, was happy with the third act. Both men agreed to be involved in the production on reading the brilliant first act, but neither felt that the third act resolved the questions raised elsewhere in the play, Gielgud finding some consolation in the fact that his own bafflement was mirrored in that of his character. Perhaps it is not surprising that their confusions communicated to the audience, more especially one hoping for a repetition of the emotional power and verbal pyrotechnics of his first Broadway success. But Albee has always taken a special and laudable pride in refusing to repeat his effects, in opting for stylistic shifts which have prevented his career slipping into the destructive repetition of his early success. So successfully did he do this, however, that his reputation continued to dwindle during the 1970s until the débâcle of his adaptation of Nabokov's *Lolita* in 1980 inspired one reviewer to beg him to terminate his role as playwright in favour of directing.

In between writing his own plays Albee has also, somewhat surprisingly, undertaken a number of adaptations. Distrustful, as he is, of the very process – 'there is a tendency to cheapen – to lessen the work that's adapted'[79] – he nonetheless followed his first Broadway success with an adaptation of Carson McCullers's *The Ballad of the Sad Café*, and *Tiny Alice* with a version of James Purdy's *Malcolm*. The first was well received; the second closed after seven performances.

Albee was an admirer of Carson McCullers's work. *The Zoo Story* plainly owed something to her short story entitled 'A Tree. A Rock. A Cloud', which appeared together with *The Ballad of the Sad Café* in a collection of her work. This had outlined a 'science of love' whereby the process of relating to people is learned first by relating to objects – a tree, a rock or a cloud. From this, the next step is to learn to love animals: 'I bought a goldfish and I concentrated on the goldfish and I loved it. I graduated from one thing to another.'[80] In *The Zoo Story* Jerry had similarly explained, 'It's just that if you can't deal with people you have to make a start somewhere. WITH ANIMALS!...A person has to have some way of dealing with SOMETHING. If not with people...SOMETHING. With a bed, a cockroach.'[81] Carson McCullers's characters – solitary, desperate for love, but located in a world which deforms such an impulse – had a natural appeal for Albee.

Carson McCullers was herself to have played a role in the production. She was actually recorded in the part of the narrator but was ill and her voice lacked the necessary power. In the Broadway production it was decided to substitute Roscoe Lee Browne, a black actor, a decision which, given the play's Southern setting, several critics found destabilising. *The Ballad of the Sad Café* (1963) begins and ends with solitariness. Peopled with gothic figures, from a grotesquely large asexual woman to a hump-backed dwarf, it is an account of the desperate need which leads to relationships but also of the solitariness which exists within those relationships. It is in a sense a story about the South (hermetically sealed against a potentially redemptive compassion), brutal and brutalising. But more than that it is offered as an account of the perversity and yet the potentially vivifying nature of love which, for all its cruelties and absurdities, has the power to transform the sensibility and end a willed isolation. What is savagely ironic in her world, however, is the lack of mutuality, the sheer consistency with which unlikes are drawn together and desire wedded to frustration.

The play is set in a small town whose nearest neighbour is the significantly named Society City. The action concerns Miss Amelia Evans, a large woman with no social graces and the will and ability to resist any man who makes sexual advances to her. Perversely, Marvin Macy, a well-known local womaniser, falls in love with her (an action which is unexplained and improbable to a degree). He reforms, abandoning both women and drink, and saves enough money to buy some land. He then proposes to Amelia who just as unaccountably accepts him. But when the marriage ceremony has been performed and they are alone together she resists his sexual advances, insisting indignantly that he sleeps on his own. He tries to win her over with gifts, even transferring his property to her. But she is unimpressed and continues to resist him, to the extent of breaking one of his teeth. In despair and anger he leaves and quickly ends up in the local penitentiary.

Meanwhile, a dwarf arrives, claiming to be Amelia's cousin. To everyone's surprise she takes him in, and, as evidence of the love which apparently now directs her actions, opens her house as a café. But Cousin Lymon simply takes advantage of her, and when Marvin returns he transfers his affection to him, though he is in turn rebuffed as a little 'runt'. When Cousin Lymon finally demands that she should make way for Marvin Macy, Amelia has to take a stand. She fights Marvin and is, indeed, winning when the dwarf joins in, securing her defeat. The two men leave and Amelia retreats into her house, closing the café, and thereafter appears only irregularly at an upstairs window. The town lapses back into its solitary condition.

This sad triangle in which people are grotesquely mismatched, tied together by an emotion which they cannot control, is both parodied and celebrated in the image of the nearby chain-gang in which 'twelve men...are together'.[82] All they share are their chains, which are both the badge of their enslavement and a symbol of their enforced community. Love, in Carson McCullers's world, is independent of the object of that love. It is in a sense an image of some inescapable absurdity. It is evidence of the need for completion and, in the terms in which she chooses to present it, the root of suffering. It can generate life or breed death. It has the same effect as Miss Amelia's alcohol: 'A man may suffer or he may be spent with joy – but he has warmed his soul and seen the message hidden there.'[83] It leads Amelia to transform her house into a café and brings a little life to the sullen town. But the frustration of that love leads her to close it again just as it takes Marvin Macy to the penitentiary. The twelve townspeople, like the twelve members of the chain-gang, are lonely but together in their loneliness. The problem is that they fail to recognise this, that they never transcend their selfishness. And in that they are contrasted to the three principal characters, for, whatever their suffering, they have glimpsed something denied even to Marvin's brother, Henry Macy, a detached observer who is immune to the backbiting and hatred of his fellow citizens but is immune too to the transforming power of love.

It is possible to see the play partly as an extension of his own earlier work *The Death of Bessie Smith*. The South is once again peopled by grotesques. It is drained of compassion, self-concerned, detached equally from moral values and historic process. But the play is more concerned with tracing the necessity for love, even while granting its destructive potential, for it is love which transforms Marvin Macy and which brings Amelia into the community, and it is the denial of that love which freezes the individual into a frightening loneliness.

In an extended aria the narrator considers the nature and power of love. In terms of the play's structure it is a redundant account of what is anyway enacted in the plot but it is a useful summary of McCullers's and Albee's positions

> What sort of thing is love? First of all, it is a joint experience between two persons, but that fact does not mean that it is a similar experience to the two people involved. There are the lover and the beloved, but these two come from different countries. Often the beloved is only the stimulus for all the stored-up love which has lain quiet within the lover for a long time hitherto. And somehow every lover knows this. He feels in his soul that his love is a solitary thing. He comes to know a new, strange loneliness. Now, the beloved can also be of any description: the most outlandish people can be the stimulus for love. Yes, and the lover may see this as clearly as anyone else – but this does not affect the evolution of his love one whit. Therefore, the quality and value of any love is determined solely by the lover himself... But though the outward facts of love are often sad and ridiculous, it must be remembered that no one can know what really takes place in the soul of the lover himself.[84]

The narrator announces that no good can come of the relationship between the three protagonists. But of course it does, if only momentarily. Amelia creates a 'special place', and for a while the town functions as a community, no matter how fragile it may be. And Albee seems concerned here, as elsewhere, to establish the connection between personal relations and public policy, as he is to balance what is given with what can still be changed. As Cousin Lymon indicates of the chain-gang, in response to Amelia's observation that 'they got no freedom', 'I know, Amelia...but they *together*...an' how they sing'.[85]

The play was praised for its 'weird, halting poetry' (*The New York Times*), described as 'beautiful, absorbing, exciting, touching and absolutely enthralling' (*New York Daily News*), and seen as a 'strange and potent drama' (The Associated Press). The superlatives seem a little misplaced. The narrator is an awkward figure who frequently offers redundant information or portentous comments. The grotesques of the McCullers novel translate awkwardly to the stage (a problem which becomes more obvious with his next adaptation, *Malcolm*), and even the language is at times mannered and unconvincing. But whatever its weaknesses Carson McCullers's fable did fit curiously well with Albee's own early plays on a thematic level, in that, like *The Zoo Story*, *The Death of Bessie Smith* and *Who's Afraid of Virginia Woolf?*, it urged the transforming power of the human relationship which is seen as the root of both despair and consolation. The source of love in *The Zoo Story*, after all, had been the grotesque landlady and her equally grotesque dog, and Jerry's hard-won insight had been the need to recognise the impulse for contact, for what he comes eventually to call 'love', behind the masks with which the individual confronts the world.

Malcolm presented an altogether more difficult task. Adapted from the work of a man who was also drawn to the grotesque and who similarly wished to probe the nature of human relationships in a world that distorts the human impulse, it relied on a series of characters and situations whose surrealistic dimensions translated poorly to the stage.

In many ways James Purdy, author, among other things, of *Cabot Wright Begins*, a mordant satire on American values, is close kin to Albee. Indeed, if anything, his denunciation of the violation of human by material values is more strident than Albee's. Consider the following:

All my work is a criticism of the United States, implicit not explicit...This is a culture based on money and competition, [it] is inhuman, terrified of love, sexual and other, obsessed with homosexuality and brutality. Our entire moral life is pestiferous and we live in a completely immoral atmosphere...I believe that the human being under capitalism is a stilted, depressed, sick creature, that marriage in the United States is homosexuality, and homosexuality a real disease, that our national life is a nightmare of noise, ugliness, filth and confusion....I don't believe America has any future.[86]

He tends to create characters who are orphans, literal and symbolic, characters who, like those in *The American Dream*, *The Zoo Story* and *Who's Afraid of*

Virginia Woolf?, are cut off from a direct contact with the spiritual values of the past and hence are especially vulnerable to what he tends to see as the corrosive values of the present. And there must have been a special attraction to Albee in a novel whose central character is an orphan who is the subject of a putative adoption by a millionaire and who has a rapid rise to success. Even the central conceit, of a person on a bench who has to be displaced, is essentially the one with which he had begun his own dramatic career, incidentally in the same year as Purdy's first novel had been published.

Malcolm is a young boy who for some reason has lost touch with his father. He had been a kind of godlike figure and hence Malcolm becomes a form of Christ, who moves towards crucifixion, albeit a particularly contemporary model of crucifixion – death by sexual excess. He is persuaded to leave his bench by Professor Cox, an astrologer, who gives him a series of addresses which, when pursued, bring the young boy into contact with a number of grotesques. Each encounter introduces him to one further aspect of the modern world and facilitates his corruption. Instead of redeeming the world he is assimilated by it, innocence not merely inviting corruption but also proving a highly marketable commodity. But this cuts both ways, for, if there is a God, He has plainly abandoned the world, sending His son painfully ill-equipped into a society whose only deity is self and only sacrament money. The corruption of Malcolm is indeed simultaneously an induction into that society as he comes to perceive the corrupting power of money (in the person of the Girards), the selfishness at the heart of marriage (Laureen and Kermit Raphaelson), and the corruption of art (Jerome and Eloisa Brace).

And that society is unambiguously presented as America. In the original production Professor Cox was dressed as Uncle Sam and Malcolm offered an American flag to celebrate his visit to a brothel. For Purdy, who believes that 'We live in the stupidest cultural era of American history',[87] it thus stands as an indictment of a world which has abandoned love and in which 'people are losing their character as real people'.[88] Indeed, the figures in *Malcolm* are fictions in the same sense as those in Nathanael West's *The Day of the Locust*. They are actors required to 'act out the parts they are meant to act out with one another'.[89] There is no longer a sense of the real to constitute the foundation of moral experience. Life follows art. And the result for both writers is apocalypse as the characters are accommodated to their own fictions. When one of the characters, Madame Girard, observes that texture is all and substance nothing she is inadvertently describing her own world. Character is so thoroughly dissembled, language so completely attenuated, oblique and vacuous, plot so contingent, that the process which Purdy and Albee alike ascribe to the social world has infiltrated his art. This is a logical enough development but one which poses problems for the writer intent on offering a social critique. The ironic ending of both novel and play (the one concluding with an empty tomb and the other with a mock ascension) leaves no space for the recuperation of values. Art becomes less commentary than ironic enactment. God becomes no more than a minor character-actor in the advertising industry ('a middle-aged emphatically distinguished man, who might have posed for sparkling water advertisements'). Where in his earlier plays Albee had retained some purchase on the real, no matter how tenuously, now the very concept of the real has been abandoned. It is, in other words, a much darker vision than he had permitted himself before, and as such it reflected a shift in his own position exemplified by *A Delicate Balance* which appeared later in the same year. And an interest in the actual process whereby individuals and societies shape the worlds which they inhabit, create the fictions which they subsequently choose to regard as realities came to absorb him in plays like *Box*, *Quotations from Chairman Mao Tse-Tung* and *Listening*. *Malcolm* was not a success in that Albee failed to find a dramatic correlative for Purdy's surrealistic figures, but it was perhaps important in suggesting the directions which his work might subsequently take. And if he was not yet ready to examine the implications of the erosion of art by the moral anarchy which he posited beyond its confines, this, too, was a subject to which he would return.

The world which Albee observes is entropic. Its basic impulse is disintegrative. His subject is what Agnes, in *A Delicate Balance*, describes as 'the gradual... demise of intensity, the private preoccupations, the substitutions'.[90] Relationships dissolve, individuality collapses. The 'regulated great gray life' supplies refuge from the sharpness of loss, a loss which is the fundamental image of Albee's work. The difference between *Who's Afraid of Virginia Woolf?* and *A Delicate Balance* lies in the fact that the former presupposes that a radical change is possible; the latter that 'It's too late'. The dawning day is indeed an image of some hope in *Who's Afraid of Virginia Woolf?*; in *A Delicate Balance* it is ironic, a denial of the insight which comes with the release of nocturnal demons. It is not that it is impossible to oppose this disintegrative impulse but that the individual has lost the will to do so. Instead he transforms existence into a simple act of waiting for extinction.

A Delicate Balance (1966) is concerned with a crisis in the lives of Agnes and Tobias. Over the years they have allowed themselves to slip into a passionless and largely untroubled routine. The repeated marital failures of their daughter Julia do not for the most part disturb their equanimity. Indeed, in a sense, those failures seem to imply their own relative success, as the drunkenness of Agnes's sister, Claire, seems to imply their own sobriety. Their lives have settled into a rut. The language of love no longer contains any substance. Language, indeed, becomes a substitute for, rather than a description of, reality. But this delicate balance is disturbed by the arrival of Harry and Edna, who have suddenly been shaken by their perception of

17. Jessica Tandy and Hume Cronyn in *A Delicate Balance* at the Martin Beck Theatre, New York, 1966.

'the terror', an experience which they cannot bring themselves to name but which seems to have been a glimpse of the sheer contingency of existence. It is an experience which, like that which affects Eliot's protagonist in *The Family Reunion*, comes

> Not in the day time
> And in the hither world
> Where we know what we are doing
> There is not its operation...
> But in the night time,
> In the nether world[91]

They present a demand for friendship and love. Commitments are required, causalities insisted upon. Their need is a last challenge to Tobias to acknowledge a responsibility beyond his own daily survival. *A Delicate Balance* is in fact Albee's version of Eliot's *The Family Reunion* as *Tiny Alice* has been his version of *The Cocktail Party*. But where Eliot gave literal form to the Furies, here they become an indefinite sense of terror. They are internalised until the pressure of the moment forces a schizophrenic division – Agnes and Tobias becoming, in effect, Edna and Harry.

The play is offered both as an examination of the failure of individual commitment, which has social, indeed national, implications ('We're not a communal nation...giving, but not sharing, outgoing, but not friendly'[92]), and as an account of that collapse of personal and social meaning which simply compounds a metaphysical absurdity. The failure of love is repeated, indeed accelerated, by the next generation. The clear need is to oppose this disintegrative drive without capitulating to a sense of order which is in fact no more than mere routine, without denying the force and reality of loss, and without succumbing to nihilism. The possibility exists. This much is clear from Claire's distinction between herself and a genuine alcoholic: 'they couldn't help it; I could, and wouldn't...they were sick, and I was merely...wilful'.[93] And here once again is a crucial distinction between Albee and the European absurdists. For Albee, absurdity is a wilful product of a failure of courage and imagination. It is a consequence not of metaphysical determinism but of the systematic denial of those human qualities which constitute a possible defence against the facts of entropy and death. Indeed, in a story about his relationship with a cat (which clearly parallels that about Jerry and the dog in *The Zoo Story*) Tobias poses a central question: what is the extent of one's obligations to others? He describes his relationship with a cat which had withdrawn its affection from him. His response had been to see this as an accusation. Love had turned into a kind of hate, a need to destroy the cat rather than face something in himself which could account for its behaviour. Now, in retrospect, he concludes, much as Jerry had done, that 'I might have tried harder. I might have gone on, as long as cats live.'[94] This is essentially the obligation in which he has equally failed with his fellow human beings. Self-pity and greed have become dominating principles. And so the moral and the lexical world collapse in concert. No longer desiring communication, indeed fearing the vulnerability that it implies, the characters degrade language to the point at which it is no longer required to do more than conceal the depth of betrayal, or bridge the gap between the apparent and the real.

In a sense the night-time demons dislocate the personalities and beings of Agnes and Tobias. At the beginning of the play Agnes speculates that she 'might, some day, or early evening I think more likely – in some autumn dusk – go quite mad'.[95] This would, however, she insists, 'be simple paranoia. Schizophrenia, on the other hand, is far more likely.'[96] The play, set on just such an autumn evening, in fact witnesses just such an event. Harry and Edna are in effect the embodiment of that suppressed terror which lies beneath the placid surface. And in the course of the play they become increasingly dominant, in effect acting as Tobias and Agnes, dispensing drinks, slapping their friends' daughter as though she were their own, asserting their proprietorial rights over the house. But the madness also constitutes a natural extension of Tobias's and Agnes's slow drift towards the placid but vacuous world of the totally uninvolved, a denial of human realities which is scarcely distinguishable from insanity. For Agnes admits to the ambiguous attractions of a position which, by the end of the play, has, in effect, become her own. She sees the process as that of 'becoming a stranger in...the world...quite uninvolved'.[97] The risk she runs and to which she eventually succumbs, is that of moving beyond some irrevocable point at which simple evasive strategy becomes definitional, at which the denial of reality becomes a necessary impulse. Tobias, as Julia remarks, has sunk to cipher. The guiding principle becomes that identified by Agnes when she remarks that her principal function is 'Maintenance..."To keep in shape",'[98] to prevent things falling apart. It is an order which is not presented as desirable. It relies on the members of the family enacting their roles and nobody destroying the delicate balance of forces; it turns on a required sustaining of bourgeois verities. And yet, paradoxically, it is Agnes who is allowed to perceive the destructive forces with clarity even if her desire for order eventually makes her deny the reality of what she sees. She recognises clearly enough the 'awful din'[99] of the family's self-concern claiming, what the others already cannot, that she is 'blessed and burdened with the ability to view a situation objectively' while she is in it – the claim equally of the writer who can say with Agnes that 'if I shout, its merely to be heard...above the awful din of your privacies and sulks'[100] – and regret only, as another character was to do in a later play, that 'no one listens'.[101] It is Agnes who recognises the loss of energy, the growing privatism, the retreat from the real. 'We become', she remarks, 'allegorical'. It is she who observes that 'the individuality we hold so dearly sinks into crotchet',[102] and who recognises that the process of living has been surrendered to the next generation who seem the cutting edge of the real but who, in truth, elaborate their own evasions, deploy their own panoply of self-deceits. Her strength has, indeed, sustained the 'delicate balance' which is not merely one between love and hate (as it had been when he used that same phrase in 'The City of People') but one between sanity and insanity, a world of reality, pain and ambiguous passions, and a homogenised existence drained of meaning, bereft of threat because without real feeling. But the effort of will which distinguishes Agnes is directed only to sustaining a status quo which is itself destructive. Her very contempt for those who surround her compounds the reductivism which she denounces. For the truth is that she accepts the invasion of her home with equanimity because she has arrived at that placidity against which she issues her warnings. She sees with clarity but lacks the will or the imagination to change.

Tobias, on the other hand, struggles with his demons because a spark remains of a moral imagination not completely extinguished by a lifetime of withdrawal; and sexual withdrawal is presented as an image of retreat from human contact, of the sterility of his stance, as it had been in *The American Dream*, *Who's Afraid of Virginia Woolf?* and *Tiny Alice*. The spilling of his seed stands as a symbol of an individual and a society which has become intransitive. And this sexual withdrawal is a response to his fear of pain. The death of their child many years before had provoked a determination to aspire to that invulnerability which can only be attained through a retreat into the inanimate. The truth he wishes to evade is once again that central assertion of Albee: that consciousness is pain, that vulnerability is an essential component and evidence of animate existence. And the static nature of Albee's plays, the congealing opacity of the *mise-en-scène*, the threatening occlusions of a material world which is deliberately required to stanch the flow of experience, the unpredictable contingency of experience, all stand as conscious images of his characters' desire to freeze time and to control space and identity. The figures who move through this fixed space are themselves aspects of that space. Their central strategy is one of survival through reduction. The womb–tomb image is dominant. Julia returns to 'the cave' which the other characters fear to leave, as Peter had defended his bench, and as Honey had retreated to the bathroom. But this strategy leaves them vulnerable to the violation of that territory. Albee's method is akin to Pinter's or, earlier, to Eliot's. The sanctum is invaded. Space becomes abyss. Realistic characters in realistic settings are subjected to dislocations which occur in the substratum. The plays treat this moment of crisis. The characters' lives are focussed to a point which, most typically, Albee sees in the image of a fulcrum. They are in a state of precarious balance. They are caught at a dubious apogee from which they can only decline into destructive self-deceit or discharge their energy in a serious attempt to deal with the fact of decline. Tobias (ageing father and husband), Jerry (the 30-year-old hippie), George (the middle-aged professor whose fantasy son's twenty-first birthday is about to precipitate him into lonely middle age), Julian (no longer young, and poised uncertainly between the grace of the church and a more secular consecration) are all caught at crucial moments of decision. At stake is their self-definition and behind that a whole moral vision; hence the social critic who so often breaks into the metaphysics of the plays.

Inherently liberal in his convictions, Albee assumes that social forms and objectives, ethical texture and mood, are the product of an individual response to social and metaphysical circumstances (though as his career developed this conviction was increasingly placed under pressure). And yet the effect of his ever more baroque approach to character was in some sense to undermine the humanism of his own convictions. His insistence on the need to drive through illusion, to shatter a surface equanimity, to reach for relationships born out of need but based on a mutual apprehension of reality, is at odds with the vision of character which he deploys. His figures are reduced to language not simply because this is their primary resort but because this is equally Albee's strength. And Albee requires language to work rather too hard, substituting words for the human substance.which constitutes the premise and the objective of his work but not its method. Character is stunted by under use. This is a theme of the plays. The arrested development of the insane is an image which recurs throughout (*Who's Afraid of Virginia Woolf?*, *Tiny Alice*, *A Delicate Balance*, *All Over*, *Listening*). But it is equally a fact of his own work as he has become more interested in ideas than people (an accusation which Sartre had once directed at Camus).

Nor does he choose to dramatise the social and moral world which he advocates. His plays remain unresolved. Ostensibly this is for the same reason that Bellow's novels remain open-ended: that is, it is the essence of liberal ideology that it needs a sustained tension rather than a dialectical method, since synthesis carries the risk of stasis. The interests of self and society, mind and imagination, are in many respects antithetical and yet the rights of both must be maintained. There is a necessary tension, a commitment to continued struggle, to negotiating conflicting demands rather than accepting a synthesis which must prove destructive. And yet the structure of Albee's play implies just such a drive towards synthesis, though this is never presented as wholly unambiguous. A new level of commitment is urged, a new engagement of the real, and acknowledgement of the centrality of human relationships. But this is never dramatised. The action never takes us beyond the moment of perception. The fear, clearly, is that what he presents as promise may prove to be threat. So that it becomes impossible to dramatise the world invoked by *The Zoo Story* and *Who's Afraid of Virginia Woolf?*, which rests on the possibility of restored harmonies and the closing of personal and social spaces. In *A Delicate Balance* that possibility seems anyway to have disappeared.

A Delicate Balance is an intensely personal play, not remote from his family experiences, and in some ways it rehearses his own conception of the function and fallibility of art. The Tobias who sits on his own looking back over the events of the immediate and distant past, and recognises the impulse to 'reconstruct, with such...detachment, see yourself...Look at it all...play it out again, watch',[103] is acknowledging a temptation which is equally that of the artist: indeed, it is equally that of the human mind itself which, as he implies in *Listening*, is concerned with the process of invention no less than the writer who simply mimics that process. And the truths offered by theatre, truths presented in a darkened space, are as likely to be dissipated by the return of light, routine and time as are those which come to the individual in moments of solitude – those night terrors dramatised by *A Delicate Balance*. When Tobias regrets that 'when the daylight comes the pressures will be on, and all the insight won't be worth a damn', he is equally anticipating the deliberately anti-climactic ending and acknowledging the fragility of art whose constructions are unlikely to withstand the pressures of actuality. Though Robert Brustein described the play's conclusion, which he took to be a replay of that in *Who's Afraid of Virginia Woolf?*, as 'one of those vibrato rising sun lines familiar from at least a dozen such evenings',[104] he failed to detect the irony which the play's action has given to Agnes's statement that 'when the daylight comes again...comes order with it',[105] for that order is no more than the vacuous existence which they had previously lived. For they are like Eliot's characters in that they:

> are all people
> To whom nothing has happened, at most a continual impact
> Of external events.

They are people who:

> have gone through life in sleep.
> Never woken to the nightmare...[106]

As Agnes confesses, 'We manufacture such a portion of our own despair...such busy folk'.[107] It would be hard to imagine a clearer statement of Albee's own position.

Edna and Harry are the mirror into which Agnes and Tobias look, not merely in the sense that this could be said of the pairs in *Who's Afraid of Virginia Woolf?* but to the extent of their being *alter egos*, the externalisations of their own suppressed selves. As Edna observes, 'Our lives are...the same'.[108] The mirror is, of course, a central metaphor of the theatre, which has often claimed to hold the mirror up to life; and so the audience is invited to observe, is offered a version of the truth, a disturbing glimpse of our own lives. 'You can sit and watch. You can have...so clear a picture, see everybody moving through his own jungle...an insight into all the reasons, all the needs...the dark sadness.'[109] But Albee's confidence in the transforming power of theatre is no longer what it was in the early plays. Audiences do not surrender their human fallibilities on entering a theatre. They, too, prefer 'known quantities', a situation in which 'the drunks stay drunk; the Catholics go to Mass and the bounders bound. We can't have changes – throws the balance off.'[110] And so his conviction that art may have the power to transform seems to have been eroded. The audience, invited to stare into the mirror in the darkened theatre, is as likely to welcome the return of 'normality' when 'the insight won't be worth a damn' as Agnes and Tobias.

In *A Delicate Balance* Albee seems to suggest that the alarming truths, in particular those relating to mortality, are concealed behind a language of conviviality and affection. But, as Agnes acknowledges, 'Time happens, I suppose. To people. Everything becomes...too late, finally. You know it's going on...up on the hill; you can see the dust, and hear the cries and the steel...but you wait; and time happens. When you *do* go, sword and shield...finally...there's nothing there...save rust; bones; and the wind.'[111] Evasion of human commitment, fear of loss, terror of the pain which is an inevitable concomitant of living, drives the self into an isolation which inevitably leads to the destruction of that self. And so the individual denies himself the only consolation capable of transforming his situation, and Edna acknowledges the destructive egotism which is the basis of this false strategy. 'For our own sake; our own...lack. It's sad to know you've gone through it all, or most of it, without...that the one body you've wrapped your arms around...the only skin you've ever known...is your own — and that it's dry...and not warm.'[112] Thus, in an interview, Albee has said that *A Delicate Balance* is essentially concerned with people who 'have not made the distinction' between self and society, 'and who have to suffer the consequences of not making the distinction. They have discovered', he insists, 'that after a certain point they have become paralysed and can't change when they want to.' Its ending he regards as 'ironic; it is so totally hopeless'. And in his mind his later play, *All Over*, is 'examining the same thing from a different point of view' in that it 'is an examination of people who have been thwarted wilfully by one person and have not created their own identities'.[113]

What is not apparent from this account, or from the rather pretentious English production, is the play's humour. It is one of Albee's funnier works, though the humour is heavily ironic and self-conscious. In the case of Claire it is a defensive tactic, a means of refusing to take herself seriously, and indeed here, as in *Who's Afraid of Virginia Woolf?*, it suggests a degree of detachment from experience which is the essence of their problem. Nonetheless, if the humour is functional it does serve to render an otherwise somewhat ponderous text more acceptable to an audience not renowned for its love of metaphysics. This did not stop Robert Brustein attacking it in *The New Republic* as a mere collection of bric-à-brac, or *Newsweek* from denouncing its inflated dialogue and resort to cliché. And there is some truth in this. His characters do tend to speak in quotation marks and are prone to pseudo-poetic utterances. In Eliot's plays the verse form established a context which justified such rhetoric; Albee's American prose seems overloaded. And though his own concern for rhythm goes some way towards creating a sense of ritual which can sustain an elevated language it is finally insufficient to support it.

In 1922 Max Eastman remarked that 'I feel sometimes as though the whole modern world of capitalism and Communism and all were rushing toward some enormous efficient machine-made doom of the true values of life'.[114] It was a conviction felt no less acutely forty years later by Edward Albee. To be sure there was now an apocalyptic component to this fear, which is translated into a threatening imagery and a vision of character and language under stress. But the threat was more directly to human values. To Irving Howe that was expressed through the failure of the intellectual: 'Some intellectuals, to be sure, have "sold out"...But far more prevalent and far more insidious is that slow attrition which destroys one's ability to stand firm and alone...Our world is neither to be flatly accepted or rejected: it must be engaged, resisted and − who knows, perhaps still − transformed.'[115] It is a similar conviction which leads Albee to make the intellectual the focus of his attention. The conformity of Peter in *The Zoo Story* and of the characters in *The American Dream* was merely the most obvious expression of a collapse of morale more fundamental than could be implied by a bourgeois capitulation to materialism, more fundamental and yet more subtle. As Howe remarked in his essay on 'The Age of Conformity', 'Gradually we make our peace with the world, and not by anything as exciting as a secret pact...and we learn, if we learn anything at all, that betrayal may consist of a chain of small compromises, even while we also learn that in this age one cannot survive without compromise. What is most alarming...is that the whole idea...of a life dedicated to values that cannot be realized by a commercial civilisation − has gradually lost its allure.'[116] This was precisely the process which Albee had set out to dramatise in plays like *Who's Afraid of Virginia Woolf?*, *A Delicate Balance* and *All Over* and which he projected to the point of apocalypse in *Box* and *Listening*. It was an accusation levelled at the liberal intellectual and hence, by a logical process, at the artist himself, who becomes a critical figure, himself implicitly accused of a potential betrayal, of necessarily employing a language which itself bears the marks of equivocation, temporising and deceit. George and Martha's 'creation' of a fantasy child, their retreat into invention, is not without relevance to the writer's own invented world. That doubt, hinted at in this early work, moves to the centre of a play such as *Box*, while in *The Man With Three Arms* (1983) he seems to confess to his own failure to alert his audience and to sustain his own efforts to use fiction as an agent of truth. Yet the artist remains a crucial figure, and language a necessary channel of communication, a public symbol of the link between people separated less by experience than fear. And this is the essence of a tension in his work: language as concealment, language as desperate attempt to establish contact; fiction as game, retreat, defence against the real, and fiction as moral exemplar, a means to dramatise human need and the possibility of action.

These are the poles of his art. The confident structures of drama are invaded by a sense of insecurity which is pressed at times to the point at which character is disassembled. Just as Marx had regretted a progress bought at the cost of character and a collapse of will, so Albee has chosen to create a theatre in which the sustaining of a moral self becomes a central theme. That it is equally vulnerable to the forces which it indicts is some kind of evidence for his assertions, but it is also of course potentially a contradiction as increasingly he chose to substitute abstractions for the human complexity, the tangible human realities and the moral density whose decay he regretted. And that was especially clear in *Tiny Alice*. Increasingly, such freedom as he could envisage was displaced onto the imaginative process itself. By degrees only the control of tone and rhythm, the careful structuring of language, implied that dominance of the self over experience which originally he had wished to imply through the elaboration of character. The irreducible reality which he had proposed as the basis of individual identity and moral action devolved into a series of exemplary gestures, deft and controlled forms which implied little more than the presence of a shaping intelligence with the power to sculpt dramatic forms if not convincingly to articulate a social experience. In *Who's Afraid of Virginia Woolf?* his liberal commitment was expressed through character, through the logic of the plot and through a language ultimately rendered transitive through pain. Twenty years later it relied on the mere presence of the writer behind the text.

When Iris Murdoch objected, in a 1961 article, that contemporary literature tends to assume an easily apprehended empirical world in which for 'the hard idea of truth we have substituted a facile idea of sincerity',[117] she identified a kind of debased Romanticism wedded to a simplified liberal model which was not remote from that offered by Albee in *The Zoo Story* and to some extent in *Who's Afraid of Virginia Woolf?* We hardly derive a sense of the complexity of the moral being or the opacity of the individual from these plays, only the reality of their suffering and the possibility of change. For Iris Murdoch 'the connection between art and the moral life has languished because we are losing our sense of form and structure in the moral world itself'. Albee's early plays clearly constituted a kind of moral fiction and a case could be made for the disintegrative mode of his plays, in which character collapsed into role and action into symbol, being a reflection of his sense of the failure of form and structure in the moral world.

The intellectual, though not dramatic, weakness of his early plays lay in the simplified model of reality and the intensely rational view of the individual which they presented. Iris Murdoch argued that 'We need to turn our attention away from the consoling dream necessity of Romanticism, away from the dry symbol, the bogus individual, the false whole, towards the real impenetrable human person. That this person is substantial, impenetrable, individual, indefinable, and valuable is after all the fundamental tenet of Liberalism.' Albee shares this conviction, but the process of his early plays is perhaps rather too concerned with demystification, too committed to Platonic notions of the real, too convinced that an individual is capable of rendering up the essence of his individuality in language or in symbolic action. Reality is seen rather too much as a given whole, a cluster of facts, a non-contingent view of experience. Though he attacks the false consolations generated by society or the individual imagination, he fails to extend his concern to the nature of artistic form or to engage an idea of character which concedes a complexity which will not deconstruct itself into essential components. For, as Iris Murdoch insisted, 'Our sense of form, which is an aspect of our desire for consolation, can be a danger to our sense of reality as a rich receding background. Against the consolations of form, the clear crystalline work, the simplified fantasy-myth, we must pit the destructive power of the now so unfathomable naturalistic idea of character.' This is not an appeal for rounded characters; far from it. Iris Murdoch is simply reminding us of the fact that 'Real people are destructive of myth, contingency is destructive of fantasy and opens the way for imagination'. Since reality is incomplete, 'art must not be too afraid of incompleteness'. The phrase 'real people' may beg a central question but her premise, no less than Albee's, is that 'Literature must always present a battle between real people and image'. Albee's weakness is that in the person of Peter or Nick he dramatises characters flattened to the point at which they are subsumed by the image.

Only later in his career does he feel able to confront the fact identified by Murdoch, that 'art too lives in a region where all human endeavour is failure', and that only 'the very greatest art invigorates without consoling and defeats our attempts...to use it as magic'. Increasingly, however, this concern has moved to the centre of his work. Character developed not towards solidity but to an opacity which has to do with a density of unexpressible experience, while the fiction-making power of the mind has proved of increasing fascination, not simply as a generator of illusion but as the source of myth and the central mechanism of a sensibility intent on reshaping experience into form. Inevitably, therefore, art itself and even the consonance assumed between language and substance has become a vital interest.

And here the question arises as to how Albee sees character and form. For Iris Murdoch, form is prevented from becoming too rigid 'by the free expansion against it of individual characters'. A novel, she has suggested, 'must be a house fit for free characters to live in; and to combine form with a respect for reality with its odd contingent ways is the highest art of prose'.[118] The question is whether Albee creates plays fit for free characters to live in. The problem is that his characters have often surrendered such freedom as they once had.

In Albee's plays there is rarely any sense that the characters are generating the action. The action contains the play's prior metaphysic. Their function is to respond to these events, locating themselves in terms of that given. Their freedom is limited. The constricting sets – most of his plays have a single set – stand as an image, a correlative of the determinism which they are all too willing to claim but which the plays are designed to negate.

In *Who's Afraid of Virginia Woolf?* he destroys one myth in order to create another. The invented child is destroyed (perhaps the son of God) in the name of a religion of man. But there are, of course, problems about urging the significance of reality over fiction in a work which is itself fictional. George and Martha create their myth as a way of holding their lives together, imposing form where the system has begun to collapse. They are asked at the end of the play to open themselves to contingency, to accept whatever comes no matter what empty world that contingency signifies. The death of the fantasy child, like the death of God, means that everything is possible. But the position is adopted in a play which is anything but contingent, indeed which is relatively closed to contingency. The deceptions of language are denounced in a lucid and wholly articulate way. Nor is Albee simply proposing the acceptance of reality as an ultimate objective. In identifying compassion – love – as a value he is urging a degree of transcendence.

Albee's morality does not consist of identifying right courses of action, or of arriving at a transcendent self-image. His liberation does not propose a rational analysis of reality or the need to acknowledge an agreed system of ethics and political behaviour. It is essentially that described in another context by Iris Murdoch:

> Virtue is not essentially or immediately concerned with choosing between actions or rules or reasons, nor with stripping away the personality for a leap. It is concerned with really apprehending that other people exist. This too is what freedom really is; and it is impossible not to feel the creation of a work of art as a struggle for freedom. Freedom is not choosing, that is merely the move we make when all is already lost. Freedom is knowing and understanding and respecting things quite other than ourselves...The knowledge and imagination which is virtue is precisely the kind which the novelist needs to let his characters be, to respect their freedom, and to study them themselves in that most significant area of their activity, where they are trying to apprehend the reality of others.[119]

Albee's metaphysics lie in relationship. Access to being lies through inter-subjectivity. Apprehension of the other becomes a path to the self. Behind Albee stands Martin Buber and Karl Jaspers. It follows that love becomes both fact and image and the failure of love, in *A Delicate Balance* and *All Over*, strikes at the essence of identity and meaning alike. The failure of these characters lies in their tendency to opt for fantasy rather than imagination; the one substitutes, the other is generative. George and Martha's child is fantasy. Their relationship at the end of the play, the moment of fragile contact at the end of *The Zoo Story*, requires an imaginative perception, a glimpse of the mutuality which constitutes the only resource available.

Lionel Trilling has said that 'all literature tends to be concerned with the question of reality. I mean quite simply the old opposition between reality and appearance, between what really is and what merely seems.'[120] And certainly Albee has concerned himself directly with this subject. But where in the early plays he tended to accept a simple opposition such as that identified by Trilling – that is, he accepted a fundamentally liberal view of art as being concerned with identifying a reality which is at base easily perceived if painfully acknowledged (moral sense being in some way identical with common sense) – in his subsequent work things seem less clear. Increasingly he has become concerned with the question of the nature of the real, and this has inevitably led him to a consideration of the nature of theatre. The Aristotelian position has increasingly been deserted for a more complex consideration. And his own theatrical experimentation became more radical, his next play being produced not on Broadway but in a small theatre in Buffalo – a displaced version of Off-Broadway.

Box and *Quotations from Chairman Mao Tse-Tung* (1968) reflect Albee's sense of diminishing possibilities and his perception of a shift, if not in American values, then in the possibility of those values acting as transforming mechanisms. Looking back, in the late 1970s, to the beginning of his career he observed that, 'After all, Kennedy was not dead yet. The war in Vietnam had not convinced us that as a society we were capable of cynical politics. A number of things had not happened at that point.' Accordingly, he confessed that

> It may be that I am becoming less and less certain about the resiliency of civilisation. Maybe I am becoming more and more depressed by the fact that I don't think people want to make the dangerous experiment. People desire to live as dictatorships tell them to do. There is a totalitarian impulse...I suppose [this] comes from watching carefully what has been going on. After all, I would like to think that I still write out of a certain amount of anger and contempt. I don't think that has changed very much. The nature of the anger may have changed.[121]

In *Box*, Albee pushes the logic of his warnings one final stage further. He creates a post-apocalyptic elegy, a theatre without characters because it is an attempt to project the destructive tendencies of society to their ultimate conclusions. It is both a warning and a threnody. The stage is dominated by the outlined frame of a cube. No actors appear; we simply hear the monologue of a middle-aged woman whose tones are deliberately flattened so as to make it difficult to relate her to any particular locality. Her observations seem to refer to some calamity which may already have happened (the past tense predominates), thereby explaining a world bereft of people and represented by a box which may stand as an image of a coffin. There is, strictly speaking, no time. The play takes place in that timeless moment identified by Eliot in 'The Hollow Men', between the 'idea' and the 'reality', the 'essence' and the 'descent'. And the stuttering conclusion of that poem is in essence equally that of Albee's play:

> For Thine is
> Life is
> For Thine is the
> This is the way the world ends
> This is the way the world ends
> This is the way the world ends
> Not with a bang but a whimper.[122]

Albee's play ends like this:

> Nothing belongs
> (Three second silence. Great sadness)
> Look; more of them; a black net...skimming
> (Pause)
> And just one...moving beneath...in the opposite way
> (Three second silence. Very sad, supplicating)
> Milk
> (Three second silence)
> Milk
> (Five second silence. Wistful)
> Box
> (Silence, except for the sound of bell buoys and sea gulls. Very slow fading of lights to black, sound of bell buoys and sea gulls fading with the light.)[123]

The explosion which is envisaged as a constant possibility and which is finally only confirmation of a more fundamental collapse of morale and morality has perhaps already happened. The milk of human kindness is as contaminated as is the literal milk by radioactivity. The centre cannot hold. Albee, too, is a poet of the hollow men.

It is though we had caught just the final instant, without time to relate the event to its environment – the thing happening to the thing happened to. The fact that *Box* was designed to be played before and after its companion piece, *Quotations*, suggests its role as warning and epitaph, an indictment not only of a society and a race but of an art which has compounded the destructive values which it should have denounced.

In an introduction Albee proposes the twin obligations of the writer: 'to make some statement about the condition of "man" (as it is put) and, second to make some statement about the nature of the art form with which he is working. In both instances he must attempt change... The playwright must try to alter his society', and 'since art must move, or wither – the playwright must try to alter the forms within which his precursors have had to work'.[124] *Box*, however, poses the question in a more subtle form. What exactly is the function of art in a period in which history is perceived as an implacable force, in which the logic of technology has replaced morality and hence the efficacy of that art? And so the disembodied voice identifies the world of 'system as conclusion, in the sense of method as an end, the dice so big you can hardly throw them any more', a world in which 'progress is merely a direction, movement', and suggests that the inevitable consequence of this inhuman logic, given an accompanying apathy, is 'seven hundred million babies dead in the time it takes, took, to knead the dough to make a proper loaf'. Given this reality 'little wonder so many...went...cut off, said no instead of hanging on'.[125] The spiritual death which his earlier plays had identified and deplored is now seen as in part a response to a threatened apocalypse, as it had been in *The Death of Bessie Smith*, its 'great, red-orange-yellow sunset' like a fire enveloping half of the continent, and *Who's Afraid of Virginia Woolf?*, with its reference to Gomorrah and Penguin Island.

The voice recalls a time 'when it was *simple*', a world which, in theatrical terms, could adequately be represented by realism as a style, in which the individual was assumed to bear the imprint of social forces and the meticulous reproduction of detail offered a clue to public and private realities. And thus the large wooden cube, which is the only object on the stage, becomes an image on the one hand of a classical symmetry and on the other of a fastidious form, a well-made art work – a *pièce bien fait*. But such art, it is suggested, failed to warn of a fatal cancer. It implied order and control. In offering to mimic life it reflected back its own coherences to a world which otherwise was without them. The function of art, the voice implies, should have been to warn rather than to console. And so the voice laments, 'If only they had *told* us! Clearly! When it was clear that we were not only corrupt – for there is nothing that is not, or little – but corrupt to the selfishness, to the corruption that we should die to keep it.'[126] For the fear is that it 'gets to a certain point' when 'the momentum is too much'. The empty stage is the primary evidence for that.

A process which begins with 'the *little* things, the *small* cracks', eventually destroys the organism. And the function of art becomes not the pursuit of beauty but the necessity to remind us of loss, for 'When art begins to hurt, it's time to look around'.[127] But the problem is that art inevitably cauterises the very wounds which it opens up in so far as it implies order, consonance, coherence. It is potentially trapped in falsification. And to attempt to break out of the paradox is to create an art which does not present itself in Arnoldian terms, which is not 'a matter of garden, or straight lines, or even...morality'.[128] But this is to risk breaking free equally of those for whom it is designed; 'and they say, what is *that*?'[129] – an experience not unknown to Albee. Compromises have to be made: 'we give up something'.[130] The writer's responsibility may, in one of the play's more striking images, be to be the one bird flying in one direction while a billion fly the other way (Albee once described the writer's function to be 'out-of-step' with his society) but, if there is no communication, there is no purpose. The awareness of loss has to be communicated if a greater loss is to be prevented. However, that possibility has seemingly disappeared, for the fatal loss is internal and spiritual: 'we all died when we were thirty once. Now, much younger. Much.'[131]

Box, then, is narrated as though the bomb had already dropped, as though it were the recorded voice of an extinct race. But an ambiguity is retained. Since the play takes place in the timeless world between the striking of the chord and its resolution, the breaking of the bone and the pain, 'It was the memory of it, to be seen and proved later...The memory of what we have not yet known.'[132] Just as with other things which we have not seen but know to be true, this account has the truth of inevitability. Because, of course, by the nature of things if this play were in fact a product of a post-apocalyptic world it could never be written, performed or observed. Box is, therefore, an anticipated elegy of something that 'can happen here, I guess. But unprovable. Ahhhhh. That makes the difference, does it *not*. Nothing can seep here except the memory of what I'll not prove.'[133] And yet we are asked to assume that in a sense it has happened. It is like the voice of a time traveller who has seen the future and whose apocalyptic message is confirmed by the fact that the processes which will lead to that future can already be observed. Thus the other implications of the box on the bare stage become apparent. It is indeed a coffin as it is also an image of art devolved into mere craft. It is a symbol of the stage (the box stage) and beyond that of the auditorium and the theatre in which the audience already sits entombed. And yet, contradictorily, we are to presume that the writer, flying in the face of social and artistic convention, believes that even now some pre-emptive action is possible. The presumption exists in the fact of the play – a warning implies the possibility of action – but scarcely in its imagery or its language. The flaw is that the individual moral sensibility which sets the stone of history rolling is not presented as rectifiable, within the play, only as recognisable for what it is by those about to be crushed by it.

Albee's imaginative perception outstrips his moral will. The values which he appears to endorse have been evacuated from the play along with virtually everything else. We are asked by implication to reconstitute those absent values as a means to forestall the apocalypse. But the moral sensibility which this expectation implies on the part of the audience already represents a weakness in the rigour of his logic. For there are, then, it appears, still those who perceive the danger and can move to obviate it. And they are, firstly, the percipient and humane dramatist and, secondly, his sensitive and appreciative audience. Quite how this comfortable partnership has managed to remain immune to the general moral and spiritual decline is never made clear. But that it does so is a basic assumption of most, though not quite all, of his work.

Quotations from Chairman Mao Tse-Tung is a natural companion piece to Box. It takes place within the confines of the cube. There are four characters, only one of whom speaks lines written by Albee. One, a minister, remains silent throughout; a second, an Old Lady, recites a sentimental poem by the nineteenth-century American poet, Will Carleton; the third is Chairman Mao Tse-Tung, who literally recites from that familiar text of 1960s radicalism, the little red book containing the sayings of Chairman Mao. Each character is trapped inside his or her own experience. They occupy the same space but share nothing. Only the fourth character, the Long-Winded Lady, speaks Albee's lines and she offers a somewhat gnomic account of the decline of her own life, a decline which evidently took literal form when she plunged from the deck of an ocean liner into the sea. Indeed the connection between all the monologues is, once again, a sense of loss and impending apocalypse. But no one account is allowed to dominate. Indeed the separate narratives are themselves deliberately disrupted. Though originally written out in separate and continuous form, they were subsequently intercut with one another. The objective was, in some sense, as Albee has explained in a note to the published text, to arrive at a 'musical structure – form and counterpoint',[134] and certainly his punctuation is offered as a kind of musical notation. But beyond this the deliberate disruption of the narrative thrust has two central effects. It creates new meanings by juxtaposition, and it makes it impossible to reconstruct the individual texts with any clarity. The consequence is an aleatory effect as the audience is forced to re-enact the process of imposing order on disparate experience, which is in fact one of the subjects of the play itself.

Sometimes the effect is deliberately ironic. Following Chairman Mao's insistence that 'The communist ideological and social system alone is full of youth and vitality, sweeping the world with the momentum of an avalanche and the force of a thunderbolt', the Long-Winded Lady replies 'Exactly: plut!' Sometimes the voices appear to confirm one another with more conviction. But the intrusion of the voice from Box is a constant ironic reminder of the logic of their separate positions. And when the Long-Winded Lady speaks of the process of decline, 'sun...haze...mist...deep night...all the Spectrum down. Something Burning',[135] the apocalyptic implications are clear. As she asks, 'How many are expecting it!?'[136]

The dominant image is entropic. Although Albee scrupulously quotes directly from Mao there is a crucial omission from one quotation, a simile which offers a clue to the connecting tissue which Albee plainly believes to exist between the private and public world. 'The ideological and social system of capitalism', Mao had observed in the omitted passage, 'resembles a dying person who is sinking fast, like the sun setting beyond the western hills'.[137] The Long-Winded Lady is just such a person; and she describes a literal sinking which plainly stands as an apt image of the decline of her own life – as it does of the old woman in the Carleton poem who goes 'Over the Hill to the Poorhouse' as a result of the callousness of her own family and of the world in which she moves. As the voice of Box reminds us, insinuating its way into Quotations, 'It's the little things, the small cracks'.[138] A failure of humanity on the personal scale is essentially of the same kind as, and, indeed, may have a causative relationship to, the failure of humanity on a national scale.

And the illusions treasured and propounded by all of the characters – religious, political, sexual – are presented not merely as being similarly destructive but as stemming from a similar impulse. The influence here seems to be that of Freud who, in The Future of an Illusion, had said,

> man cannot remain a child for ever; he must venture at last into the hostile world. This may be called 'education to reality'.[139]

Albee's work has always been dedicated to precisely this process; while Quotations from Chairman Mao Tse-Tung would seem to be a literal enactment of Freud's observation that

> having recognised religious doctrines to be illusions, we are at once confronted with the further question: may not other cultural possessions, which we esteem highly and by which we let our life be ruled, be of a similar nature? Should not the assumptions that regulate our political institutions likewise be called illusions, and is it not the case that in our culture the relations between the sexes are disturbed by an erotic illusion, or by a series of erotic illusions?[140]

Albee has insisted that both of these related plays 'deal with the unconscious, primarily', and by this he seems to mean both the degree to which they suggest that all dimensions of human life – private, social and metaphysical – are an expression of a need which can hardly be articulated or apprehended, and that it is only on the level of the unconscious that the fragmented components of his theme can cohere. Thus the plays become less something to be consciously analysed, than an experience to which the audience is invited to submit itself. The fear to which he addresses himself and the need which generates the action exist at a level beneath that susceptible of rational analysis. And the unconscious, as the seat of the imagination, also represents the possible source of redemption. As the Long-Winded Lady remarks, 'if we control the conscious, we're either mad or...dull witted'.[141]

On one level the characters can be seen as representing the past (the Old Lady), present (Long-Winded Lady) and future (Mao), or the personal and public dimensions of human failure. The silence of the minister certainly implies his irrelevance. God is plainly dead or indifferent. And the consequence is a destructive solipsism. On another level the characters are simply fictionalised forms controlled partly by the manipulative imagination of the writer and partly by chance. Dislodged from their contexts they are drained equally of their original function and meaning. Experience, and, indeed, language, are thus exposed as arbitrary and plastic. All that remains is a consistency of imagery, a disruption of harmony, which the play's form mimics. The characters' separate accounts are dominated by the notion of space – the space between meaning and language, between family and social group, between the self and its experience. Decline is the only constant, death the logical conclusion of all narratives. But Albee has insisted that even here, in a play which he agrees is concerned with a series of alternative fictions, there remains a moral intent, suggesting that it 'offers cautionary tales about most of the characters of a certain age, and people who are still capable of change but are also capable of avoiding it'.[142] The moral world, we must presume, is projected beyond the text. It is certainly not contained within it. But, for all his insistence on the moral force of the play, it effectively evades his control. All he feels able to assert is the need not to compound the absurdity which is a product of decline and death, not to anticipate it. Thus the Long-Winded Lady describes an occasion on which she had broken her thumb and screamed before the pain had resulted. 'Before the hurt could have gone through, I made it happen. Well; we do that...Yes, we do that: we make it happen a little before it need.'[143]

For Albee, there is a crucial distinction to be made between Mao, 'who published his thoughts and didn't change his mind', the Old Lady, 'who is reciting Over the Hill to the Poorhouse and whose lines are determined', the minister who 'naturally says absolutely nothing', and the Long-Winded Lady who 'is the only one character who is capable of change'. He has insisted that 'she constantly startled me. I knew exactly what the others were going to say. They didn't surprise me at all.'[144] The problem is that while he insists that she is capable of change there is little evidence for this within the play.

For Mao, the socialist system is 'an objective law independent of man's will',[145] and history an implacable force. It leaves no more space for identity to cohere, for the individual to locate a personal and public meaning, than did the capitalist enterprise parodied by the nineteenth-century poem and exposed by the Long-Winded Lady's tale of alienation and despair, or the now impotent and mute religious determinisms. The need to submit oneself to totalitarian ideas, to religious ideals, to public myths of progress, stems, he implies, less from their self-evident logic than from a desperate need for order. After all, if everything is regarded as 'part of a...predetermination, or something that had already happened in principle – well, under *those* conditions *any* chaos becomes order. Any chaos at all.'[146] And this incubus, of course, exists no less among the members of the audience, concerned with identifying the 'meaning' of the play which they are watching and desperately rearranging the fragments to reconstitute a whole which at the very least can make sense of their decision to spend $20 and an hour of their time. The conviction that a plan exists seems the unavoidable condition of art – an implied contract with the audience. It is the paradox which Albee tries to tackle, though it must be said that he tries to have his philosophical cake and eat it.

In a sense the problem which the play poses is that offered by those *trompe-l'œil* pictures in which two images coexist but which the eye can only perceive individually. The patterns which constitute one shape disrupt those which form another. To reconstitute the monologues of *Quotations* is, unavoidably, to destroy the assonances which derive from the juxtaposition of the fragments. The various realities coexist as do the characters themselves. Albee's equivocation lies in the fact that he himself wishes to locate an underlying structure, suggesting that the play is about the necessity for change. This would be a fair description of most of his work; it is singularly inappropriate to this play which dramatises a series of closed systems, occupying the same space but independent of one another. Albee's comments notwithstanding, there is no suggestion that any of the characters is capable of change. History, art and an ineluctable egotism are too powerful to brook any dissent. The dislocations of the text are in effect those of the private and public world; they dramatise that lack of social or moral cohesiveness which is a distinguishing characteristic of the world which he pictures. The young are presented, both in the Old Lady's recitation and the Long-Winded Lady's monologue, as intensely selfish and unavoidably brutal. And the same logic which makes possible the collapse of love and concern in the family, the remarkable transmutation of love into hate or indifference, draws the race towards the annihilation promised by Mao. Totalitarianism of the self is presented as being of a piece with political totalitarianism, and the alliance with death embodied in the betrayals of love on a private level has its parallel and logical consequence in the ultimate apocalypse of nuclear warfare. The image of that final willed suicide runs throughout a play which in effect offers an eschatology of the modern age. In a world in which, as the voice of Box interjects, 'nothing belongs' (an echo of O'Neill) there is no longer any force to hold the pieces together except the imagination, but, as the Long-Winded Lady admits 'one's imagination...is poor support'.[147]

Albee has found himself enrolled in a number of public causes most especially that of dissident writers. He has commented on the plight of the artist in South Korea and in Czechoslovakia. And it is no accident that he should have chosen to concentrate on the artist for, to his mind, he is a crucial figure. Whether in a totalitarian country or in one in which consensus politics and a bland materialism define the norm, the writer is seen as representing and defining a form of freedom. The imagination creates the possibility of alternatives while the circumstances of drama in particular establish the collective nature of experience and thereby the necessity for a system of moral responsibility. As he has said:

> I find very little difference between such a closed society as the Soviet Union and an open society such as ours. In a theoretically classless society such as the Soviet Union the arts are controlled from the top, while in the United States, this theoretically corrupt, heavily classed, society, the arts are controlled by the people. It is unhealthy for the arts to exist in a society where the minds of the people are controlled from the top by bureaucrats and it is not terribly healthy for the arts to have to exist in a society of the commodity market. But I have noticed that in closed societies, where people are not allowed to have access to the metaphor, there are brave people who want access to the metaphor and will gain it at whatever cost. While in a society where there is nobody stopping free access to the metaphor we are indifferent to the treasure of the metaphor.[148]

For Albee this process is fundamental to the playwright's art. He also said, 'I think a person is born a playwright or a painter because it's a way of responding to reality, to outside stimuli and then translating them into something else'.[149] In a sense all theatre is metaphorical in that an actor's actions stand for those of a character but Albee's drama is metaphorical in another sense. His plays offer a series of allegories. Despite his denials, he is a didactic writer and his theatre a teaching mechanism. It poses questions whose answers may not lie within the work of art itself. A communal mode, it demonstrates the individual's reliance on others for the generation of meaning; a public art, it relies on the reality of shared experience for its effect. Albee's realism is charged with metaphysics, his metaphysics constrained by his liberal humanism. He began his career as a 'demonic social critic', recalling America to its liberal principles and he remains that, though America has changed and he himself has lost some confidence in the ability of art to oppose the move towards apocalypse.

I don't necessarily like the environment in which playwrights have to work in this society of ours. Not only the environment in which playwrights have to work but that in which all creative people have to work – novelists, poets, sculptors, painters. Why should anyone bother to concern himself with the state of the arts in their society? Have we not had a rough time in the last fifteen years? Have we not had a war in Vietnam which tore our society apart? Have we not seen students shot down on campus, clubbed? Haven't we seen our economy in a shambles? Haven't we seen the presidency disgraced? We've had quite a bit to concern us, things of some magnitude. But, in the face of all this, art remains of central importance...We are the only animal which consciously creates art, attempts metaphor. It is our distinguishing mark...if we turn out to be the kind of society which is unwilling to use the metaphor, to use art to instruct us about ourselves, then we are a society which is on its way downhill without ever having seen the top. Indeed if we are unwise enough not to be instructed by the arts then perhaps we do lack the will, the wisdom, the courage, to support a free society.[150]

The logic that he identifies in *Box* and *Quotations from Chairman Mao Tse-Tung* may have suggested silence as the only means to avoid collusion with the forces of death but to Albee such a silence would have constituted a final betrayal, a collaboration more total than that risked by the deployment of metaphors deeply ambiguous in their origin and profoundly disturbing in their effect.

All Over (1971) presses even closer to the fact which is the root cause of the absurdity and fear that underlies his characters' actions – death. This time the group of characters is markedly older as they gather together in the familiar hermeticism of the closed room to witness the death, or perhaps the dying, of one of their number (though he remains securely behind a screen, as the fact of death and its implications for human life are similarly kept at arm's length). Their mutual surrender of complexity and individuality is expressed in their identification with role. They are the wife, the mistress, the son, the daughter, and so on to the man whose existence has given such meaning to their lives as they have chosen to claim. They have indeed allowed themselves to become allegorical, a reductive process identified as such by Agnes in *A Delicate Balance*. And the metaphysical implications of this situation are no less clear than the social. When the invisible father, husband, friend dies, from whence can they derive their meaning? With their god dead they will be left to a task of self-definition which is beyond them because they have long since surrendered their independence and freedom. Their only virtue lies in the sheer fact of survival.

As its title suggests it is a play about the process of dying, not simply the physical fact of deterioration and death, but the collapse of form, the loss of purpose, the attenuation of connectiveness. It is concerned, like so many of his plays, with the steady erosion of selfhood, compassion and morality. Betrayal is the central motif. The wife's adultery with the dying man's best friend had sent that best friend's wife spinning into insanity. And adultery is only one image for a process which seems synonymous with that of life itself – a process equally at the heart of personal and public disintegration. As the mistress observes, in words which are reminiscent of Quentin's remarks in Miller's *After the Fall*;

> It's when it happens calmly and in full command: the tiniest betrayal – nothing so calamitous as a lie held on to in the face of fact, or so niggling as a fantasy during the act of love, but in between – and it can be anything or nearly nothing, except that it moves you back into yourself a little, the knowledge that all your sharing has been... wilful and that nothing has been inevitable... or even necessary.[151]

It is a play about the excluding self, about that rigorous egotism which Albee sees as lying at the heart of human action. As the wife recognises, even the individual's response to death is to see it in terms of its effect upon himself. 'All we've done...is think about ourselves...What will become of me...Selfless love? I don't think so; we love to *be* loved, and when it's taken away...then why *not* rage...or pule. All we've done is to think about ourselves. Ultimately.'[152] The displacement of the word 'Ultimately' gives it both an ambiguity and an absoluteness. Self-concern is not simply the irreducible fact to which we must confess; it is a priority which is terminal in its implications. Thus Albee's sense of absurdity differs from that dramatised by Camus in a play like *Caligula* in that Albee sees it as a product of a failure of nerve. For though death is inescapable, 'nothing has been inevitable...or even necessary'.[153] The entropic language of the play (references to 'winding down', 'going down', 'silence', and so on) seems familiar from Beckett's world. But, where for Beckett the absurd was metaphysical, a product of a human desire for order in a universe structured on disorder, in Albee's work the absurdity derives from the characters' wilful collaboration in a language of collapse, from the degree to which they compound a disintegrative process. In a brief story, the doctor describes the process as a love-affair with death, and finds a parallel with prisoners' fantasies about having sexual relationships with their executioners.

Albee seeks to assert the broader social and cultural implications of the play by invoking the deaths of the Kennedys and of Martin Luther King. Indeed the dying man is precisely presented as an icon of this society, his death attracting the attention of the media. To some degree, indeed, it may be possible to distinguish in the play an allegory for America itself – a country which has pulled itself 'up by its own bootstraps', which once accepted 'all the responsibility to itself, the Puritan moral soul'. And 'since we have become what we are, then the double edge is on us; we cannot back down, for we are no longer private, and the world has its eye on us'. The dying man and the flaccid society become synonymous, 'all confused and retreating, surely but withdrawn'.[154] Once again the collapse of language lies at the heart of this. Albee's own precision with words is not mere pedantry; it is an insistence that language is not only a primary mechanism of social relationships but also evidence of an underlying community of experience. But it is also a primary mechanism of evasion and deceit, a means of denying reality. And it is worth recalling that the play was a product of the Vietnam years in which not the least of the achievements of the American military lay in the systematic dislocation of language. The mistress's assault on the daughter could therefore be equally an assault on the society in which they move. 'What words will you ever have left if you use them all to kill? What words will you summon up when the day *comes*', when the need for 'Love with mercy' arrives? 'What vocabulary', she asks, 'will you have for that? Perhaps', she adds, 'you'll be mute.' And this is the real danger, for the fear is that individual and society alike will be 'lockjawed, throat constricted, knowing that whatever word you use, whatever phrase you might say will come out, not as you mean it then, but as you have meant it before, that "I love you; I need you", no matter how joyously meant, will be the sport of a wounded and wounding animal'.[155]

Death, instead of being the guarantee of absurdity, is, to Albee, the evidence of the absolute need to construct values, to locate a language, to establish relationships which can themselves generate meaning. The sheer contingency of existence requires action; it necessitates a positive response. The building of the ego, the laborious creation of a spurious self-image, the construction of private and public myths becomes merely ridiculous in the face of an existence which may collapse at any moment. But the choice is usually otherwise. As the wife observes, 'you make a lot of adjustments over the years, if only to avoid being eaten away. Anger, resentment, loss, self-pity – and self-loathing loneliness.' It is a process which destroys as it apparently consoles. 'You can't live with all that in the consciousness very long, so, you put it under, *or* it gets well, and you're never sure which. Worst might be if there's nothing there any more, if everything's been accepted.'[156] In his early plays Albee believed that this process was reversible. Now he seems to suggest that it is indeed all over for the individual and for his society. But, as his next play makes plain, Albee is loathe to give up on humanity, even if the process of life seems to have more to do with dissolution and betrayal than progress.

With *Seascape* (1975) he seems to move to a more purely Beckettian world. Like *Happy Days*, it is set amidst a stretch of sand but the ironies are pressed

18. Deborah Kerr and Barry Nelson in *Seascape* at the Sam S. Shubert Theatre, 1975. Directed by the author.

in a different direction. A middle-aged couple, Charley and Nancy, sit on a beach and examine their lives, the failure and the losses which, in Albee's world, are synonymous with the process of living. Indeed the startling nature of the plot – the two are suddenly joined by a pair of large green lizards – conceals the fact that the play covers very familiar territory. Albee, in fact, seems to be all too content to paper an old house. Thus, once again, we learn of a man who, for a period, had withdrawn his affection and attention from his wife. Once again our attention is drawn towards 'accommodation', to 'the sad fantasies; the substitutions'.[157] Again the words 'decline' and 'inertia' mark the boundaries of lives which have spiralled downwards to a present state of spiritual immobility. Like a whole line of Albee protagonists the principal characters here have learned to substitute language for action, have allowed their relationship to lose its energy and purpose even as they have to acknowledge the fact of physical deterioration. And Nancy's observation, 'So much goes...we shouldn't give up until we have to',[158] could stand as an apt epigraph to any of Albee's plays.

Albee has insisted that *Seascape*

> is a completely realistic play. Absolutely naturalistic. It is merely a speeded up examination of the processes of evolution. It is a perfectly naturalistic, realistic play. It is just that two of the characters are lizards. What is so unusual

about that?...It is not a theoretical play. It is not located in any kind of isolation the way *Quotations from Chairman Mao Tse-Tung* is, or naturalistic isolation such as *All Over*. It is very much an act of aggression, and very public.[159]

Its aggression consists primarily of confronting the audience with its own passivity. When Nancy tries to explain human emotions to the two giant lizards, who, unaccountably, have suddenly emerged from the sea fluent in English and handily available for discussions of the human condition, the list that she offers stands as a summary of human weaknesses: 'Fear. Hatred. Apprehension. Loss.' Against this she can only offer, 'Love',[160] though this apparently defies definition. Charley tellingly adds, 'frustration, anger'. The sea creatures have reached a stage in evolution when they are driven out into the world and are subjected to the beginnings of the process whereby they will become human. Under the tutelage of Nancy and Charley, therefore, they are slowly inducted into the nature of human experience. When Charley asks the female what she would feel were she to lose her mate, she becomes aware of loss for the first time and sheds her first tears, so that by the end of the play, as Albee has said, 'the sea creatures have come to the point of no return. They have learned about mortality and love and therefore they can't be what they were. They have got to continue their evolutionary process.'[161] And the consequences of that process are embodied in the figures of Charley and Nancy who together contain the conflicting elements of human personality as Albee sees it. Charley, afraid of flux, constantly aware of his mortality, wants an untroubled existence, exemplified by his desire to sink down to the bottom of the water, like Ibsen's wild duck, and conclude his life in peace. Nancy, aware of lost time, wishes to fill her years with experience. But beyond them is another possibility, another projected future and conclusion to evolution, in the form of the jet fighter which roars overhead at intervals throughout the play. It is this possibility which makes the restored relationship, on a private and public level, a moral necessity.

Nonetheless, it is clearly offered as an optimistic play in so far as it ends with the offer of help by the two humans to the emerging lizards. While acknowledging the irony implicit in the notion of progress it implies that the only option is to continue, with dignity and compassion. As Nancy insists, 'Well...we make the best of it'.[162] But it is less than convincing. At the beginning of the play she had mocked her husband for his surrender of will and imagination – '"I just want to do nothing; I'm happy doing nothing"' – and had asked, 'is that what we've...come all this way for?...The same at the end as at the beginning...Incomprehensible once more?'[163] The problem is that the question is hardly addressed by a play which is too content to leave its resolution at the level of language. Deployed as patent symbols, his characters never become much more than ciphers and hence their recommitment to the struggle never much more than a rhetorical gesture. They are an excuse for a familiar litany and the fragile basis of a theme that risks banality as it is repeated ever less convincingly. Albee's own fear of the collapse of identity and individuality is ironically realised as he proves less and less willing, and perhaps less and less able, to create characters who engage attention and even interest. It is not that one looks for realism but that his humanist laments, his insistence on human relationships and the necessity to engage the reality of human fallibility, become, in a play like *Seascape*, little more than aspects of an interior monologue spilled somewhat arbitrarily into the mouths but hardly the needs and sensibilities of his characters.

George Oppenheimer's observation in *Newsweek*, quoted on the dust-jacket, that 'This is Edward Albee's finest play' is patent nonsense. His apocalypticism is laid aside in favour of whimsy and callow optimism. His language is mannered without the tension and the resonance of his earlier work. Meaning is explicit. Events are drained of that very tactile reality which is the essence of the experience on which Nancy wishes to rebuild their lives. The characters exist on the boundaries of land and sea, past and future, pre-history and history, event and emotion, but their very abstraction makes the final reconciliation and optative mood unconvincing. Like Arthur Miller's somewhat similar allegory, *The Creation of the World and Other Business*, *Seascape* is best regarded as a consciously naive attempt to trace human imperfection to its source by unwinding the process of history and myth. His original working title for what were then two one-act plays – *Seascape* and *All Over* – was 'Life and Death'. This suggests an optimistic thrust to the former play, which is perhaps sustained by the narrative logic, but the apocalyptic imagery and the decay of human relationships suggest another fate which, in Albee's work, always seems to constitute another and equally powerful potential.

In a sense *Counting the Ways* (1976) comes out of a similar whimsical mood. A series of variations on the theme of love, deriving its title from an Elizabeth Barrett Browning poem, it examines, in a series of brief scenes, the relationship between a man and a woman, referred to simply as He and She. Advanced in his earlier plays as the source of consolation and meaning, such a relationship now becomes the subject of what amount to a series of vaudeville sketches, though, as Albee insists, these are to be played in a strictly naturalistic manner. Yet the naturalism of the acting does not imply a precise setting or a model of individual character as dense with meaning. There is no plot. The substantial realities of the early plays have disappeared as completely here as in *Box* and *Quotations from Chairman Mao Tse-Tung*. The set is severely reduced with, in Albee's words, no clutter.

The play consists of twenty scenes, punctuated occasionally by signs which are lowered on stage announcing the play's author and director and reminding the actors of their obligations. And so the discussion of love becomes precisely that, a discussion. There is no past and no present, while the woman observes that in the future 'There are two things: cease and corruption. And that's all there is to say about hence. Except, perhaps, that predestination is even more awful than... what do you call it?... "the sudden void". There's that too...'[164] Thus love becomes a defence against this process. But, as she is forced to admit, it is equally subject to this process, operating, as it necessarily does, in time. It is an appetite which dulls with the senses. The question is whether the knowledge of its ultimate failure justifies faith in its present efficacy, whether its immediate physicality destroys its spiritual content.

Again Albee's theme is disintegration, the erosion of memory, the collapse of order, the dulling of emotions, the exhaustion of purpose, a 'slow falling apart'.[165] The dominant images are a wilting rose and separate beds. Life begins to parody itself and the essence of parody lies in its power to diminish. And so the human experience is not best defined by pain, but by loss. 'If you can get *away*, if you can *watch* your emotions, you know that pain is a misunderstanding: it's really loss: *loss* is what it's really about.'[166] Pain becomes the sudden consciousness of that loss. It is the evidence rather than the essence of that decline. And so the process of life becomes an equivalent of that theatrical deconstruction which has increasingly been a mark of Albee's work. His characters are left stranded without plot, drained of personal histories, denied complexity, severed from ambiguity, without passion. Language has detached itself from function. Dialogue becomes a game or a formal linguistic pattern rather than an engagement of selves. The process is essentially that identified by the man when he observes that 'Most of it's slow and after the fact and has to do with going on *without* something, something we thought was necessary...essential...but then discovered it merely made all the difference, one *could* go on if one really wanted to.'[167] Eliot's Hollow Men are never far away in Albee's work. The void is not, finally, external to the individual. It, like the grace of God, is within. Life is thus presented as the process whereby the individual comes to realise the truth of this as the various strategems designed to deny it fail. Indeed these strategies are assimilated into the process, becoming further evidence of it. And so, the man observes, the time comes when 'We are each other's rod',[168] and the separation of those once united by love (symbolised firstly by separate beds and then separate rooms) becomes primary evidence of that loss which is the basic process of life. Failing the apparent consolations of the private life, the individual can only turn to the arbitrary systems of the public world – the assertion of social patterns or scientific principles invoked to deny chaos. But such a coding of order is purely arbitrary. It is, as the woman admits, simply a 'veneer' and as a gap opens up between the assurances of mathematics, social etiquette, the formal structures and the reality of experience, so 'civilisation...will collapse'.[169]

And the theatre is not exempt from this. It, too, is a deceptive system. As Shakespeare had observed – in another play which exploited this reflexive device: 'as imagination bodies forth / The forms of things unknown, the poet's pen / Turns them to shape and gives to airy nothing, / A local habitation and a name.'[170] The man and the woman are both presented as actors fully aware of their audience, on occasion addressing that audience directly. The play, therefore, stands, in part at least, as Albee's recognition of his own role as accomplice in the process of self-deceit, of the power of art to deny the very processes which it wishes to identify.

In T. S. Eliot's *The Confidential Clerk*, Sir Claude aspires to the world of art, a world in which 'I believe you will go through the private door / Into the real world...'[171] The actual world 'begins as a kind of make-believe/ And the make-believing makes it real.'[172] But for one of the characters at least there is an inner world, a 'secret garden',[173] in which, were he religious, God would walk, a fact which would transform the outer world into reality. Without that there is always the fear that 'the flowers would fade...And the walls would be broken', a loss consequent upon the collapse of human relations. This was, in essence, precisely the image which Albee was to pick up in his radio play *Listening*.

In *All Over*, the wife recalls a garden which had been attached to an old house in France, a garden which 'had been planned, by careful minds', and which 'resembled nothing so much as an environment', which was, in fact, simply 'a world of what it was'.[174] It was an ordered world subsequently destroyed by fire, as the pattern of her life had been equally destroyed by the fact of death and by the destructive reality of personal treachery. In *Box*, Albee associates the idea of a garden with 'straight lines, or even...morality'.[175] Classicism implies order. But it is an arbitrary order. Once the controlling mind is withdrawn the natural logic is towards a kind of disorder.

Clearly, for Albee, as for Eliot, the garden exists as image. In 'Ash Wednesday' Eliot describes the garden, 'Where all loves end', where 'all love ends',[176] a place where 'the garden god, / Whose flute is breathless', presides. This is where the poet calls on the 'spirit of the fountain, spirit of the garden'. The image reappears in a different context in the 'Four Quartets' in which the opening stanza describes an eternal present in which:

Footfalls echo in the memory
Down the passage which we did not take
Towards the door we never opened
Into the rose garden.[177]

Within the formal garden is a drained pool which only the imagination can fill, a place where time is focussed to a point.

Albee's *Listening* is set in just such a garden, dominated by a dried-up fountain and presided over by a garden god. Time is equally suspended. The static nature of the play is a consequence both of a suspension of historical process and a loss of spatial and temporal referents.

Originally written as a radio play, *Listening* carries a very specific stage direction. The play takes place within the space created by a semi-circular wall which, tellingly, Albee describes as a kind of stone cyclorama. In other words the set has deliberately theatrical overtones. In the foreground is a large fountain and above it a monster head in half relief, the spigot of the fountain emerging from the mouth. At its most obvious this setting is an image of a world which has lost its ordered grace, a world in which the ordering principle has been lost, the mind which conceived that order being now dead or removed. In other words we are dealing with allegory. What once had been an ordered garden, 'clipped and trained and planned', in which the fountain had flowed and the 'monster, or God' had been functional − 'Very much as promised... Very much as stated... Very much as announced... Very much as imagined'[178] − is now a ruin. The final phrase is deliberately reductive. For the biblical assurance collapses into simple invention as the formal garden has devolved into chaos, the fountain become arid. On a social level what had once been 'personal', the expression of an individual will, has now become what is apparently an anonymous institution, possibly a mental hospital. Meaning has drained out of this world on a social and a metaphysical level. The mansion itself may even owe its shape in some degree to chance. The Man, who at the beginning of the play contemplates the meaning of his setting, speculates that it may have been 'brought over − stone by stone, numbered, lettered, misnumbered, mislettered'.[179] It is a world of dead secrets, as, indeed, in some respects, it transpires, are the lives of those who inhabit it and who contemplate 'what might have been and what has been'. In Eliot's words, '...As we grow older / The world becomes stranger, the pattern more complicated / Of dead and living... And not the lifetime of one man only / But of old stones that cannot be decyphered.'[180] The world they inhabit is, apparently, a mental hospital, as, in 'East Coker', Eliot suggests, 'The whole earth is our hospital / Endowed by the ruined millionaire.'[181] But where for Eliot an intense religious quest lies behind his awareness of a vacant earth, for Albee it is the basis of a more secular quest.

The present is seen as being problematic. The Woman remarks, 'How do you know who's what!?'[182] Their present roles are doubtful. They are apparently a nurse, an institutional cook and a patient but these are perhaps delusions, ordering devices to make sense of their situation. The past is equally problematic. The 'nurse' and the 'cook' may or may not have had a relationship. The Girl repeatedly begins but does not complete a sentence, which hints at a previous experience that cannot be confirmed. The Woman's assumption, that she 'starts it in the middle of some...conversation we've not had; or, have had, and I can't remember',[183] is itself an expression of her own desire for completion, for a sense of progression which will invest the present with some meaning. 'Get behind that sentence, that's all you have to do. Find out what precedes.'[184] Like the protagonist of Pynchon's *V* she looks for a lexical key to experience. At other times the key seems to lie in personal experiences or in an abstract model of perfection (the Girl's sense of the colour blue as a clarifying device – a feeling of sudden beauty which implies the loss, the imperfection of normality – some lost order). But the order is more apparent than real.

Albee offers a parable about the contingent nature of reality in the form of the Woman's story about the disappearance of her grandfather. On his failure to come home the family had interviewed all those who claimed to have seen him on the day of his disappearance. Though their stories were mutually incompatible the family, believing in rationality, has plotted the disparate sightings on a map to establish the place where reality existed. In fact, of course, it was simply the point of intersection of a series of competing fictions. Clearly this is offered not only as a model of the place where the three characters find themselves but equally of the universe which they inhabit. The simple models of reality to be found in the early plays now defer to a paradigm which acknowledges the sheer contingency of the world which they inhabit. And yet, even given this fact, I suspect that Albee would still associate himself with the Woman's observation (omitted from the published text) that she would rather face the fact of death fully conscious, recognising its implications for her life: 'I opt', she explains, 'for being awake – all of it, the pain, the consciousness, the terror, the hideous loss, all of it – for the privilege...the dubious privilege of being allowed to see it through: the last thing, after all.'[185]

We learn also of a girl who had apparently come to the institution because, like Julian before her, she felt that 'Reality is too *little* for me'.[186] This institution, like Julian's church, is apparently a religious one, presided over, so the Woman implies, by a 'Sister'. And yet it seems to be unfaith rather than faith which is on offer, a ceremony and a performance without audience.

Throughout the play a voice interjects, offering a sequence of numbers, from one to twenty (in the radio production, appropriately enough, it was Albee's voice). For most of the play the characters are apparently oblivious to this effect – an effect which foregrounds the theatricality of the piece. But then it suddenly becomes apparent that the characters can indeed hear this, that they are, in other words, fully aware of participating in a play. The effect is to underline the arbitrariness of their roles, the performed selves which they present. It also adds a twist of irony to a play concerned with listening, with the necessity to pay attention. It is at this moment that, on a linguistic level, the Woman and the Girl exchange roles, the latter borrowing the former's reiterated insistence on the need to listen.

The play ends with the Girl's imminent death. As the Woman recounts an occasion in the past when she had slit her wrists, so she repeats the gesture, almost as if this were the past which is being recounted. As Albee has said, 'In a play like *Listening* who is to say where the reality exists?'[187] The only apparent development in the play is indeed in the state of the girl who is on the verge of death as it ends. Death, perhaps, is the only reality. Everything else is problematic. Any meaning is projected. The system which describes the girl as mad and the woman as sane is itself purely arbitrary. Other patterns are possible. The real is simply a series of acted roles, a set of presumptions.

Albee has confessed that *Listening* is in many ways a private play – a confession to which he was forced by the incomprehension of audiences. But to some degree that bafflement is a conscious strategy. For while he continues to insist on the need to take life straight, to remain fully conscious to the pain and the loss whose frisson is in some degree the evidence for existence, he also mocks the notion that some transcendent meaning, some holistic explanation, will reward a mind finely tuned to the nuances and ironies of that world. Reality may consist of pain; meaning does not. As he has said, 'language is both the disguise and the nakedness', and because his characters 'tend to be far more articulate than a lot of people's characters, that is their problem, I suppose, and therefore they more skilfully disguise it with language'.[188] Reality will not reveal itself wholly through language. *Listening* is gnomic. Like *Quotations*, it deliberately resists an attempt to reconstruct a simple model of the real. But it is hard to see it as an effective dramatic piece. He wants to claim the poet's right to compact language, to generate oblique images and to work on the subconscious through the control of rhythm and tone. But this is rather easier in the radio than the stage version, while it is interesting to note that the Eliot he seems to model himself on or derive his inspiration from here is the poet rather than the dramatist. The work seems more private because it is the poet rather than the playwright who dominates. Its static quality, a logical enough expression of a play concerned with memory (like Pinter's and Beckett's more recent work), runs the risk of boring rather than intriguing its audience. And this is because, unlike Pinter and Beckett, he has largely surrendered his command of humour. He has not solved the problem of dramatising tedium without being tedious, of creating reified characters who command attention, of creating a play in which action is impossible or meaningless but which nonetheless contains its own internal tension. The play is a plea for awareness. It is an assertion of the need to value those experiences and those qualities whose human necessity becomes apparent when they are lost to time. Unfortunately the urgency is lost in the unfolding metaphors whose coherences were further obscured in the stage version.

Albee has objected that 'I have been accused of becoming hermetic in my later work and that my concern with language is getting a bit problematical for some people. Well, tough. But this ignores the fact that some of my plays are absolutely straightforward. *Listening* was a fairly hermetic piece. *The Lady from Dubuque* which does raise metaphysical questions is a relatively straightforward piece. *Counting the Ways* is a perfectly straightforward piece so that I move from the hermetic to the straightforward.'[189] It was a curious confession for a playwright to make. Though he enjoys the immediacy, the danger and the contact of the theatre, the fact that it is a real rather than a synthetic experience, the theatricality to which he confesses surely works against this. And this is the essence of the objection to work which makes few concessions to the audience and which seems to obviate both immediacy and contact, creating myths rather than dramatic tension. He has said that 'Most of the action in most of my plays is intense action. I am interested in ambiguity and ambivalence. These are things that don't necessarily filter through consciously but get at people through the back of their heads.'[190] Though this is an accurate enough account of his method with respect to a play like *Listening* it begins to sound a little like special pleading. He is plainly right in insisting that he exerts 'enormous structural and rhythmic control' over his work. This much is very evident in the radio version of the play. But too often this is at the expense of coherence — the rhythmic and arhythmic pulses of communication having to carry the weight of meaning.

The Lady from Dubuque (1980) reiterates the themes of his earlier plays almost at the level of parody. The hysterical tone is partly a consequence of characters pressed beyond a naturalistic poise and partly a result, I suspect, of a collapse of confidence on Albee's part. His own social analysis is now so bleak that it cannot conceive a model of character which can sustain his redemptive impulse. His distrust of human motives and the language which people deploy is such that the agencies of redemption, or oblivion, are those same abstract figures which he had himself employed earlier, in *Tiny Alice*, and which Eliot had used in *The Cocktail Party* and *The Family Reunion*. But while for Eliot such figures sprang from a coherent spiritual world in which he was prepared to place his faith or to which he was prepared to grant real autonomy, for Albee such figures become little more than *alter egos*, extensions of the writer's own messianic impulses. They speak with the writer's own authentic voice while his other characters are all too often trapped within the flaccid world which defines the limit of their freedom. As his career has advanced this stance has seemed progressively less acceptable.

His characters seem condemned to a world which the writer alone can transcend. They are wooed by forces whose clarity of insight seems intimately related to their immunity to human processes. They are urged to embrace the need to accept the real by figures who seldom become anything more than abstractions. It is, therefore, scarcely any wonder, perhaps, that their lessons are so steadfastly resisted. Albee continues to warn the world against a fate which he apparently no longer sees any way of avoiding.

As in *Who's Afraid of Virginia Woolf?* and *All Over* a group of people come together for a ritual exorcism of illusions. The appearance of sociability is quickly exposed as a sham. The void at the heart of the relationships is revealed. The dominant fact of their lives is once again loss. Hints of personal extinction and public apocalypse abound. Fear of this generates the need for communion but also seems to deny access to it. His characters are pressed towards stereotype not merely by the alienating circumstances of their existence but also by a writer who seems to feel that a description of one of them as 'your average bland housewife' and another as 'balding perhaps; average' is an adequate description of their possibilities. He had, of course, deployed such figures before in his work – most particularly in *The American Dream* and *The Zoo Story* – but in the case of the former it was in the context of an expressionistic satire and in the latter it was a portrait of a man whose character could be rendered opaque by intense experience. Here this confidence appears lacking and Albee seems to have substituted contempt for compassion. In one sense his characters in this play are what mankind has become, the play running down the curtain not only on the American dream but on the whole dream of human advancement. But it also seems to mark some final stage in Albee's personal battle to sustain faith in the characters which he creates.

The Lady from Dubuque, like so much else of his work, is about 'winding down'. Its central character, Jo, described as a frail, lovely, dark-haired girl in her early thirties, is dying, apparently of cancer. But in a sense this is merely an extreme form of the slow death which is life, as it is of the disintegration of social form and the slow collapse of language which are equally in evidence. As the play opens, a group of 'friends' are playing games, but the surface communality is easily fractured, as is the ostensible realism of the play (the audience is directly addressed by the characters). The apparent security of the house is invaded, as it had been in *A Delicate Balance*, by figures whose mission is in some respects reminiscent of that in *Tiny Alice* – except that here they seem to represent the embrace of death, that surrender of will and imagination which he has spent his career in indicting and which, in *Box* and *Quotations from Chairman Mao Tse-Tung*, he had projected to the point of apocalypse. The petty betrayals, the denials of friendship and the refusal to grant reality to death, create a logic which slowly unwinds in what is in effect another litany of human betrayal, another requiem for the lost liberal dream of a morally responsive self, for a world poisoned at source by self-interest and fear. The characters announce their love for one another only to deny it by their actions. The empty games and bitter arguments, as in so many of his earlier plays, are a substitute for genuine contact. In the world which Albee describes, friends exist 'because we need a surface to bounce it all off...Because it's too much trouble to change it all.'[191] And the political extension of this is underlined when a few lines later the name of Richard Nixon is invoked – a man, it is suggested, whom no one will admit to having voted for. The dying of affection, the decline of the body and the loss of political commitment are presented as parallel realities and they do, in fact, blend so that when Sam, husband to the dying Jo, speaks of his wife's decline it becomes simultaneously an account of the collapse of society: 'Each day, each night, each moment, she becomes less and less. My arms go around...bone? She...diminishes. She moves away from me in ways!...The thing we must do about loss is, hold onto the object we're losing. There's time later for...ourselves. Hold on!...but, to what? To bone? To air? To dust?'[192] To what, indeed? His wife is taken from him by two strangers, one of whom claims to be her mother (the woman returning to the womb), the other of whom is a Negro whose blackness is a constant point of reference and who is presented as an image of death (echoes of Pinter perhaps).

The parallel, of course, is not complete. If death cannot be resisted, if some final metaphysical absurdity is undeniable, it is plainly not necessary to compound this on a social level. And this seems to be the point which one of the strangers makes, as it is in so many of Albee's previous plays. 'If you have a fire going', she asks, 'do you...abandon it, and hope for the best? Civilizations have gone down that way you know.'[193] Indeed she is more specific than this, citing the fate of Russia and then America itself. What in his earlier work had been subtext here becomes text. Thus, she observes of 'this bewildered land of ours', the 'last of the democracies', that one day a 'real Nixon will come along',[194] and recounts a prophetic dream, thereby extending references which appear in *The Death of Bessie Smith*, *Who's Afraid of Virginia Woolf?*, *All Over*, *Box* and *Quotations from Chairman Mao Tse-Tung*:

> I dreamt I was on a beach at sunset – with friends... And all at once...it became incredibly quiet; the waves stopped, and the gulls hung there in the air... Such silence. And then it began; the eastern horizon was lighted by an explosion, hundreds of miles away – no sound! And then another, to the west – no sound. And within seconds they were everywhere always at a great distance – the flash of light, and silence... We knew what we were watching, and there was no time to be afraid. The silence was...beautiful as the silent bombs went off. Perhaps we are already dead; perhaps that was why there was no sound.[195]

When Sam unnecessarily observes that 'that was the end of the world' Elizabeth replies with what is clearly offered as a summary of the play: 'I thought that's what we were talking about. (*To the audience*) Isn't that what we were talking about?'[196] It is, in effect, what he has spent most of his career talking about and it is thus scarcely surprising that his tone should have become more shrill, his confidence have leached away and his trust in human resistance have atophied, since all that stand between *The Zoo Story* and *The Lady from Dubuque* are twenty years of foreign wars, domestic corruption and an intensified nuclear threat.

Once again, he is concerned with the fate of American revolutionary principles – though not with the fate of liberal abstractions. Thus liberty, dignity and possession are dismissed as mere 'semantics'. The essential question as enunciated by Elizabeth is 'Who am I?', for that question is clearly antecedent to all others and without that knowledge 'how can you possibly know who I am?'[197] But where once identity had turned on a simple acknowledgement of the real now a character who asserts that 'Things are either true or they're not' is mocked. Although Albee has said of the play that he remains concerned here 'as to exactly where reality exists', that reality is now more problematic than it had been in *Who's Afraid of Virginia Woolf?* Indeed the lady from Dubuque may or may not come from Dubuque and is, anyway, herself something of a fiction, her name deriving from the fictional figure invoked in the *New Yorker* magazine. The very unreality of the play itself is underscored by the fact that the characters address the audience. The only inescapable truths are the fact of existence and the termination of that existence. But those truths create other necessities – the necessity for compassion and the necessity for the artist to create. *The Lady from Dubuque* is not a successful play. It is in effect a pastiche of his earlier work, but it does act as a summary of concerns which had occupied him for twenty years and stands as a testament to his darkening view of human possibility.

Edward Albee dominated the American theatre of the 1960s. His brilliantly articulate calls for a reinvigorated liberal humanism, his dramatic parables of the need for the restoration of human values on a public and private level, struck just the right note for the Kennedy years, as did his hints of a threatening apocalypse. By turns witty and abrasive, and with a control over language, its rhythms and nuances, unmatched in the American theatre, he broke new ground with each play, refusing to repeat his early Broadway success. But that refusal to compromise (even, on occasion, to make those compromises necessary to public performance) slowly eroded his support. He was essentially an Off-Broadway playwright who (with a few exceptions) continued to insist on Broadway productions of his plays. The effect was the gradual eclipse of one of America's most powerful and original playwrights.

Albee began his career as a poet and a putative musician. The marks of this are plain to see in the sustained arias, the contrapuntal rhythms, the crescendos and diminuendos of his texts. *Quotations from Chairman Mao Tse-Tung* was actually envisaged as a kind of string quartet, in which one instrument remained silent. Nor was it without significance that the single most important literary influence should have been Eliot, not simply in the sense of a precise control and poetic condensation of language, but also in so far as he shared his sense of a contemporary world bereft of values. And beyond Eliot was Beckett. Albee has said that 'I suspect that my fascination with language, to the extent that it exists, must stem from my first readings of Beckett. Nobody in twentieth-century theatre has been more precise in the use of language, more careful and more telling in the splitting of infinities.' He has said of language that 'It is imprecise but, if you ask people to pay more attention to it, it helps...language is both the disguise and the nakedness...we communicate and fail to communicate and make clear basically by language...My characters tend to be far more articulate than a lot of people's characters. That is one of their problems I suppose.'[198]

Albee's gifts to the American theatre have been considerable. Asked in 1979 to assess them himself, he said:

> I have tried to occasionally do something if not to expand then at least to bend the boundaries of the nature of the dramatic experience. I have tried to do that in some of the more experimental plays, maybe view the dramatic form from the way other people haven't quite done it before and that might be useful. It is certainly interesting to me. Whether or not I have changed other people's minds about their short-sightedness and all the rest I don't know. I think you can always affect the recipient of what you do consciously or unconsciously, and more often unconsciously. I like to think people are forced to rethink some things as a result of the experience of seeing some of my plays, that they are not left exactly the way they came in.[199]

But his achievements go beyond this. He has made articulateness not merely a method but a subject. He has tackled issues of genuine metaphysical seriousness in a way that few American dramatists before him have claimed to do, and done so, for the most part, with a command of wit and a controlled humour which has not always characterised the work of O'Neill, Miller and Williams. He has set himself the task of probing beneath the bland surface of contemporary reality and created a theatre which at its best is luminous with intelligence and power. He has a musician's sense of rhythmic structure and tonal subtlety. Though his themes have remained remarkably consistent, attenuated only by a growing sense of despair at contemporary wilfulness, he has never been content to repeat an effect. Theatricality, indeed, has moved to the very centre of his concern as he has increasingly detected in it not simply a means of imaginative transformation but a central strategy for those who seek to reassemble experience into a form which they can acknowledge and a system which can give them a central role in their own invention. The failure which he has documented has been one of imagination no less than of will and moral being. But though he persists in issuing his warning of personal and national decline, though he continues to create plays which imply the need to reinvent those values abandoned through self-concern or simple apathy, he carries ever less conviction while his plays have proved of diminishing interest to the audience he would wish to reach.

To a degree Albee's work self-consciously addresses an American dilemma. He has said that 'I am basically concerned with the health of my own society...I have always thought of the United States as a revolutionary society and our revolution is supposed to be a continuing one, one of the few very slow revolutions that is not bogged down in bureaucracy and totalitarianism.'[200] Yet, while he has confessed to remaining fairly optimistic about the United States he has also admitted to 'becoming less and less certain of the resiliency of civilization', acknowledging that *Who's Afraid of Virginia Woolf?* was a product of 'a period in which people in the United States thought anything and everything was possible'.[201] However, behind the fascination with the fate of American revolutionary principles lies a metaphysical concern for if he was interested in the degree to which people willingly subordinated themselves to social myths he was also committed to exploring the nature of other myths. 'I have always been concerned', he said in an interview in 1980, 'as indeed I am in my new play *The Lady from Dubuque*, as to exactly where reality does exist. I don't know whether our theatre is concerned with that but I am.'[202] Albee, too, has split his infinities, and if that has led him beyond the boundaries of a theatre 'so closely allied to commerce...that it is meant to be an entertainment owned by its recipient',[203] then he sees that as one of his prime responsibilities to a theatre which he occasionally despises but to which he remains dedicated. For although he has acknowledged that film is the most popular contemporary form he is 'convinced that the public knows instinctively that film is a synthetic experience, a synthetic manufactured experience incapable of change, but people go to the theatre thinking that it is a dangerous present tense experience. They can change.'[204] This is equally a basic assumption of Albee's theatre.

Notes

Introduction

1 Tennessee Williams, *Five Plays* (London, 1962), pp. xv–xvi.
2 Robert E. Morsberger, *James Thurber* (New York, 1964), p. 190.
3 Erich Fromm, *The Art of Loving* (London, 1957), p. 29.
4 *Ibid.*, p. 31.
5 *Four Plays by Tennessee Williams* (London, 1957), p. x.

Tennessee Williams

1 F. Scott Fitzgerald, *The Crack Up and Other Pieces and Stories* (Harmondsworth, 1965), p. 39.
2 Tennessee Williams, *Memoirs* (New York, 1975), p. 252.
3 Harold Hobson, *The Sunday Times*, 27 February 1983, p. 49.
4 Benjamin Nelson, *Tennessee Williams: The Man and his Work* (New York, 1961), p. 7.
5 *Ibid.*, pp. 7–8.
6 Alan Perlis, *Wallace Stevens: A World of Transforming Shapes* (London, 1976), p. 39.
7 *Ibid.*, p. 80.
8 Tennessee Williams, *Where I Live* (New York, 1978), p. 1.
9 Paul Valéry, *The Art of Poetry*, trans. Denise Folliot (London, 1958), pp. 226–7.
10 *Where I Live*, p. 1.
11 Benjamin Nelson, p. 14.
12 Tennessee Williams, 'Candles to the Sun'. Typescript in Humanities Research Center, the University of Texas at Austin.
13 *Ibid.*
14 *Where I Live*, p. 12.
15 Dramatists' Guild Readers' Reports. Typescript in Humanities Research Center, the University of Texas at Austin.
16 *Where I Live*, p. 12.
17 All extracts from this play are taken from the typescript of 'Fugitive Kind', Humanities Research Center, the University of Texas at Austin.
18 Tennessee Williams, 'Death is a Drummer'. Typescript in Humanities Research Center, the University of Texas at Austin.
19 *Memoirs*, p. 100.
20 Benjamin Nelson, p. 39.
21 Tennessee Williams, 'Battle of Angels'. Typescript in Humanities Research Center, the University of Texas at Austin.
22 Tennessee Williams, 'Stairs to the Roof'. Typescript in Humanities Research Center, the University of Texas at Austin, p. 3.
23 *Ibid.*, pp. 9–10.
24 *Ibid.*, pp. 13–14.
25 *Ibid.*, p. 84.

26 Tennessee Williams, 'Dos Ranchos'. Typescript in Humanities Research Center, the University of Texas at Austin, pp. 279–81.
27 Tennessee Williams, 'The Spinning Song'. Typescript in Humanities Research Center, the University of Texas at Austin.
28 Tennessee Williams, 'The Front Porch Girl'. Typescript in Humanities Research Center, the University of Texas at Austin.
29 *Ibid.*
30 Jean Gould, *Modern American Playwrights* (New York, 1966), pp. 241–2.
31 *Four Plays by Tennessee Williams* (London, 1957), p. ix.
32 *Ibid.*, p. 1.
33 *Ibid.*, p. ix.
34 *Ibid.*, p. i.
35 *Five Plays by Tennessee Williams* (London, 1962), p. 324.
36 Tennessee Williams, 'If You Breathe, it Breaks! or Portrait of a Girl in Glass'. In Humanities Research Center, the University of Texas at Austin.
37 *Four Plays*, p. 62.
38 *Ibid.*, p. xi.
39 *Five Plays*, p. 127.
40 *Ibid.*, p. 128.
41 *Ibid.*, p. 129.
42 *Where I Live*, p. 103.
43 *Four Plays*, pp. 2–3.
44 Jo Mielziner, *Designing for the Theatre* (New York, 1965), p. 124.
45 Mark Haworth-Booth, *E. McKnight Kauffer: A Designer and his Public* (London, 1979), p. 75.
46 *Where I Live*, pp. 12–13.
47 *Ibid.*, p. 14.
48 *Ibid.*, p. 13.
49 *Ibid.*, p. 35.
50 *Ibid.*, pp. 36–7.
51 *Ibid.*, p. 34.
52 *Ibid.*, p. 44.
53 *Ibid.*, p. 60.
54 *Ibid.*
55 *Ibid.*, p. 16.
56 *Ibid.*, p. 21.
57 *Ibid.*, p. 22.
58 *Ibid.*, p. 19.
59 Ms Dated September 1943. Humanities Research Center, the University of Texas at Austin.
60 Tennessee Williams, 'The Spinning Song'. Humanities Research Center, the University of Texas at Austin.
61 All extracts from this play are taken from the typescript of 'Interior: Panic', Humanities Research Center, the University of Texas at Austin.
62 *Four Plays*, p. 77.
63 D. H. Lawrence, *Lady Chatterley's Lover* (Harmondsworth, 1961), p. 5.

64 *Four Plays*, p. 147.
65 Tennessee Williams, 'The Lady of Larkspur Lotion', in *Twenty-Seven Wagons Full of Cotton* (New York, 1966), pp. 70–1.
66 *Four Plays*, p. 136.
67 Jo Mielziner, p. 141.
68 *Four Plays*, p. 105.
69 Tennessee Williams, 'A Streetcar Named Desire'. Typescript dated 5 April 1947 in Humanities Research Center, the University of Texas at Austin.
70 In Toby Cole, ed., *Directing the Play* (Indianapolis, 1953), p. 296.
71 *Ibid.*, p. 297.
72 *Ibid.*, p. 296.
73 *Four Plays*, p. 109.
74 In Toby Cole, p. 301.
75 *Ibid.*, p. 302.
76 *Ibid.*, p. 305.
77 *Ibid.*, p. 306.
78 *Ibid.*, p. 308.
79 *Ibid.*
80 *Memoirs*, p. 205.
81 Donald Windham, *Tennessee Williams' Letters to Donald Windham 1937–1958* (New York, 1977), p. 93.
82 Mary McCarthy, *Sights and Spectacles 1937–1958* (London, 1959), p. 132.
83 *Where I Live*, pp. 29–30.
84 *Four Plays*, p. 169.
85 *Ibid.*, p. 197.
86 Draft of article in Humanities Research Center, the University of Texas at Austin.
87 *Ibid.*
88 *Ibid.*
89 *Ibid.*
90 *Ibid.*
91 *Ibid.*
92 'The Play of Character'. Typescript in Humanities Research Center, the University of Texas at Austin.
93 In Benjamin Nelson, p. 154.
94 Tennessee Williams, 'The Rose Tattoo'. Kitchen sink draft. Typescript in Humanities Research Center, the University of Texas at Austin.
95 *Four Plays*, p. 232.
96 *Where I Live*, p. 56.
97 *Ibid.*
98 *Ibid.*, p. 112.
99 *Memoirs*, p. 101.
100 *Four Plays*, pp. 231, 233.
101 Bernard Shaw, *The Complete Plays of Bernard Shaw* (London, 1931), p. 540.
102 *Where I Live*, p. 68.
103 *Ibid.*, p. 52.

104 *Four Plays*, p. 234.
105 *Ibid.*, p. 275.
106 *Ibid.*, p. 279.
107 *Ibid.*, p. 288.
108 *Ibid.*, p. 289.
109 *Ibid.*, p. 290.
110 Tennessee Williams, 'Some Qualifications'. Typescript in Humanities Research Center, the University of Texas at Austin.
111 Tennessee Williams, 'Lyric Theatre: A Faith'. Typescript in Humanities Research Center, the University of Texas at Austin.
112 In Benjamin Nelson, p. 178.
113 *Four Plays*, pp. 288–9.
114 *Ibid.*, p. 289.
115 *Ibid.*, p. 317.
116 *Ibid.*, p. 319.
117 *Where I Live*, p. 54.
118 *Memoirs*, p. 167.
119 Benjamin Nelson, p. 205.
120 In *Ibid.*, p. 213.
121 *Memoirs*, p. 169.
122 *Five Plays*, p. ix.
123 *Ibid.*, p. xvi.
124 *Ibid.*, p. 47.
125 *Ibid.*, p. 48.
126 *Ibid.*, p. ix.
127 *Ibid.*, p. 61.
128 *Where I Live*, pp. 72–3.
129 *Five Plays*, p. 84.
130 *Ibid.*, p. 87.
131 *Ibid.*, p. 92.
132 Tennessee Williams, 'Cat on a Hot Tin Roof'. Typescript in Humanities Research Center, the University of Texas at Austin. I, 34.
133 *Ibid.*, III, 39.
134 In Robert A. Martin, ed., *The Theatre Essays of Arthur Miller* (Harmondsworth, 1978), pp. 189–94.
135 *Five Plays*, p. 94.
136 'Cat on a Hot Tin Roof'. Typescript, I, 34.
137 *Ibid.*, III, 34.
138 *Ibid.*, III, 22–3.
139 *Ibid.*, III, 21–2.
140 *Five Plays*, p. 305.
141 Jean Genet, *Reflections on the Theatre*, trans. Richard Seaver (London, 1972), p. 64.
142 *Four Plays*, p. 338.
143 *Ibid.*, p. 248.
144 Tennessee Williams, *Sweet Bird of Youth* (London, 1959), p. 18.

145 *Ibid.*, pp. 7–8.
146 *Ibid.*, p. 42.
147 *Ibid.*, p. 67.
148 *Ibid.*, p. 79.
149 *Ibid.*, p. 90.
150 *Ibid.*, p. 91.
151 *Ibid.*, p. 92.
152 Tennessee Williams, *The Night of the Iguana* (London, 1963), p. 48.
153 *Ibid.*, p. 44.
154 *Ibid.*, p. 58.
155 *Ibid.*, p. 87.
156 *Ibid.*, p. 86.
157 *Ibid.*, p. 90.
158 *Ibid.*, p. 103.
159 Tennessee Williams, *Plays* (vol. 5, New York, 1976), p. 70.
160 *Ibid.*, p. 62.
161 *Ibid.*, p. 160.
162 *Ibid.*, p. 199.
163 *Ibid.*, p. 289.
164 Tennessee Williams, *Dragon Country* (New York, 1970), p. 214.
165 *Ibid.*, p. 138.
166 *Ibid.*, p. 141.
167 *Ibid.*, p. 18.
168 *Ibid.*, p. 21.
169 *Ibid.*, p. 30.
170 *Ibid.*, pp. 51–3.
171 *Plays*, vol. 5, pp. 217, 294, 296.
172 Tennessee Williams, *Out Cry* (New York, 1973), p. 16.
173 *Ibid.*, p. 8.
174 *Ibid.*, p. 11.
175 *Ibid.*, p. 19.
176 *Ibid.*, p. 23.
177 *Ibid.*, p. 36.
178 *Ibid.*, p. 47.
179 *Ibid.*, p. 62.
180 *Ibid.*, p. 66.
181 *Ibid.*, p. 67.
182 *Ibid.*, p. 72.
183 Tennessee Williams, *Sweet Bird of Youth and Other Plays* (Harmondsworth, 1962), p. 9.
184 *Where I Live*, pp. 169–70.
185 *Ibid.*, p. 171.
186 Tennessee Williams, *Vieux Carré* (New York, 1979), p. 16.
187 *Ibid.*, p. 65.
188 *Ibid.*, pp. 49, 51.
189 Donald Windham, p. viii.

190 Tennessee Williams, *Clothes for a Summer Hotel: A Ghost Play* (New York, 1980), p. 22.
191 *Ibid.*, p. 21.
192 *Ibid.*, p. 32.
193 *Ibid.*
194 *Ibid.*, p. 48.
195 *Ibid.*, p. 52.
196 Tennessee Williams, 'Secret Places of the Heart'. Typescript.
197 Jean Genet, p. 68.
198 *Ibid.*
199 *Where I Live*, p. 68.
200 Hart Crane, *The Collected Poems of Hart Crane* (New York, 1933), p. x.
201 *Five Plays*, p. 10.
202 *Ibid.*, p. 27.
203 In Donald Windham, p. 307.
204 *Where I Live*, p. 125.
205 *Memoirs*, p. 117.
206 *Ibid.*, p. 230.
207 *Ibid.*, p. 247.
208 Tennessee Williams, *Androgyne, Mon Amour* (New York, 1977), pp. 29–30.
209 David Mamet, *Rolling Stone*, 14 April 1983, p. 124.

Arthur Miller

1 Arthur Miller, *Collected Plays* (London, 1958), p. 53.
2 *Ibid.*, p. 52.
3 Arthur Miller, 'One of the Brooklyn Villages'. Typescript in Humanities Research Center, the University of Texas at Austin.
4 William Kozlenko, *One Hundred Non Royalty Radio Plays* (New York, 1941), p. 26.
5 Robert A. Martin, ed., *The Theatre Essays of Arthur Miller* (Harmondsworth, 1978), pp. 8–13.
6 Interview with the author.
7 *Ibid.*
8 *Ibid.*
9 Arthur Miller, *Incident at Vichy* (New York, 1965), p. 181.
10 Federal Theatre Readers' Reports. Federal Theatre Archive, George Mason University.
11 Arthur Miller, 'They Too Arise'. Humanities Research Center, the University of Texas at Austin, p. 40.
12 *Ibid.*, p. 41.
13 *Ibid.*, p. 42.
14 *Ibid.*, p. 64.
15 *Ibid.*, p. 65.
16 *Ibid.*, p. 35.

17 *Ibid.*, p. 65.
18 *Ibid.*, p. 45.
19 Arthur Miller, 'The Golden Years'. Humanities Research Center, the University of Texas at Austin. II, 24.
20 *Ibid.*, II, 27.
21 *Ibid.*
22 *Ibid.*, III, 19.
23 Arthur Miller, 'The Half-Bridge'. Humanities Research Center, the University of Texas at Austin, p. 33.
24 *Ibid.*, I, 42.
25 *Ibid.*, I, 43.
26 *Ibid.*, I, 44.
27 *Ibid.*, I, 44–5.
28 *Ibid.*, I, 45.
29 *Ibid.*, II, 15.
30 *Ibid.*, II, 15–16.
31 *Ibid.*, II, 27.
32 *Ibid.*
33 *Ibid.*, III, 1:15.
34 *Ibid.*, III, 1:14.
35 *Ibid.*, III, 2:30.
36 Arthur Miller, Notebook ms in Humanities Research Center, the University of Texas at Austin.
37 Arthur Miller, *After the Fall* (London, 1965), pp. 100–1.
38 Interview with the author.
39 *Collected Plays*, p. 113.
40 *Ibid.*, p. 119.
41 *Ibid.*, p. 135.
42 Interview with the author.
43 *Collected Plays*, p. 133.
44 Arthur Miller, Notebook for *All My Sons*.
45 Arthur Miller, *Focus* (New York, 1945), p. 150.
46 Arthur Miller, *The Man Who Had All the Luck* in *Cross-Section: A Collection of New American Writings*, ed. Edwin Seaver (New York, 1944), p. 508.
47 *Ibid.*, p. 517.
48 *Ibid.*, p. 527.
49 *Ibid.*, p. 501.
50 *Ibid.*, p. 500.
51 *Ibid.*, p. 528.
52 *Ibid.*, p. 535.
53 Arthur Miller, *A View from the Bridge and All My Sons* (Harmondsworth, 1961), p. 168.
54 *Ibid.*, p. 167.
55 *Ibid.*, p. 102.
56 *Ibid.*, p. 122.
57 *Ibid.*, pp. 121–2.
58 *Ibid.*, p. 170.

59 *Ibid.*, p. 171.
60 Interview with the author.
61 *Ibid.*
62 Arthur Miller, 'In Memoriam', in Humanities Research Center, pp. 1–2.
63 Arthur Miller, Notebook for *Death of a Salesman*.
64 *Ibid.*
65 *Ibid.*
66 *Collected Plays*, p. 134.
67 *Ibid.*, p. 140.
68 *Ibid.*, p. 139.
69 Arthur Miller, 'Death of a Salesman', early draft, in Humanities Research Center, the University of Texas at Austin.
70 *Collected Plays*, p. 192.
71 *Ibid.*, p. 191.
72 *Ibid.*, p. 149.
73 'Death of a Salesman', early draft.
74 Arthur Miller, Notebook.
75 *Collected Plays*, p. 217.
76 *Ibid.*, p. 52.
77 C. W. E. Bigsby, *Confrontation and Commitment: A Study of Contemporary American Drama 1959–1966* (London, 1967).
78 *Collected Plays*, p. 130.
79 *Ibid.*, p. 184.
80 F. Scott Fitzgerald, *The Great Gatsby* (Harmondsworth, 1950), p. 188.
81 Arthur Miller, 'The Hook', p. 76. Typescript in Humanities Research Center, the University of Texas at Austin.
82 *Ibid.*, p. 77.
83 Arthur Miller, adaptation of Henrik Ibsen's *An Enemy of the People* (New York, 1951), p. 34.
84 In Robert A. Martin, p. 17.
85 *Ibid.*, p. 19.
86 *Ibid.*, pp. 17–18.
87 *Ibid.*, pp. 39–40.
88 Eric Bentley, *Thirty Years of Treason* (New York, 1973), pp. 482–3.
89 *Collected Plays*, p. 227.
90 *Ibid.*, p. 249.
91 *Thirty Years of Treason*, p. 820.
92 *Collected Plays*, pp. 326–8.
93 In Robert A. Martin, p. 295.
94 In *Ibid.*, pp. 172–3.
95 Interview with the author.
96 Arthur Miller, 'The Crucible', early draft in Humanities Research Center, the University of Texas at Austin.
97 *Collected Plays*, pp. 248–9.
98 *Ibid.*, p. 246.
99 *Ibid.*, pp. 43–4.
100 Interview with the author.

101 Joseph Wood Krutch, *American Drama Since 1918* (New York, 1957), p. 325.
102 Arthur Miller, Notebook for *The Crucible*, Humanities Research Center, the University of Texas at Austin.
103 *Ibid.*
104 *Ibid.*
105 *Ibid.*
106 *Ibid.*
107 *Ibid.*
108 *Collected Plays*, p. 41.
109 Arthur Miller, Notebook for *The Crucible*.
110 Arthur Miller, 'Untitled Play', dated September 1952, Humanities Research Center, the University of Texas at Austin.
111 *Ibid.*
112 *Collected Plays*, p. 44.
113 Letter from Tennessee Williams to the State Department; in Humanities Research Center, the University of Texas at Austin.
114 Arthur Miller, Notebook for *Death of a Salesman*.
115 Arthur Miller, 'On Social Plays', in *A View from the Bridge* (New York, 1955), p. 48.
116 *Collected Plays*, p. 51.
117 *Ibid.*
118 Interview with the author.
119 *Ibid.*
120 *Ibid.*
121 *Ibid.*
122 Arthur Miller, 'On Intellectuals'; in Humanities Research Center, the University of Texas at Austin.
123 *After the Fall*, p. 73.
124 *Ibid.*, p. 50.
125 Interview with the author.
126 *Ibid.*
127 *Ibid.*
128 *After the Fall*, p. 26.
129 *Ibid.*
130 Interview with the author.
131 *After the Fall*, p. 127.
132 *Ibid.*, p. 113.
133 Victor Navasky, *Naming Names* (London, 1982), pp. 217–18.
134 *Ibid.*, p. 391.
135 Interview with the author.
136 *Ibid.*
137 Arthur Miller, *Incident at Vichy* (London, 1965), p. 199.
138 *Ibid.*, p. 200.
139 *Ibid.*, p. 174.
140 Walter Wager, ed., *The Playwrights Speak* (New York, 1968), p. 13.
141 *Ibid.*

142 *Ibid.*, p. 16.
143 Arthur Miller, *The Price* (New York, 1968), p. 117.
144 In Walter Wager, p. 216.
145 *The Price*, p. 109.
146 *Ibid.*
147 *Ibid.*
148 In Walter Wager, p. 192.
149 Tom Driver, 'Strengths and Weaknesses in Arthur Miller', in *Discussions of Modern American Drama*, ed. Walter Meserve (Boston, 1965), p. 110.
150 Arthur Miller, 'Morality and Modern Drama', in *Death of a Salesman: Text and Criticism* (New York, 1967), p. 181.
151 *Ibid.*
152 Friedrich Dürrenmatt, 'Problems of the Theatre', in *The Context and Craft of Drama* (San Francisco, 1964), p. 265.
153 *Death of a Salesman: Text and Criticism*, pp. 144–7.
154 *After the Fall*, p. 33.
155 *Ibid.*, p. 91.
156 *The Price*, p. 18.
157 *Ibid.*, p. 78.
158 *Ibid.*, p. 110.
159 In Tom Driver in *Discussions of Modern American Drama*, p. 107.
160 *The Price*, p. 110.
161 *Ibid.*, p. 117.
162 *Ibid.*, p. 37.
163 *After the Fall*, p. 127.
164 In Walter Wager, p. 6.
165 *After the Fall*, p. 12.
166 *The Price*, p. 82.
167 *The Playwrights Speak*, p. 7.
168 *The Price*, p. 84.
169 *Ibid.*
170 In Walter Wager, p. 10.
171 *Ibid.*
172 James E. Ethridge and Barbara Kopala, eds., *Contemporary Authors* (vols. 17–18, Detroit, 1967), p. 269.
173 Arthur Miller, *Playing for Time* (New York, 1981), p. 62.
174 *Ibid.*, p. 124.
175 *Ibid.*, p. 100.
176 *Ibid.*, p. 150.
177 *Ibid.*, p. 33.
178 In Robert A. Martin, pp. 187–8.
179 *Collected Plays*, p. 160.
180 *Ibid.*, p. 124.
181 *Ibid.*, pp. 164–5.
182 *Ibid.*, p. 168.
183 *Ibid.*, p. 170.

184 Arthur Miller, 'The Archbishop's Ceiling'. Typescript from author, 1, 24.
185 *Ibid.*, II, 5.
186 *Ibid.*, II, 20.
187 *Ibid.*
188 *Ibid.*, II, 23.
189 *Ibid.*, I, 14.
190 *Ibid.*, II, 24–5.
191 *Ibid.*, II, 44.
192 *Ibid.*, I, 45.
193 *Ibid.*, I, 20.
194 Interview with the author.
195 Arthur Miller, *Some Kind of Love Story* (New York, 1983), p. 3.
196 *Ibid.*, p. 39.
197 Arthur Miller, *Elegy for a Lady* (New York, 1982), p. 5.
198 *Ibid.*, p. 6.
199 *Ibid.*, p. 11.
200 *Ibid.*, pp. 12–13.
201 Arthur Miller, 'The American Clock'. Typescript from author. 1, 2.
202 In Robert A. Martin, p. 179.
203 'The American Clock', II, 5.
204 *Ibid.*, II, 48.
205 *Ibid.*, II, 49.
206 In Robert A. Martin, p. 19.
207 Interview with the author.
208 Susan Sontag, *Against Interpretation* (New York, 1966), p. 151.
209 In Robert A. Martin, pp. 178–9.
210 *Ibid.*, p. 180.
211 Humanities Research Center, the University of Texas at Austin.
212 Interview with the author.
213 In Robert A. Martin, p. 135.
214 *Collected Plays*, p. 54.
215 In Robert A. Martin, p. 170.

Edward Albee

1 Anon, 'Albee: Odd Man in on Broadway', *Newsweek*, 4 February, 1963, p. 51.
2 Edward Albee, 'Nihilist', *The Choate Literary Magazine*, XXXII, 22.
3 Edward Albee, 'Schism', *The Choate Literary Magazine*, XXXII, 110.
4 *Ibid.*, p. 95.
5 Edward Albee, 'Preface', *The American Dream and The Zoo Story* (New York, 1963), pp. 7–8.
6 Edward Albee, 'Introduction', *Box and Quotations from Chairman Mao Tse-Tung* (London, 1970), n.p.
7 *The American Dream and The Zoo Story*, p. 11.

8 *Ibid.*
9 Interview with the author, September 1980.
10 *The American Dream and The Zoo Story*, p. 21.
11 *Ibid.*, p. 37.
12 *Ibid.*, p. 47.
13 Interview with the author.
14 *The South Bank Show*, Thames Television, 8 February 1980.
15 *Ibid.*
16 C. W. E. Bigsby, *Confrontation and Commitment: A Study of Contemporary American Drama* (London, 1967), p. 23.
17 Edward Albee, *The Sandbox, The Death of Bessie Smith with Fam and Yam* (New York, 1963), p. 59.
18 *Ibid.*, p. 1.
19 *Ibid.*, p. 51.
20 *Ibid.*, pp. 70–1.
21 *The American Dream and The Zoo Story*, pp. 53–4.
22 Interview with the author.
23 *The American Dream and The Zoo Story*, pp. 53–4.
24 Oswald Spengler, *The Decline of the West*, vol. 2, trans. C. F. Atkinson (London, 1926–8), p. 104.
25 Interview with the author.
26 *Ibid.*
27 Fyodor Dostoevsky, *Notes from Underground*, trans. Andrew R. MacAndrew (New York, 1961), p. 104.
28 Carl Gustav Jung, *The Undiscovered Self*, trans. R. F. C. Hall (New York, 1957), pp. 21–2.
29 Edward Albee, *Who's Afraid of Virginia Woolf?* (Harmondsworth, 1965), p. 100.
30 *Ibid.*, p. 63.
31 *Ibid.*, p. 65.
32 *Ibid.*, p. 93.
33 *Ibid.*, pp. 106–7.
34 *Ibid.*, p. 111.
35 *Ibid.*, p. 119.
36 *Ibid.*, p. 138.
37 T. S. Eliot, *The Cocktail Party* (London, 1950), p. 123.
38 *Ibid.*, pp. 129–30.
39 *Ibid.*, pp. 85–6.
40 Carl Gustav Jung, pp. 114–15.
41 *Ibid.*, p. 117.
42 Edward Albee, 'Who's Afraid of Virginia Woolf?', early version in New York Public Library, Lincoln Center.
43 Diana Trilling, 'The Riddle of *Who's Afraid of Virginia Woolf?*, in *Edward Albee*, ed. C. W. E. Bigsby (Englewood Cliffs, N.J., 1975), p. 87.
44 Erich Fromm, *The Sane Society* (Greenwich, Conn., 1967), pp. 35–7.
45 *Ibid.*, pp. 127, 134.
46 *Ibid.*, p. 167.

47 *Ibid.*
48 Karl Jaspers, *Man in the Modern Age*, trans. E. Paul and C. Paul (London, 1959), p. 49.
49 *Ibid.*, p. 50.
50 *Ibid.*, p. 51.
51 *Ibid.*, pp. 81, 83.
52 *Ibid.*, p. 176.
53 *Ibid.*, pp. 176–94.
54 *The South Bank Show.*
55 *Ibid.*
56 Ms in New York Public Library, Lincoln Center.
57 Interview with the author.
58 Herbert Kohl, *The Age of Conformity* (New York, 1965), pp. 233–4.
59 Interview with the author.
60 *Ibid.*
61 Carl Gustav Jung, pp. 47–8.
62 Edward Albee, *Tiny Alice* (New York, 1965), p. 45.
63 *Ibid.*, p. 167.
64 *Ibid.*, p. 105.
65 *Ibid.*, p. 106.
66 *Ibid.*, p. 107.
67 *Ibid.*
68 *Ibid.*, p. 85.
69 *Ibid.*, pp. 168–9.
70 T. S. Eliot, *The Cocktail Party*, p. 118.
71 *Ibid.*, p. 122.
72 *Ibid.*
73 *Ibid.*
74 *Ibid.*, p. 126.
75 *Ibid.*, p. 166.
76 Henry Hewes, 'The *Tiny Alice* Caper', in *Edward Albee*, ed. C. W. E. Bigsby, p. 103.
77 *Ibid.*
78 *Ibid.*, pp. 110, 112.
79 Digby Diehl, 'Edward Albee Interviewed by Digby Diehl', *Transatlantic Review*, XIII (Summer, 1963), 57.
80 Carson McCullers, *The Ballad of the Sad Café and Other Stories* (Boston, 1951), p. 138.
81 *The American Dream and The Zoo Story*, p. 34.
82 Edward Albee, *The Ballad of the Sad Café* (London, 1965), p. 150.
83 *Ibid.*, pp. 14–15.
84 *Ibid.*, p. 116.
85 *Ibid.*, pp. 112–13.
86 Webster Schott, 'James Purdy: American Dreams', *The Nation*, 23 March 1964, p. 300.
87 *Ibid.*, p. 302.

88 Warren French, 'The Quaking World of James Purdy', in *Essays in Modern American Literature*, ed. Richard E. Longford (Stetson University Press, 1963), p. 113.
89 James Purdy, *Malcolm* (London, 1960), p. 147.
90 Edward Albee, *A Delicate Balance* (New York, 1966), p. 82.
91 T. S. Eliot, *Collected Plays* (London, 1962), pp. 121–2.
92 *A Delicate Balance*, p. 92.
93 *Ibid.*, p. 26.
94 *Ibid.*, p. 37.
95 *Ibid.*, p. 4.
96 *Ibid.*, pp. 9–10.
97 *Ibid.*, p. 3.
98 *Ibid.*, p. 80.
99 *Ibid.*, p. 81.
100 *Ibid.*
101 *Ibid.*, p. 82.
102 *Ibid.*
103 *Ibid.*, p. 127.
104 Bigsby, *Edward Albee*, p. 136.
105 *A Delicate Balance*, p. 170.
106 T. S. Eliot, *Collected Plays*, p. 65.
107 *A Delicate Balance*, p. 126.
108 *Ibid.*, p. 166.
109 *Ibid.*, p. 128.
110 *Ibid.*, p. 144.
111 *Ibid.*, p. 164.
112 *Ibid.*
113 Interview with the author.
114 Quoted in Irving Howe, *A World More Attractive: A View of Modern Literature and Politics* (New York, 1963), p. 216.
115 *Ibid.*, p. 255.
116 *Ibid.*, p. 256.
117 Irish Murdoch, 'Against Dryness: A Polemical Sketch', in *The Novel Today*, ed. Malcolm Bradbury (London, 1977), pp. 23–31.
118 Quoted in A. S. Byatt, *Degrees of Freedom: The Novels of Iris Murdoch* (London, 1965), p. 186.
119 Iris Murdoch, 'The Sublime and the Beautiful revisited', *Yale Review*, 49 (December 1960), 170.
120 Quoted in R. J. Nelson, *Play Within a Play: The Dramatist's Conception of his Art* (New York, 1971), n.p.
121 Interview with the author.
122 *The Complete Poems and Plays of T. S. Eliot* (London, 1969), pp. 85–6.
123 Edward Albee, *Box and Quotations from Chairman Mao Tse-Tung* (New York, 1968), pp. 73–4.
124 *Ibid.*, n.p.
125 *Ibid.*, p. 5.

126 *Ibid.*
127 *Ibid.*, p. 6.
128 *Ibid.*, p. 9.
129 *Ibid.*
130 *Ibid.*
131 *Ibid.*
132 *Ibid.*
133 *Ibid.*
134 *Ibid.*, p. 15.
135 *Ibid.*, p. 72.
136 *Ibid.*, p. 29.
137 Mao Tse-Tung, *Quotations from Chairman Mao Tse-Tung* (New York, 1967), p. 13.
138 *Box and Quotations from Chairman Mao Tse-Tung*, p. 41.
139 Sigmund Freud, *The Future of an Illusion*, trans. W. D. Robson-Scott (London, 1928), p. 86.
140 *Ibid.*, p. 59.
141 *Box and Quotations from Chairman Mao Tse-Tung*, p. 60.
142 Interview with the author.
143 *Box and Quotations from Chairman Mao Tse-Tung*, p. 24.
144 Interview with the author.
145 *Box and Quotations from Chairman Mao Tse-Tung*, p. 35.
146 *Ibid.*, p. 38.
147 *Ibid.*, p. 61.
148 *South Bank Show.*
149 *Ibid.*
150 *Ibid.*
151 Edward Albee, *All Over* (London, 1972), p. 16.
152 *Ibid.*, pp. 109–10.
153 *Ibid.*, p. 16.
154 *Ibid.*, p. 59.
155 *Ibid.*, pp. 64–5.
156 *Ibid.*, p. 102.
157 Edward Albee, *Seascape* (New York, 1975), p. 25.
158 *Ibid.*
159 Interview with the author.
160 *Seascape*, p. 88.
161 Interview with the author.
162 *Seascape*, p. 40.
163 *Ibid.*, p. 9.
164 Edward Albee, *Counting the Ways and Listening* (New York, 1977), p. 8.
165 *Ibid.*, p. 19.
166 *Ibid.*, p. 26.
167 *Ibid.*, p. 27.
168 *Ibid.*, p. 32.
169 *Ibid.*, p. 41.

170 William Shakespeare, *A Midsummer Night's Dream*, Act v, Scene 1.
171 *The Complete Poems and Plays of T. S. Eliot*, p. 465.
172 *Ibid.*, p. 464.
173 *Ibid.*, p. 473.
174 *All Over*, p. 97.
175 *Box and Quotations from Chairman Mao Tse-Tung*, p. 8.
176 *The Complete Poems and Plays of T. S. Eliot*, p. 92.
177 *Ibid.*, p. 171.
178 *Counting the Ways and Listening*, p. 57.
179 *Ibid.*, p. 58.
180 *The Complete Poems and Plays of T. S. Eliot*, p. 182.
181 *Ibid.*, p. 181.
182 Radio Production script, p. 16.
183 *Ibid.*, p. 14.
184 *Counting the Ways and Listening*, p. 75.
185 Radio Production script, p. 51.
186 *Counting the Ways and Listening*, p. 114.
187 Interview with the author.
188 *Ibid.*
189 *The South Bank Show.*
190 *Ibid.*
191 Edward Albee, *The Lady from Dubuque* (New York, 1980), p. 35.
192 *Ibid.*, p. 30.
193 *Ibid.*, p. 35.
194 *Ibid.*, p. 61.
195 *Ibid.*, p. 67.
196 *Ibid.*
197 *Ibid.*, p. 64.
198 Interview with the author.
199 *Ibid.*
200 *Ibid.*
201 *Ibid.*
202 *Ibid.*
203 *The South Bank Show.*
204 *Ibid.*

Bibliography

Books and Articles

Albee, Edward. *A Delicate Balance*. New York, 1966
　All Over. London, 1972
　Box and Quotations from Chairman Mao Tse-Tung. London, 1970
　Counting the Ways and Listening. New York, 1977
　'Nihilist', *The Choate Literary Magazine*, xxxii (1946), 22
　Seascape. New York, 1975
　The American Dream and The Zoo Story. New York, 1963
　The Ballad of the Sad Café. London, 1965
　The Lady from Dubuque. New York, 1980
　The Sandbox, The Death of Bessie Smith with Fam and Yam. New York, 1963
　Schism, The Choate Literary Magazine, xxxii (1946), 87–110
　Who's Afraid of Virginia Woolf?. Harmondsworth, 1965
Anon. 'Albee: Odd Man in on Broadway', *Newsweek*, 4 February 1963, p. 51
Bentley, Eric. *Thirty Years of Treason*. New York, 1973
Bigsby, C. W. E. *Confrontation and Commitment: A Study of Contemporary American Drama*. London, 1967
　Edward Albee. Englewood Cliffs, N.J., 1975
Bradbury, Malcolm, ed. *The Novel Today*. London, 1977
Byatt, A. S. *Degrees of Freedom: The Novels of Iris Murdoch*. London, 1965
Cole, Toby, ed. *Directing the Play*. Indianapolis, 1953
Crane, Hart. *The Collected Poems of Hart Crane*. New York, 1933
Diehl, Digby. 'Edward Albee Interviewed by Digby Diehl', *Transatlantic Review*, xiii (Summer, 1963), 57–72
Dostoevsky, Fyodor. *Notes from Underground*, trans. Andrew R. MacAndrew. New York, 1961
Driver, Tom. 'Strengths and Weaknesses in Arthur Miller', in *Discussions of Modern American Drama*, ed. Walter Meserve. Boston, 1965
Dürrenmatt, Friedrich. 'Problems of the Theatre', in *The Context and Craft of Drama*. San Francisco, 1964
Eliot, T. S. *Collected Plays*. London, 1962
　The Cocktail Party. London, 1950
　The Complete Poems and Plays of T. S. Eliot. London, 1969
Ethridge, James E., and Kopala, Barbara, eds. *Contemporary Authors*. Vols. 17–18, Detroit, 1967
Fitzgerald, F. Scott. *The Crack Up and Other Pieces and Stories*. Harmondsworth, 1965
French, Warren. 'The Quaking World of James Purdy', in *Essays in Modern American Literature*, ed. Richard E. Longford. Stetson University Press, 1963
Freud, Sigmund, *The Future of an Illusion*, trans. W. D. Robson-Scott. London, 1928
Fromm, Erich. *The Art of Loving*. London, 1957
　The Sane Society. Greenwich, Conn., 1967
Genet, Jean. *Reflections on the Theatre*, trans. Richard Seaver. London, 1972

Gould, Jean. *Modern American Playwrights*. New York, 1966
Haworth-Booth, Mark. *E. McKnight Kauffer: A Designer and his Public*. London, 1979
Hobson, Harold. *The Sunday Times*, 27 February 1983, p. 49
Howe, Irving. *A World More Attractive: A View of Modern Literature and Politics*. New York, 1963, rep. Freeport, 1970
Jaspers, Karl. *Man in the Modern Age*, trans. E. Paul and C. Paul. London, 1959
Jung, Carl Gustav. *The Undiscovered Self*, trans. R. F. C. Hall. New York, 1957
Kozlenko, William. *One Hundred Non Royalty Radio Plays*. New York, 1941
Krutch, Joseph Wood. *American Drama Since 1918*. New York, 1957
Lawrence, D. H. *Lady Chatterley's Lover*. Harmondsworth, 1961
McCarthy, Mary. *Sights and Spectacles 1937–1958*. London, 1959
McCullers, Carson. *The Ballad of the Sad Café and Other Stories*. Boston, 1951
Mao Tse-Tung. *Quotations from Chairman Mao Tse-Tung*. New York, 1967
Martin, Robert A., ed. *The Theatre Essays of Arthur Miller*. Harmondsworth, 1978
Mielziner, Jo. *Designing for the Theatre*. New York, 1965
Miller, Arthur. *A View from the Bridge and All My Sons*. Harmondsworth, 1961
   After the Fall. London, 1965
   Collected Plays. London, 1958
   Focus. New York, 1945
   Incident at Vichy. London, 1965
   'Morality and Modern Drama', in *Death of a Salesman: Text and Criticism*. New York, 1967
   'On Social Plays', in *A View from the Bridge*. New York, 1955
   Playing for Time. New York, 1981
   The Price. New York, 1968
Morsberger, Robert E. *James Thurber*. New York, 1964
Murdoch, Iris. 'The Sublime and the Beautiful Revisited', *Yale Review*, 49 (December 1960), 247–71
Navasky, Victor. *Naming Names*. London, 1982
Nelson, Benjamin. *Arthur Miller*. New York, 1970
   Tennessee Williams: The Man and His Work. New York, 1961
Perlis, Alan. *Wallace Stevens: A World of Transforming Shapes*. London, 1976
Purdy, James. *Malcolm*. London, 1960
Schott, Webster. 'James Purdy: American Dreams'. *The Nation*, 23 March 1964
Shaw, Bernard. *The Complete Plays of Bernard Shaw*. London, 1931
Sontag, Susan. *Against Interpretation*. New York, 1966
Spengler, Oswald. *The Decline of the West*, vol. 2, trans. C. F. Atkinson. London, 1926–8
Trilling, Diana. 'The Riddle of *Who's Afraid of Virginia Woolf?*', in *Edward Albee*, ed. C. W. E. Bigsby. Englewood Cliffs, N.J., 1975
Valéry, Paul. *The Art of Poetry*, trans. Denise Folliot. London, 1958
Wager, Walter, ed. *The Playwrights Speak*. New York, 1968
Williams, Tennessee. *Androgyne, Mon Amour*. New York, 1977
   Dragon Country. New York, 1970
   Five Plays by Tennessee Williams. London, 1962
   Four Plays by Tennessee Williams. London, 1957

Bibliography

Memoirs. New York, 1975
The Night of the Iguana. London, 1963
Out Cry. New York, 1973
'The World I Live In', *The Observer,* 7 April 1957
Sweet Bird of Youth. London, 1959
'The Lady of Larkspur Lotion', in *Twenty-Seven Wagons Full of Cotton.* New York, 1966
  The Plays of Tennessee Williams. Vol. 5, New York, 1976
  Twenty-Seven Wagons Full of Cotton. New York, 1966
  Vieux Carré. New York, 1979
  Where I Live. New York, 1978
  Clothes for a Summer Hotel. New York, 1980
Windham, Donald. *Tennessee Williams' Letters to Donald Windham, 1937–1958.* New York, 1977

Unpublished material

Humanities Research Center, the University of Texas at Austin

Dramatists' Guild Readers' Reports
Miller, Arthur, Notebook for *Death of a Salesman*
  First Draft of *Death of a Salesman*
  'In Memoriam'
  'On Intellectuals'
  'One of the Brooklyn Villages'
  'The Crucible'
  Notebook for *The Crucible*
  'The Golden Years'
  'The Half-Bridge'
  'The Hook'
  'They Too Arise'
  'Untitled Play', September 1952
Williams, Tennessee, 'A Streetcar Named Desire', dated 5 April 1947
  'Battle of Angels'
  'Candles to the Sun'
  'Cat on a Hot Tin Roof'
  'Death is a Drummer'
  'Dos Ranchos'
  'Fugitive Kind'
  'If You Breathe, it Breaks! or Portrait of a Girl in Glass'
  'Interior: Panic'
  Letter to the State Department
  'Lyric Theatre: A Faith'
  'Some Qualifications'
  'Stairs to the Roof'

Bibliography

'The Front Porch Girl'
'The Play of Character'
'The Rose Tattoo'. Kitchen sink draft
'The Spinning Song'

Federal Theatre Archive, George Mason University

Federal Theatre Readers' Reports on 'They Too Arise'

New York Public Library, Lincoln Center

Albee, Edward, 'Who's Afraid of Virginia Woolf?'

Typescripts

Miller, Arthur, 'The American Clock'. Typescript supplied by author
'The Archbishop's Ceiling'. Typescript supplied by author
Williams, Tennessee. 'Secret Places of the Heart'. Screenplay supplied by Keith Hack

349

INDEX

For obvious reasons this index does not include entries under Albee, Miller or Williams.

Index

Index

Index

Index

355